Contents

PART 2 Tourism Profiles and Behaviour

PART 3 Sustainable Tourism

PART 4 The Introduction of the Euro

PART 5 Research and Methodology

TOURISM STATISTICS
International Perspectives and Current Issues

Edited by

PROFESSOR J. JOHN LENNON

continuum
LONDON • NEW YORK

Also available from Continuum

Roger Bray and Vladimir Raitz: *Flight to the Sun*
Stephen Clift and Simon Carter (eds): *Tourism and Sex*
Christine Doolan: *Applying Numbers and IT in Leisure and Tourism*
Bill Faulkner, Eric Laws and Gianna Moscardo (eds): *Tourism in the Twenty-first Century*
Malcolm Foley and J. John Lennon: *Dark Tourism*
Malcolm Foley, J. John Lennon and Gillian Maxwell (eds): *Hospitality, Tourism and Leisure Management*

Continuum

The Tower Building
11 York Road
London SE1 7NX

370 Lexington Avenue
New York
NY 10017-6503

www.continuumbooks.com

First published 2001
This edition published 2003

British Library Cataloguing-in-Publication Data
A catalogue record for this book is available from the British Library.

ISBN 0-8264-6501-3

Typeset by BookEns Ltd, Royston, Herts.
Printed and bound in Great Britain by Bookcraft (Bath) Ltd, Midsomer Norton, Bath

Notes on Contributors

Andrea Alivernini is an official in the Statistics Department of the Ufficio Italiano dei Cambi and since 1995 has been working on the UIC sample survey on international tourism.

Paul Allin is Head of Statistics and Social Policy in the Department for Culture, Media and Sport (DCMS), which is the UK department responsible for tourism, and he chairs the statistics working group of the OECD tourism committee. He has worked in several other departments, including setting up the first statistics unit at the Equal Opportunities Commission. Paul was a member of the Council of the Royal Statistics Society from 1990 to 2000, including six years as one of the honorary secretaries, and he is secretary of the Statistics Users' Council.

Joan Bennett is a senior consultant with CAG Consultants, a small independent sustainable development consultancy. She specializes in sustainable development indicators, the integration of sustainable development into local government policy and management, and sustainability appraisal of strategic plans.

Antonello Biagioli is Head of the Statistics Department and former Head of the Foreign Exchange Department of the Ufficio Italiano dei Cambi. Prior to joining UIC, he was a member of the Research Department of the Banca d'Italia. He is a member of various international bodies and committees dealing with methodological and analytical statistical matters (European Union, European Central Bank, IMF).

Herman Bos previously worked for the Royal Dutch Automobile Club and was counsellor for tourism investment and promotion at the Ministry of Economic Affairs. Since 1985 he has been Research Manager with the Netherlands Board of Tourism.

Steven Boyne is a researcher with the Leisure and Tourism Management Department of the Scottish Agricultural College (SAC). He is currently involved with research into various aspects of tourism including tourism impacts, VFR tourism, local labour markets and tourism and food.

Ann-Kristin Brændvang is an economist and Executive Officer of Statistics Norway, Division for National Accounts.

Raf De Bruyn has been in charge of the Research Department of the Tourist Office for Flanders (Toerisme Vlaanderen) since 1993. His principal fields of work are marketing intelligence, spatial development plans and intra-regional relations.

Rosa Aza Conejo is Professor of Economics at the Universidad de Oviedo and is Director of the Escula Universitaria 'Jovellanos' (Business and Economics, Public Management and Tourism), and is co-director of the postgraduate degree course in tourism at the Universidad de Oviedo.

Javier de la Ballina is Professor of Marketing Research in the University of Oviedo and is Sub-director of the Sistema de Información Turística de Asturias (SITA).

Eduardo A. del Valle Tuero is Co-ordinator of the Sistema de Información Turística de Asturias (SITA).

Petter Dybedal has been Senior Research Economist, Institute of Transport Economics, since 1982. His fields of interest are tourism economic impacts, various topics on tourist attractions, freight transport demand and international logistics.

José M. Estébanez is Professor of Statistics and Operative Investigations at the Universidad de Oviedo.

Enrique Loredo Fernandez is Professor of Business Organization at the Universidad de Oviedo.

Helen Ford is currently the Market Intelligence Manager at the English Tourism Council (ETC). Helen joined the ETC in September 1998 and had previously been working for the British Tourist Authority.

Anne Graham is Senior Lecturer in Tourism and Air Transport at the University of Westminster. She specializes in, and has over fifteen years' experience of, demand modelling and performance benchmarking in tourism and air transport.

Anthony Harrison is a Business Development Consultant within the Moffat Centre for Travel and Tourism Business Development at Glasgow Caledonian University. His industry background has been mainly in the hotel sector in the UK and France holding several management posts, but he has also worked with several tour operators. He has been a visiting lecturer at both Napier University in Edinburgh and Glasgow Caledonian University, teaching mainly in the areas of Strategic Management and International Tourism. The main focus of his research has been tourism distribution systems, culminating with investigations into the impact of the internet on such systems. Other recent research has involved specialist tourist markets, in particular the UK backpacker market and business travel. Within his present post, he is involved in research, consultancy and training with both public and private sector organizations, including the Scottish Tourist Board, Area Tourist Boards, Local Enterprise Companies and individual tourism operators. He has worked on projects ranging from strategy development for Tourist Boards to individual feasibility studies, management training programmes and business development advice for many operations.

Rebecca Hawkins completed her PhD at Bournemouth University before embarking on a career in tourism. With experience of working in tourist boards and tourism companies, she embarked on her career in 1992, when she took up a post as the Senior Researcher for the World Travel & Tourism Environment Research Centre, examining the implications of sustainable development for the tourism industry. Later becoming Deputy Director of the Centre, she was responsible for examining the environmental policies and programmes of many of the world's largest travel and tourism companies. Subsequently, Rebecca has established a business (Synergy) with two fellow directors to examine the implications of sustainable development for a number of sectors, and has been responsible for projects such as an initiative with IHEI and WWF to develop a tool to help benchmark their environmental report and an examination of tourism certification programmes. She retains her academic interests and is the Research and Consultancy Fellow at Oxford Brookes University.

Brian Hay is Head of Research in the recently formed Tourism Futures department of Visit Scotland. He is a member of the Tourism Society and the Market Research Society. Before working for the STB he was a teaching/research assistant at Texas A&M University where he taught undergraduates some of the first courses in tourism. Before that he was a planning officer with the West Midland County Council working on the development of countryside recreation. He is a vice-chair of the Board of Management of Telford College. He also supervises postgraduate students at UHI and Queen Margaret University College, and is an external examiner for both Napier University and Glasgow Caledonian University.

Anton Jacobus started his career at the Free University in Brussels (VUB) where he was responsible for several co-operation projects with countries of the CIS. After this he started at the tourism department of the province of West-Vlaanderen (Belgium) where his first assignment was to lead the research unit. Currently, he is working as tourism product development co-ordinator for the Belgian Coast. His main publications deal with the leisure and tourism trends in the Belgian market.

David James spent twelve years in the airline industry, followed by 25 in the public sector in Canada and the United Kingdom, holding a variety of senior appointments prior to establishing Global Tourism Solutions (UK) Ltd in 1997. His main interests in tourism have been marketing, research and development. During the last twenty years, his focus has been on the development of robust local tourism indicators, and he has created a local tourism Economic Activity Model (STEAM), which is in wide use both in the United Kingdom and internationally. He has authored and co-authored a number of papers on this topic and on the developing need for local sustainable tourism indicators.

Anka Javor has worked in different departments of the Central Bureau of Statistics for the past 23 years. For the last ten years she has worked as a Head of Trade and Tourism Department, which includes distributive trade, foreign trade and tourism.

Steinar Johansen is an economist and has been Research Manager, Norwegian Institute for Urban and Regional Research (NIBR), since 1995.

Ivana Kalčić works at the Central Bureau of Statistics in the Trade and Tourism Department. She conducts surveys in distributive trade and tourism statistics. She is specially engaged in the research of private accommodation statistics.

J. John Lennon is the Moffat Chair in Travel and Tourism Business Development based at Glasgow Caledonian University. He is the Director of Moffat Centre, the largest University-based research and business development centre in the UK. He has over 20 years' experience of the tourist industry at an operational, management and strategic level. He has led a number of major research projects for global, international and national organizations and companies.

David Litteljohn is Director of Research and Scholarship in the Caledonian Business School, Glasgow Caledonian University, Scotland. He has a wide and varied interest in the development of the tourism and hospitality sectors and has published in the area of corporate strategy in hospitality and tourism.

Iain MacLeay is currently head of the International Passenger Survey branch at the Office for National Statistics (ONS). He is responsible for all aspects of the survey. He joined the statistical office in 1991, has worked on the UK national accounts and has been responsible for leading the seasonal adjustment and time-series analysis team at the ONS.

Mara Manente is Director of CISET. Her main fields of interest are the macroeconomics of tourism, the study of the economic impact of tourism, tourism demand analysis and forecasting, and tourism statistics. She is a consultant to many national and international tourism institutions in Italy and abroad (ISTAT, Eurostat, World Tourism Organization, etc.), and a member of AIEST (Association Internationale des Experts de Sciences Touristiques) and TRC (Tourist Research Centre).

Emilio Torres Manzaneda is Professor of Statistics and Operative Investigations in the Universidad de Oviedo.

Antonio Massieu was formerly Deputy Director of the Spanish Institute of Tourism Studies and also worked with the World Tourism Organization as Chairman of the Statistics Steering Committee. He became Chief of Statistics and Economic Measurement of Tourism with the World Tourism Organization during 1999. The United Nations Statistical Committee (UNSC) adopted the publication *Tourism Satellite Account (TSA): Recommended Methodological Framework* during 2000, with which he was deeply involved. He sees a need to motivate countries to develop further satellite accounts to include regional systems, input–output models and the development of employment modules to emphasize tourism's job-creating capabilities.

Scott Meis is currently Director of Research with the Canadian Tourism Commission and previously held a similar position within the Canadian National Park System. He has also worked in a university research institute and as a private industry research consultant. He has been an active member of the Professional Market Research Society and the Travel and Tourism Research Association for more than ten years. He has also served as Chairman of the Statistics Steering Committee of the World Tourism Organization, Chairman of the Ad Hoc Experts Group in Tourism Economic Accounts of the Organization for Economic Co-operation and Development (OECD) and Vice-

Chairman of the Statistical Working Party of the Tourism Policy Committee of the OECD. He has also served on the Research Committee of the Pacific Asia Travel Association and is a past president of the Canadian Association of Applied Social Research.

José Santos Dominguez Menchero is Professor of Statistics and Operative Investigations at the Universidad de Oviedo.

Victor T. C. Middleton had a marketing background with international consumer goods companies before becoming research and marketing planner for the British Tourist Authority. He then became one of the first UK academics in tourism at university level, before becoming an international management consultant, holding several appointments as a visiting professor around the world. The author of *Marketing in Travel and Tourism* (3rd edn.) and *Sustainable Tourism: A Marketing Perspective* (with Rebecca Hawkins), he was the first Director of the World Travel and Tourism Environment Research Centre established at Oxford Brookes University by the World Travel and Tourism Council in 1992. He is recognized internationally for his work in tourism on marketing, statistical measurement, sustainability and heritage management.

Kevin Millington has his own tourism consultancy firm, Acorn Consulting, which is based in East Sussex, UK. He specializes in tourism statistics, the development of tourism information databases, marketing studies, market research and the future of tourism. He undertakes most of this work in Africa, the Middle East and the UK.

Laurie Newton is an independent environmental consultant with more than 25 years' IT experience in both academic and commercial sectors, including research into food policy issues in sub-Saharan Africa. Following work on a number of pioneering projects in electronic publishing, in 1990 he co-founded and became technical director of a scientific software company. He now specializes in the analysis and interpretation of information in support of sustainable development policies. His current research interests are sustainable agriculture and rural development.

Giovanni Guiseppe Ortolani is an official in the Statistics Department of the Ufficio Italiano dei Cambi. He specialized in Operation Research and Decision Strategy at the Faculty of Statistics at the University of Rome. Since 1996 he has been the Chairman of the Eurostat taskforce on travel balance of payments.

Eva Aranda Palmero is an economist specializing in the field of tourism statistics. She is responsible for the Spanish Domestic and Outbound Tourism Survey (*Familitur*), carried out by the Instituto de Estudios Turísticos (Institute for Tourism Studies) within the Ministry of Finance, Spain. She has worked as an external consultant for international organizations like the OECD and Eurostat.

Luis Valdés Pelaez is Professor of Applied Economics in the Universidad de Oviedo and Director of the Sistema de Información Turística de Asturias (SITA). He is also Co-director of the postgraduate degree course in Tourism at the Universidad de Oviedo and President of the Associacion Espanola de Expertos Cientificos en Turismo (AECIT).

Jan Van Praet has been working in the Research Department of the Tourist Office for Flanders (Toerisme Vlaanderen) since 1993. His principal fields of work are marketing intelligence and European relations.

Paul Richardson has taught English at university in Iceland and was a professional translator. He then specialized in commercial development of rural tourism and is currently a consultant in this field and is involved in several EC projects.

Geoff Riddington is Reader in Transport Economics at Glasgow Caledonian University. His main interests are in Transport Forecasting and Choice Modelling. This work forms part of a larger project forecasting transport demands by purpose (work, leisure) and mode (car, train etc.). The overall project aims to predict the effect of changes in economic and environmental factors on transport demand in Scotland.

Mic Rogers is a director of the NOP Research Group Limited, and Managing Director of NOP Solutions. From 1970 until the very last year of the British Tourist Authority's sponsorship of the *British National Travel Survey* in 1998, Mic Rogers was involved in that survey. He worked on the original development of the *British Home Tourism Survey* for the tourist boards of mainland GB in the early 1970s and was responsible for that survey until its close in 1988. NOP then won, and retained under his management, the contract for the design, implementation and reporting of the *United Kingdom Tourism Survey* on behalf of the four UK national tourist boards, from its inception in 1989 through to the completion of its final year as a personal interview survey in 1999.

Carlos Romero-Dexeus is an economist specializing in tourism statistics, and is responsible for the Spanish Border Survey of Inbound Tourism (*Frontur*) and Tourism Expenditure (*Egatur*) which the Instituto de Estudios Turísticos within the Ministerio de Economia (Spain) carries out. He has worked as an external consultant for the World Tourism Organization (WTO) in the Madrid, Guatemala and Amman seminars, with regard to the implementation of the Tourism Satellite Account (TSA) and for Eurostat within the MEDTOUR programme (Egypt).

Isabella Scaramuzzi is Research Manager at COSES Consortium for Research and Training. Her main field of research is analysis and planning of tourism locations. She is also an expert in retail and urban development. Since 1978, she has made studies of Venice and the surrounding area. She has also been a consultant for Municipalities and EU projects in tourism development, training and communications. Since 1990, she has been a lecturer in Tourism Planning at DUET, University of Venice, and at CISET Master.

A. V. Seaton is Whitbread Professor of Tourism Behaviour and Director of the International Tourism Research Institute at the University of Luton. He has researched, consulted and taught in over 50 countries, written five books and numerous articles. His main interests are tourism marketing and behaviour, battlefield tourism and socio-literary aspects of tourism.

Antonio Martínez Serrano is a civil servant and director of the programme involving the collation of statistics in the tourism and service sectors in the National Statistics Institute. He is currently Head of Statistics at the Institute of Tourism Studies.

Colin Sinclair is currently working in teaching and learning support at Chester College of Higher Education. He is completing a PhD thesis in Modal Choice Modelling from Glasgow Caledonian University. He is a member of the Scottish Transport Studies Group and the Transport Economics Research Group at Glasgow Caledonian University.

Roel Wittink started his career at the University of Utrecht in 1985. Since 1991 he has worked at Statistics Netherlands. Until 2000 he worked as Co-ordinator of Tourism and Leisure Industry. He currently works in the research and development department of Statistics Netherlands.

Ian Wright is a Senior Associate Director of BMRB International, where he specializes in travel and tourism research. He has previously worked at British Airways as Research and Planning Manager. Since March 2000 he has been responsible for the United Kingdom Tourism Survey, conducted on behalf of the four National Tourist Boards of the UK.

Acknowledgements

The editor would like to acknowledge the generous sponsorship of the 5th International Forum on Tourism Statistics (from which this text originates). Specifically, I would like to thank the following key organisations:

British Tourist Authority
English Tourism Council
Scottish Tourist Board/Visit Scotland
London Tourist Board
Northern Ireland Tourist Board
OECD
EUROSTAT
The Department of Culture, Media and Sport, UK Government
Glasgow Caledonian University (Caledonian Business School)
Greater Glasgow and Clyde Valley Tourist Board

In addition I would like to acknowledge the assistance of Moffat Centre staff in the administration of the conference, notably Marina Martinolli and Claire Bereziot.

Introduction

This edited collection of papers on the general theme of current issues in International Tourism Statistics is derived from the highly successful fifth International Forum on Tourism Statisticians that was hosted by the Moffat Centre for Travel and Tourism Business Development at Glasgow Caledonian University from 19–23 June 2000. It provided a forum for over 200 specialists in the field to discuss and elaborate on common themes, problems, methodological issues and systems. As the fifth such forum in the last ten years it is internationally accepted as the major gathering on tourism statistics and this occasion in Glasgow produced over 50 papers of which a large number on pertinent, contemporary issues are published in this text.

The five themes of the of the text are:

- Statistical Information Needs for Tourism and the Tourism Small Firm
- Tourism Profiles and Behaviour
- Sustainable Tourism
- The Introduction of the Euro
- Research and Methodology

These themes have allowed a range of authors to offer an impressive range of data from truly international perspectives. Much of the material has both international and global relevance and the text is strengthened by the practical bias of some contributions offering case-analysis examples to illustrate issues and contexts.

PART 1 – STATISTICAL INFORMATION NEEDS FOR TOURISM AND THE TOURISM SMALL FIRM

This part is introduced appropriately, by Massieu of the World Tourism Organization (Chapter 1). The chapter deals with fundamental issues in the national development of the tourism statistical infrastructure and the way in which the relatively recent development of data collection and measurement in this area has not been underpinned by a common conceptual framework. The chapter by Meis (Chapter 2) provides a valuable comparative aggregate analysis of five countries' tourism economies in the context and rationale of Tourism Satellite Accounting. The critical importance of international comparability is demonstrated and the need for more horizontal accounts is evident. Chapter 3, by MacLeay, details the methodology and results of the 1998 UK International Passenger Survey. This contribution considers the latest developments in survey technology and examines how the survey can be integrated to provide a range of valid research data. The contribution by Bos and Wittink deals with inbound tourism in The Netherlands and the difficulties faced in an 'open'-border nation of the European

Union (Chapter 4). The realistic issues of organization, financing and participation are discussed, and a useful sample questionnaire is included. Regional, sectoral and local statistical information needs are dealt with in the remainder of Part 1. The dearth of statistical data on rural tourism micro-enterprises is the subject of the chapter by Richardson (Chapter 5). The lack of reliable statistical information and related interpretation is seen as a contributing factor in the lack of development in the sector in the period 1989–99. Developing a foundation for the compilation of tourism statistics is the focus of the chapter by Millington which deals with a case-study project in Botswana wherein fundamental data sources are being established in order to provide reliable and relevant statistical information for dissemination and planning purposes (see Chapter 6). The practical emphasis and comment in respect of transferring knowledge and ability in collection and collation of data has application in many nations evolving such systems. Chapter 7 by Johansen, Sørensen, Brændvang and Dybedal discusses the outcome of a research project considering tourism impact at a regional and local level. A range of models based on regional tourism satellite accounts are considered. Chapter 8, by Jacobus, De Bruyn and Van Praet, looks at tourism statistical collation in a federal structure wherein community-level organization is vital. The regional examination of coastal tourism offers a variety of products and indicators of a declining tourist market. Finally, Chapter 9, by Javor and Kalčić, reviews the significance of the private-accomodation sector in influencing tourism statistics and measurement of tourism flows in the Republic of Croatia.

PART 2 – TOURISM PROFILES AND BEHAVIOUR

The second part of this book looks at how statistical information can help with the understanding of the market place. Chapters consider types of visitors, travel buying, accommodation-buying trends and visitor-attraction profiling. Chapter 10 by Litteljohn focuses on developing a better future understanding of business traced by consideration of *business styles* (the structure and practice of organizations which generate travel needs) and *lifestyles* of travellers. Chapter 11 provides a geographical case analysis of the relationship between the rural Scottish Visiting Friends and Relatives market, tourism and migration, and the potential for growth in intra-EU travel. Chapter 12, by Harrison and Lennon, is concerned predominantly with the travel-buying process and relatively uncritical application of certain data sources and methodologies in order to anticipate future scenarios. The final chapter (13), by Lennon, utilizes data from the visitor attractions work conducted by the Scottish Tourist Board and the Moffat Centre for Travel and Tourism Business Development to profile visitor behaviour and expenditure in visitor attractions and offers a model product life cycle for visitor attractions. The latter has particular relevance in EU nations which have seen significant growth in this sector in recent years.

PART 3 – SUSTAINABLE TOURISM

Part 3 opens with a chapter (14) by Allin, Bennett and Newton that describes the process by which the first set of national tourism indicators are being derived in the UK. National data remains unavailable for many recorded indicators and the authors are hopeful most should become feasible if relevant organizations can be persuaded to modify their data collection/analysis. The second chapter in this part (15), by Middleton and Hawkins, questions the validity of national indicators of more sustainable tourism and proposes instead a framework of local indicators to be utilized by private- and public-sector organizations involved in tourism. The importance of local indicators is reaffirmed in Chapter 16 by James, which details the progress of the British Resorts Tourism Working Group in developing local sustainable tourism indicators in the context of a wider European local sustainable tourism indicators project. The final chapter in this part (17), by Graham, considers the use of tourism statistics to measure demand and is illustrated by a case study of the UK.

PART 4 – THE INTRODUCTION OF THE EURO

Part 4 of the text looks at the impact the introduction of the euro has had on tourism within the national economies of Italy and Spain. The first chapter (18) by Biagioli, Ortolani and Alivernini explores the role of price factors in tourism receipts. The impact of international tourism receipts in Italy's balance of payments is accompanied by an econometric analysis of a general model in which Italy's tourism receipts are related to (a) relative tourism prices in Italy (*vis-à-vis* main countries of origin/competitor countries); and (b) the aggregate income of origin countries. Finally, the influence of price factors for travellers from 'euro-zone' countries and non-'euro-zone' countries is categorized according to a variety of key variables (e.g. country of residence, gender, age, accommodation used etc.). The second chapter on the euro, by Serrano (Chapter 19), explores the implications of euro introduction and the consequent need to establish new tourism expenditure surveys in Spain.

PART 5 – RESEARCH AND METHODOLOGY

The fifth and final part of the text deals with Research and Methodology issues in a range of national and international environments. The first chapter (20), by Hay and Rodgers, outlines the adopted methodology of the four UK Tourist Boards in measuring the volume and value of tourism in the UK. Useful discussion of the challenges faced and the practical solutions adopted over the period 1998–9 are offered. The second chapter (21), by Ford and Wright, deals with how the UK Tourism Survey will move forward with some key changes to methodology discussed by the chapter authors. The Spanish context is explored in the next two chapters. Chapter 22 by Romero-Dexeus considers the major statistical analysis conducted on inbound tourism to Spain and the methodological aspects involved in this. Chapter 23 by Palmero focuses on the panel-type statistical survey method (*Familitur*) utilized to examine the tourism behaviour of Spanish residents. Finally, the regional Spanish context is examined through a case analysis of Asturias by Valdés *et al.*, in Chapter 24, in which a new model for measuring regional tourism expenditure and total tourism 'production' is explored. One source of problematic data on accommodation supply is explored in Chapter 25, by Manente and Scaramuzzi. Specifically, they examine the lack of information on second homes and rental accommodation in official statistics. A case analysis of the coastal resorts of the province of Venice is used to illustrate the problem.

Chapter 26, by Riddington and Sinclair, considers the utilization of the Scottish National Travel Survey 1972–97 as a means of illustrating the evolution of leisure travel in Scotland. This chapter indicates how a less well-known large government survey can offer significant findings on areas clearly relevant to tourism. The final chapter (27), by Seaton, considers the use of research in destination marketing. Utilizing a number of international case studies to appraise key performance indicators in behaviour and communication effects, it provides a contemporary and topical final chapter.

J.J. Lennon
Glasgow, UK
August 2000

PART 1
STATISTICAL INFORMATION NEEDS FOR TOURISM AND THE TOURISM SMALL FIRM

PART I

1

A System of Tourism Statistics (STS): Scope and Content

Antonio Massieu

PREFACE

The term 'System of tourism statistics' (STS) appears, for the first time, in the introduction to the *Tourism Satellite Account (TSA): Methodological References*[1] when mentioning that, apart from being a new statistical instrument, the TSA must be analysed as 'a building process to guide countries in the development of their own system of tourism statistics, the main objective being the completion of the TSA, which could be viewed as a synthesis of such a system'.

Nevertheless, a full definition, with this or any other similar wording, does not appear in this document or in other documents previously published by the World Tourism Organization (WTO). It must be remembered that in the *Recommendations on Tourism Statistics*,[2] under section 7 'The need for tourism statistics', it was indicated that 'some countries and industries have already established a wide and diverse range of tourism data sources, with varying concepts and definitions to meet these needs, while other countries have not yet developed significant *statistical systems for tourism*.'

Moreover, further to the approval of these *Recommendations* by the United Nations Statistical Commission (UNSC), it was stressed, in relation to the United States of America, that the term *tourism statistical system*,[3] as used in that study, relates to 'the set of data collection programs that encompass all three forms of tourism to, from and within the US and provide measures of visitors' volume and expenditure, as well as the

---

[1] Document approved by the United Nations Statistical Commission, New York, USA, 29 February–3 March 2000.
[2] WTO–UN *Recommendations on Tourism Statistics*, statistical papers, series M, No. 83, New York, 1993.
[3] Implications of the UN–WTO Tourism Definitions for the US Tourism Statistical System (WTO, 1996).

characteristics of the trips and visitors. Some of the data required for the system to be comprehensive are supplied by agencies in other countries.'

This lack of definition is due to the fact that the process followed until now, in relation to the development of tourism statistics, is recent, and also because the corresponding development of the statistical infrastructure has not enabled us, in many cases, to go further into the creation of a rigorous conceptual framework in this area of statistics.

INTRODUCTION

The National Statistical System (NSS) encompasses a series of statistical functions that correspond to a group of bodies that conduct statistical work. The coverage and extension of these systems at any given time can be ascribed to a series of elements such as:

- the organization and legal structure of the institutional units that produce statistics (mostly public);
- the administrative mechanisms and legally established links between these and the Central Unit;
- the statutory or non-statutory nature of certain statistical sources and administrative controls which generate information that is liable to be used for statistical purposes; and
- the human and material resources assigned to statistical tasks in these producing units.

The overall aim of the NSS is to provide users with reliable, consistent and appropriate statistical data relative to the country's socio-economic structures and developments, at different territorial levels, and which is geared to international comparisons with the results obtained in the different countries. To this end, the NSS must include, in addition to all the statistical sources existing at a given time, other methodological and instrumental elements that are necessary for its development.

Both on account of its aim and content, the NSS must therefore reconcile statistical information systems at the various state, infra-state and international levels, through appropriate co-ordination and integration, to which end a centralizing body must be set up. For the purposes of this task, *reconciliation* is taken to mean the controlling activity that makes it possible to ensure that a particular process meets the purpose assigned to it within the overall System; *co-ordination* is taken to mean the function that serves to balance statistical programmes from the twofold standpoint of activities and projects; *integration* is a function geared to ensuring the connection and assembly of the different statistical products.

From the perspective of this document, the following aspects should be highlighted with regard to the integration function: *instrumental elements* (international concepts, definitions, classifications and standards), on the one hand, and *integrated statistical information systems* (systems of national accounts and socio-demographic statistical systems) on the other. Of the two, the System of National Accounts (SNA) is, doubtless, the most developed. In this respect, it would be desirable for a greater balance to be achieved between the two systems in the future, insofar as they are interrelated through certain concepts, definitions and classifications, and, to some extent, because the separation of economic and social statistics is, in part, conventional, since many statistical variables are, at the same time, of an economic and social nature, or affect both economic and social issues without distinction.

It is worth highlighting that beyond the obvious fact that the number and type of available functions condition the level of development of integrated systems, a reciprocal relationship also exists, since integrated systems require a consistency and rigour in the preparation of basic statistics, providing the conceptual framework required to design the instrumental elements of the integration: definitions and classifications. Consequently, integrated systems (applied by virtue of the corresponding international standards) become the centre of gravity for statistical work in all areas.[4]

It is on the basis of this approach that a System of Tourism Statistics (STS) should be understood, i.e. as that part of the National Statistical System whose aim is to provide the user with reliable, consistent and appropriate statistical information on the socio-economic structure and developments of the tourism phenomenon and which can, in turn, be integrated with all the other economic and social statistics at different territorial levels (state, infra-state and international).

THE STRUCTURE OF THE SYSTEM OF TOURISM STATISTICS (STS): GENERAL OVERVIEW

Elements

As with the comments relative to the National Statistical System, the content of the STS is structured on the basis of the following elements:

- statistical sources;
- methodological references;
- instrumental means available.

Taken together, we will call these three elements *statistical operations*, insofar as they all denote a set of activities which are of a statistical nature.[5] Consequently, we will consider as part of the STS not only those operations that stem from the collection of individual data and lead to the presentation of aggregate results in the form of tables or indexes, but also the many others that are either necessary for the implementation of these operations or without which the overall information required to analyse tourism activity could not be tackled with the necessary rigour.

The statistical operations thus considered can be *classified* on the basis of diverse criteria:

- the existence or non-existence of individual data capture;
- the method used to obtain the primary data on the basis of which statistics are prepared (direct data capture or use of administrative registers and documents);

---

[4] For general reference, see José Quevedo Quevedo 'Integration of statistical information: instrumental elements and integrated systems', 10th Inter-American Conference on Statistics, Aguascalientes, Mexico, November 1990.

[5] In other words, these activities are characterized by the capture, processing, sorting and dissemination of a set of structured data for a specific purpose and which conform to minimum conditions of rigour in these phases of their implementation.

- the degree of exhaustiveness in data collection;
- the vehicle for and form of accessing information; and
- other instrumental elements related to the statistical infrastructure *per se*.

By combining these criteria, different types of *statistical operations* can be identified:

1. related to statistical methodology:
   - basic concepts of tourism statistics (those contained in the *Recommendations on Tourism Statistics*, 1993);
   - classifications (of tourism products and activities such as the Standard International Classification of Tourism Activities (SICTA) and the List of Specific Tourism Products (STP); and
   - methods and procedures (statistical and computer) to improve statistical production (nomenclators, use of 'geographical information systems' (GIS) etc.);
2. related to information sources:
   - statistics derived from surveys (such as surveys of overnight stays, travel surveys, structure of tourism enterprises etc.);
   - statistics derived from a register or which have their source in administrative processes (such as the information generated by the air-traffic regulation authorities);
   - censuses or directories (such as the list of collective accommodation establishments); and
   - statistical syntheses (such as national accounting systems, input–output tables and the balance of payments);
3. related to the storage and dissemination of the data obtained:
   - databases (with final results from one or various statistical sources); and
   - publications (with a particularly numerical content in relation to tourism activity and which may incorporate quantitative data from various sources, e.g. statistical sources *per se*, econometric forecasts, market research studies etc.).

Focus

The development of the STS in the various countries is, presently, exclusively geared (barring possible exceptions I am unaware of) to the economic analysis of tourism activity where non-monetary indicators hold pride of place and are, therefore, used by different types of agents for their respective focuses (whether macro- or micro-economic, for the purpose of designing tourism products, marketing etc.). However, besides being a particularly relevant factor in relation to the generation of jobs, public resources and local development, tourism also has a destructive impact on the environment.

Some countries and international organizations are already aware that we cannot continue to turn a blind eye to the fact that tourism activities can cause considerable damage to the environment as a result of the pressure to which they subject it (as a result both of specific types of flows – emissions, use of raw materials, etc. – and of specific types of infrastructures) and the qualitative change which is taking place in this respect, and which translates into an alteration of original environmental conditions.

But it is not just the environment that is at stake; other tourism resources, such as the artistic and cultural heritage, are also under threat.

In all these cases, there is a growing demand for the design of a *complementary statistical approach* which generates indicators that can contribute to identifying these types of pressures, stemming from the premise that we are dealing with a set of resources with similar characteristics (among which attention should be drawn to their singularity, vulnerability and exploitation at levels that can cause them to be damaged or even to disappear).

Design

WTO has played an important guiding role in the design of the STS. Indeed, the International Conference on Travel and Tourism Statistics, 24–28 June 1991, in Ottawa, and the subsequent publication of the *Recommendations on Tourism Statistics* in 1993, have made an overriding contribution to STS development. These *Recommendations* are the first example of international standardization relative to tourism statistics and emphasize their importance insofar as they define concepts and include basic classifications for their subsequent operationalization.

In the past, the World Tourism Organization (WTO) has also contributed to the development of tourism statistics through the preparation of technical manuals on (a) concepts, definitions and classifications (b) tourism expenditure (c) domestic tourism and (d) collection and compilation of tourism statistics, and also by providing countries with technical assistance and by disseminating the aforementioned *Recommendations*.

More recently, with the approval of the United Nations Statistical Commission of the draft Tourism Satellite Account (TSA), a new international standard has become available, providing a new statistical instrument whose operational character is a synthesis shared in common with National Accounts.

This long work process was aimed at four objectives:

- to promote a better knowledge of tourism and, more specifically, the quantification of its economic impacts;
- to contribute to the development of international statistical standards as a support to the design of relevant policy perspectives and commitments, through the proposal of appropriate recommendations;
- to direct members to their gradual implementation presenting general guidelines for it;
- to support this development through technical co-operation with WTO Member States.

Although it is not the competence of WTO to determine the procedures used to develop the recommendations approved, I consider it to be of interest to highlight the great usefulness of designing the STS, using the present economic focus, from a unitary perspective.

Generally speaking, STS development is understood as the greater or lesser number of statistical operations available; this is a useful approach for defining feasibility studies insofar as it is very important to ascertain whether the level of statistical information is sufficiently broad in scope to go about measuring the economic impacts of tourism. This focus should be rounded off with a methodological approach geared to formulating action proposals relative to ways and means of developing an STS with this goal in mind (to which end, the conceptual framework used for the design of the TSA should be borne in mind).

From this standpoint, the following methodological outline could be useful:[6]

1. a definition of the *general aim*, using a statement sufficiently broad in scope, e.g. *the creation of those statistical indicators that make it possible to quantify the economic impacts of tourism at national level.* Since any approach to the tourism phenomenon must, necessarily, stem from the perspective of demand, the main focus of attention should therefore be travel by persons outside their usual residence for the following purposes:
    *   leisure, recreation and holidays;
    *   visiting friends and relatives;
    *   business and professional;
    *   health treatments;
    *   religion/pilgrimages;
    *   other reasons.
2. Since these trips translate into the use of a set of elements without whose existence or concurrence they could not be made (or could not at least have taken place with the same intensity), it can be said, using the analysis of productive structures by way of comparison, that it is necessary to identify the nature of those elements or factors without whose concurrence it is not possible to obtain the corresponding output (in our case, trips by people) and that, by the same token, it is not by increasing them that this output would necessarily be increased (or at least, not necessarily in an efficient manner).
3. Among these factors it is necessary to identify tourism resources (nature, heritage structures etc.), tourism infrastructure (hotels, restaurants, facilities, computer equipment), tourism enterprises, the workforce associated with the tourism industries and, finally, the maintenance and conservation of these resources and infrastructures. On the other hand, steps should be taken to identify other types of factors associated with organization and management, which would include public bodies, public–private co-operation projects and non-profit organizations, assistance programmes and other factors not mentioned above.
4. Finally, there are other factors which should be considered as fixed and/or unconnected with the achievement of this aim; more specifically, even though their impact is relevant in this respect, their modification would only be possible from a long-term perspective. Basically, these factors are tied in with the *institutional framework* which, in a broad sense, we have associated with the level of a country's statistical infrastructure.

Barring exceptions, an approach of this type has never been used for STS design and, therefore, does not tend to have any general focus. Conversely, the number of statistical operations associated with tourism has been gradually extending to meet specific demands but not on the basis of a general approach designed by a centralizing body. There are various reasons for this, among which the following should perhaps be highlighted:

*   the traditional divorce, in all too many cases, between the national tourism administration and national statistical offices;

---

[6] For a more general reference, see the System of Statistical Indicators for Analysing the Economy of Tourism (SINTUR) programme of work presented by the Instituto de Estudios Turísticos for the period 1998–2000. Working document no. 15, Madrid, November 1997.

- the horizontal nature of tourism activity;
- the fact that statistical operations are costly and take a considerably long time to mature; and
- the exceptional fact that the sources of information generated by other units which are not national statistical offices are of a statistical nature.

Consequently, for one reason or another, the truth of the matter is that the gaps which exist in this respect can often be ascribed to the absence of a technical body with the necessary human and material resources, and with specific competence to undertake the design and implementation of a statistical creation and co-ordination project in the field of tourism.

Results

The aim of the overall results derived from an STS would be to *improve our knowledge of reality*, which is what it attempts to represent and measure. This is for various purposes:

1. To *facilitate* the taking of more suitable decisions on the part of the various social agents. Although it is true that there are many instances, both in public and private management, in which the taking of decisions cannot be delayed until the results of rigorous research studies become available, it is equally true that only a broad and continuous flow of periodical statistical information can engender a knowledge of reality, an opinion of what is going on and why and, equally important, ways and means of endorsing, justifying and contrasting the measures that need to be adopted.
2. To *facilitate* international comparisons which, in many cases, are of a regulatory nature and must therefore be performed.
3. To *facilitate* research in the different fields.

To this end, the results should meet a series of requirements, e.g.:

- they must be reliable and represent the part of reality they claim to represent (i.e. they must not diverge from it to any great degree);
- they must be produced promptly and swiftly if the aim is not just to provide statistics for historical and research purposes but rather to contribute to the management and decision-making process;
- they should be produced on a regular basis, that is not only as one-time estimations but also as ongoing statistical processes, combining the compilation of benchmark estimations with more flexible uses of indicators to enhance the usefulness of the results;
- data should be comparable over time within the same country, comparable among countries, and comparable with other fields of economic activities;
- data should be internally consistent and presented within macro-economic frameworks recognized at the international level; and
- both the results obtained and the manner used to prepare them should be accessible to all users, i.e. the principle of neutrality must be applicable in this respect.[7]

---

[7] This and other aspects are referred to in the *Fundamental Principles of Official Statistics*, United Nations, New York, 1994.

Not all STS results are expressed in monetary terms. Indeed, in the vast majority of countries the results expressed in monetary terms are limited in scope and mainly concern:

- total tourist expenditure per visitor category, classified on the basis of the following functional categories: travel, holidays and package tours; accommodation; food and drink; transport; leisure, cultural and sports activities; purchases; others;
- foreign currency receipts generated by inbound tourism and, secondarily, foreign currency expenditure by outbound tourists; and
- production accounts of activities traditionally considered to be tourism activities: international transport; hotels, cafés, restaurants; travel agencies.

Conversely, non-monetary indicators are those with a more long-standing tradition in the field of tourism statistics and are consequently more numerous:

- from the standpoint of demand: number of travellers according to their demographic characteristics, the origin and destination of the trip, the principal form of transport used, length of stay, purpose of visit etc.;
- from the standpoint of supply: number of accommodation units by characteristics; number of arrivals and number of overnight stays; for countries where access by non-residents is mainly by air: number of flights, number of seats available, load factor; indicators of frequentation of the sites visited etc.; and
- employment in what are traditionally considered to be tourism activities: international transport; hotels, cafés and restaurants; travel agencies.

Nowadays, these indicators are generally presented as a collection of data without any conceptual or formal link. Some of them are generated by administrative sources (particularly border police in the case of data relative to entries and departures) while others are generated on the basis of statistical operations designed for this purpose.[8]

Users

Tourism, described as the activities of persons travelling to and staying in places outside their usual environment for not more than one consecutive year for purposes not related to the exercise of an activity remunerated from within the place visited, is an activity which has grown substantially over the last quarter of the twentieth century as an economic and social phenomenon. Statistical information on the nature, progress and consequences of tourism is based mainly on arrivals and overnight stay statistics as well as Balance of Payments information which do not grasp the whole economic phenomenon of tourism. Consequently, governments, businesses and citizens do not receive the accurate information necessary for effective public policies and efficient business operations. Valid information on the role tourism plays in national economies throughout the world is particularly deficient, and credible data concerning the scale and significance of tourism is needed.

As of today, the type of data on tourism required both by the public and the private

---

[8] For a more general reference see 'Les Comptes Satellites du Tourisme: Une proposition de l'Organisation mondiale du tourisme pour intégrer l'analyse du tourisme dans le cadre de la Comptabilité Nationale'. Communication presented by Mrs Marion Libreros (WTO expert) to the Association Française de Comptables Nationaux, Paris, January 2000.

sector has changed in nature. Besides quantitative information on the flow of visitors (such as arrivals and overnights) and the descriptive information on the conditions in which they are received and served, countries now need robust information and indicators to enhance the credibility of the measurements concerning the economic importance of tourism.[9]

Generally speaking, STSs generate information relative to different spheres of analysis:[10]

- *general tourism activity at national level* – this is the most traditional approach and is obviously of a macroeconomic nature, the most regular sources of information in all countries being the Balance of Payments and registers of arrivals of non-resident visitors;
- *activity in the three tourism segments (domestic, inbound and outbound)* – travel surveys designed specifically for this purpose are usually the main source of information in this respect;
- *activity of tourism enterprises and/or establishments* – broadly speaking, the aim is to reflect the gross business characteristics of tourism enterprises; normally, information is available in this respect and is generated in microeconomic-type programmes conducted by national statistical offices, but needs to be customized in an appropriate way; and
- *follow-up and/or design of tourism products* – the statistical information is, to a large extent, generated by the actual demand surveys.

Possible users of the information generated by the STS correspond to a very varied typology:

- the central administration – besides the national statistical office, the tourism administration and the central bank – insofar as it prepares the Balance of Payments in most countries – (these being the three basic agents that produce the statistics for the STS), there are also other bodies responsible for the creation and maintenance of transport infrastructure, the regulation of the various forms of passenger traffic, industrial relations etc.;
- the regional administration, which in many cases has specific competences relative to various areas of tourism development;
- units responsible for tourism promotion;
- business associations and sector unions;
- enterprises that provide tourism activities;
- specialized consultancy firms;
- institutional investors; and
- university departments etc.

These units use the results obtained for specific purposes, insofar as their institutional aims diverge; some of them, in addition to being users, are also units that produce

---

[9] For a more general reference see *Tourism Satellite Account (TSA): Methodological References*, as approved by the United Nations Statistical Commission, New York, 29 February–3 March 2000.

[10] Canada has generated various studies on the usefulness of the enormous amount of information generated by the STS for the different users. A complete and updated example is 'A research and development program for improved tourism industry decision making'. Technical paper by the Canadian Tourism Commission, November 1999.

information. The following list, therefore, represents a fairly habitual picture of this combination of situations among the various tourism agents:

1. NTO (also provincial, regional or local tourism offices):
   - overall responsibility for tourism economic, social development and accountability within geographic region;
   - promoting the country or destination in appropriate markets;
   - national strategy and policy development;
   - business services research;
   - aiding industry development;
   - aiding product development;
2. NSO (national statistical offices) (also provincial, regional and sometimes local statistical offices):
   - gathering, processing and organizing data;
   - standards for data collection and analysis;
   - developing analytical tools;
   - encouraging consensuses on data collection priorities;
   - disseminating data and information;
3. associations (international, regional, local; sub-sector-specific, generic):
   - encouraging consensuses on industry issues and interests;
   - disseminating information;
   - advocacy of collective interests;
4. enterprises (multinationals, nationals, local enterprise, local establishment):
   - maximize returns and profits;
   - minimize costs and losses;
   - increase shareholder value;
   - increase leverage and assets.

International comparability of results

Among other competences, WTO is responsible for proposing to the United Nations International Standards for tourism statistics, with a view to facilitating international comparability of the results generated through the application of the recommendations approved. This is the case of the *Recommendations on Tourism Statistics* 1993 and the more recent (March 2000) recommendations relative to the Tourism Satellite Account. Moreover, WTO regularly asks countries for sets of results, these being what form the basis of comparable information.

International comparability is an aim in itself and one which needs to be achieved on a gradual basis for reasons that may appear obvious but are perhaps worth specifying nonetheless:

- because it requires the prior establishment of specific recommendations relative to the concepts, definitions and classifications required to structure the frame of reference for the corresponding System of Tourism Statistics;
- because countries have unequal levels of statistical infrastructure, as a result of which it would be unrealistic to expect the pace at which these recommendations are introduced and the actual coverage of those applied to be uniform; and also
- because the specific operationalization of these concepts and definitions by each country can condition, *a posteriori*, the credibility of the corresponding comparison.

Consequently, on considering the level reached in the international comparability of basic tourism statistics, the development of each national STS provides an initial benchmark for analysing the extent of the progress hitherto made in this field. Both WTO and EUROSTAT[11] have published exercises in this respect, based on conventional measures such as the sending out of structured questionnaires to be filled in by the respondent and on the basis of which it is possible to identify the general features of those statistical operations used to estimate these concepts and definitions. An analysis of the questionnaires used in these operations and the procedures used to break down and record the information gathered – the actual generation of results etc. – would make it possible to underline relevant differences regarding the way in which the concepts and definitions that form part of international standards function.

WTO has launched a process of internal reflection on how to develop a more active role in this field, both in relation to the specific tourism operations that are essential for analysing tourism activity – as is the case with the demand surveys used to quantify the characteristics of the three forms of tourism (domestic, inbound and outbound[12]) – and in relation to the reception and subsequent dissemination of their results and those of other operations that the various countries submit to the Organization on a regular basis.

---

[11] WTO Methodological Supplement to world tourism statistics, Nice, France, 1999; and EUROSTAT Progress Report on methodological developments in the EEA countries of tourism statistics following the implementation of the Council Directive 95/57/EC, July 1999.
[12] WTO–UN Recommendations on Tourism Statistics, Statistical Papers, Series M, No. 83, New York, 1993, para. 11.

2

Towards Comparative Studies in Tourism Satellite Accounts[1]

Scott Meis

ABSTRACT

Governments throughout the world are beginning to understand the benefits of using and applying satellite accounting to tourism as a way to estimate and measure the socio-economic and employment impacts of this sector on the economy in general. With Canada's Tourism Satellite Account (TSA) leading the field, other countries have completed or initiated similar projects to measure the economic significance of tourism in their national economies. To date, no-one has examined the emerging results of such studies or attempted to compare how their tourism sectors compare with those of competing countries.

This chapter presents an initial comparative aggregate analysis among five countries: Canada, United States, Mexico, New Zealand and Norway. The chapter compares in more detail, specific facets of the tourism economies of three of the five countries – Canada, United States and Mexico – which already have experience in measuring the weight of tourism in their national economies. The chapter examines the scope and objectives of the three satellite accounts, with their specific conceptual limitations and data challenges. The analysis highlights the need for further study and refinement of the three TSAs to bring them into closer agreement with the recently approved common conceptual framework of the United Nations, the World Tourism Organization and the European Community. To realize fully the benefits of consistent and comparable

---

[1] The author wishes to thank the staff members of both Statistics Canada and the Canadian Tourism Commission who have contributed over the years to the development of the Canadian Tourism Satellite Account. Key among the staff at Statistics Canada have been Kathy Campbell, former Director of Education, Culture and Tourism at Statistics Canada, and the various Chiefs of Research in National Income and Expenditure Accounts, respectively John Joisce, David McDowell and Jacques Delisle.

results on the economic significance of tourism in national economics, still further developments and revisions are needed. The final section examines further future developments envisaged in the Canadian and international contexts.

INTRODUCTION

Three major challenges confronting any national government or national industry organization related to tourism have been, first, to develop a coherent, shared and defensible view of what it represents – a national tourism industry sector – with clear definition and scope; second, to measure credibly the current situation of the sector in the national economic context; and third, to compare the size, structure and competitive share of the tourism sector with other national economies and the overall global tourism phenomenon. Formerly, these tasks seemed particularly daunting because, statistically speaking, the 'tourism industry', or, more precisely, the 'collection of tourism industries identified in the tourism sector' does not exist as a distinct entity in the statistical system. The data on various aspects of the economic activities associated with tourism are present in the statistical infrastructure, but they are fragmented and dispersed. Thus, they are transparent, disintegrated and incoherent as a whole.

In response to this challenge, in July 1994 Statistics Canada released a new analytical tool for the Canadian tourism industry, the Tourism Satellite Account (TSA). In taking this step, Canada followed and extended the earlier work of France in formulating the concept of satellite accounts in general, and piloting a satellite account for tourism in particular.

The study, completed in 1994 by Statistics Canada, established definitively that tourism is an important sector of activity in the Canadian economy. It revealed, for the first time, the full scope and interrelated structure of the collection of tourism products and industries that make up the economic activity of the tourism sector. It showed that tourism contributed a greater share of the value generated by the Canadian economy than was previously believed. It also showed that tourism represents a significant export sector for Canada. Additionally, it showed that the employment effects of tourism were proportionately even greater than its share of gross revenues or value added. Finally, the study suggested that joint marketing alliances with non-traditional partners could play a more important role than previously understood in promoting the competitiveness of Canadian tourism products.

This chapter provides an overview of the Canadian and other countries' experiences with this new statistical instrument, the Tourism Satellite Account (TSA), and compares aggregate results from five countries: Canada, Mexico, New Zealand, Norway and USA. It then compares in more detail some facets of the economic structure of tourism in Canada with those of Mexico and the United States. Next, it presents some of the conceptual and data limitations inherent in such comparisons. The final section outlines the implications of the findings emerging from this comparison as well as the further developments required before the benefits of such international comparisons can be fully realized.

HISTORY AND RATIONALE OF THE TSA

Canada's interest in this new tool dates back to 1984, when a broader Canadian vision of the French concept of 'satellite accounts' first emerged as a conceptual proposal of the Canadian National Task Force on Tourism Data. Initiated by the Canadian industry and key government stakeholders, including representatives from the industries, associations, government agencies and academic institutions interested in tourism, the Task Force was formed to develop the programmes and mechanisms to ensure the provision of the required information for enhancing the strategic planning, marketing management and profitability of the industry. Based on a successful feasibility study, completed as a working paper, the 1989 final report of the Task Force recommended that Statistics Canada develop a Tourism Satellite Account (TSA). This recommendation was driven by the need for a statistical instrument which would provide an accurate means of measuring and assessing the importance of tourism, and that would also allow valid comparisons with other industries.

Several years of research work led to a proposal on a set of detailed guidelines for the creation of a Canadian Tourism Satellite Account. These guidelines were presented at the International Conference of Travel and Tourism Statistics held in Ottawa, Canada, in June 1991. In 1993 the World Tourism Organization and the United Nations Statistical Commission adopted the Canadian vision as a recommended conceptual starting point for future work in developing tourism satellite accounts as a distinct comprehensive system for ordered socio-economic data pertaining to tourism linked with the System of National Accounts.

The quest for a new approach to measuring tourism in Canada was stimulated by the conclusions of Canadian National Task Force on Tourism Data, some fifteen years earlier in 1984–6. It concluded that Canada needed a better way of measuring the impact and significance of tourism in the national economy. More credible, consistent and relevant measurements were required than previous demand-side estimates and related economic impact models. A new approach was needed that would overcome the limitation that tourism was not an established category of either supply or demand in the official System of National Accounts. Tourism commodities and tourism industries were not distinctly identifiable. The measures that did exist at the time were not comparable with other industries nor with the total economy nor even, most importantly, with our competitors in an increasingly global tourism economy, nor with the totality of that global tourism economy in general.

In addition to identifying why a new approach was needed, the Canadian industry task force also identified the intended end uses or application requirements: (a) advocacy and awareness raising; (b) marketing; (c) investment, operations and management; and (d) manpower development, education and training.

The task force also proposed a new statistical instrument that would redress the current gaps and meet the industry's needs for more information – a Tourism Satellite Account. And they carried out an initial feasibility study of the concept, its applicability and potential benefits. The newly proposed tool seemed to be both possible to build and suitable to provide answers to the persistent industry questions that had eluded government and industry decision-makers and advocates to that date. What is the real magnitude of tourism in the national economy? What are the total tourism expenditures? Is it possible to identify a trend in these expenditures? What is the inflation rate for tourism commodities? How does it compare with inflation in the economy as a whole? What proportions of expenditures are made by foreign and domestic visitors? Is it changing? To what extent does tourism contribute to the output of goods and services within the overall economy? How many businesses are affected? How many jobs are generated? What government revenues are attributable to tourism? What is the return on government and industry investments in tourism marketing and development?

Since then others have taken the idea further. The Organization for Economic Cooperation and Development and the World Tourism Organization both developed generic versions of the new instrument. Then, in the summer of 1999, in Nice, WTO and OECD presented their TSA frameworks to the World Conference on the Measurement of the Economic Impact of Tourism. The conference asked them to harmonize the two frameworks into a common conceptual framework to take forward to the United Nations Statistics Commission. And then, finally, in March 2000, the Commission endorsed the joint conceptual framework as a new international technical standard.

Coincidental with the advancement of the conceptual development work, a number of other individual countries have also completed similar projects. These, in succession, have included Sweden and the Dominican Republic in 1996; Norway, Poland and Singapore in 1997; USA, Mexico and New Zealand in 1998; and, most recently, Chile in 1999. Other countries have projects currently under development including Australia, Spain and Cuba, while still others (including Fiji, India and the United Kingdom) have project proposals currently under consideration.

THE CANADIAN TSA

What exactly is this new statistical instrument? First and foremost, it is an account – a summary of the observed results of measurements of all the transactions between visitors and suppliers of services and products to visitors in the national economy. An account of the economy is different from a model of the economy. It consists primarily of observed data rather than assumed relations or formulae from other times and places. The instrument produces as end results a set of statistics measuring the structure and scope of tourism outputs, expenditures and employment.

In its broadest form, the Canadian Tourism Satellite Account was envisaged as a comprehensive multi-layered information system which collects, orders and interrelates statistics describing all significant statistical aspects of tourism. However, it does this in a very special way; it collects and organizes that tourism data according to the 'real world' economic transactions between producers and consumers of tourism products from which they originate, such as the purchase of a hotel room or an airplane seat. The account uses the monetary values of the commercial transactions rather than physical quantities such as visitors, rooms, seats or passenger-miles as the basic subject of focus. Monetary values provide a common metric through which all the various tourism activities can be compared and summed.

The account uses and combines data from both the supply of, and demand for, various commodities. It links these data with a larger conceptual framework of the national economy – the established input–output accounts of a country's system of national accounts. This framework provides the means of relating tourism to the total economy and all other industries in that economy. For the first time, the initial results, based on 1988, the most recent year for which the maximum amount of data was available, revealed the full details of tourism's position in the national economy in that year.

The 1994 Statistics Canada TSA study showed that tourism was a significant generator of revenues in the Canadian economy. The study provided a way to measure directly both the totality of tourism consumption and the added value to the economy from tourism, both within the tourism sector itself and outside the collection of tourism industries. The Canadian TSA is statistically and conceptually consistent with the Canadian system of national accounts used to calculate gross domestic product (GDP), the measure of industry value added or, in other words, the net output of goods and services in the Canadian economy.

Thus the release of the initial results of the TSA, Canada's new statistical instrument for analysing the economic significance of tourism, also demonstrated that the concept of a tourism industry is no longer merely an abstract theoretical idea that could not be measured or demonstrated in the economy. The results showed that tourism has a legitimate, visible and significant standing in the Canadian national economy. Furthermore, the fact that these results were released separately by Statistics Canada provided the objectivity and credibility for both the results themselves and the associated findings and conclusions.

TOWARDS AGGREGATE INTERNATIONAL COMPARISONS

As noted above, a number of other countries have also recently completed similar tourism satellite account development studies for their national economies. From Canada's perspective, the most important among these include our immediate neighbours and competitors for international tourists – the United States and Mexico. Other noteworthy examples include Norway and New Zealand – two other mid-sized nations that compete with Canada for a share of the nature-based product-activity segment of the long-haul leisure travel market. This chapter compares, for the first time, the aggregate results of the various initial tourism satellite account projects from these five countries. It then compares in more detail results of different facets of the tourism economies in Canada, United States and Mexico.

There are, however, a few precautionary comments to be made first. The various accounting projects were carried out at different stages in the evolution of the emerging common conceptual framework. Canada's followed shortly after the release of the World Tourism Organization/United Nations *Recommendations on Tourism Statistics* covering the definition and classification of tourism phenomena. It preceded, by several years, the first drafts of the emerging conceptual frameworks developed by the OECD and the WTO respectively. On the other hand, the projects of the United States, Mexico, New Zealand and Norway were all completed after the circulation of initial drafts of the emerging OECD and WTO standards. As a result the boundaries, as well as some of the terminology and underlying assumptions, are not necessarily equivalent across all five countries.

In addition, the data for each of the accounts are for different years. Canada's are for 1988; Mexico's and the United States' are for 1992; while New Zealand's and Norway's are for 1997 and 1998 respectively. The differences in years may not be a major factor, however, as the change over time is likely to be fairly small and the overall scope of the accounts and the availability and quality of the data may make the differences in years less important. Nonetheless, it is hoped that these data will provide an initial rough quantitative comparison of tourism in the five countries.

The initial results from the five very different and diverse countries indicate that tourism translates into significant and amazingly consistent levels of total output, value added and employment. In Canada, GDP attributed to tourism expenses amounts to about 2.2 per cent of total GDP and employs about 5 per cent of total direct employment. Furthermore, the total output in 1988 of CDN$30.3 billion tourism expenditures in Canada was, for comparison purposes, equivalent to about 5 per cent of total GDP. Comparable figures for the United States and Mexico are 2 per cent and 6.5 per cent for direct tourism GDP and 3.3 per cent and 6 per cent, respectively, for direct tourism employment. Similarly, comparable figures are seen for New Zealand and Norway with 3.4 and 4.3 per cent of GDP, respectively, and 4.1 and 6.8 per cent of employment. Thus, from these figures, while tourism represents an important economic phenomenon in all five countries, it would appear to be more important in Mexico, Norway and New Zealand than in Canada or the United States.

As noted above, tourism represents an important economic phenomenon in all five countries with quite similar levels of relative significance. Furthermore, this similarity in economic significance emerges despite rather large differences in the scale of total tourism demand in each country, with the USA leading with US$230.8 billion, Mexico and Canada following at US$30 billion and CDN$30.1 billion, followed by Norway and New Zealand at K50 billion and NZ$9.1 billion, respectively.

As with tourism GDP, in all five countries the proportionate scale of the total output of tourism expenditures was relatively similar with unadjusted final demand ranging from a high of 28.9 per cent of GDP in New Zealand to a low of 5.6 per cent in Norway. However, adjusting for the non-tourism components of these industries changes the figures significantly, particularly for Canada and New Zealand which fall to 5 per cent and 10.5 per cent of GDP, respectively. In Canada's case, this is principally the result of the drop in land transportation which, in aggregate, is very important in Canada but which has substantial non-tourism outputs.

Looking at the relative influence of international tourism reveals that New Zealand leads, with non-residents accounting for almost half of total tourism demand, followed by domestic households at 39 per cent. Government and business spending was less than 15 per cent. In comparison, in Canada and United States domestic travel is the mainstay of the tourism economy with non-residents accounting for less than a quarter of total tourism demand. Government and business were slightly larger at 25 per cent and 35 per cent, respectively, of household demand. Similarly, in Mexico, non-residents account for less than 25 per cent of total demand, but it is not yet possible to differentiate domestic personal demand from domestic business and government travel expenditure in the figures released in their initial version of the satellite account.

COMPARISONS OF DETAILED ECONOMIC FACETS OF TOURISM

A more detailed examination of selective economic facets in three of the five countries – Canada, Mexico and the United States – reveals that for all three countries, hotels and restaurants combined are by far the most important. This time Mexico leads with initial figures indicating that, combined, they amount to almost two-thirds of tourism characteristic value added, while in the United States the combination amounts to nearly one half and in Canada 40 per cent. For other lesser industries there are significant differences across the three countries. In Canada and the United States, air transportation accounts for about one quarter of tourism value added while land transport accounts for an additional 8 per cent, bringing the total transportation value added up to almost a third of total tourism value added. Particularly surprising in Canada was the relatively high 19 per cent contribution to tourism value added from other non-characteristic industries, mainly in the retail sector. In the United States, while the nomenclature is different, initial results reveal an 8 per cent contribution to tourism value added. In Mexico, while this retail factor is not significant, it is replaced by an 8.2 per cent contribution to tourism value added from the manufacturing sector, mainly from the manufacture and sale of local craft goods.

Another aspect of tourism revealed by the TSA GDP calculations is the possibility of discovering where tourism ranks relative to other leading industrial sectors of the economy in terms of their respective share of overall national GDP. In Canada's case, initial results indicated that tourism ranked eleventh, not first as stressed by some industry advocates. This is a respectable position and still ahead of many leading primary commodity- and manufacturing-based industries in Canada such as agriculture and related services, logging and forestry, fishing and animal trapping, as well as the extractive industries of petroleum and natural gas, if treated separately. Unfortunately, similar precise rank comparisons have not yet been revealed in the initial results reported by either the United States or Mexico.

Another facet of the tourism economy revealed by the TSA is the mix of commodities or services bought by visitors. In Canada, transportation accounts for 40 per cent of characteristic tourism demand, with air transport accounting for a full third of these commodities, compared with only 24 per cent in the United States. Conversely, tourism spending on accommodation, food and beverage services was quite comparable, amounting to 14 per cent and 16 per cent, respectively, in Canada and 16 per cent and 15 per cent in the United States. On the other hand, tourism spending on other tourism commodities was much more important in the USA, at 33 per cent, but was only 10 per cent in Canada. Tourism spending on other non-tourism commodities, principally retail, was significantly more important in Canada at 20 per cent than the United States at 12 per cent. Directly comparable data are not yet available from the initial results of the Mexican TSA.

Another new comparable feature of the tourism economy emerging from the tourism satellite accounts is the proportion of the total supply of characteristic tourism commodities consumed by visitors. Once again, data on these facets of the tourism account is available from the initial results produced by Canada and the United States but is not yet available in the results produced from the initial Mexican satellite account. For example, in Canada's case these tourism shares vary greatly from one commodity to another with tourism demand accounting for almost all (98 per cent) of the supply of travel agency services; a large share (93 per cent) of air transportation services, a lower share (86 per cent) of water transportation services and a minor share of recreation and entertainment services (24 per cent), taxi services (22 per cent) and food and beverage services (21 per cent), respectively. By comparison, in the US case, tourism demand accounts for a much larger proportion of the total domestic supply of water transport (96 per cent), taxis services (46 per cent) and recreation and entertainment services (36.5 per cent).

LIMITATIONS

As noted above, the validity of these initial comparisons is limited by the fact that at the time these initial tourism satellite accounts were being developed there was, as yet, no comprehensive approach or established standards for the treatment of tourism activities and expenditures in a manner that was fully integrated with the 'core' national accounts of the economy. Existing standards at the time included the World Tourism Organization/United Nations *Recommendations on Tourism Statistics*, covering the definition and classification of tourism phenomena, as well as the OECD's *Manual of Tourism Economic Accounts*, developed some years previously.

As a result, while a consistent approach to some tourism measurement issues existed, many other areas were still in dispute. Areas of general consistency in the five accounts reviewed here include the broad conceptual definitions of tourism trips and tourism expenditures. Areas of inconsistency emerge, however, on close examination of the operational definitions of characteristic tourism commodities, characteristic tourism industries, tourism capital, overall tourism demand and direct tourism specific employment. As a result, the boundaries, as well as some of the terminology and underlying assumptions, are not necessarily equivalent across all five countries.

As noted previously, the data for each of the accounts are also for different years, but this may not be a major factor, however, as the change over time is likely to be fairly small and the overall scope of the accounts and the availability and quality of the data may make the differences in years less important.

One particular major data gap mentioned in all of the initial accounts is the problem of insufficient specification of tourism demand in both domestic and international visitor surveys. This finding is not all that surprising when one considers that the source surveys in question preceded the development of the accounts and their associated detailed information requirements. Similarly, all five countries report difficulties in assessing tourism use of domestic fixed capital formation. In addition, Mexico and Canada both note the absence of key data on the costs of production from certain key industries. These include restaurants, bars and nightclubs in the case of Mexico, and taxis, convention centres and recreation and entertainment enterprises in the case of Canada. Similarly, Canada, USA and Mexico all suffer from a lack of information on vacation homes in their initial account, while Canada and Mexico, in particular, note a problem with limited information on tourism's use of the financial services industry.

FUTURE DEVELOPMENTS

The considerable emerging body of work reported to date from the research and development of tourism satellite accounts is still only the beginning. A number of further implementation steps are currently in progress or being planned for the future. In the short term, one immediate priority for the next year is for the UN Statistics Program and World Tourism Organization to publish and distribute the new approved standard common conceptual framework. Then, these new standards and the associated set of technical and training materials need to be distributed and promoted throughout the global statistical community, as well as with tourism industry leaders. As one step in this direction, Canada is planning, in partnership with the World Tourism Association, a global conference scheduled for 3–10 May 2001, in Vancouver, Canada, devoted exclusively to the subject of tourism satellite accounts, their implementation and applications. The World Tourism Organization is also working with various leading partner countries to set up regional TSA orientation seminars. Lastly, Canada and the other leading countries with established tourism satellite accounts need to review and study the 'fit' of their current accounts with the new TSA standards.

In the medium term, still further implementation and development work is required. The various leading countries will need to revise their existing accounts, where necessary, to bring them into greater harmony with the new standards. This step is essential if we are to realize fully the promise of international comparability discussed in this chapter. Then further detailed training seminars, and possibly even technical assistance programmes, will need to be implemented by international organizations and leading countries to assist newcomers with limited resources and experience in getting started. Lastly, the World Tourism Organization will need to complete its outstanding project to update and extend the existing *Recommendations on Tourism Statistics* dealing with tourism definitions and classifications, including the existing Standard International Classification of Tourism Activities and the proposed Tourism Product Classification.

In the longer term, further research and development work on satellite accounts is envisaged. The final endorsement of the United Nations Statistics Commission will be needed on the proposed revisions and extension to the current *Recommendations on Tourism Statistics*. Work is also underway within the OECD and among leading countries to develop a number of extensions and applications to the TSA. Most noteworthy here is the current work of OECD to develop a tourism labour force module as an extension to the account. Other future extensions currently under consideration include the development of conceptual linkages with the emerging System of Environment Accounts as well as less ambitious projects, such as developing a profile of characteristic information relating to all enterprises within the tourism sector. In Canada, for example, current work in progress is examining the distributions of the tourism enterprises and establishments in terms of their size and their financial characteristics.

CONCLUSION

In summary, tremendous progress has been made in the past decade in research and developing the tourism satellite account as the first established satellite to the System of National Accounts. As such, at both international and national levels the TSA has met the original industry objective of improving the statistical credibility and comparability of tourism in the national economy. Clearly, however, further research and development work is still required if the remaining outstanding visionary goals of international comparability are to be fully realized. The analysis undertaken in this review should be regarded as formative, an indication of the types of comparative analysis that could be possible when more harmonized accounts and more complete data are available. It is hoped that it can be seen that the TSA represents a powerful analytical tool and that the initial data for the five countries examined here have shown tourism to be a significant economic force in all five economies. At the same time, some of the initial differences that have emerged among the five countries raise new questions about the scope, structure and evolution of tourism in its various national and regional contexts.

BIBLIOGRAPHY

Beaulieu-Caron, L. (1997) 'National tourism indicators: a new tool for analysing tourism in Canada'. *Travel-log*, Statistics Canada, Catalogue no. 87-003-XPB, Winter, pp. 1–6.

Evensen, T. N. (1998) *Satellite Accounts for Tourism in Norway, Preliminary Draft*. Division of National Accounts, Statistisk sentralbyra, Statistics Norway, 7 May.

Lapierre, J. and Hayes, D. (1994) *The Tourism Satellite Account*. National Accounts and Environment Division, Technical Series Number 31, Statistics Canada. July.

Lapierre, J. and Wells, S. (1991) 'A proposal for a satellite account and information system for tourism'. Paper presented to the International Conference on Travel and Tourism Statistics, Ottawa.

Meis, S. and Lapierre, J. (1994) 'Measuring tourism's economic importance – a Canadian case study'. *Travel and Tourism Analyst*, **2**, 79–89.

Meis, S. and Wilton, D. (1998) 'Assessing the economic outcomes of branding Canada: applications, results and implications of the Canadian Tourism Satellite Account'. Proceedings of the 29th annual conference, Travel and Tourism Research Association, 10 June, Fort Worth, Texas, USA.

Ministère du Commerce, de l'Artisanat et du Tourisme (1979) 'Le compte satellite du tourisme: présentation des cadres comptables et de la premiere estimation de la défense intérieure de tourisme'. Regards sur l'économie du tourisme, 4eme trimestre.

National Accounts Division (1999) *Tourism Satellite Account 1995*. Statistics New Zealand, Wellington, New Zealand, June.

National Task Force on Tourism Data (1989) *Final Report*. Statistics Canada, Ottawa.

National Task Force on Tourism Data (1991) *Tourism Satellite Account: Working Paper No. 3*. Statistics Canada, Ottawa.

Okubo, S. and Planting, M. A. (1998) 'US Travel and Tourism Satellite Accounts for 1992'. Survey of Current Business, Economics and Statistics Division, Bureau of Economic Office, US Department of Commerce, Washington, DC, 13 July.

Organization for Economic Cooperation and Development, Tourism Committee, Statistical Working Party (1998) *A Tourism Satellite Account for OECD Countries (Draft)*. Paris, October.

Planting, M. A. (1998) 'The development of a travel and tourism satellite account for the US: input–output accounts'. Paper presented at the Travel and Tourism Research Association Conference, 10 June.

Sistema de Ceuentas Nacionales de Mexico (1999) *Cuenta Satelite del Tourismo de Mexico 1993–1996*. Instituto Nacional de Estatdistica, Geografia e Informatica, Aquascalientes, Mexico.

Statistics Canada (1999) *National Tourism Indicators: Historical Estimates, Fourth Quarter 1998*. System of National Accounts, Statistics Canada, Catalogue no. 13-009-XPB, March.

United Nations/OECD/International Monetary Fund/World Bank/European Statistical Commission (1993) *System of National Accounts*. New York, Paris, Washington, Brussels/Luxembourg.

Wilton, D. (1996) *A Comparison, Explanation and Reconciliation of the Estimates of the Economic Significance of Tourism in Canada by the WTTC and Statistics Canada in the Tourism Satellite Account*. Canadian Tourism Commission, Ottawa.

Wilton, D. (1998) *Recent Developments in Tourism as revealed by the National Tourism Indicators*. Canadian Tourism Commission Research Report, June.

Wilton, D., Joyal, S. and Meis, S. (1997) 'The economic significance of tourism: comparing Canada and WTTC Estimates'. *Proceedings of the Third International Forum on Tourism Statistics*. OECD, Paris.

WTO (1994) *Recommendations on Tourism Statistics*. World Tourism Organization, Madrid.

WTO (1995) *Technical Manual #2: The Collection of Tourism Expenditure Statistics*. World Tourism Organization, Madrid.

WTO (1998) *A Satellite Account for Tourism (4th Draft)*. World Tourism Organization, Madrid.

3

Disseminating the Results from the UK International Passenger Survey (IPS)

Iain MacLeay

This chapter details some background to the methodology used in the International Passenger Survey (IPS) and some results from the 1998 survey which show that more than 25 million visits were made by overseas residents to the UK, with over 50 million visits made by UK residents abroad. The chapter then illustrates the latest developments that have been made to allow easier access to the survey results. These are now available on paper, on CD-ROM, on the web and from marketing agents. The chapter provides some examples, showing how you can use the IPS to answer a variety of questions. Example include: What proportion of business travellers to France use the Channel Tunnel?; How many Belgian residents make day trips to the UK?; and How much do residents from the US spend per night on visits to the UK?

BACKGROUND

The International Passenger Survey (IPS) is a large multi-purpose survey that collects information from passengers as they enter or leave the United Kingdom. It is carried out by the Office for National Statistics (ONS) for a range of public and private sector organizations.

The main aims of the IPS are to:

- collect data on both spending in the UK by overseas residents and spending by UK residents abroad – respectively used as credits and debits in the travel account of the UK balance of payments;
- provide detailed information about overseas visitors to the UK for tourism policy;
- provide data on international migration;
- collect travel information on routes used by passengers as an aid to aviation and shipping authorities.

The IPS answers the questions of who goes where, when, why and how. Results are published regularly on a monthly, quarterly and annual basis. Summary data are produced monthly, with more detailed information available on a quarterly and an annual basis.

The IPS results are based on face-to-face interviews with a sample of passengers as they enter or leave the UK by the principal air, sea and tunnel routes. Travellers passing through passport control are selected randomly for interview. Nearly 263,000 interviews were conducted in 1998, representing about 0.2 per cent of travellers. The interviews were conducted on a voluntary and anonymous basis, with a response rate of 81 per cent. The survey covers both adults and children.

SAMPLE DESIGN

The IPS sample is stratified to ensure that it is representative by mode of travel (air, sea or tunnel), route and time of day. Interviews are conducted throughout the year. The frequency of sampling within each stratum is varied according to a number of factors, but primarily on the variability in tourist expenditures recorded, the volume of migrants and the costs of interviewing. For example, where the expenditure quoted on a particular route varies greatly across respondents, a higher sampling frequency is used to enable a more satisfactory estimate to be produced. Similarly it is cheaper, due to the volume of passengers, to conduct interviews at the large airports than at seaports.

Some questions on the survey are asked of all of the passengers interviewed, whilst others are restricted to certain specific sub-groups. Information on the spending and length of stay of UK residents abroad and overseas residents in the UK is only collected on the return leg of a visit. This is because actual spending and length of stay are required, and these may differ from the respondents' intentions when they start their visit. In 1998, 67,000 interviews were carried out with overseas residents departing from the UK and 55,000 with UK residents arriving back from abroad.

The details collected on the survey are used by ONS, along with other sources of information, to produce overall national estimates of the number and expenditure of different types of travellers. A complex weighting procedure is used to do this, which takes into account various factors in order to improve the estimates.

The IPS uses a multi-stage sample design that is carried out separately for air, sea and tunnel travel. The underlying principle is that in the absence of a sampling frame of travellers, time shifts or sea crossings are selected and then travellers are systematically chosen at fixed intervals within these shifts or crossings.

The main UK airports are always included in the sample. Smaller airports are reviewed each quarter for inclusion. This depends on the volume of international traffic at those airports. Sea routes are treated similarly to the smaller airports in that they are included or excluded in the sample based on the size of their international traffic.

At all the airports, a certain number of shifts are sampled randomly each quarter, stratified by time of day and by day of the week. Passengers are counted as they cross a predetermined line and, now and then, one is interviewed. At some sea ports, passengers are sampled on the quayside as they embark or disembark. The sampling approach is similar to that at the main airports as the timing of the interviewing shift is selected randomly. At other sea ports, interviewers travel on the boats and sample passengers systematically. For tunnel routes, the method is different for passenger trains and vehicle shuttles. Passenger trains are treated in a similar way to airports, where time shifts are selected and then a sampling interval used within a time shift. In contrast, for vehicle shuttles, crossings are randomly selected and interviewing takes place on board the shuttles themselves.

PRODUCING NATIONAL ESTIMATES

The interviews are grossed to total numbers on a quarterly basis using a complex weighting system. The method of grossing the interviews to national estimates varies depending on the method of travel.

Main airports (Heathrow, Gatwick and Manchester)

An initial weight is given to each interviewee, which indicates the number of people that they represent in the traffic flow. This is calculated by combining information on the number of shifts run, the sampling interval used and the number of possible shifts that could have been run in the time period. This weight is then adjusted to take account of non-contacts during the interviewing time and people who refuse to be to be interviewed. Further adjustment within country of residence and nationality is then made to allow for interviews in which only minimum information is collected. The assumption is that these respondents are similar to those of a similar residence and nationality status who provide fuller information. These contacts are not used in the later stages of the weighting system. Adjustments are then made for passengers that arrive outside the eligible times for sampling – for example, during the night-time period – based on information from the Civil Aviation Authority (CAA). The resulting weights are then summed to give estimated total passenger flows from the IPS sample data. These total flows are then scaled to bring them into line with actual numbers of international passengers passing through the main airports, as produced by the Civil Aviation Authority (CAA). Passenger flow figures are adjusted before scaling to excluded 'airside interliners' (passengers in transit to another flight) who do not pass through passport control and so, technically, do not enter the country. The weights are then finally adjusted to allow for any imbalance in the sample. This involves comparing arrivals and departures for countries and ports over a rolling year and, if the two totals are further apart than can be explained by standard errors, the weights of the relevant contacts are adjusted to reflect this.

Smaller airports, sea ports and the Channel Tunnel

For the other ports, sample figures are directly scaled to known passenger flows. For smaller, or residual, airports these figures come from the CAA, while for the sea ports, traffic information comes from the Department of Environment, Transport and the Regions (DETR). Data for traffic on the Tunnel routes is provided directly by the Tunnel operators.

Monthly weighting

Data are also processed on a monthly basis, via a more simplified processing system.

This means that earlier results can be made available, though detailed breakdowns of these are not produced.

RESPONSE RATES

Sample surveys such as the IPS rely on achieving high levels of response from the public, since non-respondents may have different characteristics of travel and expenditure patterns compared to those who do respond.

In 1998, 81 per cent of respondents provided complete or partial responses, with a further 7 per cent supplying a minimum response. Different response rates are achieved at different UK ports of entry, with higher response normally achieved on the Channel Tunnel, and with slightly lower rates obtained at the main air terminals.

QUALITY OF THE SURVEY DATA

The IPS is a sample survey and is therefore subject to some uncertainty. Standard errors are calculated for estimates from the IPS. The estimate of the total number of overseas residents' visits to the UK (excluding visits from the Irish Republic) in 1998, as a whole, had a 95 per cent confidence interval of ± 3 per cent. The confidence interval for their spending was ± 3.4 per cent. For the numbers of UK residents going abroad, the confidence interval was ± 1.8 per cent and for their expenditure ± 2.1 per cent.

In addition to sampling errors, there may also be non-sampling errors on the estimates produced by the IPS.

RESULTS FROM THE 1998 IPS

The following table summarizes the key results from the IPS.

	Visits	Nights	Spending
Overseas residents' visits	25,745,000	230.8 m	£11,573 m
UK residents' visits	50,872,000	509.2 m	£19,489 m

On their visits, overseas residents stayed an average of nine nights, spending £54 per day, totalling £487 per visit. UK residents stayed an average of ten nights on visits abroad, spending £38 per day, totalling £383 per visit. A large number of breakdowns of this top level are available, some of which are detailed later.

MONTHLY IPS RESULTS

Results from the IPS are produced monthly, approximately seven weeks after the end of the reference month; so results for March are published in the middle of May. Only summary data is available at this time, containing information on the number of visits from residents of North America, western Europe and the rest of the world, and their total spending in the UK. Similarly, the number of UK residents' visits abroad is broken down into those same three groupings and their total spending abroad is calculated.

DISSEMINATION OF MONTHLY DATA

This data is made available via an ONS First Release, which tabulates the historical monthly time series. This was traditionally made available from the ONS Press Office via subscription, or from the ONS Statfax – fax retrieval service. These dissemination channels are still available.

However, in addition to these methods, two new ways of obtaining the data in this release are now available. The release is now uploaded to the ONS website and can be downloaded as a PDF file. Also the data is loaded onto the National Statistics Statbase system. Time series data for the eight key series (overseas residents' visits to the UK; UK residents' visits abroad – both for visits and spending; and both unadjusted and seasonally adjusted) is shown monthly back to 1986. This data can either be viewed on screen or downloaded in a CSV (comma separated variable) format.

Publication dates are pre-announced via the ONS's National Statistics Updates.

QUARTERLY IPS RESULTS

More detailed data from the IPS are made available once it has been processed via the IPS quarterly processing system. These results are made available within five months of the end of the quarter, so data for quarter 1 2000 will be available in August of this year. Detailed information is available at this stage showing the numbers, nights stayed and spending of visitors, broken down by country of origin/visit, purpose of visit, mode of travel, age and gender of traveller. Analyses are also available grouping people by their duration of stay and port of entry/exit to the UK. Information is also available about in which regions of the UK overseas visitors have stayed while on their visit to the UK.

DISSEMINATION OF QUARTERLY DATA

This data is made available in a number of different formats and levels. A complete dataset is produced with weights attached to each interview conducted during the quarter. These weights can be summed to produce estimates of the number of visits to or from specific countries. The spending recorded can be multiplied by the weights and then summed to give an indication of the spending in that country or by residents of that country in the UK. This dataset is then sold to customers and to marketing agents for resale to others. The IPS marketing agents are listed in the Appendix.

A quarterly IPS business monitor is produced, tabulating key results from the quarter on a time series basis (MQ6 – overseas travel and tourism). This publication is available on subscription from the Stationery Office. Quarterly information is shown on both overseas residents' visits to the UK and of UK residents abroad, giving a breakdown of visits by mode of travel, country of residence/destination and purpose of travel. Information is also shown on spending and the number of nights stayed by the traveller. Also, a breakdown is shown of the number of overnight visits to the regions of the UK broken down by area of residence of the overseas visitor.

In addition, specific customer prints and bespoke reduced datasets are produced that allow customers to analyse the latest quarterly data.

ANNUAL IPS RESULTS

IPS results are revised on an annual basis at the end of the year, when methodological and definitional changes are taken into the processing system. These are normally made available in September of the following year.

Detailed information is available at this stage. Standard variables include:

- mode – main method of travel;
- quarter of travel;
- package – whether package trip or not;
- purpose of visit;
- country of residence for overseas visitors;
- spending on visit;
- nights spent on visit;
- country of visit for UK residents;
- age group;
- nationality of traveller;
- UK port used;
- overseas port used;
- vehicle used;
- flight type;
- class of travel.

In addition, analysis of other data is available. For example, in 1998 the IPS asked questions on the type of accommodation that overseas visitors to the UK stayed in while on their visits to the UK. From 1999, IPS data will be available showing the types of anti-malarials taken by UK residents on their visits abroad. Separate analyses could be made showing whether business or holiday travellers are more likely to take tablets than those visiting friends or family.

DISSEMINATION OF ANNUAL DATA

This data is made available in a number of different formats and at different levels. Revised quarterly datasets are produced with weights attached to each interview conducted during the quarter. These datasets are then sold to customers and to marketing agents for resale to others.

The main IPS publication, *Travel Trends*, is produced based on these revised quarterly datasets. This annual publication, available from the Stationery Office, contains a large volume of IPS tables detailing visits, spending and nights by combinations of the key variables shown above. This publication also contains a great deal of time series data, with annual data shown for the last twenty years and quarterly data for the last five years. Detailed tables are shown for the most recent year, showing, for example, spending per day of UK business travellers abroad by country of destination. *Travel Trends* also includes some commentary on the numbers. Bespoke customer prints (analyses for customers based on their own specifications and definitions) are produced at this stage and sent to customers. Examples of these are detailed breakdowns by age, sex and duration of stay.

In the last few years the IPS have produced *Travel*pac, a CD-ROM database product that allows users to perform more detailed analysis of the annual dataset than is possible from the tables within *Travel Trends*. For example, in *Travel Trends* the number of visits by UK residents to France is broken down by mode of travel, so that the number using the Channel Tunnel can be ascertained (4.6 of the 11.5 million visits made). Also, the number of visits to France is broken down by purpose, so that the number on business trips can be calculated (1.4 of the 11.5 million). However, if you wish to know how many business travellers used the Tunnel then this can only be done from *Travel*pac or from the complete IPS dataset (537,000 of the 1,419,000 business visits).

The variables included in the *Travel*pac are:

Year: year of travel
Quarter: quarter of travel
Mode: air, sea or Tunnel
Duration of stay: how long the visitor stayed in the country
Flow: arrivals by UK residents, departures by UK residents and the same for overseas residents
Weight: the number of trips the record represents
Country visited: the main country of visit (or country stayed in the longest) by UK residents abroad
Residence: the main country of residence of visitors to the UK
Purpose of visit: the main purpose of the visit
Package: whether on a package trip or not
Stay: nights stayed
Expenditure: expenditure (excluding fares) in £ sterling
Age: age group
Gender: male or female

Key annual IPS data are now also available via the National Statistics Statbase system. Key data are loaded annually and can be downloaded in CSV or other formats.

EXAMPLES OF INFORMATION AVAILABLE FROM THE IPS

From the details listed in earlier paragraphs it can be seen that there is a considerable amount of data to be found within the IPS. This paragraph contains a few tables and charts to illustrate the breadth of data contained.

More visitors came to the UK in 1998 than any other country. The UK also attracted many visitors from the rest of Europe. These visitors went to different regions of the UK and information on their spending patterns was recorded. The following chart shows where they spent money whilst in the UK.

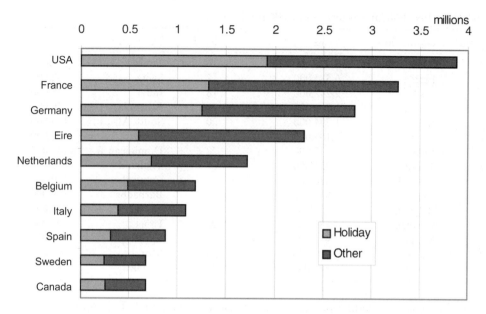

Figure 3.1 Visitors' top ten countries of residence and number of visits to the UK

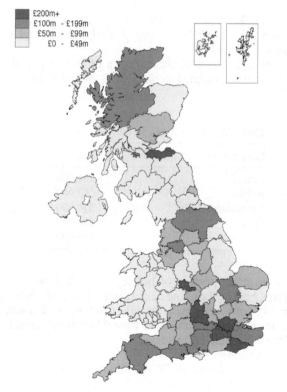

Figure 3.2 Overseas residents' spending in the UK by county/region of visit

Table 3.1 1998 holiday destinations of UK residents

Rank	Destination	Visits	Rank	Destination	Visits
1	Spain	8,895,000	16	Tunisia	331,000
2	France	6,530,000	17	Switzerland	302,000
3	USA	2,247,000	18	India	235,000
4	Greece	1,709,000	19	Australia	166,000
5	Italy	1,294,000	20	South Africa	166,000
6	Portugal	1,163,000	21	Mexico	157,000
7	Ireland	1,137,000	22	Dominican R.	143,000
8	Turkey	957,000	23	Thailand	140,000
9	Netherlands	886,000	24	Czech R.	119,000
10	Cyprus	851,000	25	Barbados	109,000
11	Belgium	739,000	26	Norway	100,000
12	Germany	587,000	27	Israel	96,000
13	Malta	418,000	28	Egypt	95,000
14	Austria	409,000	29	Morocco	91,000
15	Canada	344,000	30	Jamaica	82,000

Breakdowns of spending per day and per visit are calculated. The top-spending US visitors stayed an average of nine nights on their visits to the UK, spending £638 at an average of £73 per day.

The IPS also covers UK residents' trips abroad. Table 3.1 lists the top 30 holiday destinations as recorded by the IPS in 1998. Clearly, Spain and France remain our favourite destinations.

This list can be viewed in terms of the duration of these stays abroad. The top five destinations for short breaks, defined here as visits of less than four nights away, are shown in Table 3.2.

Table 3.2 Short-break holiday destinations

Destination	Visits
France	3,281,000
Belgium	592,000
Netherlands	574,000
Spain	314,000
Germany	190,000

As can be seen, a large proportion of holiday visits to France, and our other near neighbours, were short breaks. Looking at duration of stay of visits, the IPS shows that nearly four million day trips were made by UK residents to France, and nearly half a million to Belgium. In the same period there were 700,000 day trips by French residents to the UK and 375,000 by Belgian residents.

PLANNED DEVELOPMENTS FOR THE IPS

A number of developments are currently underway or planned for the coming year. The following paragraphs summarize the key projects that will impact on the IPS.

Changes to be introduced for 1999 results

Interviewing on Irish routes: the IPS commenced interviewing of passengers on routes to and from Ireland in April 1999. These data are currently being analysed and it is hoped to release them, with revised 1999 data, later this year. Interviews are being conducted at both air and sea terminals.

New weighting methodology: a study conducted by the Methodology Unit of the Social Survey Division of ONS recommended that some changes be made to the weighting system used for the IPS. These changes have been tested and will be implemented for the revised 1999 results.

Changes that will affect 2000 results

Foreign language questionnaires: following research conducted in 1999 it was estimated that 2 per cent of IPS interviews are adversely affected by language difficulties. In order to convert minimum responses (those where very little information is collected) to partial responses, it was shown that a questionnaire in the traveller's own language was needed. A self-completion questionnaire has been designed and is being used in the 2000 IPS. Foreign-language questionnaires in 2000 have been produced in French, German, Spanish, Italian, Greek, Portuguese, Japanese, Mandarin, Cantonese and Russian.

Changes that will affect later years' results

Evaluation of out-of-hours traffic: currently the IPS covers approximately sixteen hours of passenger traffic. Traffic outside these hours is not sampled but is accounted for in the IPS weighting system. Sampled traffic for each terminal and direction is grouped into ten regions of the world, defined by the flight origin and destination. Figures for the volume of unsampled traffic are obtained from the Civil Aviation Authority (CAA), and the sampled traffic is weighted up within the region group to account for this. The chief assumption of the weighting is that daytime and nighttime passengers within this group are similar. However, the unsampled traffic is not evenly distributed across the country groups and it is known that particular types of flights are being missed.

A research project is currently being conducted to test these assumptions. The research will assess whether it is necessary to collect information on a regular basis, out-of-hours, or whether adjustments need to be made to the current weighting mechanism, or whether the current treatment is sufficient. These data will be analysed during 2001 and final recommendations will be made in the autumn of 2001.

NEW DEVELOPMENTS IN DISSEMINATION

In addition to some of the methodological issues discussed above, the IPS is planning to make some changes in dissemination practices to make the data more accessible and useful to our customers and potential customers.

Monthly outputs

The key change in the IPS monthly outputs is the bringing forward of the publication of monthly results by one week from July 2000. The data shall now be available at 9.30am on the second Friday of the publication month. Data for May will therefore be available on 14 July, and June data available on 11 August, etc.

Quarterly outputs

A review is currently underway of the quarterly publication (MQ6 – overseas travel and tourism). Options under consideration include making this product available electronically for download from the National Statistics website. It is also planned to make more data available on a quarterly basis via Statbase.

Annual outputs

The main developments being considered at the moment are with regard to making databases available for customers to perform their own analyses. A more user-friendly interface has been developed for the *Travel*pac product. This should be available in November 2000 to coincide with the release of the next edition of *Travel Trends*.

In addition to *Travel*pac, the IPS is planning to produce a larger database for distribution that includes more variables than those covered in the existing product. Additional variables that are being considered for this product are:

UK port used: UK air- or sea port used
Overseas ports: overseas ports used
States of residence: region of residence for overseas visitors to the UK for selected countries
UK county: county of residence for UK residents
Nationality: nationality of traveller
Persons: number of people travelling in spending group
Number in vehicle: number of people in vehicle
Type of flight: whether scheduled or charter flight
Class of air travel: whether first, business or economy.

APPENDIX

IPS marketing agents

MDS TRANSMODAL
5–6 Hunters Walk
Canal Street
Chester CH1 4EB
Tel: 01244 348301
Fax: 01244 348471
E-mail: queries@mdst.co.uk
    MDST@compuserve.com
Web: www.mdst.co.uk

SH&E LTD
210 High Holborn
London WC1V 7BW
Tel: 0207 242 9333
Fax: 0207 242 9334
E-mail: ips@sh-e.co.uk
Web: www.sh-e.com

INFORMATION RESEARCH
NETWORK
Davis House
129 Wilton Road
London SW1V 1LD.
Tel: 0207 416 8107
Fax: 0207 828 2030
E-mail: irnxxx@easynet.co.uk
Web: www.interstat.co.uk

OFFICE FOR NATIONAL
STATISTICS
International Passenger Survey
Room B2/12
1 Drummond Gate
London SW1V 2QQ
Tel: 0207 533 5765
Fax: 0207 533 6154
E-mail: ips@ons.gov.uk
Web: www.statistics.gov.uk

4

Inbound Tourism in The Netherlands in 1999

Herman Bos and Roel Wittink

1. INTRODUCTION

Data on the demand side of the tourist market in The Netherlands is scarce. During the last 25 years information on inbound tourism for the country as a whole has been published only rarely. In 1979 and 1984 the survey on inbound tourism was conducted by interviewing tourists at the border on leaving The Netherlands. One of the consequences of opening up the borders between the countries in the European Community was that conducting a border survey on tourism became very complicated. In 1993/94 an inbound tourism survey was conducted using a new interview approach. Tourists from abroad were interviewed at the moment of checking out of their accommodation. During every interview period, ten foreign-tourist parties were interviewed on the day of leaving (an interview period is defined as one week and a tourist party is defined as a person travelling alone or a group of people travelling together who have collective spending during the trip). One member of the tourist party was interviewed. When many foreign tourists left at the same time, a time-span of ten to fifteen minutes between every interview was observed. To create a research population of accommodation establishments it was possible to make use of the data of the survey *Tourism Accommodations* from Statistics Netherlands, which reveals information on the number of guests and their overnight stays by country of residence, on a monthly basis. Moreover, this survey also reveals supply-side information of 95 per cent on the accommodation establishments in The Netherlands. In 1999 this method was applied for the second time.

The 1999 survey, however, shows some significant changes in comparison with the 1993/94 survey. First of all, there was a significant change in financing of the inbound tourism survey. This change, and its implications on the questionnaire, is the subject considered in section 2. In section 5 the survey on inbound tourism of 1999 is compared with this survey of 1993/94 in three aspects: response rates; content of the questionnaires; and the question 'Does the postulate of the 5-minute interview still hold?' The focus in sections 3 and 4 is on the steps that had to be made in order to create populations of accommodation establishments appropriate for, and willing to, co-operate with the survey. The chapter ends with a discussion on inbound tourism.

2. POLICY ASPECTS, ORGANIZATION AND FINANCING

The need for a new survey on the structure of demand of inbound tourism was included in an inventory by the Ministry of Economic Affairs on the needs for, and priorities of, tourism research. It was decided that a new survey every four years was needed, as it is nearly impossible for The Netherlands to obtain data otherwise on a regular base. The decision includes the assumption that the structure of demand changes only very slowly and that continuous tracking is not essential. At the same time, a new policy on the responsibility for basic tourism research, and how to finance this research programme, came into being. Annual data is needed on holiday-making among the Dutch population and on the arrivals of visitors from abroad by country of origin (including the type of accommodation used, the time of year and the distribution over the various regions). These are financed fully by the government, though the holiday survey is part of a multi-client survey for which the Foundation for Continuous Holiday Research (CVO) is responsible and which can be regarded as a good example of public partnership in tourism research.

For the bigger, less frequent surveys, i.e. on inbound tourism and day trips, the Ministry of Economic Affairs is, within the framework of conditional investments, now only prepared to pay 50 per cent of the costs involved. The benefiting industry has, for their part, to show its interest by its willingness to finance the other half of the costs. The industry is regarded as another party, not being the Ministry of Economic Affairs. As only a limited number of parties have adequate budgets to participate substantially, the funding of that 50 per cent is problematic to organize. Only by convincing major possible benefactors did we finally succeed in a break-even budget. It will be clear that, in order to gain their support, special questions of interest had to be considered.

Costs and fundraising

The total cost of the survey was calculated as approximately €500,000. The largest part, €320,000, is for the actual fieldwork done by a research company with experience of the first survey on inbound tourism in 1993/94. Statistics Netherlands requires €180,000 for their services.

The Ministry of Economic Affairs (A) contributes €250,000, The Netherlands Board of Tourism (B) €125,000.

The remaining part is financed by the following participants:

C. the National Board for Hotels, Restaurants, Bars and Catering (Hotel and Catering Industry Board) (€45,000);
D. the Ministry of Agriculture, Environment and Fisheries (€22,500);
E. the Ministry of Transport and Water Management (€22,500);
F. the Ministry of Education, Culture and Science (€22,500);
G. KLM Royal Dutch Airlines (€22,500);
H. the organization for entrepreneurs in campsites, holiday dwelling and recreation-parks (Recron);

I.   the organization of inbound tour operators (ANVR-VRI).

The last two organizations pay €1000, in order to show 'moral' support.

Rationale for participating and subsequent questions

No specific questions were included by the Ministry of Economic Affairs. The Ministry, however, is particularly interested in the total spend, considering that the travel balance of payments includes much other spending apart from just travel. The Hotel and Catering Industry Board is particularly interested in the level of satisfaction with accommodation, services and consumer-friendliness as are Recron and NBT. The Ministry of Agriculture, Environment and Fisheries is very interested in the appreciation of nature and landscape, this being their responsibility as part of their policy on outdoor recreation. Their policy, in general terms, is related to the needs of the Dutch population, but a better understanding of the views of visitors from abroad is regarded as most welcome. The Ministry of Transport and Water Management continuously studies the transportation of the national population, but as they lack adequate data on transportation of foreign visitors in the country, the study is most welcome in order to gain a better knowledge in this area. It is incumbent on the Ministry to ensure that this information is of value in attracting foreign visitors. The NBT can provide useful insight into the success or failure of this aim, because of its emphasis and expenditure on cultural facilities. Though KLM has a good knowledge of their passengers, additional information on the use of competitors is of interest to them. For this survey this is more related to emotional reasons for visiting the country.

   The NBT already has good information on the motives of summer holiday-makers, but lacks adequate data outside the main season. The summer data is based on face-to-face questioning at the borders, but a nationally representative sample could, in a general way, not be cost effective.

3. INBOUND TOURISM IN PRACTICE

The 1999 survey does not cover all types of accommodation. To create the research population we made use of the data of the 'Tourism Accommodations' survey. The lower limit for every identified accommodation category in that survey is five bed places for hotels and similar establishments, and twenty bed places for tourist campsites, holiday dwellings and other collective accommodations. Although it does not cover all accommodations, the volume of this population is at least 95 per cent of the total capacity. The result was that the population under research totalled 6290 accommodation establishments (see Table 4.1).

   Tourists were selected for interview by a two-step sampling model. In the first step we selected those accommodation establishments which had reported to Statistics Netherlands more than 365 guests from abroad in 1998. This step resulted in a population of 840 accommodation establishments which were qualified to serve as the sample. In the next step, 1000 interview periods were distributed at random over a sample of 840 accommodation establishments. In this second step we took account of the following variables: the number of foreign guests in the accommodation; type of accommodation; region; and the distribution of the guests during the year.

Table 4.1 Accommodation establishments in 'Tourism Accommodations' in 1998

	Number of accommodation establishments according to the survey Tourism Accommodations	Number of accommodation establishments with at least 365 guests from abroad in 1998	Number of accommodations to be visited for interviews
Hotels and similar establishments	2,788	601	196
Tourists campsites	2,035	130	80
Holiday dwellings	708	75	46
Other collective establishments	759	34	25
Total	6,290	840	347

Table 4.1 shows that this method resulted in a sample of 347 tourism accommodations, where 10,000 tourist-party members were to be interviewed. Of this total, 4920 were to be interviewed in hotels and similar establishments, 2220 in holiday dwellings, another 2150 on tourist campsites and 710 in youth hostels and other collective accommodations. Every accommodation was visited at least twice by the interviewers. The large accommodations had to be visited eleven times, maximum, for hotels and similar establishments, ten times for tourists campsites, twenty times for holiday dwellings and fourteen times for other collective establishments. A consequence of this maximum number of visits was that some accommodations had to be visited more than once during a month. The maximum number of visits we allowed was four, i.e. 40 interviews per accommodation per month.

4. THE CO-OPERATION OF ACCOMMODATIONS: FROM PLAN TO REALIZATION

At that stage we had the names and addresses of 347 accommodation establishments at which we had planned 10,000 interviews in total. These interviews had to be realized during 1000 visits distributed during 1999. The main question for the next stage of the survey was, 'Is every selected accommodation establishment prepared to co-operate?' In order to answer this question we sent out a letter to the contact persons of the selected accommodations which were known from the monthly survey Tourism Accommodations of Statistics Netherlands. In that letter we announced the survey Inbound Tourism to be held for 1999 and mentioned our intention to visit them once or several times during the year for interviewing the guests from abroad at the moment of their checking out of the accommodation. Next to that, we assured the informants that each interview would not take more than five minutes. Finally, we announced that we would contact them after a fortnight by phone in order to obtain their willingness, or their refusal, to co-operate.

In the case of refusal, we developed the following rules: select another accommodation establishment in the population with at least 365 guests from abroad in 1998 and try to find an accommodation that fulfils the following conditions: the accommodation

Table 4.2 Willingness of the accommodations establishments to co-operate

	Number of accommodations				
	Planned	Realized	Refusals in total	Substitutes	Allocated interview periods
Hotels and similar establishments	196	169	101	41	81
Tourists campsites	80	75	12	5	14
Holiday dwellings	46	40	9	2	20
Other collective establishments	25	24	1	0	2
Total	347	308	123	48	117

must fall in the same stratum, must have about the same number of guests from abroad in 1998 and must be in the same region. The conditions must be fulfilled in that order. If it is not possible to find another accommodation as a substitute for the original accommodation, the following procedure had to be followed: select a co-operative accommodation which is most similar to the refusing one in terms of stratum and region. In case of the availability of more than one alternative, we gave preference to that accommodation which has the highest foreign-guests quota. That quota is the number of foreign guests in 1998 divided by the number of already allocated interview periods.

The result of this part of the Inbound Tourism survey was that we faced the least problems among the other collective establishments (see Table 4.2). From only one accommodation came a refusal to co-operate, and those two interview periods were allocated to two different accommodations. The co-operation of the tourist campsites and holiday dwellings was rather good. The refusals amounted to fifteen, 20 per cent of the number of planned accommodations. The number of interview periods that had to be reallocated remained restricted to fourteen. The willingness to co-operate was the least for the hotels and similar establishments. From the original sample, 68 accommodations were not willing to receive our interviewers. For eighteen it was not possible to find a suitable substitute. For the remaining 50 refusals from the original population, we eventually found 41 substitutes. For the other nine refusals, after searching for another substitute it turned out to be an impossible task. The 81 interview periods of those 27 accommodations were reallocated among the willing accommodations.

5. INBOUND TOURISM OF 1993/94 AND 1999 IN COMPARISON

When we compare the survey of 1993/94 with the survey of 1999 there are similarities and differences. In this section we restrict ourselves to the discussion of three fundamental changes and their implications on (the design of) the survey on inbound tourism of 1999. The first and most important implication of the change in the financing of the survey was that the number of interviews had to be restricted to 10,000. A second change was that the participation of market parties implied a number of additional questions that had to be asked of the tourists. And, finally, this augmented questionnaire raised the question, Are tourists willing to answer these questions and is it still possible to answer the whole questionnaire within the compulsory time limit of five minutes?

Response rates

The yearly number of guests from abroad has grown in the period 1993–9 from 6.2 million foreign guests to almost 10 million. A part of the increase resulted from an improvement in methodology. The number of planned interviews for the Inbound Tourism Survey, however, decreased from 14,000 in 1993/94 to 10,000 in 1999. The implication of these changes is that one interview represented about 450 foreign guests in the survey of 1993/94, whereas one interview in the survey of 1999 counted for 1000 foreign guests. One of the consequences is that it is not possible to maintain the same publication scheme, and therefore the same reliability level, as was in operation in 1993/94.

This information makes clear that it was a matter of the highest importance that the realization of interviews should resemble, as closely as possible, the planning of the interviews. It caused us to extend the rules for the interviewers. Instead of making one visit on a specific settled day to a specific accommodation and interviewing ten foreign guests, we allowed more visits. These additional visits had to be held in the same month and on the same day of the week, until ten interviews were completed. In the case that the first visit made a second visit impossible in the same month, the interviewers could go back to the accommodation on the next day in the same month until ten interviews were held.

The fieldwork of the first survey on inbound tourism was done between October 1993 and October 1994, and resulted in a total of 10,436 interviews, as can be seen in Table 4.3. This number implies a response rate of 75 per cent. The fieldwork of the survey held in 1999 resulted in 8016 interviews which could be used for rounding up. Better results among the hotel and similar establishments, and especially among the holiday dwellings, implied a response rate for all accommodation establishments in 1999 of 81 per cent.

Table 4.3 Interviews among tourist parties for the Inbound Tourism Survey of 1993/94 and 1999

| | Number of interviews | | | | Response rate | |
| | Planned | | Realized | | Percentage | |
	1993/94	1999	1993/94	1999	1993/94	1999
Hotels and similar establishments	7,000	4,920	5,395	4,032	77	82
Tourist campsites	3,000	2,150	1,902	1,420	63	66
Holiday dwellings	3,000	2,220	2,387	2,060	80	94
Other collective establishments	1,000	710	752	504	75	71
Total	14,000	10,000	10,436	8,016	74	81

The questionnaires

The idea of the questionnaires of 1993/94 and 1999 (see Appendix) is much the same: most of the questions were maintained and some questions were maintained but simplified. Nevertheless, there were some significant changes in the questionnaire: it has been augmented, with questions on the following subjects: means of transport in The Netherlands; type of reservation and the time between reservation and stay; main motive and second-best motive for the holiday in The Netherlands; activities during their stay; level of satisfaction with their accommodation; the service and their stay in general; and what was appreciated the most and the least in The Netherlands. These additions resulted in an increase of the number of questions from 16 to 21.

The five-minute interview

The fact that the questionnaire had been expanded under the influence of the wishes of the participants did raise questions concerning the willingness of the foreign guests to answer these questions, and also whether it is possible to maintain our postulate that the interview will take no longer than five minutes.

As can be seen from Table 4.4, the average of five minutes was still a good estimation of the time for interviewing a foreign guest, with a slight deviation for the time needed for the interviews at other collective establishments. The score for the maximum time taken for an interview shows that some guests were actually on holiday and that some of them were pleased to be interviewed.

Table 4.4   The interview time

	Mean	Standard deviation	Minimum	Maximum
	Time in seconds			
Hotels and similar establishments	291	242	29	3,190
Tourist campsites	325	335	11	5,802
Holiday dwellings	282	323	22	7,407
Other collective establishments	390	419	50	5,829

A three-category split for the interview time – less than five minutes, five to ten minutes and more than ten minutes – shows that more than half of the interviewed foreign guests on other collective establishments were prepared to spend more than five minutes to give an interview (see Table 4.5). The same was the case for 45 per cent of the interviewed campsite guests from abroad and even for more than one third of the guests in holiday dwellings and in hotels and similar establishments.

6. INBOUND TOURISM CONTINUED

The objective of the survey Inbound Tourism 1999 was to gain insight into the composition of the foreign-tourist stream coming to The Netherlands by geographical

Table 4.5 The interview time in three categories

	Less than 5 minutes (%)	5 to 10 minutes (%)	10 minutes (%)
Hotels and similar establishments	64	31	5
Tourist campsites	56	36	8
Holiday dwellings	64	30	5
Other collective establishments	46	41	13

region, reason for coming, age, the pattern of stay, the volume of the tourist party, the motive for visiting The Netherlands, the level of satisfaction and the pattern of spending etc. The outcome of the survey is that we have a clear impression now of the profile of the foreign tourists visiting our country. The survey is essential in acquiring a more complete overview of the Dutch tourist industry and, together with the results of the survey of 1993/94, it is possible to make a start on an historic analysis which opens the possibility of developing trends and forecasting. Moreover, it enables policy-makers to develop plans and policy for creating an even better climate for foreign tourists visiting The Netherlands. The results are sufficiently encouraging for us to conclude that it is worthwhile to continue an accommodation approach to inbound tourism research.

Nevertheless, there remain some problems to be solved. In the survey Inbound Tourism 1999 foreign tourists were interviewed at the moment of checking out of the accommodation. One of the implications of this method is that the population under research didn't include tourists on day trips and those who resided on a boat, in their second home or exclusively with family and/or friends, and those who visited The Netherlands on a cruise. The question is in what way the categories of tourists can be monitored to make our overview more complete.

Another improvement can be found in the increased willingness of the accommodation establishments to co-operate. Likewise the willingness of the foreign tourists to answer the questions. Finally, the actual and potential participants have to find sufficient motivation, in the outcomes of the survey and its implications, to finance the next inbound tourism survey in 2003.

APPENDIX

Survey Inbound Tourism 1999

1a.   In which country do you live?
      Germany . . . . -01
      Belgium . . . . -02
      Great Britain . . . . -03
      Luxembourg . . . . -04
      France . . . . -05
      Spain . . . . -06
      Italy . . . . -07
      Switzerland / Austria . . . . -08
      Sweden / Norway / Finland . . . . -09
      Denmark . . . . -10
      Another country in Europe . . . . -11
      USA . . . . -12
      Canada . . . . -13
      Other America (Central and South) . . . . -14
      Japan . . . . -15
      Other Asia . . . . -16
      Australia, New Zealand, Oceania . . . . -17
      Africa . . . . -18

1b.   In which Bundesland (Germany), in which province (of Belgium) or in
      which part of Great Britain do you live?

GERMANY
Baden-Württemberg . . . . -11
Bayern . . . . -12
Berlin . . . . -13
Brandenburg . . . . -14
Bremen . . . . -15
Hamburg . . . . -16
Hessen . . . . -17
Mecklenburg-Vorpommern . . . . -18
Niedersachsen . . . . -19
Nordrhein Westfalen . . . . -20
Rheinland-Pfalz . . . . -21
Saarland . . . . -22
Sachsen . . . . -23
Sachsen-Anhalt . . . . -24
Schleswig-Holstein . . . . -25
Thüringen . . . . -26

BELGIUM
Antwerpen . . . . -31
Brabant (incl. Brussel) . . . . -32
Henegouwen . . . . -33

Limburg. . . . . -34
Luik. . . . . -35
Luxemburg . . . . -36
Namen . . . . -37
Oost-Vlaanderen. . . . . -38
West-Vlaanderen . . . . -39

GREAT BRITAIN
North (Northern Ireland, Scotland, North England). . . . . -41
Middle (Wales, North West, Yorkshire and Humberside, East and
West Midlands) . . . . -42
Greater London area. . . . . -43
South (East Anglia, South West or South East, but not Greater
London). . . . . -44

2   Please indicate on this card to which category you belong:

Travelling alone:
Younger than 25 . . . . -01   → 4
Between 25 and 39 . . . . -02   → 4
Between 40 and 54 . . . . -03   → 4
55 or older . . . . -04   → 4

Two partners travelling without children:
Oldest partner younger than 25. . . . . -05   → 4
Oldest partner between 25 and 39 . . . . -06   → 4
Oldest partner between 40 and 54 . . . . -07   → 4
Oldest partner 55 or older. . . . . -08   → 4

Two partners travelling with a child/children:
Oldest partner younger than 25. . . . . -09
Oldest partner between 25 and 39 . . . . -10
Oldest partner between 40 and 54 . . . . -11
Oldest partner 55 or older. . . . . -12

One adult travelling with a child/children:
Oldest adult younger than 25 . . . . -13
Oldest adult between 25 and 39. . . . . -14
Oldest adult between 40 and 54. . . . . -15
Oldest adult 55 or older . . . . -16

**Other, e.g. two couples or two or more friends, acquaintances or
relatives travelling together:**
Oldest person younger than 25. . . . . -17
Oldest person between 25 and 39 . . . . -18
Oldest person between 40 and 54 . . . . -19
Oldest person 55 or older. . . . . -20

Don't know/unknown . . . . -21

3.   How many people are you travelling with (including yourself)?

Number of people:

4a.   How many nights did you spend in this accommodation?

Number of nights spent in this accommodation:

4b.   How many nights will you spend in Holland during this trip,
<u>including your stay in this accommodation?</u>

4c.   What is the total number of nights during this trip, <u>including</u>
<u>the number of nights in Holland?</u>

5.   Please indicate with which means of transport you travelled to Holland.
Car, motorbike, camper . . . . -01   → 7
Coach . . . . -02   → 7
Bicycle, moped . . . . -03   → 7
Ferry (without your own means of transport). . . . . -04   → 7
Train . . . . -05   → 7
Plane . . . . -06   → 6
Other, i.e.:. . . . . -07   → 7

6.   Which airline did you fly with, if you arrived in Holland by plane?
(Participant G)
KLM. . . . . -01
KLM partner (e.g. NorthWest, Alitalia, AirUK). . . . . -02
Other airline (e.g. BA, SAS, AA) . . . . -03
Don't know. . . . . -04

7.   Which is the <u>main</u> means of transport with which you travelled
within Holland?
(Participant E)
Car, motorbike, camper . . . . -01
Coach . . . . -02
Bicycle, moped, on foot . . . . -03
Taxi . . . . -04
Bus, tram, underground . . . . -05
Train . . . . -06
Other, i.e.:. . . . . -07

8.   Are you a member of a group tour?
No . . . . -1
Yes . . . . -2 → 10a

9a.   How did you book your stay in this accommodation (or how was
your stay booked)?
(Participants B, C, H, I)
In advance, directly with the accommodation . . . . -1 →9b

In advance, through an organisation (e.g. travel agent / reservations centre) in own country . . . . -2 →9b
In advance, through an organisation (e.g. travel agent / reservations centre) in Holland. . . . . -3 →9b
Upon arrival at the accommodation . . . . -4 →10a
In another way, i.e.: . . . . -5 →10a

9b. How long prior to travelling did you make the reservation?
Less than 1 month ago. . . . . -1
Between 1 and 3 months ago. . . . . -2
Longer than 3 months ago . . . . -3
Don't know (any more) . . . . -4

10a. Have you stayed in Holland previously, during another trip?
(Participant B)
Yes . . . . -1
No . . . . -2 → 11

10b. How often have you travelled to Holland during the past three years and stayed overnight (not including this trip)?

Number of times:

11. Please indicate the <u>main</u> reason for this trip to Holland.
Holiday (including a weekend trip, midweek stay, etc.). . . . . -1 → 12
Visiting friends or relatives . . . . -2 → 14
Business trip: trip for your work (not a congress!) . . . . -3 → 14
Accompanying someone who is on a business trip (not a congress) -4 → 14
Participation in a congress . . . . -5 → 14
Accompanying someone who is participating in a congress. . . . . . . -6 → 14
School or study trip: trip for your study . . . . -7 → 14
Accompanying someone who is on a school or study trip . . . . -8 → 14
Stop-over on the way to another country . . . . -9 → 14
Another reason . . . . -10 → 14

12. What **gave you the idea** to spend your holiday in Holland?
(more than one answer possible) **(Participant B)**
Read about Holland in a newspaper/magazine . . . . -1
Saw a television programme on Holland . . . . -2
Heard a radio programme on Holland . . . . -3
As a result of a TV commercial . . . . -4
As a result of a radio commercial. . . . . -5
The advice/stories of friends/relatives . . . . -6
As a result of visiting a travel agency. . . . . -7
As a result of visiting a holiday fair . . . . -8
Information from the Netherlands Board of Tourism . . . . -9
Information from a VVV (local tourist office) . . . . -10
Through Internet . . . . -11
No special reason/just wanted to visit Holland (again). . . . . -12
Another reason, i.e. . . . . -13

13a. How would you, in general, characterise your motive for your holiday in Holland?
Please give your main motive first. **(Participants B, D, F)**
City trip . . . . -1
Beach holiday. . . . . -2
Holiday on the inland waterways . . . . -3
Holiday in the countryside (i.e. not a city trip, not a beach holiday or a holiday on the inland waterways). . . . . -4
Touring through the country . . . . -5
Cultural holiday. . . . . -6
Active holiday (cycling, walking). . . . . -7

13b. What is the next most important characterisation of the motive for your holiday?
(Participants B, D, F)
City trip . . . . -1
Beach holiday. . . . . -2
Holiday on the inland waterways . . . . -3
Holiday in the countryside (i.e. not a city trip, not a beach holiday or a holiday on the inland waterways). . . . . -4
Touring through the country . . . . -5
Cultural holiday. . . . . -6
Active holiday (cycling, walking). . . . . -7

14. Which of the following did you do during your stay?
(more than one answer possible)
(Participants B, C, D, E, F, H, I)
Had a meal in a restaurant. . . . . -1
Had a drink in a bar/ café . . . . -2
Fun shopping . . . . -3
Visited Amsterdam . . . . -4
Visited The Hague, Rotterdam, Utrecht. -5
Visited smaller cities and towns . . . . -6
Visited a museum . . . . -7
Attended a concert . . . . -8
Attended a theatre performance . . . . -9
Visited/looked at buildings worth seeing, old parts of cities/small villages. . . . . -10
Took trips by car. . . . . -11
Cycling. . . . . -12
Walking . . . . -13
Swimming . . . . -14
Sailing, surfing, canoeing. . . . . -15
Spent time in a wood or nature reserve . . . . -16
Visited an amusement park . . . . -17
Visited a zoo. . . . . -18
Visited an event (e.g. a festival, major exhibition). . . . . -19
Visited/attended a flower exhibition/gardens/flowerparade . . . . . . -20
Attended a (major) sports tournament . . . . -21
Went on an organised excursion by coach . . . . -22

I will now ask you some questions about your spending.

You are travelling with . . . . persons

15. Can you indicate the <u>total amount</u> of money spent by these persons?
No . . . . -1 **19a** →
Yes . . . . -2 **16** →

16. Did you and/or your travelling companions (to whom the amount
of money spent relates) pay in advance (at home) for your stay
in this accommodation?
No . . . . -1 **18a** →
Yes, accommodation costs only. . . . . -2 **17** →
Don't know . . . . -4 **18a** →

17. What was the amount of money paid in advance for accommodation
costs?

CURRENCY:
Dutch guilder . . . . -01
German mark . . . . -02
English pound . . . . -03
Belgian/Luxembourg franc . . . . -04
American dollar . . . . -05
French franc . . . . -06
Italian lire . . . . -07
Spanish peseta . . . . -08
Swiss franc . . . . -09
Swedish crown . . . . -10
Danish crown . . . . -11
Euro . . . . -12
Other, i.e.: . . . . -13

AMOUNT :
(please round off the amount)
Don't know . . . . -14

I would now like to ask you how much your party spent
<u>during</u> your stay in this <u>accommodation</u> in Holland.

18a. Which currency do you want to use for your answer?
CURRENCY:
Dutch guilder . . . . -01   18b
German mark . . . . -02
English pound . . . . -03
Belgian/Luxembourg franc . . . . -04
American dollar . . . . -05
French franc . . . . -06
Italian lira . . . . -07
Spanish peseta . . . . -08
Swiss franc . . . . -09

Swedish crown. . . . . -10
Danish crown . . . . -11

Other, i.e.: . . . .
Don't know. . . . . -13   19a
Prefer not to tell . . . . -14

18b. Please indicate per category on this card how much you and you
party have spent during your stay in this accommodation?

Category:	Amount spent:
1 Accommodation, food and beverages	. . . .
2 Transport within Holland	. . . .
3 Admission fees, excursions	. . . .
4 Purchases, souvenirs	. . . .
TOTAL AMOUNT SPENT:	. . . .

18c. According to your statement, you and your party have spent . . . . during
your stay in this accommodation
Is that approximately correct?
No. . . . . -1   **18b AGAIN →**
Yes . . . . -2   **19a**   →

19a. How satisfied are you about the accommodation in which you have just
stayed?
Please give a mark from 1 to 5; 1 being very dissatisfied, 2 dissatisfied,
3 neither dissatisfied nor satisfied, 4 satisfied and 5 very satisfied
(Participants B, C, H)

19b. How satisfied are you about the service / customer-friendliness in Holland
in general?
Please give a mark from 1 to 5; 1 being very dissatisfied, 2 dissatisfied,
3 neither dissatisfied nor satisfied, 4 satisfied and 5 very satisfied

19c. How satisfied are you, in general, about your stay in Holland?
Please give a mark from 1 to 5; 1 being very dissatisfied, 2 dissatisfied,
3 neither dissatisfied nor satisfied, 4 satisfied and 5 very satisfied

20. What did you appreciate most during your stay in Holland?
    Only <u>one</u> reply is possible. **(Participants B, C, D, E, F, H)**
    The people, friendly population, atmosphere. . . . .   -1
    Amsterdam . . . .   -2
    The coast . . . .   -3
    Peace and quiet . . . .   -4
    Nature and landscape. . . . .   -5
    Cultural history. . . . .   -6
    Cycling . . . .   -7
    Pubs/restaurants/accommodations . . . .   -8
    Attractions/events . . . .   -9
    Large and small cities and towns. . . . . -10
    Don't know/ nothing . . . . -11

21. What did you least appreciate during your stay in Holland?
    Only <u>one</u> reply is possible
    (Participants B, C, H)
    Don't know / there is nothing I appreciated least . . . .   -1
    Transport and traffic problems (such as traffic jams, parking, sign-
    posting). . . . .   -2
    Filthiness (such as graffiti, rubbish in the streets or on the beach) .   -3
    Price level . . . .   -4
    Quality accommodation(s). . . . .   -5
    Quality restaurants . . . .   -6
    Bustle . . . .   -7
    Criminality/unsafe feeling/drugs/porno/sex. . . . .   -8
    Service level / customer-friendliness . . . . -10
    Something else which you appreciated least . . . . -11

THANK YOU VERY MUCH FOR YOUR CO-OPERATION

5

Rural Tourism Micro-enterprises (RTME) Sector Statistics: The Need for and Current Lack of Statistics in RTME

Paul Richardson

INTRODUCTION

The purpose of this chapter is to cast light on statistics in the RTME sector from the point of view of an insider. The author of the chapter started working full-time in rural (farm) tourism marketing and development, almost by chance, in the mid-eighties. He then lived on a farm in South Iceland, working as a professional translator and offering short horse-riding tours in the summers – at a time when there were almost no tourism enterprises run by members of the local community. After joining the Farm Holidays Association he was elected to the board and then elected president, mainly because of his experience of writing promotional material in English for the Icelandic tourism industry. For the next twelve years he worked on developing the farm holidays sector, which now has a chain of guesthouses and farm hotels all round the country, marketed by a tour-operator company owned mainly by the providers. He was also elected first president of the European Federation for Farm and Village Tourism in 1991. Subsequently, the author has worked as a rural tourism consultant in a number of former Soviet-bloc countries, most recently in Poland, Russia (Kamchatka) and Latvia. He has led an EC Leonardo da Vinci project that aims at targeted dissemination of vocational training for rural tourism at a European level, and is the technical co-ordinator for a fifth EC Framework Information Technology Project called VMART. This project started officially on 1 November 2000. VMART uses ICT for marketing and development purposes for the RTME sector and will also establish a structure that will enhance the quality and availability of RTME statistics.

The opinions expressed in this chapter are not based on an academic study of the RTME sector at a European level but on the author's own experience and on his discussions with practitioners in a number of European countries during the last decade. The opinions are insights and should be taken as such, bearing in mind that there are, doubtless, exceptions to what is presented here.

THE HYPOTHESIS

The hypothesis is that the RTME sector as a whole has not advanced in accordance with its potential during the past decade and that this failure can be attributed, in part, to a lack of reliable information. In addition, there is a lack of informed interpretation of what does exist in the way of statistics. Reliable information and statistics are prerequisites for elaborating feasible development strategies and for gaining the funding necessary for the successful implementation of such strategies

SUMMARY

The chapter will deal briefly with the background to RTME development and with the sector in perspective as part of the whole tourism offer. Categories of useful statistics will be defined and examples given of their availability according to the author's experience. The author will also comment on examples of methodology of collecting statistics for the RTME sector and on actions that need to be taken at national or local level that would help improve the quality of statistics. Finally, there will be a view on how better statistics will enhance the RTME sector.

BACKGROUND

During the last decade there have been great advances in tourism, both in terms of economic growth and in terms of advances in the use of telematics. Large amounts of money, from public and private sources, have been spent on regional development in Europe, often specifically targeted at tourism. Looking back at this decade, it is fair to say that there was no lack of vision for rural tourism at the outset and that many current developments in tourism were predicted. If one limits oneself to the rural tourism sector one could ask why we are not more advanced today, particularly in employing the new technology for collection and dissemination of information. Other sectors have implemented their vision – particularly in IT – but progress in RTME is slower than anticipated.

RTME SECTOR IN PERSPECTIVE

At this point it is worthwhile putting the small rural operator into perspective in terms of the industry as a whole. An OECD conference on tourism management at national level was held in Mexico in November 1997. Some interesting statistics and conclusions were published in the conference documents. In Europe, 95.6 per cent of tourism enterprises in the accommodation and catering sectors have a staff of ten or fewer.

These enterprises account for 60 per cent of employment in that sector of tourism. There is a significant (unquantified) proportion of these enterprises in rural areas. One of the conclusions was that the tourism industry was fragmented in some sectors while in other sectors, like hotel chains and airlines, there was a tendency to merge, and thus create fewer and larger units. Recent forecasts on tourism trends say that the 612 million tourists of 1997 will increase to 1600 million in the year 2020, and that the growth areas will be tourism – where the attraction is related to natural environments – ecotourism and activity tourism. Individual entrepreneurs with a small staff traditionally develop the basic service units for eco- and activity tourism.

USEFUL STATISTICS AND CURRENT AVAILABILITY

The kind of statistics needed at a European level are as follows.

The number of providers

This would appear to be a fairly simple task, but there are many reasons why the figures given by official sources are usually not accurate for the smallest of providers or units. Larger establishments, traditionally, use part-time, unregistered providers for overflow, and these providers start to get business direct. They are usually not included in official figures. In some regions, like the south of Spain, the official requirements and fees to be paid by operators are higher than the small providers can support so they continue to fulfil demand without being officially registered. Many small operators will remain invisible in order to avoid taxation. The task of finding all the small providers and maintaining up-to-date information about their offers is usually seen as too time-consuming by the authorities who find it easier to ignore them. Summer cottages or apartments in private ownerships may be leased or may be subject to a time-share agreement. They are, to a certain extent, part of the tourism offer, but are usually not registered as such. There are even organizations that own many cottages, rented internally to their staff, that are not counted in the tourism offer. In Iceland this is a common scenario and there are many examples of these dwellings having been leased on the open market without appearing in the statistics for the tourism offer. This is doubtless also the case in many eastern European countries where institutions and enterprises traditionally provided subsidised summer camps for their staff.

Types and quality of units

Many of the above-mentioned factors also influence the accuracy of statistics on types and quality of units. Another problem with these statistics is that it is expensive to maintain an up-to-date database for so many small units, and the information is often not validated by an independent party. Nor is there a standardized manner of describing the smallest accommodation in the same way that hotel accommodation is described by the larger hotel brands.

Number of beds

The capacity of the units in the RTME sector is less well defined than that of the hotel industry, not only because many of the units are invisible but also because some units are not classified as holiday accommodation. There are also examples in many countries of a cut-off point, e.g. maximum eight beds, where the proprietor's status with regards to, for example, statutory fire precautions, changes. The size of his operation may also affect his tax status or requirements regarding provision of toilet facilities. Complying with certain requirements may be expensive, so it can be in the interests of the proprietor to appear smaller than he actually is.

Occupancy

It is clear that the lack of accurate statistics on the above-mentioned aspects confuses any attempts to estimate occupancy in a meaningful way. There is also less professionalism among the smallest of providers in registering occupancy and a high level of bookings that do not go through a sales agent. It is normal to expect that a certain proportion of direct bookings will not be registered, though this will vary greatly from country to country.

Profit/loss

Calculations on the profitability of RTME enterprises often indicate a poor return on investment, but this will vary greatly depending on the market realities in each instance. There is a great need to study this aspect in a wider context. The general picture gained will be negative, though the enterprises may, collectively, be profitable for the region or for the family concerned in that they avoid the cost of uprooting and starting afresh in an urban area. It is also in the interests of these micro-enterprises to show as small a profit as possible on paper, unlike larger public companies whose boards must show the shareholders and potential investors good profits.

RTME equity development

When calculating the feasibility of RTME enterprises, there is a tendency to concentrate on the Profit and Loss Account and to ignore the assets on the balance sheet, because, on the one hand, some assets can be difficult to estimate and on the other, the proprieter may not wish to make regular adjustments to some assets. Another factor is that many RTME businesses are in a continuous process of expansion or property improvement. The costs of these improvements are often registered in the Profit and Loss Account, rather than as an investment, which means that the enterprise will show less profit and will not show improved assets. It would also be very unusual for these small enterprises to show any Intangible Fixed Assets, which could be the good will, market contacts, established products and knowledge that the enterprise has gained over a period of years. A rule of thumb in the RTME sector is that you have to invest at least three years of work before you start showing significant success in your marketing. Statistics on equity development in the RTME sector are scarce. This is a serious deficiency when examining economic performance in the sector over a period of years because, with many small family enterprises, the main financial gain would be seen in the form of increased equity, were it calculated in a realistic manner.

Proportion of tourism offer

Without reliable statistics on the number of providers and on their offer, it is impossible to calculate what percentage the RTME sector represents of the whole tourism offer.

Number of jobs created and tax revenue generated by RTME

These factors are difficult to calculate because of the way tourism spending spreads throughout the community. Such calculations have doubtless been done, but the author has not encountered them specifically for the RTME sector in the countries and regions in which he has worked. As a rule of thumb, it is said that 30 per cent of a tourist's spending is at his place of accommodation and the remaining 70 per cent for other goods and services, excluding air travel to the country in question, in the case of foreign visitors. It is fair to say that statistics are needed on these aspects.

SUMMARY OF AVAILABILITY AND RELIABILITY OF STATISTICS ON RTME

The factors that govern availability and reliability of statistics could be summarized as follows:

- The cost for local government to regulate very small units is high and the authorities may not see this regulation as cost-effective.
- The RTME provider will usually see little advantage in providing data about his business, other than purely promotional data.
- Advisers and researchers are usually unable to validate basic data they receive, and do not have sufficient experience of the business to sense what data to question. The methodology of questioning the validity of basic data is essential in this sector.

WHAT THE LACK OF RELIABLE STATISTICS MEANS FOR THE RTME SECTOR

The tourism industry depends, to a large extent, on infrastructure provided initially for other purposes and used by other sectors – infrastructure usually provided from public funds. In the case of the RTME sector this is even more true than for larger tourism enterprises, which makes it highly dependent on decisions on which it has almost no control. The lack of reliable statistics that would show the economic significance of the sector means that long-term (public sector) planning will be inhibited with respect to the needs of RTME.

Investments in infrastructure beneficial to RTME could be justified if such statistics were available. Employment policy could take account of the potential of RTME as an 'engine for growth' in rural areas suffering loss of population and, therefore, with an acute need to create new jobs for the future.

The lobbying position of RTME is weak when competing for development funds with other branches of tourism or with other industries. When the stated economic gains of RTME development are not supported by clear statistics they will be ignored in the face of solutions presented by larger, more easily defined enterprises. The investment needed for development of RTME will not be easily found when financial institutions cannot clearly see where the profit lies in the sector. Feasibility studies need to incorporate good knowledge of the factors governing the business, for which accessible statistics are mostly unavailable today.

In terms of marketing, a lack of reliable, validated information on RTME products and services will affect the quality image of the sector. Quality of information is becoming increasingly important, if not vital, with the advent of e-commerce.

WAYS OF GATHERING STATISTICS

Actions Required at National/Local Level

Statistics on the size and nature of the offer

Actions required to improve the quality of staistics would include registration and categorization of all accommodation offered on the open market. As is already the case in many countries or regions, the providers, associations and marketing agents are involved in this process. They see such registration as part of the implementation of quality control, which benefits the whole sector. Another action that should be taken is that the authorities should adopt a policy of ensuring quality of information for their region. Much RTME promotion is publicly funded so the authorities can exercise the right to validate information in some way before disseminating. Authorities can also extend health and safety requirements to cover all providers who offer products or services on the open market. These actions will contribute towards recording the size and the nature of the offer and towards defining its quality.

Statistics on economic performance

Public funding is common for the development of RTME enterprises and infrastructure. Through co-operation with the associations or agents of providers, the authorities should support research that will aim at quantifying the real economic performance and potential of the sector. This can only be done by involving those who have commercial experience of the sector (at least in the first instance) because of the lack of statistics. One action would be co-operation with sales agents and associations in devloping criteria for feasibility studies.

How statistics will improve the situation

Many factors related to the development and operating environment of RTME would improve with improved statistics. Decision-making and provisions affecting RTME by public bodies or enterprises will be enhanced, not least in terms of the infrastructure and regional marketing. Reliable statistics will make it possible to produce well-informed business plans and feasibility studies which, in turn, will make it easier for providers to raise investment capital and to attract new capital into the region. In terms of tourism at a national level, the potential significance of rural tourism will vary greatly from country to country. In some countries, particularly those that are sparsely populated, the attendant improvements in the RTME sector will greatly enhance the national offer. It will open new opportunities for the development of activity and eco-tourism, which are recognized as the growth sector of the coming decades.

6

From Safaris to Satellites – Building the Statistics Base in Botswana

Kevin Millington

INTRODUCTION

Botswana is a destination that is not immediately associated with tourism. Many travellers are unaware of its exact location, and many more do not know what kind of product it offers. However, whilst it does not have a coastline, Botswana is well situated in the southern part of Africa, between the better known destinations of South Africa, Zimbabwe and Namibia.

Around the size of France, but with a population of only 1.5 million, Botswana offers an attractive tourism product to travellers who are increasingly looking for out-of-the way, back-door locations. Botswana's national parks are undoubtedly among Africa's wildest, characterized by open spaces, and even the most popular parks are dominated by wilderness. In addition to the parks, the Okavango River flows in from Namibia and soaks into the Kalahari Desert sands, forming the 15,000 sq. kms of convoluted channels and islands that comprise the Okavango Delta. The area is a haven for wildlife.

Last year, Botswana attracted 750,000 tourists, with the principal generating markets being South Africa, Zimbabwe, Namibia, Zambia, the United Kingdom, the USA and Germany. Visitor expenditure was estimated at around £175 million and it is estimated that tourism's contribution to the national economy represents around 8 per cent of GDP. This is some considerable way behind mining which contributes around 36 per cent.

Economically, Botswana was catapulted into new realms with the discovery of diamonds in 1967. Although most of the population remains in the low-income bracket, this mineral wealth has provided the country with enormous foreign-currency reserves. In the late 1980s, Botswana achieved the world's second highest rate of economic growth, and the pula remains Africa's strongest currency.

With Botswana's mineral wealth, and also its extensive export of beef, the development of the tourism industry tends to be rather low-profile. In part, this is because there has been little measurement of the economic impact of tourism in the country and the importance of the industry is not fully understood or appreciated by policy-makers within the government.

With the development of a tourism satellite account for Botswana the situation could be very different. A TSA is a set of data which enable tourism to be measured in a similar way to the system of national accounts for traditional industries such as agriculture, manufacturing and mining. Clearly, such an account could highlight the significance of the tourism industry in Botswana. Consequently, the Department of Tourism in Botswana is keen to develop its own tourism satellite account. However, before a tourism satellite account can be implemented, a considerable amount of data relating to the industry needs to be collected, and this data collection needs to be maintained on an annual basis in order for the account to be kept up to date.

Botswana, like many other countries in Africa, the Middle East and, to an extent, Asia, has few formal procedures for the collection of tourism statistics and, consequently, any statistics they do have tend to be either out of date, incomplete, or inaccurate. Statistics are often collected in an ad hoc manner and are rarely stored centrally. Typically, data is collected and stored on a spreadsheet or text file. Any subsequent data collected are often stored in separate files and, consequently, comparisons and trends between data sets are rarely made. Unless data is stored in an orderly manner in one location, such as a specific tourism database, the weight of the data is diminished and, often, opportunities to correlate one set of data with another are lost.

The Botswana Tourism Statistics Development Project is a study funded by the United Nations Development Programme and executed by the World Tourism Organization. The project commenced in November 1999 and will run for one year. The aims of the project are to:

- establish a set of procedures for the collection, processing and dissemination of tourism statistics;
- transfer know-how to the management staff of the Department of Tourism in Botswana;
- enhance to the utmost the reliability and usefulness of the statistical data gathered; and
- computerize the statistical department of the Department of Tourism by developing a database to store, retrieve and maintain the statistics.

The project, whilst aiming to develop the statistics base in Botswana, could equally apply in many other countries worldwide. Several countries are in the same situation as Botswana and are facing the same problems regarding the deficiency of data, difficulties with data collection and the lack of knowledge regarding interpretation and presentation of the data that is available. The brief in Botswana was not only to develop the statistics base, but also to ensure that the country will be well set to start developing, with careful guidance, a set of tourism satellite accounts.

The tourism statistics database that we have developed over the last year is essentially made up of four basic components:

- visitor arrivals statistics;
- accommodation statistics;
- visitor expenditure statistics; and
- statistics related to the tourism supply.

VISITOR ARRIVALS STATISTICS

Tourist arrivals statistics are the most fundamental measure of tourism in a country, and whilst visitor expenditure ultimately has greater importance, visitor spend is difficult to calculate without knowing the number of tourists entering the country, and also their relevant characteristics.

Throughout the world, one of the most simple and most recognized sources of tourism statistics is the immigration registration form completed by an international traveller at the point of arrival and departure, popularly known as the entry and departure card (E/D card). These cards provide a convenient and normally already existing source of information which provides a range of information of relevance for the planning, marketing and monitoring of tourism. Thus it is normally possible to retrieve from E/D cards such statistics as the actual number of foreign visitor arrivals, a breakdown of tourist arrivals by country of residence and purpose of visit, or data on the intended or actual duration of stay of the visitor, their sex, age, mode of travel and any multiple cross-tabulations of these.

Obviously, such information can only be retrieved and utilized confidently by the public and private tourism sectors if the immigration E/D card system is properly established and operated effectively by means of computer-processing. This includes:

- complete and reliable registration of *all* travellers passing through *each* of Botswana's points of entry/exit, by air, road or rail;
- regular and timely collection of the cards from all border posts;
- reliable computer-processing of the collected data; and
- timely publication and dissemination of standard statistical tables on arrival and departure statistics in general, and on tourist arrivals in particular.

As is customary in many countries throughout the world, the Immigration Department of Botswana has introduced a system to record the movement of foreigners (non-Botswana passport holders) across Botswana's international borders. The system is to a large extent based on international practice and comprises an E/D card to be completed by all persons who do not hold a Botswana passport when crossing the country's borders. However, there are several shortcomings regarding the data-collection procedures, and while these are specific to Botswana they are not uncommon in many other countries.

- In 1990 a decision was made by the Department of Immigration to exempt all Botswana passport holders from completing the form. This was introduced due to lengthy queues building up at certain border posts. Consequently, there are no detailed records kept of Botswana nationals either entering or departing the country. This is significant because a visitor is still classed as a tourist when entering a country for which they hold a passport, so long as they reside in another country. So all those Botswanans living overseas, but visiting their country for holiday or business purposes, are being excluded from the tourist arrival statistics. Information should be collected on all persons crossing Botswana's international borders.
- Currently staff are limited to using the entry card for measuring visitor arrivals as the departure card does not require the visitor to declare their actual length of stay. Therefore, we must rely on the traveller's *intended* length of stay rather than their

actual length of stay – the two are often not the same. The departure card should be amended so that the visitor is requested to enter their actual length of stay.

- The present entry and departure cards request the visitor to state the number of 'days' that they will spend in Botswana, rather than the number of 'nights', which is the usual unit used to measure length of stay. There appears to be some confusion among travellers at the border: sometimes they write in '1' to mean one day only, and sometimes it means a day and a night, but leaving early the following day. The term 'nights' should be used on the entry and departure cards.
- Tourism statistics should *not* include residents of Botswana, even if they are nationals of another country, as an international tourist is defined as residing in a country other than the one visited. At present, those people who do not hold a Botswana passport but reside in Botswana are being included in the tourist statistics. However, it is easy to remove these from the arrivals statistics database as they state their country of residence as 'Botswana' on the E/D card.
- Children entering Botswana on their mother's or their father's passports are, at present, not being included in the tourism statistics. If the parent with whom they are travelling enters Botswana for tourism purposes then the child, whatever its age, is also a tourist and should be included in the statistics. The entry and departure forms allow for the number of children accompanying a parent to be recorded. However, this data is not being utilized. Consequently, around 60,000 visiting children who are classified as tourists are not being included in the statistics.

ACCOMMODATION STATISTICS

Daily recording of room- and bed-occupancy rates, and also average lengths of stay, are vitally important for the measurement of the performance of the accommodation industry and to determine changes taking place over time. These findings enable decisions relating to the planning and development of the accommodation and tourism industry to be made.

The accommodation sector is usually measured by requesting all accommodation establishments to complete, on a monthly basis, a form which identifies the number of rooms and beds occupied on each night of the month. Additional information can be requested, such as the country of residence of these guests, and also certain revenue indicators such as turnover from room, bar and restaurant sales. This simple information can provide some very useful statistics, such as:

- the bed- and room-occupancy rates of the establishment;
- the average length of stay of guests by their country of residence; and
- the average cost of a room, and revenue generated from guests for the establishment.

The collection of accommodation statistics should, in theory, be simple. However, in practice it is riddled with problems. Principally, these are from the non-compliance of hoteliers in completing the monthly collection forms. Whilst the Tourism Act in Botswana states that each registered accommodation establishment in the country should report their accommodation statistics on a monthly basis, the regulation is generally not adhered to, and the government does not attempt to prosecute those hotels which do not comply. This results in less than 50 per cent of all accommodation establishments reporting their operational statistics. The principal fear of hoteliers is that the figures will be used by the revenue authorities for taxation purposes, so many simply prefer to keep the number of guests they receive to themselves.

In Botswana, we have been holding a number of regional meetings with hoteliers across the country to explain to them what the monthly accommodation form is for, what we in the Department of Tourism do with the completed forms, and how we will be producing quarterly accommodation reports which will be sent out to the hoteliers four times a year.

This last point is essential in boosting the number of forms that are completed nation-wide. All too often, the private sector is requested by government to complete questionnaires and surveys, but does not receive any relevant feedback. If the hotels receive well-presented and comprehensible reports that they can use for their own marketing purposes, it is more likely that they will be disposed to disseminate data about themselves in the first place.

VISITOR EXPENDITURE

The tourism industry the world over seems to be obsessed with visitor arrivals figures. However, it would be refreshing to hear someone say 'Great news, our tourist arrivals have gone down by 25 per cent, but our revenue has gone up by 50 per cent.'

The collection of visitor expenditure statistics is an important activity, as it helps to measure the economic impact of tourism in a country. After all, the positive effect tourism has on the economy is the principal reason most countries develop their tourism industries. There are various methods that can be used to measure tourism expenditure, and the most appropriate method chosen must be based on the situation in the country in question. While the use of central bank data based on foreign currency transactions can work in some instances, and expenditure models in others, often the most appropriate and useful method is to undertake a visitor survey on a sample of tourists as they leave the country.

It is important to remember that all borders must be surveyed in proportion to the number of tourists that cross each one. Consequently, air, land, rail and sea borders, where appropriate, must be covered. Seasonality also needs to be considered, and with the tourism industry in most countries having peak and low seasons, it is essential to conduct a survey during each season.

The advantage of carrying out such visitor surveys is that they can be used to collect information in addition to visitor expenditure statistics. Information such as trip itineraries, visitor impressions and ratings can be sought at the same time as part of the survey, and these can embellish the picture that is painted of the tourism industry from the data collected within the entry and departure cards. The main problem with visitor surveys is funding. Most tourism departments simply do not build into their annual budgets a line for visitor surveys. The consequence is, of course, that data does not get collected. The funding problem is exacerbated by the lack of technical know-how regarding the planning and execution of such surveys. In Botswana, we hope to have trained our counterparts sufficiently to plan and carry out visitor surveys in the future, but, unfortunately, I anticipate the insufficient funding of such surveys to be an ongoing problem.

Another purpose of a visitor survey is to make amends for some of the inadequacies of the visitor arrival statistics. As I have mentioned above, the use of entry and departure cards is not always entirely satisfactory for the measurement of visitor arrivals, as often these forms are designed by the immigration department, who have little understanding of tourism statistics. The visitor survey effectively allows us to take a sample of our visitor arrivals, and to extract their trip characteristics and personal profiles. In Botswana, it has allowed us to measure:

- the *actual* length of stay of visitors; and
- the number of Botswana *nationals* resident overseas but visiting Botswana for holiday, VFR or business purposes.

Neither of these items can be collected from the entry and departure cards.

TOURISM SUPPLY

It is useful to have data on the capacity and characteristics of tourism supply, i.e. the hotels, tour operators, travel agents, tourist shops, museums, attractions etc. However, defining the tourism sector is not an easy task due to the very composite nature of the tourism industry, and as a result of the great diversity of the business establishments which produce goods and services for sale to tourists. The problem is compounded by the fact that the goods and services produced by tourism-related business establishments are sold not only to foreign visitors but also to local residents as well. Therefore, the employment and revenues generated by these establishments cannot be attributed solely to tourism.

However, for all practical purposes, the above problems can be overcome by isolating the business establishments which have been set up solely or principally to cater for the needs of the foreign visitors. An inventory of these establishments can help the tourism authorities to choose target markets that seek the goods and services the country's tourism sector offers. The number, location and description of tourism supply establishments also serve as a basis for producing facility directories for tour operators, travel agents and visitors. Such directories are effective marketing tools for the tourism authorities and also the private sector.

Analysing these data sources can also alert the national administrations to actual or prospective shortages of tourism services that should be redressed to accommodate growing demand, both international and domestic. Comprehensive descriptions of tourism supply establishments also assist efforts to quantify the role of tourism in the national and regional economies.

In most countries, some form of licensing procedure is required by operators within the tourism industry. If licensing procedures are adhered to strictly, the licensing department can provide a useful source of statistics regarding the tourism supply with respect to the number of units, size and turnover. In the absence of this source of data, an annual survey can be undertaken, but generally such surveys do not achieve high response rates and, consequently, do not paint a very complete picture of the tourism sector.

With either method, the problem tends to be the same as that experienced when attempting to collect monthly accommodation statistics. All too often, private sector tourism enterprises are loathed to disseminate information about their businesses. In Botswana, the proposal is to request all tourism-related enterprises to submit their annual accounts at the same time as they apply for their annual licence renewal. No audited accounts means no licence. This is being strongly opposed by the private sector that does not want to disclose its operational statistics. However, if the country wishes to develop tourism satellite accounts, this reporting procedure will have to be implemented, as it will provide a rich vein of economic related data.

THE DATABASE

To bring a disparate collection of statistics, albeit all related to the tourism industry, to life, it is essential to build a fully integrated database that can manipulate the figures, link different but related data sets together and also produce well-presented and meaningful reports and charts.

The end-users should be considered at all times. These will be not only the public sector – most immediately the tourism department itself – but other sectors within government, such as central statistics offices, who are also likely to be interested in accessing data from time to time. In addition, it is likely that the private sector will be interested in certain information for their own planning and marketing purposes.

Whilst the database should be capable of producing a number of standard reports, many of which will form the quarterly and annual tourism statistics reports, ad hoc queries are equally important. Questions such as 'How many male visitors from Italy between the ages of 15 and 25 did we receive last year?' need to be answered quickly and easily.

This leads to an interesting conundrum. Once the basic structure of the database has been developed and the data-entry forms and reports have been created, what do we do next? Do we develop a relatively simple database and let the statistics department extract the relevant data as is it requested or required? There is no right or wrong answer. However, in countries where computer-programming knowledge is limited, this option is by far the most favourable.

The most important part of any database is its structure. Once you have got this right, the key is training. Complex menu systems require considerable programming and training. It is better to channel the time spent training into the design of the database – how to amend it, how to put data in and how to get information out. This training should not be limited to one member of staff; people leave jobs or get transferred to other departments. Technical assistance that has so often been carefully prepared is also so often lost, and the department that was briefly strengthened ends up back where it started.

Finally, it is important not to lose our focus on what we are ultimately trying to achieve. In order to plan, market, develop policies and monitor a tourism industry properly, the government must have an accurate and up-to-date base of statistics. These statistics are of little use on their own; they need to be analysed and interpreted so that the most appropriate marketing decisions and policies are formulated. As with database development and maintenance, this is also a skill which requires training.

All too often, statistics are simply churned out, presented in reports in a dull tabular format, put on a shelf and rarely referred to. Statistics can be valuable. If they are presented in an interesting fashion they are considerably more useful and understandable, and, subsequently, this leads to better decision-making within the sector.

7

Tourism Statistics and Models on the Regional Level in Norway

Steinar Johansen, Knut Sørensen, Ann-Kristin Brændvang and Petter Dybedal

The Norwegian Research Council initiated a research programme on tourism in 1999. One of the focal points of the programme was to develop data and models for analysing the impacts of tourism at regional and local level. This chapter focuses on discussing how existing information can be applied, and what types of additional information are needed for developing economic impact models for tourism at the regional level. The approach chosen is to first develop regional tourism satellite accounts (RTSA) in order to ensure that production and consumption data are consistent at national and regional levels. The principles for national accounting, at both levels, are very well developed in Norway, and they will be applied to the work on RTSA. In the first part of the chapter we discuss the principles by which RTSA will be developed, and some recent results at national level are presented. Data on tourism consumption and production by industry is developed at national level (satellite account for tourism), while regional and local information is restricted to occasional studies in smaller regions. However, some information on tourists' consumption in different areas, by type of accommodation and nationality, exists. In addition to hotel accommodation statistics, there are surveys covering domestic and incoming tourism that may be used to regionalize data on tourist flows for all types of accommodation. In the second part, some methodological problems connected to implementation of consumption- and tourism-survey results, as well as national tourism statistics, are discussed.

The need for an economic model that can be used also for calculating secondary and induced impacts of tourism is evident, and the aim of the project is to develop impact models based on information provided in the RTSA. In the second part of the chapter we discuss different types of models that can be developed, focusing on the input–output type of model. Different types of regional models are presented, and we discuss how tourism can be implemented in these models.

INTRODUCTION

A few years ago, the Norwegian Research Council (NFR) initiated a new research programme on travel and tourism. This programme was a follow-up from earlier programmes on similar topics. One of the main aims of the new programme was to supply data and develop models for analysing tourism and its impact. Within the framework of the programme, the Norwegian Institute for Urban and Regional Research (NIBR), Statistics Norway (SSB) and the Institute of Transport Economics (TØI) applied for funds for a pilot project on Regional Satellite Accounts and Regional Models for Tourism. This project resulted in a report (Dybedal *et al.*, 1999), in which the existing data situation and the possibilities for developing simulation models for analysing tourism impacts were discussed. The report, together with an application for further funding for a project on *developing* data and models for analysing tourism at regional level in Norway, was accepted by the NFR in August 1999. This project will continue until the end of 2001. There are three main topics for the project:

1. developing regionalized tourism satellite accounts (TSA) for Norway;
2. developing data that can be adapted for constructing a regionalized TSA; and
3. developing a simplified input–output model for analysing the impacts of tourism at regional level.

The data situation is relatively good in Norway. Regionalized national accounts exist, and TSA on the national level has also been developed. Therefore, the challenge connected to topic 1 is to regionalize the national TSA and to ensure that the new regionalized TSA is consistent with the national TSA, as well as with the regionalized national accounts. In order to achieve these consistencies, information from other sources has to be used. Existing sources are not sufficiently developed for this purpose. We therefore look closer into how these sources of information have to be expanded with new information in order to give satisfactory coefficients for distributing the national satellite accounts (topic 2). The regional national accounts have been utilized for developing interregional and single-region input–output models in Norway. These models – or parts of them – can, if they are modified with the regional satellite account data, be utilized for analysing the impacts of tourism at regional level (topic 3). Topics 1 and 2 will be finished this year, while topic 3 needs information from 1 and 2 in order to be finished. The regional-impact model will therefore be developed next year.

REGIONAL TOURISM SATELLITE ACCOUNTS (RTSA)

The tourism satellite accounts are satellites to the national accounts, giving emphasis to tourism consumption and activities of tourism industries. In Norway, such accounts exist on a comparable basis for the period 1988–97, and some preliminary figures for 1998 have been produced. These accounts are established according to the (old) guidelines from the OECD (1991). OECD and WTO have, however, quite recently, proposed new manuals.[1] The regional tourism satellite accounts (RTSA) are to be a breakdown by region of the tourism satellite accounts.

---

[1] Eurostat document TOUR/99/42/EN (preliminary).

The main advantage of the satellite accounts approach is that the consistency and conceptual coherence from the national accounts can be applied to the tourism field as well. Comparable descriptions of tourism activities across regions call for a strong co-ordination in the definition of tourism and the principles of calculation etc. This co-ordination is not easy to find in independent projects for different regions. It is easier to achieve if figures for all regions are estimated simultaneously within a common accounting framework, as in our RTSA approach.

A traditional small-region project is often able to organize a specialized data collection for the regional activities of interest. This is often beyond the reach of an RTSA project. On the other hand the RTSA has a lot of information of a general nature for non-tourism activities that may be difficult to cover with local surveys. This is information needed to calculate impacts beyond the direct consequences within the tourism industries.[2] The RTSA has more of a top-down, macro flavour than local surveys. Calculating impacts of tourism on regional or higher levels is, however, by nature a macro-economic project.

An RTSA is not a substitute for regional tourism statistics. These types of statistics are needed as an input to the accounts. If the resources are available, one can imagine a combined use of the two approaches. The general regional tourism accounts could be combined with local data-collection for some selected tourism segments of particular local importance. The tourism satellite accounts are used for general background information and analyses.

The plan for the RTSA for Norway is to link the national tourism satellite with the production routines from the regionalized national accounts. Norway has produced regional accounts at 3–4-year intervals since 1973. These accounts are generally not up to date, but an acceleration of the production process is under way, as the main results are included in the annual reporting routines to the EU/EEA. At the moment, the latest regional accounts apply to 1993. Regional figures for 1995 are in the pipeline and production of 1997 figures has also started. The RTSA will be constructed for 1997, since much of the data for tourism consumption is weaker for earlier years. National figures for 1997 are shown in Table 7.1.

In 1997 non-residents accounted for approximately 30.5 per cent of the total tourism consumption. The tourism consumption of resident households was 49.6 per cent of the total. The remaining 19.9 per cent was related to resident industries' business travel expenditure (intermediate consumption). Final consumption by non-residents represented approximately 4.2 per cent of total export in 1997 (approximately 6.7 per cent excluding exports of crude oil and natural gas).

Table 7.1 also shows which products constitute tourism consumption, and from where these products are supplied (domestic production by industry; imports). Based on this supply pattern, we have defined a group of specialized tourism industries in the TSA. These industries are hotels and restaurants, most passenger transportation and some other industries. The tourism industries account for 72.5 per cent of total tourism consumption. Value added in the tourism industries is 4.5 per cent of total GVA, and the industries represent a somewhat larger share of persons employed: 6.7 per cent.

Our regional accounts can be used to study tourism (and other) industries. They also give information on the products made and used for intermediate consumption. This product information is the basis for the present regional economic models, which can be

---

[2] See Chapter 4.

Table 7.1 Tourism consumption expenditures at market prices. Non-residents' tourism consumption (F), resident households' tourism consumption (H) and resident industries' expenditures on business travel in Norway (B).* MNOK 1997

	F	H	B	Total
Characteristic tourism products:				
Accommodation services	3,560	2,503	2,426	8,489
Food and beverage serving services	3,287	3,866	1,188	8,341
Passenger transport services	4,294	6,338	8,752	19,384
Package tours and car rental services†	80	7,552	0	7,632
Museum, sporting activities etc.	467	975	0	1,442
Total tourism consumption of tourism products	11,688	21,234	12,366	45,288
Other products:				
Food, beverages and tobacco	2,968	0	0	2,968
Clothing and footwear	702	0	0	702
Souvenirs, maps etc.	583	275	0	858
Other transportation costs	1,755	4,229	0	5,984
(of this: petrol and oil)	1,630	3,873	0	5,503
Other commodities and services	1,373	5,275	0	6,648
Total tourism consumption of other products	7,381	9,779	0	17,160
Total consumption expenditures of tourists	19,069	31,013	12,366	62,448

* Notice that 'resident industries' total expenditures on business travel', by definition, is different from 'the total expenditures of individuals travelling mainly at the expense of private or public domestic establishments.' This is the case because a person who travels for business purposes may buy services and/or goods on his/her trip which are not paid by his/her employer, but by his/her own household.
† Gross recording of package tours

used also for the study of tourism activity. The regional accounts are weaker on the regional distribution of household consumption, and, presently, provide no information on the share consumed by tourists.

The main part of our work on RTSA will be related to the regional distribution of tourism consumption and of household consumption in general. For tourism consumption, priority will be given to relating the consumption to the county where it actually took place. This is, by assumption, the country where the demand is evident, and also where it can be related to local production. The household consumption, in general, is distributed according to the county of residence of the household. If the tourism part of household consumption can be defined, we will have a picture of an implicit net trade pattern for tourism services.

One of the advantages of linking the RTSA to the existing regional accounts is that production of the RTSA can be linked to existing routines of data production. These routines will most probably be continued in the future also. This implies that the satellites can be produced, more or less, alongside the ordinary national accounts statistics. The disadvantage is the long production period. Also, we need to work with the regional indicators that are used to distribute the national accounts figures by region. These were established without having our use of the results in mind. Although the compilation of the regional accounts are done at full national-accounts level (175 industries, c. 1000 products), the product information is generally treated in a summarized way. Normally, the same regional indicator is used for distributing all the products of an industry. The RTSA will offer an occasion to review the regional distributions, entering more information also on the product level. This has proved possible, for example, with hotels.

In the regional accounts, the main principle is that the activity is located at the region of residence of the Local Kind of Activity Units (LKAU). This is a principle that works well for most of the non-transport tourism industries. In Norway, the data is generally for the LKAUs. Some transportation industries, such as air and rail, use regional-activity indicators such as the number of passengers that enter or exit on stops in the region. This also works well for our purpose, although some industries, especially tour operators and sea passenger transport, would need a closer look. In most cases the region of production of the tourism services, as recorded in our regional accounts, would coincide with the region where the tourist consumption actually takes place.

The recording of tour-operator services is a classic challenge to tourism accountants. In our regional accounts, as in the national accounts, there is a gross recording of tour-operator services. Hence the full amount paid for the package tour is the production of the tour operator, and his expenses for transport, accommodation, meals etc. – in short, the components of the package tour – are intermediate consumption for the tour operator. This implies that the product 'package tours' is produced in the region of residence of the tour operator, while actual consumption of tourism services could well occur in other regions. Norwegian tour operators mainly organize travel abroad. In this case it is reasonable to say that the actual consumption of the services takes place abroad, with the exception of the margin of the tour operator. So the consumption could be distributed as if package tours are recorded net.

Countries within the EU and the EEA have to use a set of guidelines for producing regionalized national accounts, as they are presented in a manual produced by Eurostat (1995). There is no particular manual relating to regional tourism accounts. However, several principles can be inferred from the manual on regional national accounts. The main principle has been to apply the national guidelines to each region as if the regions were small nations. So, for instance, in the OECD guidelines that we presently use for our tourism accounts, the rule is that normal food consumption for resident tourists travelling does not belong to tourism consumption – only extra expenditure does. For non-residents, all expenditure is included. Applying this principle to a region, food consumption for tourists resident in other regions of the country is included in tourism expenditure as with expenditure of foreign tourists. To keep the link with the tourism accounts on the national scale, all tourists residing in Norway shall be classified as domestic tourists. The tourist consumption of food will, however, be different; as a large part of domestic tourism is holiday homes, this could be important. Of course, classifying food consumption as tourism consumption does not imply that the food is produced in the region, although most of the related trade probably is.

As an illustration of the tourism data that could be found presently in our regional accounts, we have assembled Table 7.2. The data are for 1993, but more recent data will soon be available. The 1993 data-set was constructed before our application to tourism was planned. The relevant data are mostly those describing the activity of industries. For the table we have grouped tourism industries in three broad groups: hotels/restaurants; (part of) transportation; and other tourism industries. As noted earlier, the strength of the regional accounts is mainly that the fourth column, representing non-tourism industries, is present, and that all industries are treated comparatively for all regions and activities. The figures show some regional differences in the importance of tourism.

From Table 7.2 we see that the tourism industries are, relatively, most important in Akershus, in the north of Norway, and in Oppland. In Akershus the importance of

Table 7.2 Gross value added, 1993, by county and tourism industry

| County | Gross value added (Mill NOK) | Percentage of total GVA of the counties that it is produced in: | | | | Non-tourism industries |
| | | Tourism industries (of which): | | | | |
		Total	HORECA	Transp.	Other tourism	
Østfold	29,151	2.7	1.0	0.7	0.9	97.3
Akershus	59,176	8.7	1.1	6.1	1.5	91.3
Oslo	141,964	5.9	1.4	1.7	2.8	94.1
Hedmark	21,865	3.8	1.6	1.3	0.9	96.2
Oppland	21,300	6.2	3.4	1.0	1.8	93.8
Buskerud	31,159	4.3	2.1	1.2	1.0	95.7
Vestfold	24,319	3.3	1.3	1.3	0.7	96.7
Telemark	20,951	4.0	1.9	1.0	1.1	96.0
Aust-Agder	12,203	3.8	1.5	1.4	0.8	96.2
Vest-Agder	21,084	4.7	1.5	2.2	1.0	95.3
Rogaland	60,530	5.0	1.6	2.3	1.1	95.0
Hordaland	60,611	6.1	1.6	3.1	1.3	93.9
Sogn og Fjordane	14,504	3.9	1.9	1.3	0.7	96.1
Møre og Romsdal	30,294	4.2	1.4	2.0	0.7	95.8
Sør-Trøndelag	33,464	5.3	1.5	2.4	1.4	94.7
Nord-Trøndelag	14,718	3.6	1.3	1.4	0.9	96.4
Nordland	28,698	5.9	1.8	3.1	1.0	94.1
Troms	18,710	7.1	2.2	3.7	1.2	92.9
Finnmark	8,855	6.8	3.0	2.2	1.6	93.2
Svalbard, Jan Mayen + North Sea oil activities	101,169	0.2	0.0	0.0	0.1	99.8
The whole country	736,957	4.8	1.4	2.1	1.3	95.2

Source: Regional accounts.

tourism can be explained mainly by the localization of transportation activities. The main airport of Norway is situated in this county, and Akershus is also the resident county of some large bus companies. Oppland has a more traditional tourism industry with a focus on HORECA (hotels, restaurants and camping) activities. The year 1993 was a good one for the tourism industry of Oppland, which expanded prior to the Winter Olympic Games of 1994. The Norwegian capital, Oslo, also had a relatively large share of activity in the tourism industry. Oslo had a lot more 'other tourism activities' than the other counties. Among these activities Oslo has a concentration of cultural activities.

COLLECTING AND PREPARING DATA FOR RTSA: A REAL CHALLENGE

The basic information needed to establish RTSA concerns tourist expenditure in each county. Initially there are two major problems: one is to estimate the total production consumed by tourists; the other is to estimate the distribution of consumption of the various types of goods and services.

There are various approaches to these problems (see, for instance, Frechtling, 1994, p. 368). However, there are two basic estimation principles. One is to use production data and estimate the distribution of the production of goods and services on tourists' consumption and non-tourists' consumption. The approach usually chosen in TSA work, however, is to use consumption data from visitor surveys and combine these with visitor statistics. Because tourists' consumption comprises products from several other industries apart from tourism industries, this is the safest way to estimate production delivered to the 'tourism industry'. An important share of the production of characteristic tourism industries is sold to those other than tourists (local consumption in restaurants, leisure parks etc.). Tourists also buy several products that are not produced by industries defined as tourism industries.

The consumption-based method used for TSA has two major steps. The first step is to collect survey data on consumption, specified on various goods and services. The Norwegian studies used in our current RTSA work (Haukeland and Grue, 1996; Flognfeldt and Onshus, 1996; Jean-Hansen, 1996) clearly demonstrate that the total consumption, as well as the distribution, of items depends on several variables. The most important are: type of holiday (characterized by type of accommodation); and, very important for RTSA calculations, type of region visited. The visitor-survey samples, hence, have to be large enough to supply representative data for these variables. The next step is to estimate total number of tourists (and length of stay) by type of accommodation for each region. Here we face some problems: Statistics Norway have produced hotel statistics and camping statistics (see, for instance, Statistics Norway, 1998) for a long time, and statistics for holiday homes have now been established. However, accommodation statistics are sufficiently reliable for hotel accommodation only. Figures for 1998 show the following distribution of holiday and leisure trips by type of accommodation, emphasizing that considerable impacts occur from other forms of tourism apart from the traditional hotel industry. By knowing both the distribution of visitors by type of accommodation for each region and the exact number of bed-nights in one of the categories, one should, in principle, get the total number of overnight stays by type of accommodation for each region. In this case, hotel data provide a reliable basis.

Information on distribution by type of accommodation also requires very reliable data, which can only be supplied from sample surveys among travellers. The implementation of the EC tourism statistics directive[3] in national statistics has secured reasonably good data on domestic travellers. However, to obtain sufficient sample size to split accommodation data by county, we had to combine quarterly surveys for two years (1997 and 1998). However, the level of reliability remains somewhat uncertain.

The EC directive requires no surveys of foreign visitors, and the national surveys on outgoing tourism in each country do not supply reliable information for small destination countries like Norway. The Institute of Transport Economics, however, conducts a yearly survey of foreign visitors including interviews at all important border crossings, ferry terminals and airports. This survey covers both holiday and business travel, and is documented in several reports (for instance Haukeland and Rideng, 2000;

---

[3] Council Directive 95/57/EC of 23 November 1995, on the collection of statistical information in the field of tourism.

Table 7.3 Holiday travellers in Norway: bed-nights by type of accommodation, 1998 (%)

	Hotels etc.	Camping	Rented/ borrowed or own cabin	Friends & relatives	Other
Norwegians	11	10	32	41	6
Foreign visitors	22	30	34	12	3

Sources: Statistics Norway Travel Survey and Institute of Transport Economics (Haukeland, Rideng 1999)

Dybedal and Rideng, 1999; Jacobsen, 1999). There are problems, however, when it comes to estimating distribution by type of accommodation for each region. The incoming holiday tourism is dominated by round trips including several counties, and it has been nearly impossible to record the exact number of days spent by each respondent in each county. Respondents are asked to name places visited and, if possible (and relevant), the major destination on the trip. However, by examining geographical travel patterns and camping capacity, number of holiday homes etc. in each county, we have reached fairly good estimates on the distribution of bed-nights by type of accommodation. The hotel statistics, which are reliable on county level also, provide the final anchor to obtain reasonably good input for the tourist-consumption estimates.

MODELLING IMPACTS OF TOURISM: THE REGIONAL LEVEL

Activities directly and indirectly connected with tourism are important to measure, both for economic and policy reasons. The size of these activities depends upon the level of tourists' expenditure, which can be thought of as exogenous to, or generated outside, the local (regional) economy. Expenditure from tourists is, therefore, to some extent a base activity to the economy in question. Our task is to measure the impact on the regional economy of the tourists' expenditure or, rather, changes in tourists' expenditure. We are *not* focusing on trying to measure to what extent regional supply of activities directed towards tourists compete with similar (tourist) activities in other regions and countries.

MODELLING TOURIST ACTIVITIES

There are several ways of measuring the impact of tourist activities. One is to adapt (economic) simulation models. Such models, or modelling systems, are simplifications of real life, and can be described as systems that – given data, assumptions, a theory and a method – calculate the impacts in question. The impacts themselves can be named 'endogenous variables'. There might be several types of modelling systems that can be used for calculating impacts for the same, or similar, endogenous variables. Within economic modelling, equilibrium and non-equilibrium models are two major categories.

When calculating the impacts of (changing) tourist activities, non-equilibrium input–output models or techniques are the most commonly used; see for instance Archer (1995), Archer and Fletcher (1996), Freeman and Sultan (1997) and Khan, Seng and Cheong (1990).

Input–output models focus on modelling flows of goods and services between different activities within the economy. This requires a certain amount of information (data). Models based on national accounts (NA) data are most commonly used. They can be general, and thus adapted for special purposes, or they can be tailor-made for specific analyses. Input–output models can be used for simulating indirect (including induced) impacts of changing activities, for instance for production or employment, given direct impacts. This is one of the major features of such models, and also the main purpose of our modelling of tourism activities.

In Norway, the NA is the database for input–output models at the national level. At the regional level, regionalized NA is most commonly used for general modelling purposes. For specific purposes, for instance for modelling impacts of tourist activities in limited regions, data have until now been collected separately, but at a certain cost.

The new RTSAs, as they are described in Chapter 3, will provide an opportunity for constructing regional models based on these data. This is a more cost-effective way of modelling impacts of tourism, but, at the same time, local information may vanish from the models. In this chapter, we discuss how existing regional input–output models in Norway may be modified in order to include information on tourism, or if alternative models may be adapted.

THE STRUCTURE OF EXISTING REGIONAL INPUT–OUTPUT MODELS

Two major categories of regional input–output models exist in Norway, namely single-region and multi-region models. Both categories are based on the regionalized NA and operate at county level.

Single region models

PANDA (see Johansen, Nilssen and Stokka, 1999) is a single-region model that has been developed for analysing regional development at county level in Norway. The input–output core is a 30 × 30 industry by industry system. Focus in PANDA is on modelling intra-regional trade flows, given (growth rates of) final demand. The final demand categories are private consumption (optional; can be endogenously determined), public consumption, investments, interregional and international exports. In addition, a final demand category called 'activities' is included. Here, activities exogenous to the regional economy can be included. Employment is determined by multiplying sectoral production and exogenously given (growth rates of) labour productivity. A shift-and-share system is included for distributing regional (county) employment by industry between municipalities. The system is quite flexible, with several exogenous handles. Each industry can be treated exogenously – the activities and final demand are exogenous – and several other handles also exist. For each new simulation, individual coefficients for intra-regional flows of goods are estimated. PANDA may also be connected, via the labour market, to a demographic model.

Multi-region (interregional) models

There are two interregional models in Norway – REGARD and REGION. Both of these models have been presented by Johansen *et al.* (1993). The models are in many respects quite similar, but there are some differences. Both models have an input–output core of around 30 industries and products. A given product may be produced in all industries. They are top-down models in the sense that their main feature is to distribute national simulations regionally. Focus is put on interregional trade, and a national trade pool with given coefficients is constructed in order to avoid the large number of equations needed for estimating trade coefficients for all commodities between pairs of regions. The regional distribution of most activities is determined endogenously. However, some activities are distributed exogenously. Final-demand activities, as well as production in some specific industries, are the most important.

REGARD operates on county aggregates and includes a demographic model, and the production in the manufacturing industries is modelled in a more sophisticated manner than a pure input–output system would. REGION operates on the county level, with a pure input–output system as the core of the model. Both systems are less flexible than PANDA, mainly because of interregional trade restrictions and fixed coefficients.

HOW CAN TOURISM BE INCLUDED IN THESE MODELS?

The RTSA provides us with several opportunities for including tourism activities in the existing models. We have two major ways of doing that: by either changing the models' coefficients (maximum inclusion), or by pre- and sub-modelling tourist consumption and tourism production respectively. The maximum inclusion involves re-estimating the entire systems of equations; by introducing new tourism equations, variables and coefficients into the input–output core of the models. This is a quite extensive and expensive way of including tourism, but it ensures, at the same time, that tourism is treated quite precisely. In the present model implementations, some tourism industries are aggregated with other industries. For example, hotels and restaurants are included in business services. Changing the system of equations will, of course, increase the models' performance when analysing impacts of tourism, but this might, on the other hand, reduce their performance when analysing other problems.

The easier way of changing the models is to construct pre-models for tourist consumption and sub-models for calculating the direct impacts for tourist industries. Pre-models could then separate tourists from different countries, with differing expenditure levels and patterns from each other. Tourist consumption, at least by international tourists, is, *per se*, exogenous to the economy and could therefore be treated exogenously. The intra-regional model (PANDA) would also treat the consumption of national tourists from other counties exogenously (as exports) and similar to international tourists' consumption. Within the interregional models, national tourism would have to be treated endogenously, as spending income in other counties would reduce the spending in the home county. This would also lead to a need for re-estimating trade coefficients in these models.

Separating tourist commodities and industries from other industries and commodities is necessary in order to be able to separate primary from secondary impacts of tourist consumption. However, if the direct impacts, and their industrial distribution, are known, it is possible to separate them from the indirect impacts in a sub-model, or after the simulations are made. This can be adapted to the single-region as well as the multi-region models and is quite inexpensive. However, some consistency problems may occur.

A simplified alternative for modelling tourism?

In addition to modifying existing models, we have also discussed the possibility of constructing a simplified input–output model for simulating impacts of tourism. This involves using information from the RTSA directly, for different categories of tourists and their expenditure levels and patterns, and for each county. The secondary, or indirect, impacts of the activities can be calculated relatively easily by using standardized multiplicators instead of simulating impacts in detail. This could be thought of as a 'local' model, where local information, for instance from surveys, can be added in each case. This model will involve no simultaneous equations, and we have already started developing a generalized spreadsheet for such a model.

An alternative to this simplified model is to use the activities in PANDA for tourist consumption, and to use the sub-model version (see previous paragraph) for separating tourist from non-tourist production. This alternative involves simultaneous equations, and is also being developed.

A SIMULATION EXAMPLE

Purely as an illustration, we have looked at how a NOK 100 million increase (1992 NOK) in tourist consumption in the county of Sogn og Fjordane (SF)[4] will influence the local economy both directly and indirectly. We have adapted the PANDA model's input–output core for SF when calculating the impacts.

Assumptions

Resource-based production (four primary production industries and mining), shipbuilding and production within the two public industries – a total of eight industries – is, by assumption, unaltered by the increased tourist consumption. All of the NOK 100 million will, by definition, be consumed within the county of SF and can be regarded as direct impacts, while secondary impacts will be distributed between SF and counties outside SF according to the estimated 'self-sufficiency' coefficients for each production industry. There are, in total, 29 industries, of which eight, by assumption, are not influenced by the change. The NOK 100 million are assumed to be purchases of goods from retail trade (20 million), hotels and restaurants (50 million), transportation (5 million), banking and insurance (5 million) and other private services (10 million). The total production value in the county (before the change) is around 30 billion (1992 NOK).

Results

The initial change is an increase in production value of NOK 100 million. In addition, a NOK 33 million secondary increase in production value is simulated using PANDA. NOK 25 million, of which seven can be found within the business services industry and

---

[4] One of 19 counties in Norway.

sixteen within the 'tourist' production industries mentioned above (in addition to the initial increase of NOK 100 million), are increases within the production of services, and NOK 10 million are increases within manufacturing production. The multiplicator value is, in other words, estimated to be 1.33, or for each initial NOK spent, a secondary increase of NOK 33 can be expected. In addition, an increase in production value just short of NOK 50 million will leak out of the county (the rate of self-sufficiency is around 40 per cent in total).

SOME CONCLUSIONS AND FURTHER WORK

In this chapter we have presented an ongoing research project in Norway where tourism statistics and models on the regional level are developed. The project tries to utilize as much of existing information as it can, together with new information when necessary, when developing a new RTSA and new tourism impacts models. One criterion for developing the RTSA is that they have to be consistent with existing national accounts and regional national accounts. The new models will be based on the RTSA.

In the autumn of 2000, the RTSA for 1997 will be finished and the data will be published. We will then continue developing models based on existing systems of input–output models. The resource situation limits us to developing a simplified model, as described in the earlier section. However, we will continue working on adapting the existing input–output structure of the single-region model, PANDA, to be able to make more simultaneous simulations in individual cases. At this stage, we have no means for developing the interregional models further, but this will be given priority when applying for further funds for research.

REFERENCES

Archer, B. (1995) 'Importance of tourism for the economy of Bermuda', in *Annals of Tourism Research*, **22** (4), pp. 918–30.

Archer, B. and Fletcher, J. (1996) 'The economic impact of tourism in the Seychelles', in *Annals of Tourism Research*, **23** (1), pp. 32–47.

Dybedal, P., Edvardsen, H., Evensen, T. N., Johansen, S., Sorensen, K. and Toresen, J. (1999) *Turismens regionale betydning – et forprosjekt*. (Regional impacts of tourism – a pilot project.) Oslo: The Norwegian Institute of Urban and Regional Research.

Dybedal, P. and Rideng, A. (1999) *Gjestestatistikk for sommersesongen 1999*. (Foreign visitor statistics summer season 1999.) Institute of Transport Economics, Oslo, Working Report 1153/1999.

Eurostat (1995) *Regional Accounts Methods: Gross Value-added and Gross Fixed Capital Formation by Activity*. Statistical document theme 1 (General statistics), Series E: *Methods*. Office for Official Publications of the European Communities, Luxemburg.

Flognfeldt, T. jr and Onshus, T. (1996) *Reiselivsundersøkelsen i Ottadalen sommeren 1995 (The tourism survey in Ottadalen in the summer of 1995)*. Lillehammer College, working paper 25/1996.

Frechtling, D. C. (1994) 'Assessing the economic impacts of travel and tourism: measuring economic benefits', in J. R. Brent Ritchie and C. R. Goeldner, (eds) *Travel, Tourism and Hospitality Research* (second edition) New York: John Wiley & Sons.

Freeman, D. and Sultan, E. (1997) 'The economic impact of tourism in Israel: a multi-regional input–output analysis', in *Tourism Economics*, **3**(4), pp. 341–59.

Haukeland, J. V. and Grue, B. (1996) *Turistenes forbruk i Norge sommeren 1995* (Tourists' Expenses in Norway in the Summer of 1995). Report 320/1996. Oslo: Institute of Transport Economics.

Haukeland, J. V. and Rideng, A. (2000) *Gjestestatistikk (1999): 'Utenlandske forretnings- og feriereiser i Norge'* (Foreign Visitor Statistics 1998: Business and Holiday Travels). Report 475/2000. Oslo: Institute of Transport Economics.

Jacobsen, J. K. S. (1999) *Utenlandsk bilturisme i det nordlige Norge 1998* (Foreign Motor Tourism in the North of Norway 1998). Report 439/1999. Oslo: Institute of Transport Economics.

Jean-Hansen, V. (1996) *Forbruksundersøkelser blant vinterturister og norske kurs- og konferansedeltakere* (Consumption Surveys Among Winter Tourists and Norwegian Conference Participants). Report 337/1996. Oslo: Institute of Transport Economics.

Johansen, S., Mønnesland, J., Mohn, K. and Sørensen, K. Ø. (1993) 'Regionalisering av beregningsgrunnlaget i Regjeringens Langtidsprogram' (Regional breakdown of national economic scenarios from the government's long term programme). Samarbeidsrapport NIBR-SSB, Oslo. (In Norwegian, with summary in English).

Johansen, S., Nilssen, I. and Stokka, A. (1999) 'Bruk av PANDA i arbeidet med regionale utviklingsprogram' (Applying PANDA when working on Regional Development Programmes). SINTEF-rapport STF A99612, Trondheim, Oslo.

Khan, H., Seng, C. F. and Cheong, W. K. (1990) 'Tourism multiplier effects on Singapore', in *Annals of Tourism Research*, **17**, pp. 408–18.

OECD, Tourism Committee, Dr Alfred Franz (1991) *Manual on Tourism Economic Accounts*. Paris: Organization for Economic Development.

Statistics Norway (1998) *Reiselivsstatistikk 1997* (Statistics on Travel 1997). Kongsvinger.

8

Regional/Local Survey on Tourism on the Belgian Coast

Anton Jacobus, Raf De Bruyn and Jan Van Praet

TOURISM IN BELGIUM: A COMMUNITY MATTER

Belgium is a federal country. Some government authorities are not maintained at federal level but through the regions or the communities. Federalization has also had an effect on the way in which the tourist authority structures are organized. There is, therefore, no national tourist board in Belgium, nor a national tourism promotion body.

The highest level of competent authority for tourism in Belgium is the community level; in practical terms, the Flemish, French and German-speaking communities. The various communities organize tourism policy autonomously according to their own judgement, for which they are responsible. From the market standpoint, it can be considered strange that a country with strong tourism does not sing its own praises. This is, however, the result of the federalization of Belgium, and the formation of communities and regions.

For the Flemish community, the public institution Tourist Office for Flanders (TOF) exists for the benefit of tourism in and to Flanders and Brussels. TOF is authorized to fulfil the legislation and to promote Flanders and Brussels as tourist destinations. TOF's marketing policy can be structured on the supply side according to three so-called macro-products: the Historic Cities, Green Flanders and the Coast.

Within Flanders there are other state-supported partners that assist TOF with implementing tourism policy, notably the provinces and the towns. The entire Belgian Coast lies within Flanders and, more specifically, within the province of West Flanders. The province of West Flanders is therefore the natural partner of TOF for shaping the marketing of the Belgian Coast at home and abroad.

THE BELGIAN COAST: AN IMPORTANT CORNERSTONE IN FLEMISH TOURISM

Some features of the tourist supply side

Description of the product

The Belgian Coast is one of the oldest tourist areas in the world. The first tourist activity was noted at the end of the eighteenth century, a period in which the emphasis was on the healing nature of a stay by the sea. At that time tourism was reserved simply for a small group of privileged people. Up to the middle of the twentieth century, the Belgian Coast would continue to develop into one of the favourite seaside resorts of the well-to-do West Europeans. With reconstruction after the Second World War, demand (influenced by increasing prosperity, better means of transport and an increase in leisure time) exploded. The coast, as a whole, lost its rather elitist character and prepared itself for mass tourism.

Geographically speaking, the Belgian Coast is bounded by north-west France and south-east Holland and extends along the North Sea for a distance of 67 km. It includes ten municipalities and has thirteen seaside resorts, each with their own character. The Belgian North Sea shore consists of fine sand and can, in some places, be up to 500 metres wide at low tide. There are further rows of sand dunes on the west coast, and there is an extensive nature reserve on the east coast bordering Holland.

A common feature of many seaside resorts is the promenade, a traffic-free deck for walking, with terraces, cafés, restaurants and shops. Various resorts are characterized by a lively night scene, with dancing, discotheques or casinos. The rise in mass tourism has meant that there has sometimes been an unbridled building craze, which at present is giving many resorts an urban character.

Statistical overview of the supply side

The supply of accommodation on the Belgian Coast is dominated by individual rented holiday homes and second homes. Individual rented holiday homes and second homes appear in the same form but differ in the sense that second homes are not usually available on the commercial market. Demand generated by second homes is, therefore, not included in the figures of the National Institute for Statistics (NIS).

Rented holiday homes and second homes are usually situated in apartment blocks, but a minority appear as villas, terraced houses or bungalows. The increase, primarily in second homes, remains physically fixed, to a great extent, to an area overlooking the Belgian Coast.

If the rented holiday homes and second homes are left aside, the number of hotels outweighs the number of other forms of accommodation. Expressed as bed capacity, this predominance is no longer recognized. Then there are the campsites that are able to offer the highest capacity (i.e. 126,000 beds; this number includes the 105,000 beds that are let on a yearly basis).

Between 1989 and 1997 the number of commercial accommodation units decreased by almost 15 per cent. This figure is determined by the loss of individual rented holiday homes, but also all other forms of commercial accommodation which saw their positions outstripped, with the exception of the holiday villages. The general decline in the number of structures resulted in a fall in the bed capacity of 6 per cent overall.

Table 8.1 Belgian Coast: Number of accommodations and bed capacity in 1989 and 1997

Type of accommodation	Number of accommodations			Bed capacity		
	1989	1997	Trend (%)	1989	1997	Trend (%)
Hotels	567	418	−26.3	25,246	19,940	−21.0
Campsites	140	134	−4.3	122,306	125,978	+3.0
Social holiday centres	46	40	−13.0	14,521	11,719	−19.3
Holiday villages	16	22	+37.5	17,462	20,985	+20.2
Youth hostels	85	72	−15.3	8,964	7,234	−19.3
Rental houses/apartments	26,742	22,861	−14.5	128,536	112,809	−12.2
Total commercial provision	27,596	23,547	−14.7	317,035	298,665	−5.8
Second Homes	27,282	43,782	+60.5	119,973	193,750	+61.5

Source: West-Vlaams Economisch Studiebureau (WES)

In the same period the number of second homes as well as the capacity of these homes increased enormously, to the tune of 61 per cent. A phenomenon that has been observed frequently is that hotels that stopped their activity were replaced with apartment blocks containing second homes and/or rented holiday homes.

Some features of demand in tourism

A dominant destination on the Belgian tourist scene

The National Institute for Statistics (NIS) noted 35,158,579 overnight stays in 1998 for Belgium. These overnight stays were recorded in hotels, campsites, holiday centres, holiday villages, youth hostels and in the rented sector. With nearly 24 million overnight stays, or 68 per cent of the total, Flanders forms the most important destination for travellers in and to Belgium. The Walloon and Brussels regions, respectively, generate 20 per cent and 12 per cent of total overnight stays.

On the supply side, the Tourist Office for Flanders (TOF) structures its marketing measures according to three macro-products: the Coast, Historic Cities[1] and Green Flanders. In 1998, the three macro-products together generated 28 million overnight stays. This corresponds to 80 per cent of all the overnight stays recorded in Belgium. The activities of TOF, therefore, relate to four-fifths of the total volume of tourist demand generated by Belgium. Expressed as overnight stays, the coast is by far the most important tourist destination to and in Belgium. With 13 million overnight stays, the coast has a total of 54 per cent of all the overnight stays in Flanders and 37 per cent of all overnight stays in Belgium.

The relationships between the macro-products differ, however, if we take the number of arrivals as variables. Here the Historic Cities clearly lead the way with 3.8 million arrivals, or 46 per cent of all arrivals recorded in the macro-products. Then follows Green Flanders, with 2.5 million arrivals, and the Coast with 2 million arrivals.

---

[1] Antwerp, Bruges, Brussels, Ghent, Leuven and Mechelen.

Table 8.2　Belgium: Overnight stays in the regions 1994–98 (× **1000**)

Region	1994	1995	1996	1997	1998	Tr.97–98 (%)	AAG94–98 (%)
Belgium	35,162	35,261	35,949	35,581	35,159	−1.2	−0.0
Flanders region	24,284	24,567	24,650	23,950	23,966	+0.1	−0.3
Brussels region	3,263	3,466	3,984	4,260	4,089	−4.0	+4.6
Walloon region	7,615	7,228	7,315	7,371	7,103	−3.6	−1.4

Source: NIS
(AAG: average annual growth)

Table 8.3　Flanders: Overnight stays in the macro-products 1994–98 (× **1000**)

Macro-product	1994	1995	1996	1997	1998	Tr.97–98 (%)	AAG94–98 (%)
Coast	14,520	14,068	14,083	13,293	13,036	−1.9	−2.7
Historic cities	5,795	5,980	6,751	7,191	7,330	+1.9	+6.1
Green Flanders	7,232	7,986	7,800	7,726	7,690	−0.5	+1.5

Source: NIS
(AAG: average annual growth)

Table 8.4　Flanders: Arrivals in the macro-products 1994–98 (× **1000**)

Macro-product	1994	1995	1996	1997	1998	Tr.97–98 (%)	AAG94–98 (%)
Coast	1,943	1,993	1,963	1,988	1,956	−1.6	+0.2
Historic cities	3,082	3,244	3,555	3,719	3,833	+3.1	+5.6
Green Flanders	2,110	2,369	2,392	2,467	2,516	+2.0	+4.5

Source: NIS
(AAG: average annual growth)

Table 8.5　Belgian Coast: Overnight stays 1970–98 (× **1000**)

Year	Number of overnight stays	5-Year Trend (a) (%)	10-Year Trend (a) (%)
1970	16,952		
1975	17,171	+1.3	
1980	14,026	−18.3	−17.3
1985	15,331	+9.3	
1990	16,170	+5.5	+15.3
1995	14,068	−13.0	
1998	13,036	−7.3	−19.4

Source: NIS
(a) with the exception of t = 1998

Table 8.6 Belgian Coast: Overnight stays by country of origin 1994–1998 (× **1000**)

Country of origin	1994	1995	1996	1997	1998	Tr.97–98 (%)	AAG94–98 (%)
Belgium	11,665	11,105	11,181	10,423	10,196	−2.2	−3.3
Foreigners	2,855	2,963	2,902	2,869	2,839	−1.0	−0.1
Germany	1,146	1,284	1,244	1,182	1,102	−6.8	−1.0
Holland	577	648	682	632	702	+11.2	+5.0
France	463	416	402	433	377	−12.9	−5.0
United Kingdom	307	273	246	289	349	+20.7	+3.3
Luxembourg	227	226	215	211	202	−4.3	−2.9
Others	136	117	114	123	108	−12.1	−5.6
TOTAL	14,520	14,068	14,083	13,293	13,036	−1.9	−2.7

Source: NIS
(AAG: average annual growth)

The differences between overnight stays and arrivals are clarified by the difference in the length of stay between the three macro-products. This amounts, on average, to 6.7 nights for the coast, 3.0 nights for Green Flanders and 1.9 nights for the Historic Cities. More individual tourists arrive at the Historic Cities than on the coast, but those on the coast stay, on average, three times longer.

In the past two to three decades, the Belgian Coast has lost about a quarter of the total tourist demand. At the beginning of the 1970s, demand fluctuated at around 17 million overnight stays, and in 1998 this had fallen by 4 million to 13 million. Although an obvious further wavering in demand was perceptible, at the end of the 1980s/early 1990s, this did not continue over the rest of the decade.

In the last five-year period, for which a complete summary is available (1994–8), the number of overnight stays per year on the Belgian Coast per year dropped by an average of 2.7 per cent.

The domestic market dominates

The market territory of the Belgian Coast is geographically relatively limited. The share of the domestic market clearly predominates, with 78 per cent of total demand. Foreign countries provide 22 per cent of tourists who stay, and these come almost exclusively from Germany, Holland, France, the United Kingdom and Luxembourg.

The loss of almost 1.5 million overnight stays over the period in question is almost entirely due to the decline in the domestic market. The foreign markets are, more or less, balanced, with the Dutch and British market as obvious growth markets, and with a loss on the German, French and Luxembourg market.

Problems with which the coast is confronted

A crumbling market

A significant problem for the Belgian Coast is the continual decline in demand for tourism. The decline in demand is not simply the result of the falling number of tourists but, primarily, of a decline in the length of time the actual tourists stay. If we compare Table 8.3 with Table 8.4, we can see that between 1994 and 1998 the total number of tourists themselves remains unchanged, but that overnight stays, annually, fell by almost 3 per cent.

As outlined above, the loss in market volume can mainly be blamed on the crumbling domestic market, primarily in the sector of the individual rented holiday homes. The Belgian Coast is, increasingly, the destination for its own population for a second holiday or short break, and, increasingly, less a main holiday destination.

The decline in the (domestic) market has internal and external causes. The internal causes are related, on the one hand, to the structural legacies of the Belgian Coast (see below), but also to inadequate and splintered promotional endeavours.

Above all, the Belgian Coast, as a traditional tourist destination, has to compete with the globalization of holiday destinations on offer today. Competition with the sun-secure destinations is no longer restricted to the coastal resorts of the Mediterranean, but charter tourism is at present reaching beaches in almost every part of the world. In addition, the expansion of this provision and the pricing structure of international competitors do not work to the advantage of the Belgian Coast.

A product in distress

A traditional tourist region like the Belgian Coast, with a long history and explosive growth due to the advent of mass tourism, is, naturally, subject to the negative effects of these phenomena. The advent of mass tourism took its toll on the natural product and the open space of the Belgian Coast. Important image-fixing infrastructures, such as the sea dike, beach area, the dunes and the layout of the seaside resorts, came under constant pressure.

The Flemish and provincial authorities acknowledged these problems. In 1997 they started a five-year programme that gave top priority to the restoration and improvement of the public domain. The radical improvement of the public domain is seen as a catalyst for attracting private investment.

The conscious programme does not simply pay attention to the open space, but also to accessible private areas such as shopping centres, sporting infrastructures, pleasure- and theme parks. With regard to existing provisions, an improvement in the quality of what is on offer is being striven for. The priority for new establishments lies in an 'all-weather infrastructure' for making the coast less dependent on the weather.

ORGANIZATION OF THE MARKET ANALYSIS

Market analysis forms an essential part of marketing policy. Adequate, reliable information must be available for each stage in the marketing process in order to enable well-founded decisions to be made. Because detailed market information about customers who visit Flanders can seldom be gathered from secondary sources, TOF has decided to obtain this through its own market analysis.

A cyclical process of analysis has therefore been started, divided up, in the first instance, according to the reason for the stay and then to the macro-product. In the first year of the cycle the entire leisure or holiday market is thus carefully examined for the three macro-products (Coast, Historic Cities and Green Flanders). In year 2 the MICE market is analysed and in year 3 the pure business sector is scrutinized (from the macro-economic rather than the consumer standpoint). Finally, up-to-date detailed information is available after three years, which is an acceptable interval in view of the cost-price of this analysis.

The coastal analysis formed a pilot project within this cyclical process of analysis (a pilot project in the sense that the Flemish and provincial partners are developing a joint marketing policy based on a market analysis drawn up together).

Thus the objectives and the concept of the coastal analysis were fixed in consultation between TOF and the Tourism and Recreation Service of the province of West Flanders. It is not insignificant that funding took place on a divided basis and that the results were interpreted, reported and used jointly. The fieldwork of the coastal analysis was contracted out to the West-Vlaams Economisch Studiebureau (WES) in Bruges.

THE BELGIAN COAST TOURIST MARKET RESEARCH 1999

Methodology

Population

There are four main groups of tourists that visit the Belgian Coast:

1.   tourists staying in paid accommodation;
2.   tourists staying in their second home;
3.   one-day visitors and excursionists; and
4.   tourists staying on their yachts.

From these groups, the first has the highest priority in tourism policy and, therefore, the population of the coastal research was restricted to this group. Tourists staying in paid accommodation are, as a group, the most marketable and have a spending behaviour that creates the highest impact on the economy.

Within this group of tourists a quota sample (cf. Table 8.7 and Table 8.8) was calculated, based on the arrivals per country of residence and per accommodation form. This resulted in the selection of six different countries of residence (Belgium, Germany, The Netherlands, France, Luxembourg and the United Kingdom), and five different accommodation forms (hotels, rental houses/apartments, campsites, holiday villages and social holiday centres).

Some combinations made no sense; e.g. social holiday centres hardly cater for foreigners, as Belgians mainly use this form of accommodation. This left us with a quota sample for eighteen different sub-groups, with at least 100 questionnaires to be collected in each sub-group. It is important to mention, however, that the number of questionnaires in the sample does not correspond to the number of arrivals for each sub-group. This difference will be corrected during the processing of the data collected.

Interview methodology

The interviews were conducted face-to-face by a team of interviewers. Our experience shows that face-to-face interviews create better results than written questionnaires or telephone interviews, certainly insofar as spending behaviour is concerned.

Table 8.7 Belgian Coast: Arrivals by country of origin 1998 (× **1000**)

Type of accommodation	Belgium	Germany	Holland	France	Luxembourg	UK	TOTAL
Rental houses/apartments	324	31	11	12	8	1	387
Hotels	491	66	51	32	20	105	765
Campsites	129	19	20	6	2	2	178
Social holiday centres	231	3	1	3	2	0	240
Holiday villages	94	56	51	17	2	9	228
TOTAL	1269	175	134	70	33	117	1798

Source: NIS

Table 8.8 Belgian Coast Research 1999 – quota sample

Type of accommodation	Belgium	Germany	Holland	France	Luxembourg	UK	TOTAL
Rental houses/apartments	300	200	100	100	100	–	800
Hotels	300	200	200	200	100	200	1200
Campsites	200	100	100	–	–	–	400
Social holiday centres	250	–	–	–	–	–	250
Holiday villages	150	100	100	–	–	–	350
TOTAL	1200	600	500	300	200	200	3000

Source: Belgian Coast Research 1999

The task of the interviewers was to contact people on the streets or in lodging accommodation on a random basis, avoiding interviewing two or more people from the same party travelling together. Except for one specific sub-group (French tourists staying in hotels) the interviewers succeeded in finding enough people to fulfil all the requirements.

Questionnaire

A first questionnaire was presented during the summer of 1998. This questionnaire was adapted and tested again during the same summer in order to have a good list of questions, which would supply us with the required marketing information.

The questions were focused on the following topics:

1. profile of the visitors;
2. characteristics of the present stay;
3. leisure activities during the stay;
4. spending; and
5. tourism information sources used.

A maximum coding was included for the possible answers for all the questions in order to make it easier to process the results afterwards. Although the questionnaire is rather long, the experience gained during the summer of 1998 shows that, on average, only a small number of answers were given compared to the large number of possible variables. This results in a normal interview time of ten to fifteen minutes.

Period of interviewing

The period in which the interviews were collected stretched from May to November 1999. During this period the different resorts were visited during three defined seasons: pre-season (May–June), high season (July–August) and post-season (September–November).

Processing of results and report

After collecting the information the results were processed by computer. A weighting factor was used to ensure that the proportions for the different nationalities were representative for actual proportions. The results will be combined in a report which will be used as one of the bases for the strategic planning for both promotion and product development.

First, there will be six separate reports, one for each country of residence, with all the variables of which some may be useful for marketing purposes. In addition, there will be two specific reports: one aimed towards the activities that tourists undertake during their stay at the coast, and another concentrating on tourist spending. These last two reports will be of great importance both for policy-making and for proving the importance of our sector to politicians.

Results

In this chapter we present a selection of the results. Obviously, not all the results obtained can be presented in such a short report. Therefore, results that might be interesting for other researchers and policy-makers in the tourism sector were selected for presentation.

Profile of the tourists

Next to a variety of profile characteristics, an interesting result was obtained concerning the kind of party in which the tourist visited the Coast. The results (see Table 8.9) show a concentration of families without children (mainly between 45 and 74 years old) and families with very young children. Families with older children seem to turn their back on the Belgian Coast.

Characteristics of the stay

One of the main questions, which this study sought to answer, concerned the choice of accommodation, i.e. do people take more than one kind of accommodation into consideration for their holiday, or do they stick to only one type of accommodation which has been decided upon before they start looking for information on the resorts and accommodation possibilities? The answer was a rather surprising one (see Table 8.10). The vast majority of tourists (approximately 95%) have never considered any type of accommodation other than the one they have currently chosen. This figure clearly indicates that, for a specific holiday, the choice between different types of accommodation seems to be rather irrelevant. This does not mean that a person will not use different types of accommodation for different holidays!

Table 8.9 Belgian Coast Research 1999: Type of visiting party

Type of visiting party	%
individual, 15–24 years old, without children	4.4
individual, 24–44 years old, without children	10.7
individual, 45–64 years old, without children	24.8
individual, 65–74 years old, without children	16.8
individual, 75+ years old, without children	6.3
families, youngest child <6 years old	21.3
families, youngest child, 6–14 years old	12.2
families, youngest child, 15–24 years old	3.2
Number of respondents	2998

Source: Belgian Coast Research 1999

Table 8.10 Belgian Coast Research 1999: Choice of accommodation

	Considered no other form of accommodation (%)	Number of respondents
Current accommodation		
Hotel	95.1	1295
Holiday village	94.3	245
Rental house/apartment	95.7	957
Campsite	97.4	229
Social holiday centre	93.3	268
Country of residence		
Belgium	94.9	2180
Holland	93.5	201
Germany	95.4	283
Luxembourg	96.1	51
France	96.4	83
United Kingdom	98.9	178
Repeat visits		
repeat visitors (a)	95.4	1902
non-repeat visitors	94.8	1130

(a) Repeat visitors are visitors who have visited the Belgian Coast at least once during the last two years
Source: Belgian Coast Research 1999

Information sources

A final aspect of the results that can be put forward in this context are the information sources used by tourists to collect information about their stay at the Belgian Coast. These results are influenced by the frequent repeat visits by many tourists (which make them less likely to seek tourist information).

The first important result represents the use of information sources per country of residence. Overall, there is one very important information source: 'information gathered through earlier experiences' (53.8%). 'Friends, family and relatives' are another major source of information (21.9%). These two most important information sources have in common that they can only be influenced indirectly by marketing efforts.

Next to these two, all other information sources seem to have a very small impact. Travel guidebooks, newspapers etc. all account for just a few percentage points of the information services. One interesting result is the 1.2 per cent for the internet, a result that is higher than that for television or travel fairs.

Finally, it is astonishing to note that almost one in five tourists seek no information at all.

Some specific results are evident between Belgians and foreigners. Foreigners seek more information trough travel guidebooks and the internet. In addition, they show a high number of 'earlier experiences', which shows that many of them are actually repeat visitors.

For reasons of marketing, the main attention goes to non-repeat visitors (because, on average, the repeat visits are very high, so we are looking for new visitors who may become repeaters). If the results of the non-repeat visitors are compared with the result for the repeat visitors we can see that almost all the 'marketing' information sources have a higher score, except for the travel fairs. When we take into consideration that a lot of visitors come back to the Belgian Coast after they have visited it once, this gives hope for further marketing measures.

But here it becomes even clearer that the earlier experience is very important, even for tourists that have not been at the coast in the last two years.

A final result deals with the number of tourists who have had contact with tourist boards prior to their stay. The local tourist boards get the highest scores both for repeat and non-repeat visitors. For the non-repeat visitors, the Flemish Tourist Board gets a good result, probably due to the foreign visitors.

Table 8.11 Belgian Coast Research 1999: Use of information sources by country of origin

Type of information source	Belgium (%)	Germany (%)	Holland (%)	France (%)	Luxembourg (%)	UK (%)	TOTAL (%)
Experience earlier visit	59.5	42.0	35.1	38.4	44.0	34.0	53.8
FFR (a)	22.7	21.9	23.5	28.0	21.6	7.5	21.9
Travel guidebooks	2.8	7.6	10.8	13.1	7.3	12.5	4.7
Newspaper advertisement	2.5	2.8	1.3	1.8	2.2	1.5	2.3
Newspaper article	2.1	2.5	1.0	2.2	2.7	4.0	2.2
Magazine article	1.1	1.9	2.1	2.0	2.2	2.5	1.4
Internet	1.0	1.8	2.4	1.6	2.0	1.5	1.2
Television	1.0	0.9	1.3	0.6	1.4	1.5	1.1
Magazine advertisement	0.4	1.6	1.8	1.4	2.9	2.0	0.8
Travel Fair	0.1	1.2	0.2	0.0	0.0	0.5	0.2
Radio	0.0	0.0	0.1	0.0	1.4	0.0	0.1
No information sources	16.2	26.6	32.3	16.1	20.2	41.5	19.9
No. respondents	2180	283	201	84	51	178	2976

(a) Family, friends and relatives
Source: Belgian Coast Research 1999

Table 8.12 Belgian Coast Research 1999: Use of information sources, repeat and non-repeat visitors

Type of information source	Repeat visitors (a) (%)	Non-repeat visitors (%)	TOTAL (%)
Experience earlier visit	65.8	32.6	53.8
FFR	20.7	24.0	21.9
Travel guidebooks	2.6	8.3	4.7
Newspaper advertisement	1.3	4.0	2.3
Newspaper article	1.3	3.8	2.2
Magazine article	0.6	2.7	1.4
Internet	0.7	2.1	1.2
Television	1.0	1.3	1.1
Magazine advertisement	0.3	1.6	0.8
Travel Fair	0.2	0.1	0.2
Radio	0.0	0.1	0.1
No information sources	12.4	33.2	19.9
No. respondents	1902	1104	2976

(a) Repeat visitors are visitors who have visited the Belgian Coast at least once during the last two years
Source: Belgian Coast Research 1999

Table 8.13 Belgian Coast Research 1999: Consultation of tourist boards, repeat and non-repeat visitors

Type of tourist board	Repeat visitors (a) (%)	Non-repeat visitors (%)	TOTAL (%)
Local Tourist Board	4.5	3.5	4.1
Provincial Tourist Board	1.1	0.5	0.9
Tourist Office for Flanders (b)	1.4	3.7	2.2

(a) Repeat visitors are visitors who have visited the Belgian Coast at least once during the last two years
(b) Including foreign offices
Source: Belgian Coast Research 1999

SOME SPECIFIC ASPECTS

Timing of the interview

The respondents were interviewed as they passed by on the waterfront, the beach or in the streets. This means that we were not sure at what moment during their stay we were interviewing them. One of the main objectives of the survey was the analysis of the spending patterns of the tourist. At first, this uncertainty in the timing of the interview caused a problem. In order to correct any errors due to timing, the spending pattern was split into two different units: spending for lodgings and spending during the day.

In addition, we intended only to interview people on their second day at the coast, otherwise they would have been at the coast less than 24 hours, which would have made their spending the previous day irrelevant. This is why we chose to select respondents by asking them whether they had already been at the coast for at least two nights, to ensure that they would have been on a holiday the whole of the previous day.

Of course, this choice has its impact on the results. First, there will be an under-representation of tourists staying at the coast for shorter periods (as they run less risk of being interviewed by one of the interviewers). Second, there is a total absence of data on people staying only for one day at the coast. The researchers are very aware of these imperfect results, which is why all the results concerning spending behaviour that have been published mainly concern daily spending. Although the results linked to other variables might also be influenced, this influence is more difficult to grasp.

Activities

Another main issue was the activities by tourists at the coast and in the countryside. We needed adults to answer most of the questions (18 years upwards). However, for questions concerning activities, we also needed younger children (12 years upwards). Because of this, the 'first birthday' method was chosen for the questions on activities. Within a party, the one who was about to celebrate his/her birthday first was chosen to answer these questions. The age limit of twelve years was put forward because we believe that children start to make their own decisions on what they do and when around this age. Younger children will mainly do what their parents suggest; older children will have their own activities and will insist on doing their activities at the coast. Next to this, the tourism sector at the coast is also considering opportunities to develop a number of products that are suited to youngsters, so we need to know what the youngsters like to do.

In practice, the interviewer had to be very strict on these matters, because often the person answering the questions in the first place (mainly the father or mother) was eager to continue answering the questions.

Brochures

When asking respondents on a beach or in a hotel lobby which brochures they possessed or had used for their trip, people tended to confuse the different kinds of brochures available. For this reason we chose to give every interviewer a copy of the front page of a brochure, so that he/she could show the front pages to the respondent. This system was tested during 1998 and proved to be very effective.

9

Private Accommodation in Tourism Statistics in the Republic of Croatia

Anka Javor and Ivana Kalčić

The aim of this chapter is to show the importance and the methods of statistical recording of tourist capacities, and actual numbers of tourists and nights in private accommodation facilities in tourism statistics within the Republic of Croatia. Because of the importance of tourism for Croatia, private accommodation is statistically recorded on a regular, monthly basis.

Although methodology is generaly harmonized with the WTO/Eurostat recommendations, data quality is affected by coverage problems with reporting units. In order to improve coverage of private accommodation in the Central Bureau of Statistics (CBS), the following measures have been undertaken:

- better co-operation with national and regional tourist boards;
- implementation of a new survey on tourists and nights in second homes and flats which are not rented (nights by owners, relatives and friends during tourism season); and
- preparation of methodology for estimating unregistered tourist flows.

IMPORTANCE OF TOURISM ACTIVITY IN CROATIA

In socio-economic development in Croatia, tourism is an important economic activity, or group of activities. There is almost no economic sphere which is not, directly or indirectly, influenced by tourism, which increases their turnover. Tourism activities influence the development of many activities, because tourism expenditures flow into catering, transport, trade, sport etc. and directly influence gross domestic product, employment, balance of payments, development of undeveloped areas and standard of living.

Croatia has a tourism tradition lasting more than 150 years, mainly thanks to the climate, natural characteristics and attractive Adriatic coast. Tourism ensures direct and indirect employment for about 180,000 people, and it accounts for 13 per cent of total gross domestic product (1998). In the balance of goods and services for 1998, the credit from tourism amounted to $US2.7 billion and 32 per cent of total credit from goods and services export, namely 69 per cent of total services exported. Debit of tourism amounted to $US0.6 billion, so total foreign-exchange earnings were $US2.7 billion. In the same year, in all accommodation facilities (which comprised of 725,000 beds), 5.5 million arrivals and 31.3 million overnight stays were made.

DATA SOURCES

Data sources for tourism include different surveys (accommodation statistics, transport statistics, household budget survey, balance of payments etc.), which are conducted by the Central Bureau of Statistics and other institutions in Croatia. The Central Bureau of Statistics is responsible for accommodation tourism statistics.

The most important survey in this area is the Monthly Report on Tourism and Nights (TU-11). Data collected by this survey include number of accommodation facilities, their capacity (number of rooms and beds), number of tourists (arrivals) and overnight stays by type of accommodation facilities and by country of residence for foreign tourists.

Number of tourists refers to the number of tourist arrivals in all accommodation facilities. Number of overnight stays refers to the number of nights that a tourist spent (or reported) in an accommodation facility. Number of beds includes permanent and auxiliary beds.

Methodology is generally based on the WTO/Eurostat recommendations for accommodation statistics. Monthly data on tourists and nights are used as short-term indicators for creating economic policy, and also for national accounts and balance of payments compilation. The survey is based on full coverage.

The survey covers commercial (rental), collective and private accommodation facilities. Collective accommodation includes hotels, motels, boarding-houses, bed and breakfast, holiday villages, inns and other food-and-lodging facilities, spas, health establishments, company-vacation facilities and vacation facilities for youth, campsites, temporary accommodation facilities (e.g. students' and pupils' dormitories which are rented to tourists during the summer), ship cabins and couchette train accommodation. Although marinas are covered by the monthly survey, from 1998, these data are presented separately.

Private accommodation covers private rooms, flats, villas and second homes, and private, non-organized campsites. The elementary data from this survey are presented in Table 9.1.

For analysis, longer data series have to be used because of the exceptional circumstances of the war years (1990–5) which caused the decrease in number of tourists and tourist nights, and on transformation of tourism accommodation into refugees centres. In 1988, Croatia had its highest number of beds, 926,300. The lowest level was registered (534,500) in 1992. During the war years, about 250,000 available capacities were destroyed or became no longer available for tourism; therefore in 1998, numbers were reduced to 1981 levels. The highest number of tourist nights was reached in 1986 (68.2 million) and the lowest level was registered in 1991. Although after 1995 tourism increases, it is still far from the level before the war. For example, the total

Table 9.1 Number of tourists, nights and beds in all accommodation establishments in Croatia

	Tourists (× **1000**)			Nights (× **1000**)			Beds (× **1000**)
	Total	Residents	Non-residents	Total	Residents	Non-residents	
1980	7,929	1,486	6,443	53,600	7,750	45,850	6,920
1981	8,333	1,513	6,820	56,573	7,715	48,858	7,285
1982	8,042	1,620	6,422	54,436	8,315	46,121	7,694
1983	8,268	1,753	6,515	54,632	8,541	46,091	7,745
1984	9,146	1,778	7,368	59,465	8,527	50,938	8,001
1985	10,125	1,790	8,335	67,665	8,790	58,875	8,203
1986	10,151	1,767	8,384	68,216	8,836	59,380	8,493
1987	10,487	1,731	8,756	68,160	8,397	59,763	8,858
1988	10,354	1,661	8,693	67,298	7,946	59,352	9,263
1989	9,670	1,580	8,090	61,849	7,383	54,466	9,228
1990	8,497	1,448	7,049	52,523	6,747	45,776	8,627
1991	2,146	800	1,346	10,158	3,394	6,764	5,970
1992	2,010	739	1,271	10,725	3,170	7,555	5,345
1993	2,363	842	1,521	12,908	3,150	9,758	5,703
1994	3,402	1,109	2,293	19,977	4,421	15,556	6,203
1995	2,438	1,113	1,325	12,885	4,370	8,515	6,093
1996	3,899	1,249	2,650	21,456	4,910	16,546	6,459
1997	5,206	1,372	3,834	30,314	5,617	24,697	6,833
1998	5,450	1,338	4,112	31,288	5,286	26,002	7,250
1999	4,750	1,307	3,443	26,564	5,215	21,439	6,709

number of nights in 1998 is only 46 per cent of the record year 1986; i.e. it is at the same level as in 1970. This rising trend came to a halt during 1999 because of the Kosovo crisis.

Comparative analysis of results from this survey with other surveys in research tourism is limited because of different approaches, definitions and coverage. If we compare data on entry of foreign travellers into the country from transport statistics with number of tourist arrivals in all rental accommodation facilities (marinas included), then the share of tourists is only about 13 per cent. According to the Survey of Foreign Tourists Expenditure conducted by the Institute of Tourism on Cross-Borders, in the observed sample the total number of travellers with paid nights is about 37 per cent. Estimates made by tourist experts from the Institute of Tourism say that about 20 per cent of tourist nights in campsites and in private accommodation are unregistered and statistically unrecorded. If number of nights is corrected to include that percentage, their share of total number of travellers is increased significantly. The conclusion is that a great part of rental tourism turnover, mainly in private accommodation, is statistically unrecorded.

Experience says that unrecorded turnover in non-rental accommodation is much greater, and even a part of rental activity is hidden within this measurement. Non-rental tourism activity is the subject of a separate statistical survey; Report on Tourists and Nights in Summerhouses and Apartments (second homes).

Table 9.2   Structure of number of tourists and nights by types of accommodation establishments

	Tourists (%)					Nights (%)				
	1980	1985	1990	1995	1999	1980	1985	1990	1995	1999
Total	100	100	100	100	100	100	100	100	100	100
Hotels	44.2	41.3	49.5	57.3	45.9	32.7	31.0	39.4	43.4	36.2
Holiday villages	5.8	6.9	8.0	10.8	9.1	7.3	8.1	9.9	15.3	11.9
Vacation facilities	9.3	9.0	8.0	2.8	2.6	13.3	12.3	10.8	3.8	3.4
Campsites	19.8	20.3	16.9	15.0	22.8	23.9	25.5	22.6	26.6	28.6
Other collective est.	7.4	8.0	7.7	9.7	5.9	7.1	2.6	3.0	4.4	2.2
Private accommod.	13.5	14.5	9.9	4.4	14.7	19.4	20.5	14.3	6.5	17.8
Residents	100	100	100	100	100	100	100	100	100	100
Hotels	41.5	40.5	55.2	68.1	62.3	23.7	21.9	39.2	58.8	50.8
Holiday villages	4.0	4.7	5.3	6.7	6.1	3.2	3.1	5.2	10.7	8.9
Vacation facilities	17.5	18.5	14.0	4.5	6.2	28.4	29.1	24.3	7.6	11.7
Campsites	11.9	13.0	4.7	3.0	3.7	17.2	21.4	10.0	8.0	8.7
Other collective est.	12.0	12.2	16.1	14.5	13.8	5.5	4.8	15.7	8.5	7.0
Private accommod.	13.1	11.1	4.7	3.2	7.9	22.0	19.7	10.8	6.4	12.9
Non-residents	100	100	100	100	100	100	100	100	100	100
Hotels	43.0	41.4	48.3	48.2	39.7	34.2	32.4	39.5	35.4	32.6
Holiday villages	6.2	9.4	8.6	14.2	10.2	8.0	8.8	10.6	17.7	12.7
Vacation facilities	7.4	7.0	6.8	1.4	1.2	10.7	9.7	8.8	1.9	1.4
Campsites	21.6	22.6	19.4	25.1	28.6	20.6	27.0	24.5	36.2	33.4
Other collective est.	8.3	7.1	5.9	5.7	3.0	7.4	2.3	1.8	2.2	0.9
Private accommod.	13.5	14.5	11.0	5.4	17.3	19.0	19.8	14.8	6.6	19.0

Table 9.3   Number and structure of beds by types of establishments

	Beds (× **1000**)					Structure (%)				
	1980	1985	1990	1995	1999	1980	1985	1990	1995	1999
Total	692.0	820.3	862.7	609.3	670.9	100	100	100	100	100
Hotels	113.2	127.8	142.9	137.8	129.1	16.4	15.6	16.6	22.6	19.2
Holiday villages	36.4	51.1	58.2	61.4	57.7	5.3	6.2	6.7	10.1	8.6
Vacation facilities	94.0	103.5	89.2	10.3	19.4	13.6	12.6	10.3	1.7	2.9
Campsites	232.7	267.0	283.7	260.5	202.0	33.6	32.5	32.9	42.8	30.1
Other collective est.	19.4	12.1	15.4	12.9	19.4	2.7	1.6	1.8	2.1	2.9
Private accommod.	196.3	258.8	273.3	126.4	243.3	28.4	31.5	31.7	20.7	36.3

PROBLEMS WITH COVERAGE OF REPORTING UNITS

Absence of quality updated register for better coverage of registered rental accommodation

In Croatia, three types of units offer accommodation services to guests: legal entities or their local units; citizens registered as crafts; and households/citizens.

The Central Bureau of Statistics keeps an administrative register of legal entities and their local units and gradually creates its business register. In the present register, all legal entities are registered regularly when they start running businesses. But any change in their status, or ceasing business, is not registered. So our register is not qualitative, and it contains a great number of non-active units. On 31 January 2000, in the Hotels and Restaurants (NACE Rev. 1) activity there were 5854 legal units, of which only 2942 were active. When conducting a survey one finds a great number of units with inaccurately stated prevailing activity. For tourism activity, local units are especially important, but their accuracy is even worse. While legal entities can be compared with other administrative registers (e.g. tax office or the Institute for Payments Transaction), a register of local units exists only in the CBS. Enterprises are not legally obliged to register their local units. Therefore it is very difficult to find all the units that deal with rental accommodation activities, although they can be regularly registered with the institution responsible (for payment of income tax, residence tax etc.), but under the wrong activity.

For citizens/crafts no official register exists. CBS uses a database from the tax office which contains all independent operators, recorded for payment of income tax. The fault of this database is the fact that it is taken from the tax office and is out of date – almost a year after the reference year – and it contains many units with wrongly reported prevailing activity.

Households/citizens which let accommodation to guests are not obliged to be registered. This part of the population, although commercial, is the most difficult to explore.

Unregistered rental accommodation (hidden economy)

This activity poses a huge problem for coverage, and is very significant for tourism. It refers mainly to private accommodation. Collective establishments are obliged to be officially registered in order to run business regularly (to open transfer accounts, to keep business books etc.).

Non-rental accommodation providing accommodation services to relatives and friends without charge

This type of accommodation, which is private accommodation, is not yet covered with the regular Monthly Survey on Tourists and Nights, but since 1996 it has been covered by a separate survey. A significant number of rental activities are hidden within it; that is reason enough to record this type of accommodation statistically. At the present time, in order to avoid paying tax, there is an intention in private accommodation to present rental activities as non-rental ones. The Ministry of Tourism and the Croatian Tourist Board are very much interested in these data sources.

Table 9.4 Average annual rate of growth/decrease of number of tourists, nights and beds

	Total (%)			Collective accommodation (%)			Private accommodation (%)		
	tourists	nights	beds	tourists	nights	beds	tourists	nights	beds
1980–85	5.01	4.77	3.46	4.76	4.48	2.52	6.55	5.93	5.68
1985–90	−3.45	−4.94	1.01	−2.38	−3.49	0.97	−10.55	−11.60	1.10
1990–95	−22.10	−24.50	−6.72	−21.18	−23.18	−3.91	−33.65	−35.44	−14.29
1995–99	18.14	19.83	2.44	14.83	16.04	−2.99	59.50	53.39	17.79

PRIVATE ACCOMMODATION

In Croatia, tourism was one of the rare economic activities in which private initiative was encouraged through the so-called 'cottage industry'. On the one hand it contributes to the standard of living, and on the other it creates a new, huge segment of 'cheap accommodation capacity', which is certainly not the aim of Croatian tourism policy. The main characteristic of Croatian tourism is an inadequate structure of accommodation facilities, so the share of primary capacities (hotels and similar establishments) in regular tourist years is mainly below 25 per cent, and 75 per cent refers to supplementary capacities (mainly camping and private accommodation – over 30 per cent each). This situation was different only during the war, when supplementary capacities were decreased drastically (annual rate of decrease in private accommodation was 14 per cent). Private accommodation, the most flexible type of accommodation, withdraws from the market in unfavourable conditions, and vice versa. In the period 1995–99 it recovered, with an annual growth rate of 17 per cent (Table 9.4).

Primary capacities are: hotels, motels, boarding-houses, holiday villages (and similar). Supplementary capacities are company-vacation facilities and vacation facilities for youth, campsites and private accommodation.

The disadvantages of private accommodation are:

- insufficient occupancy rate;
- occupancy limited to short period of time during the year;
- it does not offer possibility for complementary tourism activities;
- over 98 per cent of private capacities are located at the seaside, although in collective accommodation the situation is not much better (90 per cent) (Croatia as a central European country, a crossroad of ways and cultures, with rich history, has more space for extended tourism supply away from the sea and the sun).

According to the data in Table 9.5 it is obvious that Croatia is a typical seasonally receptive tourist country, because all capacities are used mainly in summer months, during the tourist season. Over 80 per cent of all tourist nights are in use during the four summer months. Collective accommodation accounts for about 70 per cent of total seasonal tourist nights, and private accommodation about 90 per cent. However, during the year private accommodation has an average occupancy rate of under 20 per cent and over 40 per cent in the summer (during regular years). Viewed by month within a year, private accommodation is hardly used during winter months.

Table 9.5 Occupancy rate of accommodation capacities (gross); accommodation capacities at 31 August

	Annual occupancy rate (%)					Occupancy rate for June–September (%)				
	1980	1985	1990	1995	1999	1980	1985	1990	1995	1999
Total	21.2	22.6	16.7	5.8	10.8	54.1	57.3	40.4	13.7	28.6
Hotels	42.4	45.0	40.4	11.1	20.4	82.4	84.6	76.2	20.4	45.4
Holiday villages	29.6	29.1	24.5	8.8	15.1	79.8	76.7	64.9	25.6	43.2
Vacation facilities	20.7	22.0	17.4	13.2	12.8	57.3	60.3	47.0	36.2	36.3
Campsites	15.1	17.4	11.2	3.6	10.0	45.0	50.5	32.9	10.5	29.0
Private accommod.	14.5	14.8	7.7	1.8	5.4	43.1	43.4	21.6	5.4	16.0

Table 9.6 Occupancy rate of accommodation facilities by months: accommodation capacities available for each month (%)

1999	I.	II.	III.	IV.	V.	VI.	VII.	VIII.	IX.	X.	XI.	XII.
Total	22.3	11.0	15.2	7.2	7.2	9.1	15.7	40.0	46.7	14.9	6.1	8.7	7.6
Collective	25.6	12.5	17.6	8.1	8.1	10.7	21.0	48.0	55.8	20.8	7.6	10.7	8.9
Private	14.0	1.5	0.5	0.5	1.6	1.9	4.4	25.6	30.8	4.1	0.8	0.6	0.6

Table 9.7 Average length of tourist stay by type of establishments (days)

	1980	1985	1990	1995	1999
Total	6.8	6.7	6.2	5.3	5.6
Hotels	5.2	5.0	4.9	4.0	4.4
Holiday villages	8.6	7.8	7.6	7.5	7.4
Vacation facilities	9.6	9.1	8.3	7.2	7.4
Campsites	6.9	8.4	8.2	9.4	7.3
Private accommod.	9.8	9.5	9.0	7.8	6.8
Other collective est.	5.4	2.2	2.4	2.4	2.1

Table 9.5 represents gross occupancy rate by years, since only maximum accommodation capacity for 31 August was available. Since 1999 we have collected monthly data on total available beds in all accommodation facilities having at least one tourist night in the reference month (Table 9.6).

In spite of its disadvantages, private accommodation has, relatively, great importance in the tourism supply of Croatia. In all registered rental accommodation, statistically covered, private accommodation in typical years accounts for about 30 per cent (Table 9.2), and about 20 per cent of total number of tourist nights. In 1998 there were 107,500 rooms in private accommodation, i.e. 262,300 beds, with 855,700 tourist arrivals and 6.1 million nights. Tourism experts estimate that 20 per cent of unregistered private rental accommodation is not statistically covered. Unofficial estimates for some regions amount to as much as 50 per cent. Because of all of this, it is important to properly cover this segment of our tourism supply statistically.

According to the Law on Rental Accommodation Activity, private accommodation comprises rental accommodation services in households. According to that law, a citizen or a household can let rooms, apartments and summer-houses up to a maximum of ten rooms or twenty beds. A household can also rent non-organized campsites on its own land, to a maximum of ten accommodation units or 30 guests at the same time. For running this business under our national limits, the household is not obliged to be registered as a legal entity or craft. It is required merely to get a work permit from the regional local government body responsible for tourism. These permits are not kept as a database and there is no register of households that rent accommodation facilities. It is considered that the lowering of the national limit of number of rooms or beds would cause a significant resistance, knowing that domestic populations in tourist venues build accommodations with a large number of rooms, with an intention of letting them to guests. Households can offer their facilities directly to guests or by the intervention of tourism collective establishments or travel agencies.

In our regular monthly survey we cover private rental accommodation, i.e. rented rooms and apartments in family houses or second homes and flats, and non-organized campsites on private land.

Statistical reports for households are not submitted individually, but there is a single questionnaire for all households at a city level. The questionnaires are submitted by:

- tourism collective establishments that intermediate in renting of private accommodation (e.g. hotels);
- travel agencies that intermediate in renting of private accommodation; and
- local tourist boards for private accommodation that is rented directly, without a mediator.

STATISTICAL COVERAGE IMPROVEMENT

Registered rental accommodation

In this segment the Central Bureau of Statistics co-operates very closely with the Ministry of Tourism and the Croatian Tourist Board. Regional tourist boards keep records on accommodation facilities in order to collect residence tax. Tourist boards provide us with address lists of rental collective accommodation facilities. As for private accommodation, we get a list of travel agencies that are engaged in mediation in renting of private accommodation.

A new process of categorization of accommodation facilities, which is the responsibility of the Ministry of Tourism and local government bodies engaged in tourism, is in its final stage in Croatia. As a result, a quality database of newly categorized accommodations is being established. They will provide us with lists of all facilities which satisfy new strict legal working conditions. The list can be verified with regional tourist boards.

This year (2000) the Ministry of Tourism starts a large project of establishing a unique tourist register of all accommodation facilities (including households). This register will serve as a good basis for updating statistical address lists. It can be done relatively easily for collective accommodations, but for private accommodations it will take time, as the basis for the register of private accommodations will be work permits obtained from local government bodies. It is anticipated to be a very important project in which many institutions will be engaged.

Non-rental accommodation

Since 1996 the CBS has carried out a survey of non-rental private accommodation (Report on Tourists and Nights in Summerhouses or Apartments TU-11v). The focus of this survey is owners of summer-houses and apartments, members of their families, and relatives and friends who stay in the parts of these facilities without charge. The survey is based on the records kept by town/county tourist boards for collecting residence tax. According to the Residence Tax Act, owners of summer-houses or apartments and all persons who spend their holidays during the period 15 June to 15 September in these facilities are compelled to register in a tourist board in order to provide payment of a residence tax.

A summer-house or apartment is any building or apartment (second home) which is used seasonally or temporarily. The results of this survey include the number of persons registered as accommodated in the summer-houses and apartments (owners, family members, other relatives and friends) in the period from 15 June to 15 September and the number of registered overnight stays for which residence tax is paid.

Reporting units are tourist boards at a county level. The survey covers about 130 tourist boards, mostly situated on the Adriatic coast, which have established a system of computerized residence-tax registration and payment.

From Table 9.8 it is obvious that there is a great number of foreign relatives and friends. It means that a part of rental activity is hidden within that type of accommodation. Since the inspection control of residence tax registration is very organized, the majority of guests are registered with local tourist boards (it is particularly true for foreign guests who are difficult to hide and who are, in fact, commercial guests). However, it is difficult to prove that they pay for accommodation services. In that way, households who let accommodation avoid paying income tax. In spite of fines, a proportion of domestic relatives and friends are unregistered for residence-tax payments. There is a great resistance against paying residence tax when one uses one's own summer-house or apartment for holidays only, and for which all municipal services are paid for the whole year.

This is one of the indicators of hidden commercial activity, which may urge the Ministry of Tourism and Croatian Tourist Board to make a more restrictive law in order to ensure a higher degree of rental activities registration.

Table 9.8 Tourists and nights in second homes/flats (non-rental accommodation), from 15 June to 12 September

	Tourists (× **1000**)			Nights (× **1000**)		
	total	residents	non-residents	total	residents	non-residents
1996	73.5	36.3	37.2	1074.5	773.0	301.5
1997	118.4	61.5	56.9	1788.8	1292.8	496.0
1998	135.6	76.3	59.3	2121.2	1567.6	553.6
1999	132.4	74.5	57.9	2039.1	1537.1	502.0

Unregistered rental activity

According to the estimates of the Ministry of Tourism, tourist boards and other tourist experts, about 20–50 per cent of private rental accommodation is statistically unrecorded. The CBS is preparing a revision of a survey which used to be carried out many years ago: Estimates of Unregistered Commercial Tourist Flows in Private Accommodation. The survey would be carried out each fifth year in selected tourist resorts on the Adriatic coast.

Observation units will be households that rent accommodation facilities in private rooms, apartments, villas or second homes to the tourists, and who are not registered in any official register and do not pay any tax. Tourist experts who are familiar with the local situation would be members of special commissions at county level. The members of commissions would be from local government bodies for tourism, tax offices, travel agencies, tourist boards, statistical branch offices etc.

The estimation would be done on the basis of existing data on registered tourist flows and also different data from other sources: number of registered beds for renting and nights spent in collective and private accommodation, number of days of full utilization in collective accommodation, retail-trade turnover, number of travellers from transport statistics etc. Implementation of this survey depends on available resources.

CONCLUSION

Private tourism accommodation for the Republic of Croatia has a significant importance in considering the number of available accommodation capacities and number of tourists and nights taken in that type of accommodation. In order to obtain more comprehensive and timely information on the situation and trends for users it is necessary for private accommodation to be regularly recorded on a monthly basis. In order to improve quality of statistical surveys in this area and to harmonize them with Eurostat recommendations, the CBS will undertake actions in order to ensure accurate indicators on tourist flows in the Republic of Croatia. Thanks to the planned actions for improving the coverage of reporting units, the quality of our accommodation statistics will be satisfactory and will ensure accurate indicators on tourist flows.

REFERENCES

Community Methodology on Tourism Statistics. Eurostat, 1998.
Pirjavec, B. (1998) *Economic Characteristics on Tourism*. Faculty of Economy, University of Zagreb.
Statistical Yearbook. Central Bureau of Statistics, Zagreb, 1997–9.
Tourism and Hospitality Management. Faculty of Hotel Management, University of Rijeka, 1998.
Tourism, Central Bureau of Statistics. Statistical report, Zagreb, 1980–98.

PART 2
TOURISM PROFILES AND BEHAVIOUR

10

Business Travel Markets: New Paradigms, New Information Needs?

David Litteljohn

INTRODUCTION

The work is predicated on the assumption that significant structural changes in economic and social environments in developed societies impact on tourism behaviours. To compete effectively, suppliers in private and public sectors must ensure that the appropriate information is gathered and interpreted to be able to understand underlying forces and their impact on individual travel decisions and behaviours. At certain times there will be significant shifts in behaviours which require adoption of new paradigms.

The context for the investigation is business travel. Change over a range of factors that influence markets in advanced, information societies is analysed. Past market assumptions and associated relationships between demand and economic cycles should, it is suggested, be augmented by an understanding of fundamental social and technological factors affecting *business-styles* (the structure and practice of organizations which generate travel needs) and the *lifestyles* of travellers. In this latter context differentiation between 'work' and 'leisure' activities requires attention. While it is not an aim of this work to progress in any way to a universal theory of tourism motivation, it aims to establish the need for any shifts necessary to tease out interrelationships between work and non-work travel motivations within conventional conceptions of 'business tourism'.

METHODOLOGY

The approach adopted is largely inductive. To conventional notions of economic analysis, it adds ideas from some postmodernist authors who examine the distinction between 'work' and 'non-work' and leisure time. A differentiation is made between (a) business travel and other forms of tourism; and (b) business travel and other forms of work activity. A conventional definition of the business travel market is first taken: *travel markets, primarily generated through a person's employment, related to an individual's work and professional activities.* It is seen here within a tourism context, i.e. a stay away from home of at least 24 hours (consistent with previous work, for example, Slattery and Johnson, 1990; Litteljohn and McLennan, 1997; and the *United Kingdom Tourism Statistics*). This approach will be revaluated at the conclusion of the work.

While some can see tourism, in general, as a luxury product (e.g. Wong, 1997), business tourism is related to underlying trends in productive infrastructure of regions, nations' trading blocs and, in a globalizing environment, world markets. Further, while regular holiday taking is a generally accepted phenomenon in western advanced societies, business travel is a more limited, focused activity; limited in the sense that it covers a smaller proportion of the population, and limited because motivation and flexibility is constrained by the employer. Yet business travel is not homogenous. Motivations, purchase patterns and behaviours differ by segments of the market, which are usually seen as: individual/small group travel; meeting/conference/congress markets (varying from the relatively small to major events involving many thousands of delegates); and exhibitions (extended from Opperman and Chon, 1997).

The research method turns on the notion that context and applications are as important as discipline pedigree for understanding and theory development. It borrows from what Gibbons *et al.* (1994) terms *transdisciplinarity* and Tribe (1997) refines into *extradisciplinarity* (Pearce, 1993). Among the disciplines used here are a blend of economics, industrial and consumer sociology. Work largely relies on conceptual insights provided by secondary-data statistical and industry sources and the results of a pilot study on business travel behaviour undertaken in 1998.

AN OVERVIEW OF THE IMPORTANCE OF TRAVEL MARKETS TO HOTELS AND THEIR COMPETITIVE STRATEGIES

As a sector within tourism, hotels, particularly, find financial health closely tied to movements in business markets. Many hotels, located in prime city locations, rely on business-generated travel, where volumes and prosperity are tied to the economic cycle. From the Mintel estimates given in Table 10.1 it can be deduced that the two main forms of business travel generated 46 per cent and 45 per cent of hotel turnover.

Other estimates go somewhat higher: Keynote (1997) puts the figure at 62 per cent of hotel turnover. In their analysis for 1996, Horwarth Consulting state that 61.5 per cent of hotel occupancy comes from business travellers and government officials and another 14 per cent from conference participants. Some of these differences will come from difficulties in separating different types of consumption – overnight and day-only segments. Other variances could result in the samples of hotels included in the surveys. Business travel is often seen as the preserve of more up-market hotel operations. However, Horwath's comparison between 'luxury' and 'economy' hotels shows only marginal differences in their reliance on business travel. In luxury hotels, 60.6 per cent of occupancy is generated by corporate and government organizations, while the economy sector derives 58.2 per cent from these sources. Significant differences between the two sectors exist, however, in the share of business/corporate markets taken by conference participants. In the luxury sector, conferences account for nearly 23 per cent

Table 10.1 Sources of income for hotels by type of guest, 1995 and 1997

Purpose	1995		1997	
	£ billion	%	£ billion	%
Holiday and Short break	2.8	40	3.4	42
Regular Business Travel	2.5	36	2.9	35
Conferences, courses etc.	0.7	10	0.8	10
Others	1.0	14	1.1	13
Total	7.0		100	8.2
100				

Source: Mintel Leisure Intelligence (1998) *Business travel in the UK*, June

Table 10.2 Size and value of the UK business travel market, 1998

Category	UK residents		Overseas visitors		UK total	
	Trips (million) (%)	£ (million) (%)	Trips (million) (%)	£ (million) (%)	Trips (million) (%)	£ (million) (%)
Business tourism	13.7 (11.2%)	2200 (15.7%)	6.9 (26.8%)	3820 (30.1%)	20.6 (13.9%)	6020 (15.2%)
All tourism	122.3 (100.0%)	14,030 (100.0%)	25.7 (100.0%)	12,671 (100.0%)	148.0 (100.0%)	39,372 (100.0%)

Source: British Tourist Authority and National Tourist Boards, *UK Tourism Statistics*; International Passenger Survey

of business occupancy, while in the economy sector they account for only 5 per cent (derived from Horwath, 1997).

Given the usual health warnings, the statistics give a global indication of the market and its different segments. It will be noted, however, that they treat the market broadly, while deduction shows that the two main categories identified, for convenience labelled here as 'conference/seminar' and 'other', possess different purchase and behavioural characteristics. Thus published figures directly emanating from the hotel industry fail to provide a complete view of the market. The *United Kingdom Tourism Statistics* and International Passenger Survey data (various years) that gather data directly from consumers, give overall figures for the size and value of the business travel market.

As evidenced by the differences between Tables 10.1 and 10.2, while hotels rely significantly on business travellers their penetration, at 60 per cent, could be significantly improved (hotel market value in 1997 is estimated at £3.7 billion and market value (1998) at around £6 billion). Yet even this high penetration cannot be taken for granted. Whilst hotel share of the domestic business travel overnight accommodation market has fluctuated around 60 per cent over the past fifteen years (*British Home Tourist Survey* and *UK Tourism Statistics*) their share of the market dipped three percentage points from 1994 to 59 per cent in 1996. Hotels have employed a variety of competitive strategies, including those below.

Specific brands

Upmarket business brands are an established industry feature. For example, hotels replicate airline conventions of first-class and club-class services to target business travellers.

The development of hotel chains, as opposed to independent operations, is well charted in the literature (see, for example, Littlejohn, 1997). Brands cover a spectrum of facility and location specifications but tend to be at high-facility levels and concentrated at primary commercial and communications centres.

More recently, attention has turned to mid-tier provision. Even high-spend operations have developed spin-off tiers for this market, e.g. Four Points (Sheraton) in North America. Mid-tier brands concentrate on what it is felt the market requires in personalized facilities in customer rooms, usually by economizing on the availability of public spaces.

New service provision

New technology has influenced an extension of traditional services: data ports and internet hook-ups, voicemail, cordless telephones, for example. Specialist facilities may be limited to some rooms in many properties: in others, the intention is to have them generally available. Some chains consider that the speed of technological change is such that future 'road warriors' will be self-sufficient in office and communication services. Other chains intend to provide travellers with some back-up services, e.g. Law (1998) reports that Four Seasons will ensure help for production of computer-generated presentations and language translations.

Social changes have also been addressed to varying degrees: catering for the increasing proportion of women business travellers is regularly announced. For example, after earlier attempts to feminize rooms through 'soft colour schemes' and the provision of hair-driers since the 1980s (which were found to be non-gender specific), hotels now view security services in a more sophisticated way.

Pricing and distribution

The provision of high-quality services for this sector is balanced by tension to ensure high-capacity use. This can be carried out by a number of different means: usually one form or other of discounting is applied. In the hotel industry it is common for there to be a range of corporate discount bands. Purchase scale will usually determine price offered offering large organizations a preferential position. Options provided by information technology in capacity management and distribution through the internet provide opportunities for more targeted pricing and direct customer-sales methods.

Promotional tools

Hotel chains ubiquitously employ customer loyalty and discounting practices, though it is difficult to evaluate their effectiveness. For example, the impact of frequent flyer schemes is evident from the fact that international business flyers, on average, belong to 3.5 schemes, with 30 per cent belonging to a minimum of five (OAG, 1999). As information technology allows greater sophistication in data-capture and administration, so other promotional configurations are tested. These invariably feature room upgrades, use of telephone office services and mini-bars within the room rate, and extra TV channels.

As the UK leisure facility upgrading frenzy of the 1980s showed, investment programmes are not always sound. Leisure provision was originally meant to capture and retain resident customers – particularly business travellers. However, poor returns on investment driven more by competition than market requirements were solved, as possible, by finding new, often non-resident, markets.

For public sector tourism organizations, perhaps the most attention given to the business travel market has been given through the recognition of special marketing requirements generated through the need to market destinations as major conference destinations, partly a consequence of significant public sector investment in conference facilities during the 1980s and 1990s. The development of tourist-board-supported, strategically orientated city and area conference bureaux, which helped in planning and organization as well as promotion, in Scotland has been a significant development of the past decade.

Some view trends in the UK business travel marketing cynically. Conway (1998) reports a Hogg-Robinson executive as stating that appreciation of add-ons by travellers is not necessarily shared by employers. They are more interested in basic room rates and tend to see the add-on strategy as a ploy to increase rates. If so, hoteliers must beware economic downturns. The depressed economic conditions of the early/mid-1990s led to endemic discounting. If the new add-ons have substantially increased cost bases, chains will be vulnerable to price wars. Furthermore, whereas company expenditure on business travel continues to rise in real terms, their ability to gain economies through better management of their travel budgets is called into question by O'Brien (1998) who goes on to imply that more radical measures may be necessary when he states that '[European] business travel is at a crossroads': a crossroads driven by new communication networks and through consolidation in major industry sectors.

ECONOMIC CYCLES AND TRAVEL MARKET BEHAVIOUR

Perhaps because of its relative low share of the total tourism market, business travel dynamics have attracted rather less academic attention than other areas of tourism demand. Slattery and Johnson (1990) has been a progenitor of the debate on market evolution in business travel. Controversially, in the eyes of some, he proposes a link between economic development and volumes of business travel that chain-affiliated hotels capture: the structural theory of business travel.

It is a feature of developed economies that they become increasingly service dominated. Slattery and Johnson hold that at intermediate rates of service employment growth (e.g. between 30 per cent and 70 per cent of the workforce) levels of business travel demand grow very quickly. After the 70 per cent threshold is reached, growth in business travel generated by the transition to a service economy slows. Slattery contrasts this to what he terms the Bonus Theory. The Bonus Theory can also be termed conventional market wisdom: e.g. 'The major driving force for business travel services is the economy. Growth . . . is mirrored by an increase in business activity which increases the demand for business travel services' (Mintel Leisure Intelligence, 1998). During good times volume will grow; depressions cause belt-tightening. It is difficult to argue with this latter, common-sense view. Clearly there is a relationship

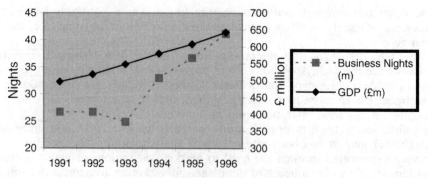

Figure 10.1 UK changes in GDP (£) and business travel (nights) 1991–6
Source: UKTS and UK economic statistics

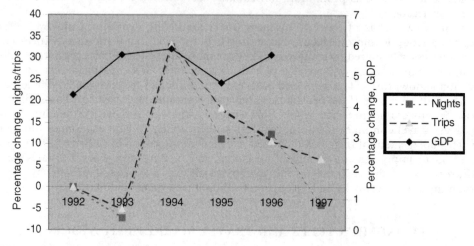

Figure 10.2 Plots of percentage annual change in business travel night and trips to percentage annual changes in GDP
Source: UKTS and UK economic statistics

between business travel and the state of an economy, though its precise nature may be difficult to predict. Assuming that a common supplier reaction is to mirror pricing strategies to variations in the business cycles (high at peaks and heavy discounting at troughs) pricing or value measures will not be used in this analysis. Rather, volume measures in business travel nights and/or trips are used. Figure 10.1 shows a generally positive relationship between GDP annual growth rates and business travel volumes.

In fact, the data presented above indicates that there may be longer-term factors at work. Figure 10.2 clearly shows a steeper decline in nights away than business trips, indicating that business trips may be getting shorter.

The Structural Theory does not banish the influence of short-term movements in an economy. Rather it overlays these on longer-term economic trends. Hughes (1993, 1995) has criticized the looseness of Slattery's analysis, while Litteljohn and MacLennan (1997) attempted to relate changes in levels of business travel in Scotland to macro-changes in the UK economy (Gross Domestic Product) from 1989 to 1995: no immediate Bonus Theory relationship was found. Rather, travel spending and levels varied erratically. The test is not conclusive in any way: data inadequacies and the conjunction of Scotland business travel to UK GDP figures could distort even relatively strong national relationships. Furthermore, during the depressed times covered by the survey, chains (and other travel suppliers) react to demand downturns by lowering prices significantly, thereby minimizing the decreases in business travel.

The study did, however, illuminate the fact that other, non-economic, forces could be important. In particular, it showed that the business travel market, while dominated in value terms by the high AB socio-economic groups, was increasingly penetrated by C1 (intermediate managerial, administrative or professional) and C2 (supervisory or clerical and junior managerial, administrative or professional) groups. The generality of annual UKTS figures has already been mentioned and meant that deeper analysis was impossible. The figures available did indicate that these travellers settled for considerably less expensive accommodation than was previously the norm when managers at slightly higher organizational levels took a higher share of the market.

Clearly, hypotheses advanced concerning business travel development are incomplete. The organizational view of business travel suggests it will be influenced by economic conditions, nature of industry, type of firm and category of travel. The indications are that there are qualitative changes happening in the UK business market, yet these changes appear to be related to more than changes in the development of service economies. Slattery's Structural Theory indicates that once 70 per cent of the economy is service-dominated, travel will lose its (supposed) relationship to service growth.

The Structural Theory suggests there is a need to move away from boom–bust explanations of business travel. It points to underlying economic trends to provide further depth of understanding. In this way it merely exchanges one barometer for another. Its predictive power also, for the years shown, appears to be patchy. While changes in GDP are mirrored by rising volume for 1993–94, other years are more variable, showing significantly greater turbulence in business travel than in GDP.

Early in the chapter it was shown that the market covers different sectors that possess different characteristics. There appears to sufficient evidence to claim that factors other than economics are affecting market volume. There may also be factors which are changing market behaviour. For example, the popularity of budget hotel accommodation with business travellers has been to referred to. This type of shift appears to have become embedded. For example, by 1998, economy class accounted for 53 per cent of all domestic flights in developed economies and 32 per cent of international short-haul flights originating from them (OAG Worldwide, reported in Travel and Tourism Intelligence, 1999).

BUSINESS TRAVEL MARKET SEGMENTS DEFINED IN ORGANIZATIONAL TERMS

This section proposes at once a more holistic view of business travel while also proposing an 'in–out' view of travel generation, rather than usual 'out–in' (i.e. business-cycle) explanation. It does this by recognizing and defining the diversity inherent in the sector. Organizations which generate travel do so in relation to their (a) aims and ethos;

(b) geographic coverage; and (c) decisions on the necessity and/or value of the business travel. In relation to (a), most texts refer to commercial and government travel. In modern economies there is also a significant voluntary sector (often dependent on public sources of finance) which will generate demand for business travel in accordance with its own needs. Point (b) relates to the extent of international travel which may become more important in a globalizing world; while (c) refers to the functional aspects of business travel.

Palpably, travel does not arise from a single organizational need. Table 10.3 differentiates market segments from an organizational perspective. It does this to get away from the product-orientated manner in which hotels often describe the market (e.g. 'conferences'). It sees business travel markets as being generated at two levels within an organization: internal and external. These two levels are further divided into activities designed to ensure the maintenance of the organization (in similar ways to those that existed in the past) and those which are directly due to changing previous *modi operandi*. Thus travel in (i) below relates to that generated by basic functions in the organization. In most manufacturing and service operations these do not directly lead to travel of people. There are examples such as transport services (air crews and some transport of road freight) where the basic functions create demand by employees for hotel services. Travel of type (ii) relates to the operational, tactical and strategic planning work that will maintain the organization. It covers a great number of business needs ranging from training to planning. External travel in (v) is those activities such as order-taking, business hospitality and other routine business travel. Travel indicated in (ii), (iii) and (vi) relates to situations when organizations decide to change the underlying pattern of their existing activities. Travel indicated in (iv) can be considered a special case: here

Table 10.3 A development of organizational types of business travel

Main area of organizational activity	Sub-area of activity	Business travel behaviour	
		Directed to maintain the organization	Directed at organizational change
1. Internal operations and interfaces	1(a) Basic functions	(i) Carry out existing functions	(ii) Aimed at – developing new functions (horizontal, vertical movement and diversification) – developing new ways of doing work
	1(b) Operational, tactical and strategic activities across all parts of the organization	(iii) Ensure that basic functions are carried out efficiently	(iv) Ensure that organization is effective
2. External Interfaces	–	(v) Service existing networks	(vi) Aimed at generating new capabilities and opportunities
3. Motivational	1(c) Incentive to perform/behave	(vii) Embed and/or develop behaviour through rewards	

travel has no functional value in own right, but is offered to encourage achievement of particular targets and goals that the organization deems appropriate.

The approach allows a greater depth to judge change of business travel from a qualitative and organizational perspective: alternative segmentation methods such as 'conferences' and 'individual business travellers', often used by industry, relate more to pricing and selling methods than to underlying travel motivations. This organizational approach, while requiring further refinement, allows distinctions to be made between:

- core/routine/maintenance type of travel. In the short term this will be the most difficult to cut back, but will also be the most attractive to substitute from an organizational perspective (partly because of its routine nature and also due to cost savings). Information Technology (IT) substitution may be important here;
- firms and industries with different characteristics and stages of development. Thus their travel patterns will differ from the 'norm', being related to meso-trends rather than macro-trends;
- travel aimed at developing/applying new knowledge, techniques and networks. This may involve internal as well as external interfaces; and
- measures which organizations use to affect behaviour. This can relate directly to travel such as incentive travel, where an employee's accomplishment of a prescribed goal is rewarded by 'a unique travel experience' (Grey Forton and Arbrioux, 1990).

This kind typology is unlikely to be used extensively by organizations in appraising their travel requirements. Possibly the areas that receive most attention at any one time (in relation to costs) relate to their stage of development and the opportunities presented to them in the external environment. However, more fundamental aspects will also be at work, and it is in this way that the typology may have more offer.

SOCIO-TECHNICAL CHANGES AND WORK ORGANIZATION

Terms such as the 'information society', 'information workers', 'the new economy' and 'the knowledge economy' jostle, in various permutations, for precedence in explaining a post-service economy where e-communication and e-commerce radicalize conventional certainties of organization, growth and innovation. Trying to predict the precise nature of change in the ways that organizations will change is a large and challenging study, and one that can only be covered generally here. Instead, this section will look at general trends in economies and organizations, leaving the impacts on individuals to be discussed later.

Researchers and commentators indicate little dissension from the notion that major shifts within organizations are occurring as a result of economic, social and technological change. However, views on the direction, level and time-scale of change are divergent. Thus it is difficult to explain changes quantitatively. Instead, this review intends to indicate the direction of change and qualitative differences that may occur in the business travel market. To start, an overview of major changes in the organization of the workforce is given. Services employment is likely to be increasingly characterized by high-technology, high-skill and knowledge-intensive occupations (OECD, 1994; Kiechel, (1993); Gill *et al.*, 1992; Coulson-Thomas, 1991). Figures 10.3(a) and 10.3(b) illustrate expected sectoral and occupational shifts in the UK.

The figures confirm the growth of 'new' service sectors in business services,

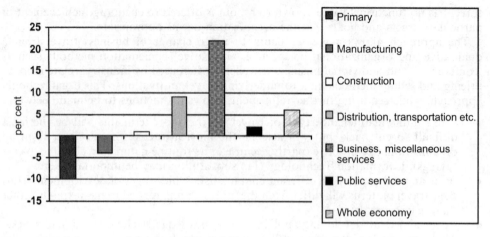

Figure 10.3(a) Percentage change in UK employment, 1994–2001, by sector

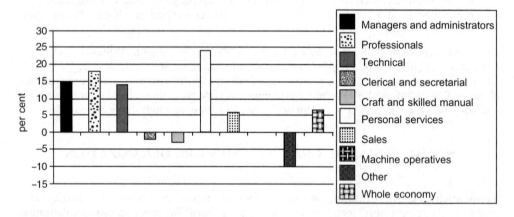

Figure 10.3(b) Percentage change in UK employment, 1994–2001, by occupation.
Source: SEN (1997)

distribution and personal services – sectors that include e-commerce 'dotcom' start-ups. Figure 10.3(b) also supports the view that there will be a change in the composition of the workforce – of note in relation to business travel is the 15 per cent rise in management and administrative staff, professionals and technical staff who are currently the groups most likely to travel. More arguably, socio-technical phenomena, such as the 'knowledge worker', have developed, a dramatic example being Handy's idea of the 80:20 society where only a small group of directly employed workers prevail (Handy, 1995), in comparison to a majority who essentially acquire, process and develop (i.e. manage) information.

In terms of adopting IT, some authors argue that employment effects are more structural than absolute, older industries and occupations making way for new service-orientated occupations, and employment overall has grown (OECD, 1994; Kiechel, 1993). Conversely, some suggest that decline of employment in primary and secondary sectors, already induced by technology, will eventually affect service and technology sectors too, leading to progressive decreases in employment (Handy, 1995; Rifkin, 1995; Aronowitz and DiFazio, 1994). Between these polar views are those who question the level and timescale of change, e.g. the extent to which corporate managers loathe to relinquish authority may stifle progress (Milkman, 1998) and the much referred-to delayering/business process re-engineering (BPR) from the mid-1980s and into the 1990s was often held up through organizational inertia and political factors within organizations. Access to skills becomes more important than owning all parts of the organization (Coulson-Thomas, 1991). This is reflected in the emergence of network relationships such as joint ventures, strategic alliances, supplier-producer collaborations, franchising, consortia and linkage agreements within channels of distribution (Cravens *et al.*, 1996).

However, there is no doubt that economic factors are already affecting the ways in which organizations work. For example, sizes of some organizations are falling through a combination of 'new computational infrastructures' and the likes of downsizing, BPR and an increase in businesses outsourcing many non-core functions (Barley, 1996; Hammer, 1993; Reich, 1993; Tapscott and Caston, 1993; Coulson-Thomas, 1991). The development of IT can, it is claimed, remove distance. The twin availability of speed in communications and the ability for ever-increasing levels of sophistication in written, audio and visual communications in the digital economy will allow teleworking at home, in satellite offices and a mix of home and office (Kurland and Bailey, 1999). Cully *et al.* (1998) report that the phenomenon of home-working is well established, with 9 per cent of all respondents to a large-scale survey in the UK reporting that they work at or from home.

Globalization trends will continue and the concept of business networks will become more viable than traditional large, vertically structured organizations. Smaller organizations, facilitated by new technology, will be highly flexible entities allowing greater input from customers and suppliers alike in business-policy development (Kiechel, 1993; Tapscott and Caston, 1993; Coulson-Thomas, 1991). The recent switch in business press from concentrating on business-to-consumer relations to business-to-business relations does not mean any reduction to changes that new technology will mediate in relationships that organizations will design with current and future e-consumers, as mediated by future trends in m(obile)-technologies. Rather it re-dresses a general lack of attention given to internet and the World Wide Web-facilitated relationships between businesses/organizations and other stakeholder organizations. These relationships could, potentially, cover the whole range of functions involved in management and business supply and development. An overview of major changes in the ways in which organizations will be managed is shown below in Table 10.4.

In this organizational world there is an identified gap in research which looks at the particular ways in which middle managers approach and execute their work (Wheatley, 1992). For example, there may be a higher ratio of managers to total employees, but their roles will be more flexible (ambiguous) and changing (uncertain) with possibly less job security or at least perceptions of lower security. In flatter, leaner, team-driven organizations, traditions of management development are open to question. In relation to white-collar employees, Haas (1999) remarks: 'the systems for managing employees, such as wage and benefit policies, training and development systems, promotion ladders, and other practices of internal labour markets, were part of the elaborate internal administration of the firm'. While Haas acknowledges the difficulties in gaining reliable data in this field, he foresees a regime (in the USA) where cafeteria approaches to benefits (including training) and more transportable benefit packages are provided to

Table 10.4 A paradigm shift in the organization of the firm

Element	Old organization	New organization
Structure	Vertical hierarchy	Network and horizontal relationships
Size	Large, many layers	Downsized, de-layered, smaller
Basis of action	Control	Empowerment
Operating environment	Static	Dynamic, changing
Decision-making	Centralized	Decentralized, disaggregated & autonomous
Work organization	Departmentalization	Multi-functional teamwork, project work
Production	On-site, owned by firm	Dispersed, outsourced
Communication	Formal	Informal, flexible
Personnel focus	Managers	Professionals, technical competency
Compensation basis	Position in hierarchy	Accomplishment, value of skills and value added
Values	Masculine	Feminine
Learning and competency of employees	Narrow and specific	Broad and continuous, flexible specialization

Source: Adapted and extended from Tapscott and Caston (1993)

management employees. Essentially, he sees external market-places replacing internal markets as a driver for managers, much as they are already for less-qualified staff. Research in the UK (Thomas and Dunkerley, 1999) confirms the reduction of internal career-planning mechanisms, though indicates that alternative mechanisms have yet to be put into place.

The attention given to supply-chain management and management employees in the latter part of this section brings out the need for increasing attention to be given to external, market-focused aspects. This points to organizations having explicit business-style strategies. For example, there is a current debate among financial organizations about their relationship with customer groups: *bricks* (branches/personal interaction with customers) v. *clicks* (web-based interaction). Within this approach, business travel can play a particular role. On the one hand it will determine the nature of contact between the organization and its suppliers. Indirectly this will also affect the opportunities/career patterns for managers. More directly, managers will be affected by the employee-based policies on management development and knowledge creation in relation to business travel.

In summing up all these changes, it is important to realize that there is no single emergent trend: 'The banal and simple truth is that there is no simple or universal direction' (Thompson and Warhurst, 1998, discussing knowledge workers).

> Underneath all the rhetoric about the new-wave management, the most important trend appears to be people working harder ... the combination of increased competitive pressures for cost reduction on private and public sector organizations, with expanded means for reducing and recording 'idle time' are leading to substantial work intensification, whether through reductions in manning levels and job demarcation, or for other reasons. (Elger, 1991)

Furthermore, many new middle managers are women. The extent to which their needs

Table 10.5 Implications for change in business travel, by travel function

Directed to maintain the organization	Directed at organizational change
Carry out existing functions Intelligent activity Significant impact as technology facilitates responsive management information systems and CIT training packages and individual-to-individual communications. Distance unimportant, interaction relatively prescribed/programmable	**Aimed at developing new functions (horizontal, vertical movement and diversification)** Intelligent and creative activity Greatly facilitated by new technology, but considerable planning requiring complex interaction including problem-solving and un-programmable personal contact from inside and outside the organization **Aimed at developing new ways of doing work** As above, though potentially even more creative, unprogrammable and people-centred
Implication: Travel likely to decrease except where: travel is part of the basic service (e.g. transport); travel is related to development and installation of new systems; ongoing training and enhancement of existing systems.	*Implication:* Travel purpose centred on increasing knowledge and personal interactions. Changes in structure etc. will often be primarily affected by expectations in the external environment, while new ways of doing work will receive a primary impetus from internal sources.

Ensure that basic functions are carried out efficiently / **Ensure that organization is effective**

Intelligent activity – requires information systems networking, benchmarking and analysis. Greatly facilitated by information-technology applications
Implication:
Travel requirements relate to levels of innovation requiring personal contact which cannot be replaced by IT-generated options, e.g. video conferencing.

Service existing external networks Intelligent and interactive relationships Information-seeking as well as information-giving; critical in establishing business style *Implication:* Carefully designed to meet customer/client relationships – part of the organization 'trade mark'. Directly related to strategies pursued in the growth/contraction of micro-markets, rather than overall economic movements. Can utilize full range of communications technology	**Aimed at generating new capabilities and opportunities** Intelligent, creative and interactive communications required *Implication:* Perceptions within organizations, relative to learning about internal and external knowledge. Centered on accessing 'new' knowledge and developing new ways of working. Requires high levels of external travel

Embed culture through rewards

Dependent on overall organization culture and reward culture of the organization. Can be related to given targets as decided by the organization, or given as a range of benefits to which employees can aspire
Implication:
Incentive travel for proscribed goals may be more difficult to operationalize than in the past as management become more flexible. Alternatives would be to make business travel itself more flexible.

are fully taken into account is not so much a matter of debate but is still a matter of gender comparison and campaigning for over three decades.

In further examining the sum effect of all these qualitative changes it is possible to view the change in Foucaultian terms. Foucault's (1988) theory is ultimately about the organization of subjects: managers in the context of this work. He draws attention to networks that 'produce' the individual and 'normalize' behaviour (i.e. create the norms by which managers carry out this portion of their lives). 'The question is to determine what the subject must be, what his condition must be, what status he must have, what position he must occupy in the real or imaginary, in order to become a legitimate subject of any given type of understanding.' The three types of power identified by Foucualt are:

- institutional power (ethnic, social and religious forms of domination)
- economic power (class system and [labour] markets) and
- subjective power (the personal struggles against subjectivity and submission).

PERSONAL PERSPECTIVES ON BUSINESS TRAVEL IN ADVANCED ECONOMIES

This short analysis draws attention to relationships between the nature of business travel and individual lifestyles. It interweaves notions of tourism, work, leisure and other social factors as they impact on managers to explore implications for business travel. The focus here is the individual and the attempt is to explore how fragmented the travel experience is and may become.

Ryan (1991) indicates that tourism is a very special type of *non-work* activity. Tribe (1997) interprets this not so much as an attempt at a global definition of tourism but an 'initial foray into [understanding] tourism motivation'. It is noticeable that Ryan's definition excludes business travel. Technical definitions of tourism are more inclusive and ensure that business travel is recognized in official statistics. Chadwick (1994) not only recognizes it but also categorizes business tourism into distinct primary activities (consultations, conventions, inspections) and secondary ones (dining out; recreation; shopping; sightseeing; visiting family and relations). While he includes sightseeing in this definition of business travel, much the greatest amount of work into tourism motivations is allied to pleasure/holiday travel and related to notions such as escape (from routine environments and behaviours). The sum of these definitions is to differentiate leisure tourism from business tourism. On the other hand it can be seen (*ibid.*) as fragmenting the 'tourism experience' into 'splinters' of work and non-work activity.

There is a tradition that sees work and leisure as diametrically opposed, or sees work as the dominant factor (see Rojeck, 1995, for an excellent analysis). This tradition holds leisure as residual or donative in relation to work. Work can be seen as distinct from leisure and home. Identities for work (Du Gay, 1996) can be considered as separate from those associated with the leisure persona. Here there is a perceptual dislocation between work activity and leisure, which is well in keeping with the ways in which tourists are counted, and many tourism theorists examine tourism behaviour. This type of approach would argue that work motivations remain the primary factor in meeting the needs of the business traveller. It follows, therefore, that business travel needs spring primarily from organizations that generate business travel. They should remain the focus of research.

Followers of a postmodern view, as embodied by Foucault, would counsel an understanding of the business travel market needs to take into account the motivations and preferences of business travellers themselves. Even conventional strategic and technical definitions of business travel see it as fragmented into three main sectors. It is fair to assume that methods of consuming the tourist experience can differ by sector. In addition, there are major external changes taking place.

At a time when communications technology is 'destroying' distance, allowing work space and leisure space to overlap; when traditions of work are changing to the extent that lifetime careers (particularly salient for managers) are less organizationally designed and are gaining greater individual/external focus; and when the traditional distinctions between work time and non-work time are blurring and employer loyalty is affected by immediate demands of work intensification and greater job mobility, it is appropriate to consider further the implications of these changes on business travel. Resonating with the organizational changes discussed within the chapter, a manager can increasingly be seen as 'entrepreneur of the self' (Du Gay, 1996) where work is part of a regime to achieve self-optimization. In other words, while work demands may intensify on managers in quantitative terms, work may not be as radically separated from leisure as has previously been the case. Extrapolating from this, it is possible to imagine that just as there are currently elements of 'home working', so there may be some 'leisure business' travel. Lifestyle choices will play an increasing role in the type of managerial employment undertaken and the way this intermeshes with other elements of lifestyle, such as family and leisure consumption. These changes do not necessarily mean major quantitative changes. They do, however, mean that there will be significant changes in the personal 'frames' that potential business travellers will bring to the way in which they approach and experience business travel.

Quantitative changes in the mixes between business and leisure travel can operate at a number of different levels:

- where a prime reason is business – on a 'person trip' basis, leisure may be introduced into business travel through the timing of the trip and/or extending the duration of the trip to take leisure/other activity into account; on a 'per trip' basis by including accompanying persons (e.g. partners) whose travel purpose is not business travel related;
- where a prime travel motive is leisure, it may be possible to introduce work related motivation/activities.

An experimental question in UKTS (1997) estimated that 6 per cent of business nights spent in the UK and 11 per cent of business nights spent by the British abroad were over and above those required solely for business purposes. As this is a one-off survey it is not possible to evaluate whether mix is changing over time. The Travel Industry Association of America (2000) report that 21 per cent of business travellers combined business and vacation on their last trip in 1999, the highest rates of 'mixing' trips being found in less-frequent travellers and women business travellers. Again in the USA Crowne Plaza Hotels commissioned a survey of 500 business travellers who went away on business at least twice within twelve months and stayed at upscale hotels 'at least one time' (Crowne Plaza, 1998). Results reported here reflect differences between male and female business travellers. Women surveyed took, on average, many less business trips away. The highest percentage of women (43%) take between three and five trips per year. Women tend to stay away one night longer than men, perhaps because 'women are twice as likely as men to extend their stay over the weekend to enjoy leisure activities, and three times as likely to being a friend or spouse'. The 1999 USA figures show that the largest proportion of business travellers are in health, legal and educational services, though also reports that the proportion of all business travellers in professional/managerial occupations declined from an all time high 55 per cent in 1994 to 47 per cent in 1999 (Travel Industry Association of America, 2000).

Again, contrary to commonly held views, not all business travel is paid for by employers: of international business travellers to the UK, 4.5 per cent of air passengers and 11.5 per cent of sea passengers do not have their tickets paid by their employing companies. Admittedly, while significant, these proportions are small. However, they may help explain the popularity of economy travel among some sectors of the business-travel market.

Underlying social constructs and contexts should also be fully investigated. In the free market, corporately downsized environment of USA, many recruiters look at potential employees in different ways than was the case twenty years ago. While evidence tends towards the anecdotal, Generation X members (c. 30 years) are seen to be hardworking and loyal, they are much more likely than previous generations to look for a more challenging jobs and better benefits such as flexible work schedules. It is here that concepts of lifelong learning, networking and flexibility flourish (Hayes, 1999). In literature, Douglas Coupland (1999), commenting on the work–life balance for which the generation strive, coined the term 'Ozmosis' (the inability of one's job to live up to one's self image). Clearly, the USA cannot be taken as representative of all countries; clearly, Generation X does not herald the end of the work ethic. On the other hand, the experience of subtle change in the USA may be appropriate for many developed societies to consider: for example, there is increasing attention in the UK to issues of work–life balance.

These trends confirm that advanced societies are likely to see a range of different motivations apparent in the business-travel market. Partly these will be influenced by the increasing feminization of the travel market. Partly it will be influenced by perceptions of travellers in the mix between business and leisure. Partly, also, it may be influenced by the need for individuals to seek new knowledge and develop new networks as they become active participants in a non-hierarchical, information-rich and information-needing society. These insights are not meant to argue towards a process of homogeneity occurring between leisure- and business-market sectors. Clearly, there are areas where overlaps are potentially higher (e.g. conference and exhibition attendance may be more flexible than regular business trips). Whatever the speed of change, the direction of change is evident: the market, whatever the constraints place on it, will move towards greater differentiation.

ORGANIZATIONAL CHANGE AND BUSINESS TRAVEL OF MANAGEMENT PERSPECTIVES: EMPIRICAL RESULTS

The study was undertaken to ascertain perceived qualitative influences on business-travel policy within organizations. Using semi-structured interviews, fifteen senior executives in major organizations across several industrial sectors in Scotland were asked to reflect on:

1.   actual work changes in their respective organizations and the perceived effects on business travel;
2.   their own travel patterns when on company business.

The executives were asked to respond based on their experiences over the last three years. Responses – gathered in summer and autumn 1997 – neither indicated a positive or a negative change for business-travel demand. Overall, executives had not experienced a clear shift in the level of business trips, either individually or for the company as a whole.

Potentially negative impacts of new communications technologies were not perceived among respondents:

- Technology had acted as an adjunct to business travel; that is, improving the business communication process rather than replacing the need for face-to-face meetings.
- Videoconferencing was available in fourteen firms. Its impact has been felt at meetings and occupations below executive level and essentially involved internal interfacing rather than external links. At the executive level, firms still require face-to-face meetings to be effective in developing business. For example, post-conference 'get-togethers' were when the real business was done.

The perception of organizational change also produced an unclear picture in relation business travel demand:

- Respondents saw themselves increasingly as network organizations with a requisite need for travel between partners. Some respondents indicated that they had formed strategic alliances with suppliers and intermediaries in recent years. This had necessitated an increase in traffic at least in the early stages of relationship-building.
- De-layering and downsizing were reported by most respondents, but this was not perceived to have replaced the need for business travel. Some personnel now travelled more, while it appeared that the positions lost had little or no business-travel content.

For the present, it appears that technology enhances communication rather than replaces business-travel needs. While technological applications are ever more sophisticated, there is still a need for travel that even highly developed means cannot substitute.

CONCLUSION

At one time, business-travel markets may have been related to economic cycles. It is likely, though by no means certain, that increasing penetration of service organizations had a disproportionately positive effect on business-travel markets. In advanced service economies, while economic change remains a very important factor in determining volumes of business travel, communication technologies at one level and macro-social trends relating to employment structures and practices at another will determine many of the 'hows' and 'whens' of business travel.

At this stage it is not considered that a paradigm change in the definition of business markets would be particularly illuminating. Rather, it is the recognition that there are a number of different markets working under the general definition that will be important to suppliers and researchers. Worthy of investigation at this level are perceptions of the relationship between leisure and work and its effect on understanding change in market composition and behaviour.

The speed of the change contained under these headings is difficult to predict and immediate quantitative effects may be not be immediately apparent. Changes in the dynamics of private and public sector employment will affect individual decisions and behaviours. As the employing organizations themselves set 'rules' of business travel they will remain a primary force. Indeed, at a policy level, government's role (taxable and non-taxable benefits) should not be minimized.

Organizations may first look to substitute that management travel which covers routine data collection and communication. This will include technology-mediated person-to-person communications and management systems, with the goal of making the organization more effective. The ways in which organizations measure their efficiency and perceive the risk of introducing new knowledge management and communication systems will be critical in driving changes in this sector of the market. This does not mean that routine, repetitive business travel will vanish: this will remain if it adds value to the organization's activities. Thus, contingent organizational factors include trends in networked organizations as well as IT impacts on management information, customer information and communication between stakeholders. To this extent, organizations may see that business travel is part of a wider communication strategy with their audiences and travel policies, rather than being distinct parts of an organization's procedures, and will become integrated in a 'business style' strategy. This may affect the nature and structure of demand rather than overall levels.

Markets will be progressively affected by changes in social perspectives. Strategic position in communications and travel adopted by organizations may well have to co-exist with a more autonomous business traveller, having set her agenda in terms of travel requirements and mixes between business, personal, professional and leisure travel. Setting personal career aims in a world where individuals build up career portfolios rather than rely on major employers to provide career ladders may increase an emphasis on professional and management conferences used to build up individual competences and contacts. Conversely, a closer connection between personal consumption and what has been traditionally seen as business travel may increase the influence of the economic cycle on these travel decisions, as related to lifestyle, and may see some elements of the new business travel as discretionary.

In meeting these new conditions, the marketing and provision by tourist suppliers will change. Already strides have been made. However, there is high reliance on boom–bust/high–low price strategy that becomes very damaging at times of low demand. Suppliers should seek to protect themselves from exposure to heavy discounting – a position which loyalty programmes are, in themselves, unlikely to counter successfully. Suppliers should take into account a more diversified market in terms of timing, gender, group size and composition. Travellers will seek not only standardization and luxury, so successful in the development of the market in twentieth century, but also flexibility, economy and novelty. In researching the dimensions, characteristics and behaviours of the market, public- and private-funded research should ensure that areas of lifestyle, work style, leisure style and business style are fully researched. In this work it is suggested that qualitative methods should have high prominence.

Clearly there is much work to be done in further researching this area. This will involve the development in areas on consumer behaviour and communications (technology and psychology). The work can be aimed at understanding how organizations work, just as much as how business travellers consume. A helpful next step will be to produce typologies and models of business travel and individual consumption that can be applied to business travel and which can then be tested and refined.

ACKNOWLEDGEMENT

I would like to thank Tony Harrison, now of the Moffat Centre, Glasgow Caledonian University, for assistance with collecting data on employment trends and the survey work with business executives.

REFERENCES

Aronowitz, S. and DiFazio, D. (1994) *The Jobless Future: Sci-tech and the Dogma of Work*. London: University of Minnesota Press.

Barley, S. (1996) 'The New World of Work'. Pamphlet, London: British–North American Committee.

Chadwick, R. A. (1994) 'Concepts, definitions and measures used in travel and tourism research', in J. R. Ritchie and C. R. Goeldner (eds) *Travel, Tourism and Hospitality Research*. New York: John Wiley and Sons.

Conway, H. (1998) 'Rewards of loyalty'. *Caterer and Hotelkeeper*, 15 January, pp. 70–1.

Coulson-Thomas, C. (1991) 'IT and new forms of organisation for knowledge workers: opportunity and implementation', *Employee Relations*, **13** (4), 22–32.

Coupland, D. (1999) *Generation X*. London: Abacus (first published in 1991 by St Martin's Press).

Cravens, D. W., Piercy, N. F. and Shipp, S. H. (1996) 'New organisational forms for competing in highly dynamic environments: the network paradigm', *British Journal of Management*, **7**(3), September.

Crowne Plaza (1998) 'Crowne Plaza Hotels travel index surveys today's "Road Warriors"', http://www.hotel-online.com/Neo/News/PressReleases1998_2nd/June/98_Crowneplaza Survey.html (survey carried out by International Communications Research).

Cully, M., O'Reilly, A., Millard, N., Forth, J., Woodland, S., Dix, G. and Bryson, A. (1998) *The 1998 Workplace Employee Relations Survey: First Findings*. Social and Community Planning Research.

Du Gay, P. (1996) *Consumption and Identity at Work*. London: Sage.

Elger. T. (1991) 'Task flexibility and the intensification of labour in UK manufacturing in the 1980s', in A. Pollert (ed.), *Farewell to Flexibility*. Oxford: Blackwell.

Gibbons, M., Limoges, C., Nowotny, H., Schwartzman, S., Scott, P. and Trow, M. (1994) *The New Production of Knowledge*. London: Sage.

Gill, C., Beaupain, T., Frohlich, D. and Krieger, H. (1992) 'Workplace involvement in technological innovation in the European Community'. *Volume II: Issues in Participation*. European Foundation for the Improvement of Living Conditions, European Union.

Grey Forton, G. and Arbrioux, C., quoted in G. Watson (1990) 'The incentive market in Europe'. *Travel and Tourism Analyst*, **3**, 65–78.

Foucualt, M. (1988) '[Auto]biography, Michel Foucualt 1926–84', *History of the Present*, **4**, Spring, (adopting the pseudonym of Maurice Florence).

Haas, W. A. (1999) 'Career jobs are dead'. *California Management Review*, **42** (1), Fall.

Hammer, M. (1993) *Reengineering the Corporation*. London: Brearly Publishing.

Handy, C. (1995) *The Future of Work*. W.H. Smith Contemporary Papers, 8.

Hayes, S. (1999) 'Generation X and the art of reward'. *Workforce*, November, 44–8.

Horwath Consulting (1997) *UK Analysis*. London: Horwath Consulting.

Hughes, H. (1993) 'The structural theory of business demand: a comment'. *International Journal of Hospitality Management*, **12** (4), 309–11.

Hughes, H. (1995) 'The structural theory of business demand: a rejoinder to Slattery'. *International Journal of Hospitality Management*, **14** (2), 117–18.

Keynote (1997) *Key Note Plus Market Report*. London: Keynote.

Kiechel III, W. (1993) 'How we will work in the year 2000'. *Fortune International*, **127** (10), May.

Kurland, N. B. and Bailey, D. E. (1999) 'Telework: the advantages and challenges of working here, there, anywhere and anytime', *Organizational Dynamics*, Autumn, 53–68.

Law, J. (1998) 'Providing the works'. *Executive Travel*, December/January, 52–3.

Litteljohn, D. (1997) 'Hotel chains and their strategic appraisal', in M. Foley, J. Lennon and G. Maxwell (eds), *Hospitality, Tourism and Leisure Management: Issues in Strategy and Culture*. London: Cassells, pp. 229–44.

Litteljohn, D. and MacLennan, D. (1997) 'Business travel markets and the role of theories: boom or bust?'. Proceedings of the 6th Annual Hospitality Research Conference, Council for Hospitality Management Education and Oxford Brookes University, pp. 204–25.

Milkman, R. (1998) 'The new American workplace: high road or low road', in P. Thompson and C. Warhurst (eds) *Workplaces of the Future*. London: Macmillan Business, pp. 25–39.

Mintel Leisure Intelligence (1998) *Business Travel in the UK*, June, London.

OAG Worldwide (1999) 'Business travel lifestyle 1999', in *Travel and Tourism Intelligence*, December, 5–6.

O'Brien, K. (1998) 'The European business travel market'. *Travel and Tourism Intelligence*, **4**, 43–54.

OECD (1994) *The OECD Jobs Study Part I: Labour Market Trends and Underlying Forces of Changes*. Paris: OECD.

Opperman, M. and Chon, K.-S. (1997) 'Convention participation decision-making process'. *Annals of Tourism Research*, **24** (1), 178–91.

Pearce, P. (1993) 'Fundamentals of tourism motivation', in D. G. Pearce and R. W. Butler (eds) *Tourism Research*. London: Routledge, pp. 113–34.

Reich, R. (1993) *The Work of Nations*. London: Simon and Schuster.

Rifkin, J. (1995) *The End of Work: Decline of the Global Labour Force and the Dawn of the Post-market Era*. New York: G.P. Putnam's Sons.

Rojeck, C. (1995) *Decentring Leisure: Rethinking Leisure Theory*. London: Sage.

Ryan, C. (1991) *Recreational Tourism: A Social Science Perspective*. London: Routledge.

SEN (1997) *Labour Market and Skill Trends 1996/1997*. Nottingham: Department of Education & Employment, Skills & Enterprise Network.

Slattery, P. and Johnson, S. (1990) *UK Hotels plc: The Decade Review*. Kleinwort Benson.

Tapscott, D. and Caston, A. (1993) *Paradigm Shift: The New Promise of Information Technology*. New York: McGraw-Hill.

Thomas, R. and Dunkerley, D. (1999) 'Careering downwards? Middle managers' experiences in the downsized organisation'. *British Journal of Management*, **10**, 157–69.

Thompson, P. and Warhurst, C. (1998) *Workplaces of the Future*. London: Macmillan Business.

Travel Industry Association of America (2000) *Survey of Business Travelers* (1999 Edition), OAG: http://www.tia.org/press/fastfacts91.stm (20/05/2000).

Tribe, J. (1997) 'The indiscipline of tourism'. *Annals of Tourism Research*, **24** (3), 638–57.

UKTS (UK Tourist Boards) (1997) *United Kingdom Tourist Statistics*. Annual Publication. London: British Tourist Authority.

Wheatley, M. (1992) *The Future of Management*. Corby: Institute of Management.

Wong, K. K. (1997) 'The relevance of business cycles in forecasting international tourist arrivals'. *Tourism Management*, **18** (8), 581–6.

11

VFR (Visiting Friends and Relatives) Tourism in Rural Scotland: A Geographical Case Study Analysis

Steven Boyne

ABSTRACT

Based around primary research in case study areas of rural Scotland during 1999, this chapter reports on the initial analysis of the collected data. Comparisons and contrasts are made between the findings of this work and a similar study conducted in Australia in 1994. The Scottish case study areas are then considered together in the light of the results from each, and the geographical and demographic differences between them. The chapter explores the relationships between tourism, migration and VFR (visiting friends and relatives) tourism and builds upon earlier work by Williams *et al.* (2000) and Williams and Hall (2000) suggesting further linkages between tourism and migration in terms of high-quality environmental characteristics and peripherality. Finally, the chapter briefly considers the potential for growth in the VFR tourism sector as the globalization of labour markets and easing of barriers to the movement of people within the European Union generate migration flows which then create the potential for VFR tourism flows.

INTRODUCTION

The importance of the VFR tourism market in Scotland has been highlighted in recent years, not least by the inclusion of VFR data in the annual United Kingdom Tourist Survey (UKTS) since 1989. In 1998, 3.1 million trips to Scotland from within the UK were taken by VFR tourists, representing 32 per cent of Scotland's domestic tourism market and accounting for £316 million, or 21 per cent of domestic tourism spending

(STB, 1999). Internationally, in 1997, VFR tourism accounted for 20 per cent of all trips to Scotland and some £137 million in spending. Less well understood, however, is the volume and value of VFR tourism in rural parts of Scotland. Seaton and Palmer (1997, p. 349) write that VFR tourism is most common in high-density, urban areas, in contrast to patterns of 'normal' recreational tourism, however, this analysis does not take into account the heterogeneity of rural communities. This research aims to investigate patterns of VFR tourism in rural Scotland using a comparative case study approach.

Building upon survey work which targeted hosts of VFR visitors, undertaken in Australia by McKercher (1996), the scope of this research is extended to investigate not only patterns of VFR visitations but also to compare the structure of VFR tourism across the case-study areas, which were chosen for their diversity of size, emigratory history, proximity to major visitor attractions and degree of peripherality. In addition to data regarding structure and frequency of visits, spending patterns, activities and trip purpose, the questionnaire included exploratory questions relating to potential social impacts of VFR tourism. Further areas for exploratory investigation include VFR trip motivation (visitors may travel specifically to see their friends or relatives, or may be primarily seeking accommodation with them) and VFR tourists' involvement with genealogical research during their trip away from home. Finally, respondents' migratory status was recorded. The survey results indicate a strong relationship between migratory status, propensity to host friends and relatives and peripherality (economic and physical) of case study area.

This chapter briefly reviews the VFR tourism research literature of the last decade and highlights some of the conceptual and methodological approaches which have been taken. Additionally, areas for further research, as highlighted in the literature and by this author, are described. The survey methods and research approach to the work undertaken in Scotland in 1999 are then described before the chapter reports on a selection of the results. The comparative elements of the research are considered briefly and contrasts with McKercher's (1996) data from Australia are made. Differences in results between the case study areas in Scotland are considered in the light of contrasting patterns of economic and physical peripherality, rural countermigration and destination area tourism and environmental characteristics. It is suggested that there exist specific interrelationships between flows of tourism, migration and VFR tourism and that in the light of closer European integration and increased intra-European labour migration, there exists the potential for significant rises in VFR tourism flows both within the EU (European Union) and internationally.

CURRENT ISSUES IN VFR TOURISM RESEARCH

Moscardo *et al.* (2000) write that it has become somewhat trite to suggest that the tourism industry and academic tourism research community have largely neglected the VFR tourism market segment. During the 1990s this sector certainly received increased attention from tourism researchers (King, 1994; Seaton, 1994; Pearce, 1995; Yaman, 1996; and Seaton and Palmer, 1997) and from some destination marketing organizations (see, for example, Morrison *et al.*, 1995, pp. 61–2). However, in comparison to holiday and business tourism, VFR tourism, hosts, destination areas, tourists and processes remain significantly under-researched.

The following table (Table 11.1) briefly describes the content and geographical

Table 11.1 The scope and content of VFR tourism literature

General domain	Author(s)	Specific foci	Geographical foci
Conceptual	Seaton (1994)	More accurate classification of category	General
	Boyne *et al.* (forthcoming)	VFR tourism and migration	Scotland/UK and general
Behaviour and trends	Seaton and Tagg (1995)	Empirical VF/VR/VFVR examination	Northern Ireland
	Yuan *et al.* (1995)	Long-haul VFR/non-VFR comparison	Netherlands and USA
	Meis *et al.* (1995)	VFR tourism and repeat visits	Canada and USA
	Braunlich and Nadkarni (1995)	VFRs and commercial accommodation	USA
	Morrison *et al.* (1995)	VFR segmentation by activities	Queensland, Australia
	McKercher (1996)	Economic impacts and regional development	New South Wales and Victoria, Australia
	Seaton and Palmer (1997)	Economic impact, behaviour and conceptualization	Scotland
	Moscardo *et al.* (2000)	VFR segmentation by activities	Queensland, Australia
Diaspora/ ethnic/ international	King (1994)	VFR, diaspora/ethnic reunion travel	Australia
	King and Gamage (1994)	Diaspora VFR and economic impacts	Sri Lanka
	Williams *et al.* (2000)	Retirement migration and social aspects of VFR tourism	UK and Southern Europe
Transport	Cohen and Harris (1998)	VFR trips and transport modal choice	United Kingdom
Mixed	Yaman (1996)	Conceptualization, trends and behaviour	UK and Australia

Source: author's compilation

coverage of much of the published research of the last decade explicitly related to VFR tourism.

While our understanding of the VFR category has been considerably enhanced over the last decade, there remain many aspects of VFR tourism requiring further research. Examples of such areas include: social, cultural and environmental impacts of VFR tourism; the relationships between VFR tourism and migration in a domestic context; VFR tourism in rural and peripheral areas; and VFR tourism outside Europe, North America, Australia and South East Asia.

In addition to further empirical research in the areas identified above, although much of the existing research contains conceptual elements, there remains a need for a coherent conceptual foundation with which to underpin studies in this sector, and to relate this sector to other forms of tourism and the wider social conditions which give rise to the VFR phenomenon. The following discussion describes some of the approaches which have been taken for the purpose of identifying and studying VFR tourists and tourism.

Seaton (1994, p. 316) points out that historically the VFR category has been regarded as a lower-value form of tourism, and therefore not meritorious of detailed research, owing to the fact that it is based on what VFR travellers do not do; that is pay for commercial accommodation, rather than any more positive criteria. In an attempt to address this knowledge gap, since 1989 the UKTS (United Kingdom Tourism Survey) has included a section relating to VFR tourism in the UK. Seaton and Palmer's (1997) analysis of the UKTS data indicates that VFR tourism is significant in terms of spending, short-break and off-season trips, destination area and demographic profile of guests. Seaton (1994) further questions the efficacy of aggregating friends and relatives together, on the basis that behaviour and impacts of guests may vary depending on the nature of their relationship to their host(s). In fact Seaton (1994) recommends three discrete categories: VF (visiting friends); VR (visiting relatives); and VFR for those guests visiting both.

Further ambiguities relating to definitions of VFR tourism are included in the UKTS methodology which defines a VFR trip as one where the *main trip purpose* is to visit friends or relatives. Seaton and Palmer (1997, p. 353) refer to these VFRs as *motivational* VFRs and point out that, from the UKTS survey, if the category is extended to also include *accommodational* VFRs (that is those guests who stayed with friends or relatives, but whose main purpose of trip was for some other reason, perhaps to attend an event or to visit a particular destination), then the number of VFR trips per annum in the UK doubles. Furthermore, Seaton and Palmer (1997, p. 354) suggest that splitting VFRs into those defined by motive and those defined by accommodation may highlight significant behavioural differences between these discrete groups of travellers.

The links between international migration and VFR tourism have been explored by, for example, King (1994) and King and Gamage (1994) who describe patterns of 'ethnic reunion' tourism to Australia and Sri Lanka and the patterns of VFR tourism therein. In Europe, Williams *et al.* (2000) have undertaken research on patterns of retirement migration from the UK to Southern Europe and the bi-directional VFR tourism flows generated by these migrations. In the context of domestic VFR travel in the UK, Boyne *et al.* (forthcoming) argue that VFR tourism trips, like any tourism trip, must take place outside the guest's normal place of residence. Thus, it is argued, with the exception of some special cases, some form of migration must take place to create the conditions under which VFR tourism can exist. Their polemic goes on to suggest, for the UK, a threshold of 15 km below which migrants are simply 'local movers', and VFR visits do not constitute 'tourism trips'.

For the purposes of this current research, however, VFR tourism has been defined simply as an overnight visit from a friend or relative, regardless of the distance travelled or the motivation of the guest. Such a definition was required due to the survey's use of respondent-completed questionnaires and the subsequent need for clarity of presentation and content. Further details of the survey methods are described below.

SURVEY METHODS AND RESEARCH APPROACH

This research was designed to accomplish two broad objectives as follows: (a) in the light of recent calls for more comparable research in the academic tourism literature (see, for example, Opperman, 2000, p. 145) the survey sought to generate similar data to that recorded by McKercher (1996) in his study of VFR hosts in the Albury Wodonga area, Victoria, Australia; and (b) to inform future empirical studies, the questionnaire included some exploratory research into potential social impacts of VFR tourism and differential effects of visitors' trip motivation. The choice of rural Scotland as the geographical locus for this work was informed by (a) the requirement to more fully understand tourism's role in, and impacts on, the economic and demographic restructuring currently being experienced in rural areas of Scotland; and (b) the need to assess patterns of VFR tourism in destination areas with diverse characteristics, as identified by Seaton and Palmer (1997, p. 354).

The survey employed case study areas which were chosen based on their characteristics in respect of the following criteria:

- varying degrees of proximity to built or natural tourist attractions;
- varying degrees of a history of emigration with potential for diaspora VFR tourism;
- varying levels of access and contrasts in peripherality;
- all should be rural[1] or semi-rural; and
- contrasting settlement sizes.

The four areas thus selected were as follows:

- Linlithgow Bridge, West Lothian: semi-rural, close to and accessible from Edinburgh;
- Kirkhill, Invernesshire: more peripheral, close to natural and mythical attractions;
- Tighnabruaich, mainland Argyll: economically and physically peripheral, natural attractions, medium level of emigration; and
- Colonsay, Argyll: island, natural attractions, high level of emigration to Canada, although high in-migration has reduced the proportion of native islanders.

During June 1999 a total of 1099 questionnaires were posted to households selected at random from the then current electoral register for each area. Of the 1064 valid addresses contacted, 364 of these households returned completed questionnaires; a response rate of 34.2 per cent.

The size of sample was chosen on the basis of (a) the response rate (38.8 per cent) to the pilot survey (conducted during April 1999 in the village of Kirkmichael in South Ayrshire); and (b) the requirement to achieve 400 responses and thus ensure that, for a given finding of 50 per cent, the 95 per cent confidence interval (95% C.I.) would be equal to ± 5 per cent. To maximize the return rate, elements of Dillman's (1978) Total Design Method were utilized for the design of the questionnaire and for administration of the questionnaire delivery and follow-up mailings. Questionnaire return was by FREEPOST and the return envelopes were coded to allow identification of non-respondents. The questionnaires themselves were unmarked and therefore anonymous. Non-respondents were sent a postcard after two weeks, and following a further twelve days another questionnaire was delivered along with an amended covering letter. Coding and analysis were carried out using SPSS (Statistical Package for the Social

---

[1] Based on Randall's (1985) definition of rural (< 100 persons per km^2). Linlithgow Bridge, chosen for its proximity to Edinburgh, is considered here as semi-rural as it possesses both urban (population density) and rural (low levels of industry, dormitory town) features.

Sciences). Extended response questions were first interpreted and then coded using content analysis.

Results

The following section addresses the results of the survey in two parts: the first reports on key results from the comparative research element which drew on McKercher's earlier work in Australia (McKercher, 1996); and the second considers a selection of these key results, and compares and contrasts these across the case study areas surveyed in the Scottish research.

The questionnaire was structured in four sections: on the front page respondents were asked if they had hosted friends or relatives in the twelve months prior to the delivery of the questionnaire; if the respondent had not, then they were asked if they had *ever* hosted friends or relatives. Depending on their answers to these questions, the respondents then each completed one of the first three sections. All respondents completed the fourth and final section on personal and demographic details. Although the respondents were ultimately self-selecting (both in terms of choosing to respond and which member of the household completed the form) the covering letter asked for the household member responsible for the majority of the household spending to complete the questionnaire in order to elicit the most accurate information relating to hosts' additional spending incurred as a result of their VFR hosting activities. Unlike McKercher's (1996) study, no questions were posed relating to visitors' spending as it was thought that hosts may not possess sufficient knowledge of their guests' spending patterns to yield a reliable set of data.

In the Albury Wodonga VFR study, McKercher only sought data from those residents who had hosted VFR guests in the twelve months prior to time of the research. For the sake of comparison, therefore, the results contained in Tables 11.2a and 11.2b are from only those respondents who had hosted VFR guests in the twelve months prior to the Scottish study (excepting the first entry in Table 11.2a – relating to the proportion of households participating in VFR travel – which for the Scotland statistic is based on all 364 respondent households).

The data collected from the remainder of the survey respondents is not dealt with here as it cannot be compared with the Australian study. Again seeking comparability with McKercher's findings, some of the data below have been analysed using both median scores and 5 per cent trimmed means. This technique has been used in cases where, due to the presence of some large outliers, the data is positively skewed; a calculation of the central tendency using a 5 per cent trimmed mean excludes the upper and lower 5 per cent of responses, thus reducing the effect of the large outliers. Using the trimmed mean as an upper indicator and the median as an estimate of the lower boundary should, McKercher suggests (1996, p. 520), provide a range of values within which the true population value will lie.

Key results from the VFR case study research

The following comparisons relating to person trips, person nights and hosts' spending are presented separately below (Table 11.2b) as the data must be (a) weighted to account for the greater population in the Scottish study; and (b) for the data relating to hosts' spending, adjusted using the retail price index to compensate for inflation between 1994 and 1999 and converted to Australian dollars (the exchange rate

Table 11.2a Key results from the VFR case study research (1)

Data		Albury Wodonga (n = 225)	Scotland (n = 272)
Households participating in VFR travel in year prior to survey		87.6%	74.7%*
Number of visits per household per annum	Median	5	6
	Trimmed mean	5.99	8.5
Trip purpose	Holiday/pleasure/for a visit	68.6%	84.3%
	Family gatherings	12.7%	6%
	Other	18.7%	9.7%
Party composition	Family	64.3%	59.6%
	Friends	30.6%	31.3%
	Mix of family and friends	5.1%	8.8%
Party size	Median	2	2
	Trimmed mean	2.4	1.8†
Length of stay	One night	22.7%	21.5%
	Two or three nights	45.9%	38.1%
	Four or more nights	31.4%	40.4%

* 74.7 per cent or 272 of *all* respondents; for Scotland total n = 364
† The trimmed mean is not an appropriate measure for party size in the Scottish example as the distribution is very close to normal (mean = 1.989; median = 2.00; mode = 2.00)
Source: McKercher (1996, p. 521) and author's original research

Table 11.2b Key results from the VFR case study research (2)

Data	Albury Wodonga case study area	Scotland case study areas	
Estimated total number of person trips in 12 months prior to survey	219,900–316,150	unweighted: weighted:	1,005,555–1,486,574 213,485–315,607
Estimated total number of person nights in 12 months prior to survey	438,000–995,000	unweighted: weighted:	3,116,667–5,576,853 661,685–1,183,995
Estimated total incremental expenditure incurred by residents when hosting friends and relatives in the 12 months prior to the surveys being undertaken	A$5.5–A$11.3	unweighted pounds sterling (million): weighted, adjusted for inflation and converted to Australian dollars (million):	£18.5–£38.7 A$8.47–A$17.73

Source: McKercher (1996, p. 521) and author's original research

employed was £1 = A$2.48 at the time of writing [April/May 2000]). Table 11.3 shows the estimated incremental spending by hosts in 'rural' and 'all' Scotland based on the data from the case study areas and population (household) data from the 1991 census, as detailed in the Scottish Rural Life Update (Scottish Office, 1996, p. 101).

Table 11.3 Estimated wider host expenditure based on case study data

Data	Case study areas (millions)	Rural Scotland (millions)	All Scotland (millions)
Estimated total incremental expenditure incurred by residents when hosting friends and relatives in the 12 months prior to the surveys being undertaken	£18.5–£38.7	£100–£209	£345–£722

Source: author's original research

Table 11.2a shows that a greater proportion of Albury Wodonga residents hosted VFR guests in the twelve months prior to the Australian study than their counterparts in the Scottish study (no account is taken here of economic factors such as currency strength in either the UK or Australia which may have influenced patterns of foreign and domestic travel to, from and within either country at the respective times of the studies). Of the 75 per cent of Scottish households who did host VFR guests, however, these tended to accommodate VFRs more frequently throughout the year prior to the study. Additionally, in the Scottish survey, a greater number of trips lasted for more than one night. In particular, the number of trips lasting four or more nights was some 9 per cent greater than in the Albury Wodonga area.

Not surprisingly, these differences in trip frequency and duration are compounded and exaggerated in the person nights and hosts' spending per year categories shown in Table 11.2b. Comparative figures for person trips remain similar; this is presumably due to the counter-balancing effect of, on the one hand, the reduced VFR participation by Scottish households (74.7 per cent compared with 87.6 per cent in Albury Wodonga) and on the other hand, the greater annual frequency of VFR visits to those households which do participate. The upper and lower estimates for the Scottish data in Table 11.2b are calculated on the same basis as McKercher's Albury Wodonga estimates using medians and trimmed means. To allow comparisons to be made with the Australian data, the Scottish figures are also weighted to counteract the fact that the population represented by the Scottish case study areas was several times greater than that in the Albury Wodonga study area.

Establishing the factors responsible for the greater frequency and duration of trips in Scotland compared to those in the Australian study was, however, not practical at the time of writing. As mentioned above, no account has been taken of the wider economic conditions present in each country at the times the respective pieces of research were undertaken, nor the myriad other factors which may be responsible; for example, cultural attitudes to VFR travel, geographical extension of friendship and kinship networks, transport infrastructure or geographical, economic and social differences between the Albury Wodonga region and the Scottish case study areas.

If we consider the Scottish results on their own, Table 11.3 shows the estimated annual incremental expenditure, based on the survey results, by VFR hosts in the case study areas, for 'rural Scotland' (as defined by Randall, 1985) and for 'all Scotland'. Taking the lower estimate for 'all Scotland' (£345 million) and comparing this with VFR visitors' spending in 1998 of approximately £453 million (STB, 1999), it can be seen that hosts' spending is not insignificant with respect to Scotland's tourism revenue. In fact, even using this lower estimate, VFR hosts' incremental spending is equal to around 76 per cent of all VFR visitors' spending in Scotland – although, as a caveat,

VFR visitor numbers as measured by the United Kingdom Tourism Survey (UKTS) may be under-represented in comparison to this survey due to the UKTS's definition of VFRs as *only those* visitors whose *main trip purpose* is to visit their friends or relatives.

Although, as identified above, it would prove a difficult and complex task to identify specific factors which may account for the differences observed between the Scottish case study areas and the Albury Wodonga area, by making some comparisons of the data between the Scottish case study areas and considering these differences in the light of the geographical diversity of these areas this chapter briefly explores some factors which may be responsible for regional variations in patterns of VFR tourism.

The Scottish case study areas

The data in Tables 11.2a and 11.2b above show that trip frequency and trip duration are both greater in the Scottish example than in the earlier Australian research. Within the Scottish results there are also variations in these data *between* the case study areas. Using analysis of variance (ANOVA) procedures, statistically significant differences were shown between case study areas for (i) trip frequency (at the 5 per cent level) and (ii) trip duration (at the 1 per cent level). The underlying trends show that both trip length and person nights per year increase with the peripherality of the case study area. Additionally, where trip frequency drops due to physical remoteness (as in the case of the Isle of Colonsay), trip length and therefore person nights per year increase as, presumably, visitors wish to maximize their 'ground time' to travelling time ratio. Tighnabruaich enjoys the greatest number of VFR tourism trips per year, probably because this area has, of the four case study areas, (a) one of highest levels of in-migrants (encouraging friends and relatives to visit) and (b) by far the highest level of economically inactive households of the case study areas (thus giving the residents greater leisure time to participate in hosting activities).

The relationship between migration, retirement migration and VFR activity has been highlighted most recently by Williams *et al.* (2000), where these authors report on the relationship between retirement migration from the UK to tourism destinations in southern Europe and the resulting bi-directional VFR tourism flows. Williams *et al.* (2000) and Williams and Hall (2000) suggest that tourists' experiences of destination areas can inform their future search spaces and thus their future retirement migration decisions. The interlinkages between these phenomena may be more complex, however. For example, the intrinsic environmental characteristics which in many cases encourage tourism development in an area, and also inform quality of life considerations in the migration decision-making process, may also render that area particularly attractive to VFR guests (who may make a choice of which friends or relatives to visit based on the attractiveness of the area in which the prospective hosts live). This process is summarized thus:

1. high quality environmental characteristics lead to tourism attractiveness and help encourage tourism activity in the area;
2. this tourism activity informs future search spaces;
3. search spaces inform migration decision;
4. migration creates potential for VFR tourism flows;
5. this potential is fulfilled due to the same high-quality environmental factors which attracted the initial tourism trips; and, finally,
6. the VFR trip may itself inform the search spaces of future potential migrants.

Fundamentally, it is the high-quality environmental characteristics that lie at the base of this process: as high-quality environmental characteristics are often found in peripheral locations, it is perhaps not surprising that remote locations are popular tourism destinations (for VFR and for migrants). This is particularly the case for those migrants at the retirement stage of life and who have little or no requirement to live close to core economic areas. This is not to say, however, that urban areas will not experience similarly high or even higher intensities of VFR tourism. Indeed, Seaton and Palmer find from their analysis of the United Kingdom Tourism Survey (UKTS) that VFR tourism 'tends to reverse the normal patterns of recreational tourism, being most common in high-density population, urban regions, rather than rural and seaside regions' (1997, p. 349). They go on to show how VFR tourism intensity varies proportionately with the size and density of a region's population. They suggest that this is due to more people having more friends and relatives and thus more potential visitors. However, other factors may exist, such as the greater ease of travel afforded by urban areas' transport links and the greater potential for event-driven trips in urban areas.

CONCLUSIONS

There exists, therefore, a distinctive relationship between VFR tourism and migration which has been explored in the literature in the context of (a) intra-European retirement migration (Williams *et al.*, 2000); and (b) domestic migration and VFR tourism (Boyne *et al.*, forthcoming). Globally, labour markets are becoming more flexible and the movement of skilled and unskilled labour is increasing (Williams and Hall, 2000, p. 9). Within the European Union, closer economic integration is sought and the movement of people within nation states is set to become easier. Therefore, as the geographic distribution of family and friendship networks increases, along with leisure time and disposable income (for some), the potential for growth in the VFR tourism sector, both within and between EU nation states and internationally, is strong.

For rural areas, in particular, in the light of the increasing proportion of the life-cycle being spent in the third age and retirement migration to areas possessing high-quality environmental characteristics (possibly with search spaces informed by tourism experiences), there exists the potential for continued increases in levels of in-migration and the resultant (bi-directional) VFR tourism flows. This research has shown that there does exist a significant economic impact from hosts' incremental expenditure during VFR tourism visits and, judging by the existing data for VFR visitors' spending, there is likely to be a greater economic impact from these visitors. In terms of social impacts, initial analysis of the exploratory data relating to the social impacts of VFR tourism in rural Scotland suggests that, in general, VFR tourism is relatively benign (it is small-scale, requires no additional infrastructure, occurs throughout the year and is not concentrated at peak tourism times and there are no employment impacts from a downturn in VFR tourism). Indeed, it may be that rural communities will experience less adverse impacts from VFR tourists and tourism than they do from many of the rural in-migrants whose relocation creates the potential for VFR tourism.

ACKNOWLEDGEMENTS

These findings are derived from research funded by the Scottish Executive Rural Affairs Department (SERAD) as ROAME research project NCR 658707.

REFERENCES

Boyne, S., Hall, D. R. and Carswell, F. J. (forthcoming) 'Reconceptualising VFR tourism: friends, relatives and migration in a domestic context', in A. M. Williams and C. M. Hall (eds), *Tourism and Migration: New Relationships Between Production and Consumption*. Kluwer Dordrecht, Netherlands: Academic Publishers.

Braunlich, C. G. and Nadkarni, N. (1995) 'The importance of the VFR market to the hotel industry'. *Journal of Tourism Studies*, **6** (1), 38–47.

Cohen, A. J. and Harris, N. G. (1998) 'Mode choice for VFR journeys'. *Journal of Transport Geography* **6** (1), 43–51.

Dillman, D. (1978) *Mail and Telephone Survey: The Total Design Method*. New York: Wiley-Interscience.

King, B. (1994) 'What is ethnic tourism? An Australian perspective'. *Tourism Management*, **15** (3), 173–6.

King, B. E. M. and Gamage, M. A. (1994) 'Measuring the value of the ethnic connection: expatriate travelers from Australia to Sri Lanka'. *Journal of Travel Research*, **32** (2), 46–9.

McKercher, B. (1996) 'Attracting the invisible tourism market: VFR tourism in Albury Wodonga, Australia', in L. Harrison and W. Husbands (eds) *Practicing Responsible Tourism: International Case Studies in Tourism Planning, Policy and Development*. Chichester: Wiley, pp. 509–29.

Meis, S., Joyal, S. and Tribes, A. (1995) 'The U.S. repeat and VFR visitor to Canada: Come again, eh!' *Journal of Tourism Studies*, **6** (1), 27–37.

Morrison, A. M., Sheaushing, H. and O'Leary, J. T. (1995) 'Segmenting the visiting friends and relatives market by holiday activity participation'. *Journal of Tourism Studies*, **6** (1), 48–63.

Moscardo, G., Pearce, P., Morrison, A., Green, D. and O'Leary, J. T. (2000) 'Developing a typology for understanding visiting friends and relatives markets'. *Journal of Travel Research*, **38**, 251–9.

Opperman, M. (2000) 'Triangulation: a methodological discussion'. *International Journal of Tourism Research*, **2**, 141–6.

Pearce, P. L. (ed.) (1995) 'Special edition: the visiting friends and relatives market'. *Journal of Tourism Studies*, **6** (1).

Randall, J. N. (1985) 'Economic trends and support to economic activity in rural Scotland'. *Scottish Economic Bulletin*, **31**, 10–20.

STB (1999) *Tourism in Scotland, 1998*. Edinburgh: Scottish Tourist Board.

Seaton, A. V. (1994) 'Are relatives friends? Reassessing the VFR category in segmenting tourism markets', in A. V. Seaton, C. L. Jenkins, P. U. C. Dieke, M. M. Bennet, L. R. MacLellan and R. Smith (eds) *Tourism: The State of the Art*. Chichester: Wiley, pp. 316–21.

Seaton, A. V. and Palmer, C. (1997) 'Understanding VFR tourism behaviour: the first five years of the United Kingdom Tourism Survey'. *Tourism Management*, **18** (6), 345–55.

Seaton, A. V. and Tagg, S. (1995) 'Disaggregating friends and relatives in VFR tourism research'. *Journal of Tourism Studies*, **6** (1), 6–18.

Scottish Office (1996) *Scottish Rural Life Update: A Revised Socio-economic Profile of Rural Scotland*. Edinburgh: HMSO.

Williams, A. and Hall, C. M. (2000) 'Tourism and migration: new relationships between production and consumption'. *Tourism Geographies*, **2**, 5–27.

Williams, A. M., King, R., Warnes, A. and Patterson, G. (2000) 'Tourism and international migration: new forms of an old relationship in Southern Europe'. *Tourism Geographies*, **2** (1), 28–49.

Yaman, H. R. (ed.) (1996) *VFR Tourism: Issues and Implications*. Proceedings from the Conference held at Victoria University of Technology, 10 October.

Yuan, T., Fridgen, J. D., Hsieh, S. and O'Leary, J. T. (1995) 'Visiting friends and relatives travel market: the Dutch case'. *Journal of Tourism Studies*, **6** (1), 19–26.

12

Over-optimistic Estimates of the Utilization of new IT in the Travel-buying Process: A Rejoinder

Anthony Harrison and J. John Lennon

INTRODUCTION

In reviewing statistical projections regarding online sales in the travel and tourism industry, two significant problems were identified. First, there is an apparent over-reliance on and misuse of one collective data source – American e-commerce consultants. Data on its own has little or no meaning, and so organizations have been able to manipulate it through dubious cross-contextualizations in order to fit it with their own policy or business objectives – or simply to sound informed and in control of information technology. Second, there is the sales projection data itself, which varies so much in scale between sources that one has to question the methodologies employed.

The purpose of this work, therefore, is to explore these two issues more fully and attempt to address the data realistically within the context of the United Kingdom and its consumers. Issues regarding the take-up of the internet for online purchasing, such as hardware ownership levels, credit/debit card penetration within the population and product complexity, have been rehearsed elsewhere and are not the subject of this chapter.

OVER-RELIANCE ON AND MISUSE OF ONE COLLECTIVE DATA SOURCE

Organizations, researchers, industry writers and business consultants wishing to communicate the impact of the internet on the sales of travel and tourism have invariably utilized figures created by American e-commerce consultants. This is mainly due to a dearth of research on the subject outside the United States. The problem with this is that the United States is significantly ahead of most of the rest of the world in terms of internet penetration and online sales (Marcussen, 1999), yet figures are rarely extrapolated to take account of this anomaly.

Francesco Frangialli, Secretary-General of the World Tourism Organization, like many other people within policy-forming organizations, has used the figures of the US-based consultants to make his point regarding online travel sales – seamlessly moving between the context of global tourism and the unique experience of one country (WTO, 1998).

Even at the single-destination level, in Scotland the Executive of the new Scottish Parliament is likewise blurring contexts in informing businesses of what they can expect in terms of online sales: 'travel industry sales via e-commerce will represent 12 per cent of world-wide travel industry sales by 2003' (Scottish Executive, 2000). On requesting the source, it proved difficult to track down where this figure originated. However, the only other source that quotes 12 per cent as the likely online travel sales contribution by 2003 is Forrester Research (1999), but this is solely for the United States market – the most advanced internet market by far!

THE ANOMALY IN ON-LINE TRAVEL SALES PROJECTIONS

As shown in Table 12.1, projections for on-line travel sales vary widely. In the USA, where internet penetration is most significant, Travel Industry Association of America (1999) estimate $6.5 billion in travel sales to come from the internet by 2001, while the consultants PhoCusWright (1999) project a figure three times as large. It may be argued that the TIA figure is what one would expect from an NTO trying to take a balanced and cautious view of the situation. However, it was another e-commerce consultant, Jupiter Communications, that was commissioned to undertake the research and who are ultimately responsible for this projection, which beggars the question: How can two respected consultancy firms who have presumably brought significant experience and resources to bear on the e-commerce question, arrive at such vastly different estimates?

Unfortunately, the methodologies that led them to their findings are the subject of copyright, so it is unlikely that anyone will ever know. Nevertheless, even the optimistic estimates mean that only 4–5 per cent of travel revenues in the USA come from on-line sales – that is as a proportion of total travel and tourism sales generated by United States consumers. However, it is more than likely that consultants are using their own individual definitions of what constitutes travel and tourism sales and, consequently, on-line travel sales proportions will vary along with projections.

European-based estimates include: Marcussen (1999) – 0.15% for western Europe; and Richer (2000) – 0.1% for the United Kingdom specifically. If projections for the

Table 12.1   Internet projections from selected sources in the USA

Organization	Projections
TIA (1999) (Jupiter Communications)	$ 6.5 billion (2001)
Jupiter Communications (1999)	$11.7 billion (2002)
PhoCusWright (1999)	$20 billion (2001)
Forrester (1999)	$29 billion (2003)

Source: Forrester Research (1999), Jupiter Communications (1999); PhoCusWright (1999), TIA (1999)

United States market of 4–5% on-line travel sales penetration in the same period are to be believed, then US businesses are receiving 40 to 50 times more on-line business as a proportion of total sales than Europe as a whole and 20 to 25 times more than the UK as an individual country. This severely questions the optimistic statements reviewed earlier regarding what the world and individual countries can expect from on-line travel sales.

One estimate for western Europe for 2002 predicts that a mere 2.2 per cent of travel sales will be made on-line, which itself would represent a fifteen-fold increase (Marcussen, 1999). This alone could be optimistic given that the Jupiter Communications projection for the USA on behalf of the Tourism Industry Association of America shows only a four-and-a-half-fold increase over the same period (TIA, 1999) and that US consumers are proven more enthusiastic users. However, it could be accounted for by the fact that the USA is further along the life-cycle than Europe in relation to the internet. If this is the case, then Europe is exhibiting growth figures that the USA experienced probably four or five years earlier. This again proves that expecting world on-line travel sales to be in double percentage figures within two to three years is highly optimistic. It is questionable whether even the USA will have attained such a proportion by then, let alone less advanced nations.

To confuse matters further, according to Jupiter Communications, US consumers purchased $6.5 billion worth of travel on-line in 1999 (Jupiter Communications, 2000) – double what they had predicted in the TIA (1999) study.

In terms of projections for the number of on-line travel buyers, one estimate for the USA is that over one third (38%) of the travel-buying population will purchase some form of travel via the internet in the future (PhoCusWright, 1999). This is confirmed by a similar response in the United Kingdom (39%) (Moffat Centre, 2000). This means that almost two-thirds will not do so and the third that will are unlikely to purchase all their travel via the internet just as they are unlikely to make existing purchases through one channel. Indeed, one travel category – airline seats – has dominated internet travel sales, as shown in Figure 12.1. This affirms that on-line travel buyers still purchase much of their travel off-line.

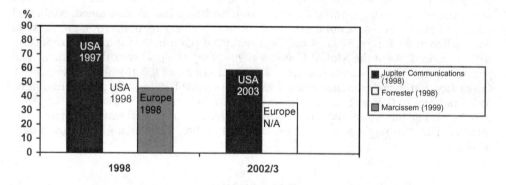

Figure 12.1 On-line air travel revenue as a proportion of total on-line travel sales

RESEARCH BY ORGANIZATIONS OUTSIDE THE UNITED STATES

The anomalies presented above regarding both revenue and numbers projections, and the subsequent use of the data by different organizations with different objectives could prove dangerous for many SMEs (Small and Medium Enterprises) in the tourism industry. One issue is that investment in the requisite technology – initial and updated – has to be made on the basis of revenue expectations that will feed into likely payback projections. For example, small firms in Scotland have to work on the basis that, as cited earlier, 12 per cent of their business will come from the internet by 2003 (Scottish Executive, 2000) – as this is the figure emanating from the key bodies responsible for tourism marketing and development in the country. However, this is the most optimistic of estimates and if, as is likely, the actuality is less – potentially up to six times less given Marcussen's (1999) projection – then the payback delivery and subsequent cashflow outcomes for small firms could be dangerous financially.

Therefore, it is essential – and would have been preferable if done much earlier – that governmental organizations in Europe – and other regions outside the USA for that matter – undertake their own research into the subject of the internet. The Travel Industry Association of America's projection – even though contracted to an e-commerce consultant – helped provide a rein on the more expansive estimates proposed by 'independent' consultants. Such a responsibility ought also to be incumbent upon similar governmental organizations involved in tourism worldwide. It also should be the responsibility of tourism consultants outside the USA to formulate and implement their own research studies rather than relying on second-hand data produced in and mainly for use within the United States.

Although there is plenty of anecdotal evidence in the press industry journals, apart from Marcussens's (1999) work there is very little in the way of European-based and industry-wide research being undertaken.

The Moffat Centre for Travel and Tourism Business Development – by whom the authors of this chapter are employed – have undertaken a UK survey of general consumer intentions towards the internet, although it does include actual estimates as to the size of the market (Moffat Centre, 2000). Rather, it has, as mentioned, confirmed US-based estimates that around one third of the travel-buying population are likely to buy on-line in the future. What is not clear is at what point in the future this proportion will be realized. As at the Moffat Centre's 1999 survey, 9.6 per cent of respondents had purchased travel items via the internet – 48 from a sample of 498 (Moffat Centre, 2000). Given that European estimates of on-line travel revenue for the same period amounted to 0.1 per cent to 0.2 per cent of total travel sales (Richer, 2000; Marcussen, 1999) then existing on-line buyers are spending a minute amount of their total travel budget via the internet. That this might become 12 per cent within three years seems ludicrous in light of this.

CONCLUSION

It is apparent that the rest of the world continues to be over-reliant on the United States when it comes to research and statistics regarding information technologies. The case in point, the internet, exemplifies this and should act as a catalyst to ensuring that all types of organizations attempt some of their own bespoke research. To a great extent issues regarding the internet are market-related; that is the key to statistical projections lies in the measurement of consumers' attitudes and intentions. Most organizations have likely been wary of undertaking their own research because of lack of expertise in the technical issues on the supply side and so have deferred to the e-commerce 'specialists' in the USA.

The danger of this has been explored through its potential impact on the small firm that is the dominant supplier and employer in the tourism industry. Such entities do not have the resources – financial or experiential – to undertake their own thorough investigations and so rely heavily on what is fed to them by way of strategy and policy statements from NTOs and commercial media coverage that necessarily feeds off the big impact statements of e-commerce consultancies.

Therefore, as many of the external business information needs of SMEs are necessarily national or regional in contextual terms, so it is that public and private sector organizations ought to provide contextually relevant information. Indeed, this is invariably case in all other spheres of tourism analysis, so why not in information technology?

REFERENCES

Forrester Research (1999) *The Internet Shows Meteoric Growth*. Cambridge, MA: Forrester Research, Inc.

Jupiter Communications (1999) '1999 On-line travel report: strategies for destination-based commerce'. New York: Jupiter Communications, Inc.

Jupiter Communications (2000) 'Triple-digit growth rates to fade in internet travel market: suppliers and agencies must lock in long-term strategies now'. http://www.jupitercommunications.com/company/pressrelease.jsp?doc=pr000414, 14 April.

Marcussen, C. H. (1999) 'Internet distribution of European travel and tourism services: the market, transportation, accommodation and package tours'. The Research Centre of Bornholm, Denmark.

Moffat Centre (2000) *UK Survey of Travel Purchasing Online*. Glasgow Caledonian University: Moffat Centre for Travel and Tourism Business Development.

PhoCusWright (1999) 'PhoCusWright e-commerce survey 1999'. Connecticut: PhoCusWright, Inc.

Richer (2000) 'Battle of the brand'. *Travel Trade Gazette*, London, 25 April.

Scottish Executive (2000) *A New Strategy for Scottish Tourism*. Scottish Parliament, Edinburgh: Scottish Executive.

TIA (1999) *Travel and Interactive Technology: a Five Year Outlook*. Washington: Travel Industry Association of America.

WTO (1998) 'A new era in information technology: its implications for tourism policies'. Address by Mr Francesco Frangialli, Secretary-General of the World Tourism Organization, OECD Conference. Seoul, Korea, 10–11 November. Madrid: World Tourism Organization.

13

Towards a Better Understanding of Visitor Attractions in Scotland: The Case of the Scottish Visitor Attraction Monitor

J. John Lennon

ABSTRACT

This chapter reports the findings and analytical projections derived from an extensive series of surveys of the Scottish visitor attraction industry. Data is drawn from the Visitor Attraction Monitor (Moffat Centre/Scottish Tourist Board, 1999, 2000), which provides a detailed picture of the Scottish visitor attraction market. The chapter highlights critical findings on visitation, development, revenue generation, seasonality and employment in a sector that is poised for growth of supply. Reference is also made to the rapidly changing environment within which attractions must now operate in the UK. Against this context, some preliminary analysis of attraction life-cycles and operating typologies are considered.

AN INTRODUCTION TO THE SECTOR

Attractions are at the heart of tourism and in 1999 some 40.8 million visitors were recorded entering attractions in Scotland (Moffat Centre/Scottish Tourist Board, 1999). Their presence is central to other tourism services and their successful operation is both complex and central to Scotland's tourism product. According to Gunn (1979) attractions provide two primary functions ; namely they (a) entice and stimulate interest in travel; and (b) offer visitor satisfaction from the travel product.

The Scottish Tourist Board (STB) offers the following definition of a visitor attraction:

> A permanently established excursion destination, a primary purpose of which is to
> allow public access for entertainment, interest or education, rather than being

142

principally a retail outlet or a venue for sporting, theatrical or film performances. It must be open to the public for published periods each year, and should be capable of attracting tourist or day visitors as well. (STB, 1991, p. 1)

While a typology of attractions remains debatable (see, for example, Inskeep, 1991; Lew, 1987) the following useful generic typographic categories are offered by Swarbrooke (1998). Fundamentally, attractions can take the following forms and can constitute:

1. features within the natural environment;
2. man-made buildings, structures and sites that were destined for a purpose other than attracting visitors, such as religious worship, but which now attract substantial numbers of visitors who use them as leisure amenities;
3. man-made buildings, structures and sites that are designed to attract visitors and are built to accommodate their needs, such as theme parks; and
4. special events.

Other attempts to classify attractions have been offered on the basis of ownership, catchment, usage, location, size, market and relative uniqueness (for further discussion see Swarbrooke, 1998; Cooper, Fletcher, Gilbert, Sheperd and Wannhill, 1998).

This chapter will utilize the extended classification of the Moffat Centre/Scottish Tourist Board employed in the Visitor Attraction Monitor (1998, 1999). It is based upon a classification developed by the Tourist Board over the period 1984–97 and is detailed below:

- castles
- churches, abbeys and cathedrals
- country parks
- distilleries
- gardens
- historic heritage sites
- historic houses
- industrial and craft premises
- interpretation and visitor centres
- monuments
- museums and art galleries
- pleasure cruises and boat trips
- railways – steam and miniature
- wildlife, zoos, safari parks and farms
- other.

This will form the foundation upon which some of the sectoral analysis reported in the first part of this chapter is reported.

METHODOLOGY

The STB has conducted an annual postal survey of Scottish Visitor Attractions from 1982 to 1997. Since 1998 the Visitor Attraction Monitor (VAM) surveys have been conducted by the Moffat Centre for Travel and Tourism Business Development, Glasgow Caledonian University, on behalf of the Scottish Tourist Board. Attractions included in the 1999 VAM are those where attendance can be reasonably accurately recorded. This includes those who have electronic/mechanical analysis as well as others who make a reasonable estimate based on previous knowledge or sample counts. For the 1999 Visitor Attraction Monitor, 994 visitor attractions in Scotland were contacted. Of those contacted, questionnaires were returned by 793 (a response rate of 80%) and a selection of the analytical data is presented below.

Inevitably, any survey is only as good as the information supplied and the authors have some concerns about the value of estimated visitor numbers from certain attractions. Other data requests were equally dependent upon robust internal information systems; for example, the dwell-time data request (how long customers spent in various elements of the operation) was, in the majority of cases, dependent upon estimates. However, a number of operators have continued to invest in a review of this aspect of visitor behaviour and the question serves to indicate the importance of secondary aspects of attraction operations (i.e. catering, retail etc.). Methods of recording visitor numbers have become more sophisticated in recent years, and the 1999 Visitor Attraction Monitor information was derived as follows:

Table 13.1   Recording methods for Scottish visitor attractions

Recording method	Percentage of visitor attractions utilizing methods below
Ticket analysis	40.6%
Manual count	33.3%
Mechanical/electronic	13.1%
Sample estimate	7.8%
Other	5.2%

The main alternative (Other) methods of recording visitor numbers were visitor books and honesty boxes (for admission/donations).

The VAM also attempts to compare attraction performance with other macro-tourism indicators but fails to provide detailed breakdown of key areas such as customer profile and customer origin. Inevitably, such customer analysis remains relatively crude without detailed intercept surveys being conducted. However, within the parameters of the research brief, the high response rate and the wide range of usable data provides a useful illustration of the Scottish visitor attractions industry.

THE SCOTTISH ATTRACTION SECTOR (1999)

The ownership of visitor attractions in Scotland is detailed in Figure 13.1.

Of the 734 attractions detailed in this report, some 32 per cent were privately owned, with some 21 per cent in local authority ownership. Historic Scotland, with 9 per cent of visitor attraction stock, and The National Trust for Scotland with 8 per cent of attraction stock, maintain a significant presence.

Scotland's stock of attractions according to the Moffat Centre/Scottish Tourist Board classification is broken down as shown in Figure 13.2.

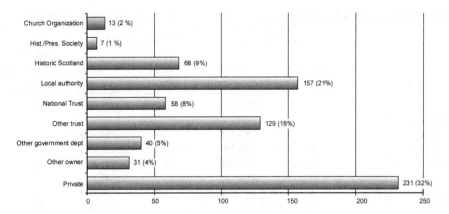

Figure 13.1 Ownership of visitor attractions in Scotland in 1999
Source: Visitor Attraction Monitor (1999), Moffat Centre/Scottish Tourist Board 2000

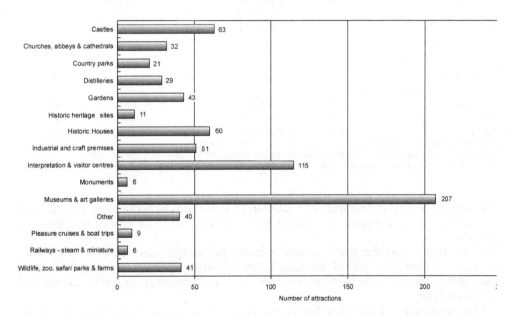

Figure 13.2 Total number of attractions in Scotland by sectoral type
Source: Visitor Attraction Monitor (1999), Moffat Centre/Scottish Tourist Board 2000

Figure 13.2 shows the clear dominance of museums and art galleries (207) in the Scottish attractions sector followed by interpretation and visitor centres (115). These two sectors account for 44 per cent of all of the attractions in the survey. Volume of attendance illustrates the significance of free admission operations and the relative popularity of sectors.

Table 13.2 Analysis of paid and free admission attractions by sector and visitor numbers

Type of attraction	Paid admission		Free admission		Total no. of attraction sites
	No. of sites	Total attendance	No. of sites	Total attendance	
Castles	60	3,463,983	3	25,724	63
Churches, abbeys & cathedrals	17	283,468	15	256,489	32
Country parks	6	844,243	15	8,960,764	21
Distilleries	21	620,266	8	245,944	29
Gardens	33	489,812	10	1,745,983	43
Historic heritage sites	8	177,881	3	36,005	11
Historic houses	53	1,391,143	7	60,037	60
Industrial & craft premises	15	184,899	36	853,876	51
Interpretation & visitor centres	58	2,960,236	57	3,060,895	115
Monuments	5	233,740	1	2,192	6
Museums and art galleries	75	1,591,581	132	7,948,243	207
Pleasure cruises & boat trips	8	14,220	1	3,803	9
Railways – steam & miniature	6	155,349	0	0	6
Wildlife, zoos, safari parks & farms	28	1,240,479	13	761,615	41
Other	23	1,910,921	17	1,146,161	40
Total	416	15,690,221	318	25,107,611	734*

* This table is derived from 734 respondents providing usable data in this category in 1999
Source: Visitor Attraction Monitor, 1999, Moffat Centre/Scottish Tourist Board 2000

The highly seasonal distribution of visitation to attractions in Scotland is illustrated in the best fit curve in Figure 13.3 which links quarterly analysis totals for illustrative purposes.

While this is not methodologically correct, and simply links median attendance totals, it is used for each of Scotland's Area Tourist Boards to illustrate seasonal fluctuations and compare to the average for the 734 attractions included in this element of the analysis.

The significance of the May–September period is very clear with the most marked seasonality evidenced in the Highlands and Islands region, whereas the key cities (Glasgow and Edinburgh) appear to show less marked seasonality. If one compares quarterly average attendance to UK and overseas holiday statistics, a degree of commonality is present (Table 13.3).

The majority of visits (71%) to attractions in Scotland occur in the summer months, from April to September. This broadly reflects the seasonal nature of the Scottish tourism industry although for UK holiday-makers, the October–December period of 1999 was clearly very popular. The average paid entrance attraction charges across Scotland are charted each year in order to understand price movement and fluctuation. These are detailed in Table 13.4.

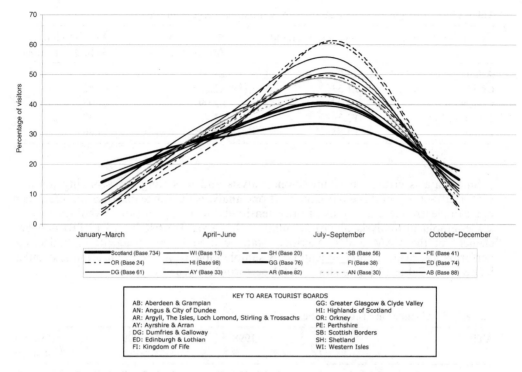

Figure 13.3 General overview of seasonality of visitor attractions by ATB

Table 13.3   Quarterly distribution of visitors in 1999

| | Visits to attractions | | UK holiday trips to Scotland | | Overseas holiday tourists to Scotland |
	1998 (%)	1999 (%)	1998 (%)	1999 (%)	1998 (%)
January–March	13	15	12	15	5
April–June	31	31	30	25	24
July–September	40	40	38	33	58
October–December	16	14	20	28	13

Base: 669 attractions which submitted questionnaires in 1998 and 1999
Sources: Visitor Attraction Monitor (1999), Moffat Centre/Scottish Tourist Board (2000)
        Visitor Attractions Survey (1998 and 1999), United Kingdom Tourism Survey (1999)
        International Passenger Survey (1999)

Table 13.4   Average admission charges to Scottish visitor attractions

Type of customer	Average Scotland	Average charge ASVA member	Average charge STB/QA member
Adult	£3.06	£3.25	£3.04
Child	£1.53	£1.62	£1.52
Concession	£2.02	£2.09	£1.97
Group (adult)	£2.36	£2.42	£2.32
Family	£4.25	£4.54	£4.26

Such data is critical in competition analysis and in setting entry pricing for new visitor attractions in this environment. If one analyses the range of prices on offer, then one can clearly see indications of price sensitivity at the upper price bandings.

Geographical analysis of visitor numbers by Area Tourist Board (ATB) is a key element of the VAM and is a critical statistic used by many agents in budgeting, performance review and commentary. A sample table from the publication is detailed below as in Table 13.5 and shows ATB performance year on year.

Table 13.5   Changes in visitor numbers 1998–1999 by ATB

ATB	1998	1999	1998–99 % change
Aberdeen and Grampian (85)	2,880,830	2,757,967	−4%
Angus and City of Dundee (27)	724,187	714,102	−1%
Argyll, The Isles, Loch Lomond, Stirling and the Trossachs (71)	3,508,741	3,444,800	−2%
Ayrshire and Arran (29)	1,788,967	1,637,695	−8%
Dumfries and Galloway (55)	651,874	640,779	−2%
Edinburgh and Lothians (66)	7,537,488	7,751,222	3%
Kingdom of Fife (35)	1,239,622	1,256,922	1%
Greater Glasgow and Clyde Valley (72)	14,790,910	14,717,694	0%
Highlands of Scotland (88)	3,072,406	2,961,684	−4%
Orkney (21)	317,941	310,470	−2%
Perthshire (38)	1,414,538	1,304,390	−8%
Scottish Borders (55)	924,909	933,124	1%
Shetland (18)	95,055	97,499	3%
Western Isles (9)	124,110	121,287	−2%
TOTAL	39,071,578	38,649,635	−1%

Source: Visitor Attraction Monitor (1999), Moffat Centre/Scottish Tourist Board 2000
Base: Some 669 attractions, returning questionnaires in 1998 and 1999 with usable data in this category. Number of attractions in each ATB in brackets

In order to extend analysis on visitor trends, respondents were asked to cite key factors affecting performance in the 1999 period of operation. The most popular positive factors influencing visitor numbers were detailed as follows:

- Marketing   19%
- Special Events   19%
- Signage   13%

The most common negative factors quoted were:

- Weather   22%
- Economic (strength of the pound)   28%

In order to build on the qualitative element of analysis, a further telephone interview survey of some 45 attraction operators (representing approximately 6% of stock) covering the full range of geographical regions, sectors and ownership of attractions was conducted to provide a 'snap-shot' of opinion in early 2000. Interviews were conducted around a standard database of questions. Questions were 'open-ended' and designed to allow interviewees to elaborate on and discuss further, areas of relative importance to their operation.

A critical element of the Visitor Attraction Monitor analysis which is central to the understanding of profitable operation is revenue distribution. Some 68 per cent of visitor attractions responded to this enquiry in 1999 (Moffat Centre/Scottish Tourist Board, 1999). Data on admission, catering and retail based on the Scotland-wide sample is sectorally analysed in Table 13.6 below.

Industrial and Craft Premises show the greatest average spend followed by the Distillery sector. The poorest total spend is evident in the Historic Heritage Sites (free admission) and the Museum and Galleries sector (free admission). Admission price averages vary significantly across the industry with the Pleasure Cruise/Boat Trip sectors achieving the highest spend per visitor.

In catering terms, the Wildlife, Zoo, Safari Park (free admission) operators achieved the greatest spend. This is possibly related to dwell-time for this sector which is longer than average and usually results in increased catering expenditure. Other sectors achieving high catering expenditure are Distilleries (paid admission) and Gardens (free admission). In the retail area, it is clear that Industrial and Craft Premises (free admission) evidenced the most significant expenditure levels. Other high retail spends were achieved in the following sectors: Distilleries (paid); Distilleries (free); Gardens (free).

Revenue levels in these sectors reflect the serious investment in retail areas, notably: spatial allocation; merchandising; display; and range of products on offer.

Polarization is continuing to occur in retail revenue generation levels. Generally, those sectors who have invested least in the development and operation of retail areas are receiving the smallest return in terms of visitor expenditure. Significant growth in expenditure category 'Other' is evidenced. This constitutes relatively expensive hire/purchase elements such as: equipment hire; boat hire; and horse-riding tuition.

The Visitor Attraction Monitor also requests data on how long visitors spend in various aspects of the operation. Some 68 per cent of visitor attractions responded to this question and the average breakdown of dwell-time was derived for Scottish attractions (Table 13.7).

Table 13.6 Distribution of gross revenue in Scottish visitor attractions (1999)

Sector		Admission average per person (£)	Catering average spend per person (£)	Retail average spend per person (£)	Other average spend per person (£)	Total visitor spend per person (£)
Castles	Paid	2.03	2.25	1.60	1.38	7.26
Churches, abbeys	Paid	1.51	1.50	1.08	–	4.09
& cathedrals	Free	–	2.02	2.15	1.06	5.23
Country parks	Paid	2.10	–	–	–	2.10
	Free	–	4.50	1.73	1	7.23
Distilleries	Paid	2.26	6.03	10.93	–	19.22
	Free	–	–	11.33	–	11.33
Gardens	Paid	2.10	2.10	1.99	–	6.19
	Free	–	4.03	8.13	–	12.16
Historic heritage	Paid	1.38	1.89	1.50	1.42	6.19
sites	Free	–	–	–	–	–
Historic houses	Paid	2.42	1.34	1.43	0.56	5.75
	Free	–	0.75	1.11	2.00	3.86
Industrial &	Paid	1.67	1.82	1.82	11.24	16.55
craft premises	Free	–	2.22	13.46	8.49	24.17
Interpretation &	Paid	2.35	2.75	2.12	3.05	10.27
visitor centres	Free	–	1.86	4.07	0.32	6.25
Monuments	Paid	1.54	–	1.27	–	2.81
Museums &	Paid	1.63	1.63	1.81	–	5.07
art galleries	Free	–	1.62	1.22	0.67	3.51
Pleasure cruises & boat trips	Paid	8.59	5.28	1.06	–	14.93
Railways – steam & miniature	Paid	2.53	–	0.50	–	3.03
Wildlife, zoo,	Paid	2.85	1.25	2.14	–	6.24
safari parks, farms	Free	–	4.50	6.99	14.74	26.23
Other	Paid	3.64	1.56	1.20	1.58	7.98
	Free	–	2.04	1.28	–	3.32
National average		2.57	2.45	3.78	3.04	11.84

Table 13.7   Average visitor dwell-time in Scottish visitor attractions

Aspect of operation	Average dwell-time
Attractions	80 minutes
Retail	20 minutes
Catering	28 minutes
Other	34 minutes
Total	2 hours 42 minutes

The 'Other' category incorporates interpretive trails, play areas, family related facilities etc., usually located outside of the attraction and used to extend the visitor experience. It is notable that the non-attraction elements (Retail, Catering and Other) account for up to 1 hour and 22 minutes of dwell-time, thus reinforcing the importance of non-core elements to attraction operation, revenue generation and visitation.

The employment level in the Scottish Visitor Attraction sector is not significant and is detailed in Table 13.8 below:

Table 13.8   Employment in visitor attraction in 1998–9

	1998	1999	% change 1998–99
Full-time permanent	2303	2429	5%
Part-time permanent	1110	1044	–6%
Full-time seasonal	886	1035	16%
Part-time seasonal	1488	1431	–4%
Total paid employment	5787	5939	3%
Unpaid volunteers	2835	2888	2%

Source: Visitor Attraction Monitor (1999), Moffat Centre/Scottish Tourist Board (2000)
Base: 669 attractions which submitted questionnaires in both 1998 and 1999

In 1999 an increase in total paid employment was recorded at 3 per cent, with unpaid volunteers also increasing by 2 per cent over the period. There appears to be a reduction in part-time permanent and part-time seasonal staff over the period with clear growth in full-time seasonal employment evident. Full-time seasonal staff are the favoured resource that possibly serves to accommodate the highly seasonal pattern of visitation evident in Scottish Visitor Attractions.

SCOTTISH AND UK ATTRACTIONS: TOWARDS 2000

The Visitor Attraction Monitor confirms that the visitor attraction sector in Scotland achieved significant growth towards the end of the last millennium. The opening of the Royal Museum and Museum of Scotland (1998), the Former Royal Yacht Britannia (1998), Dynamic Earth (1999) and Shaping a Nation (2000), all in Edinburgh, gave the capital an increasingly strong amalgam of attractions. April 2001 will see the opening of the Science Centre and the Loch Lomond Project (Lomond Shores) in the West of

Scotland. Such developments in Scotland must be seen against a considerable growth in the attraction sector UK-wide. Middleton (1998) noted that 50 per cent of the UK's attraction stock of approximately 6000 have opened since 1980. This growth pattern has rapidly accelerated towards the end of the century and such growth has undoubtedly been catalysed by funding availability. Since the 1980s, the availability of European Regional Development Funds, for many parts of the UK able to demonstrate the need for economic regeneration, has been a key facilitator of development. Indeed, tourism development has been used in many applications as a critical factor in building the case to gain such funds and stimulate growth and employment. The second major UK catalyst to development of visitor attractions has been the availability of National Lottery and Millennium Commission funding, which in a large number of cases has been used to partially fund many of the developments listed in Table 13.9.

Table 13.9 Attractions planned/in development in England

General location	Project title/site	Total investment (£m)
Manchester	Visions Centre	1.0
London	Soccer Hall of Fame	15.0
	Imperial War Museum	28.5
	Tate Modern	106.0
Salford	Lowry Museum	96.0
Mansfield	Making It!	3.5
Liverpool	Museums	34.0
	Wildflower Centre	3.3
	Pondlife Centre	3.8
	National Discovery Centre	91.5
Merseyside	Snowdome	40.0
	Glass Museum	14.0
	Courthouse	4.0
Stoke	Ceramica	3.2
	Wedgewood	6.2
Glos./Stroud	Ledbury Park	N/K
Bristol/Bath	Bath Spa	313.5
	Weston Helicopter Museum	0.6
Doncaster	Earth Centre	125.0
Portsmouth	Renaissance	86.6
Newcastle	Centre for Life	54.0
Bracknell	Weather Watch	3.6
Sheffield	Centre for Popular Music	15.0
Cornwall	Eden	106.0
Leicester	Space Centre	46.0
Norwich	Technopolis	62.0
Hull	The Deep	39.9
Rotherham	Magna	51.0
Kings Lynn	North Sea Haven	4.0
Derby	Discovery	13.0

Table 13.10 New attractions experiencing problems (since 1998)

Title	Location	Development cost (£m)	Lottery funding (£m)	Comment
National Centre for Popular Music	Sheffield	15	11	Insolvency pending
The Earth Centre	Doncaster	100	50	50% completed. Redundancies occurred in month 4 of operation
The Lowry	Salford	100	66	Under development. Emergency Manager appointed. Insolvency possibility
The Renaissance of Portsmouth Harbour	Portsmouth	80	40	Under development, cost significantly over budget
National Glass Centre	Sunderland	17	10	Redundancies continue
Making It!	Mansfield	3.5	2	Under development: location could be problematic
The Millennium Dome	London	850	449	Visitation levels scaled down from 12m to 7m. Senior management replaced, sponsorship commitment in doubt, Millennium Commission accepts that it has lost all of the £538 million offered in 'development loans'

This funding catalyst is considerable with millennium funding alone contributing over £700m to UK attraction development during the five-year period 1997–2002. The extent to which the range of attractions, either opening or planned, is related to consumer demand, remains questionable. Given the number of operational problems which have occurred in a number of new developments both the demand projections and feasibility studies may well be questionable. Table 13.10 lists some of the most contentious developments with some comments on areas of difficulty.

It is undoubtedly the case, given the problems above, that many visitor number projections in such attractions have been simply exaggerated in order to maximize grant aid. However, under-performance may also be due to the inability of many of the traditional format 'new' attractions to compete in an increasingly diverse market. Stevens (2000) and Middleton (1998) argued that demand for 'traditional' attractions is now in decline and competition has intensified. Visitor attractions increasingly find themselves competing with a new range of leisure products that stretch the traditional visitor attraction definition. Increasingly, across the UK, attractions have been developed in association with other sectors of the leisure industry. Retail and entertainment definitions are increasingly blurred as these sectors merge and shopping becomes a primary activity in leisure time, both for visitors and host communities. The 'family entertainment centres', now being developed throughout the UK, offer a range of retail, entertainment, leisure and sometimes incorporate 'traditional' attractions in an all-weather facility, in either out-of-town or urban locations. Such centres offer consumers a variety of facilities and services that can formulate a destination amalgam, strong enough to pull visitors to a location and hold them for a significant period of their leisure time. These developments comply with UK leisure behaviour in the late 1990s. Shopping has become a major activity of visitors and, in the US, retail centres are increasingly identified as tourist attractions. Leisure behaviour is becoming characterized by increasing pressure on an individual's time, as work demands become greater. As a consequence, leisure time is reducing and those facilities offering a variety of functions and services at one location stand to gain much in this scenario. Deloitte and Touche (1998) provide evidence that suggests, given the choice between a multiple leisure development and a more traditional stand-alone attraction, the latter appears a less and less attractive option. Such threats to the attraction sector have been the subject of scrutiny by a number of agencies (see for example CBI, 1998; Deloitte and Touche, 1998; Scott Wilson, 1996). There would appear to be a general consensus that the competitive environment has intensified as leisure time has diminished.

TOWARDS A VISITOR ATTRACTION LIFE-CYCLE

Given such concern alongside the continued growth in major attractions, the Moffat Centre has carried out explanatory research on the average life-cycle achieved by new attractions which have opened in Scotland over the period 1988–98. Data has been analysed from those attractions achieving visitor numbers of more than 10,000 per year and who are able to provide a level of robust and continuous data since the date of opening. From this data a graphical illustration of visitation has been developed, which covers a consolidated four-year period (see Fig. 13.4).

The sample of new attractions opening over the period where data was available amounted to 37 with some 21 (57%) being paid and some 16 (43%) being free admission. The sample did not include country parks, pure retail operations, monuments, castles, churches, abbeys and cathedrals. All other Visitor Attraction Monitor classifications of attraction were included. Notably seasonal attractions opening over the period accounted for 48 per cent of the sample. A consolidation of visitor numbers charted from a uniform year of opening gives a prototype life-cycle for visitor attractions. This is based upon average attendance of the sample of 37 across four years and is illustrated below in a best fit curve of average visitation levels.

In Figure 13.4 both free and paid admission attraction visitation is combined to provide a consolidated average. A life-cycle is emergent with growth evident in years 1–2 and with decline evident after year 3. In Figures 13.5 and 13.6, similar average annual achieved visitor numbers are shown for both paid and unpaid attractions over the period 1988–98.

Paid attractions on average show a greater tendency to maintain a degree of stability in visitor numbers across the initial three to four years of operation.

Clearly for non-paid admission attractions the four-year period indicates clear growth in year 1, reaching maturity in year 2 with the decline and stabilization of visitor numbers occurring in years 3 and 4. Such life-cycles represent one type of evolutionary scenario within a range of possibilities. The consolidated average invariably disguises the stronger and weaker operators and each of the 37 contributing attractions was also

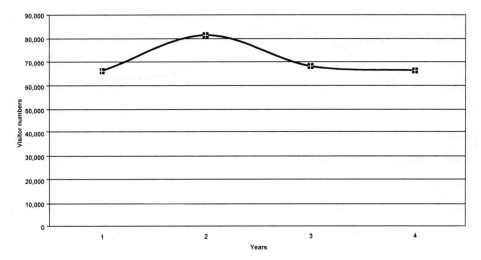

Figure 13.4 Consolidated average attendance levels – paid and free attractions in Scotland (opening and trading 1988–98)

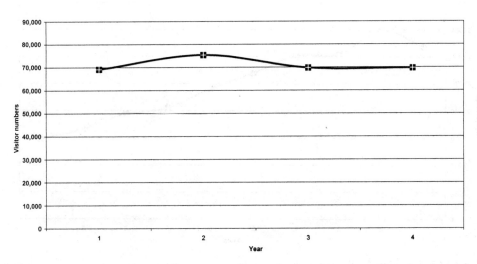

Figure 13.5 Consolidated average attendance levels – paid attractions in Scotland (opening and trading 1988–98)

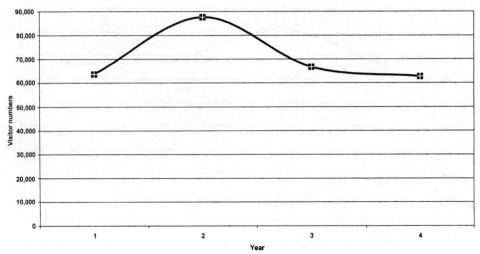

Figure 13.6 Consolidated average attendance levels – free attractions in Scotland (opening and trading 1988–98)

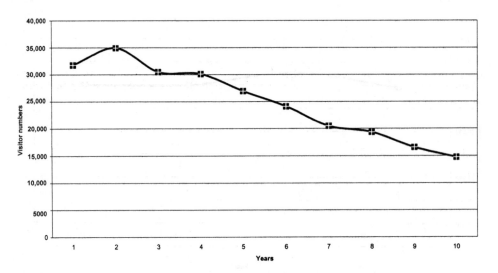

Figure 13.7 Typology A: Attraction decline cycle

graphed for illustrative purposes. This provided a number of typologies (outlined below) that help illustrate attraction performance in the late 1980s and 1990s. The following three categories are representative of major elements of the sample and are illustrative of visitation levels. They are graphed from a uniform year of opening (detailed as year 1) in order to provide anonymity for attractions.

In Typology A (Figure 13.7) the pattern of visitor numbers shows a peak in year 2 of operation with a clear decline following in year 3 onwards. At the end of the period it is apparent that achieved visitor numbers are less than half of the highest annual visitation level. Attractions in this category have usually seen very limited investment in

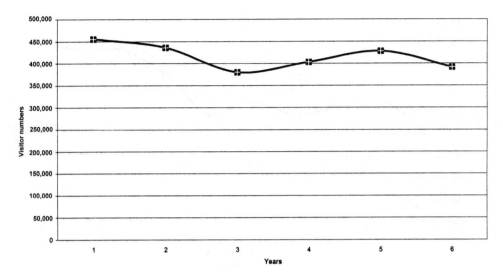

Figure 13.8 Typology B: Year 4 revivalists

the facility after opening. Thus a traditional decline curve is symptomatic of static operations that choose not to innovate or extend the visitor offer as the market becomes increasingly sophisticated. There were a number of attractions analysed which corresponded to this typology and it is representative of a management orientation common in the public sector in Scotland that is characterized by non-investment and non-development of the facility. In more extreme circumstances funding is continually reduced on a yearly basis resulting in an even more rapid decline.

The graphical representation of Typology B (Figure 13.8) is typical of many attractions that anticipate a potential decline in visitor numbers occurring sometime between years 3 and 4. Accordingly a new element/feature of the operation is added or a major refurbishment is conducted. This is invariably accompanied by significant marketing activity in order to cause an upturn in visitor numbers in year 4 of operations. The weakness of this approach is that the re-investment cycle in the attraction is rarely planned beyond year 3 and 4 resulting in decline in visitor numbers in latter years of operation.

In Figure 13.9 (Typology C) the curve is representative of a minority of Scottish visitor attractions that have been willing to systematically undertake reinvestment, product diversification, upgrade and redevelopment and consequently see visitor growth over the life-cycle period. The programme of constant innovation and a cycle of systematic reinvestment in the facility provides the unusual scenario of an attraction constantly exceeding initial-year performance. Such positive results are rare in the Scottish visitor attraction sector but are not unknown in large international theme parks and world leaders in the field. Clearly, the message of systematic reinvestment and upgrade and attempting constantly to innovate and extend the product has seen results in other parts of the world.

The weakness with this approach is that given the nature of the graphical illustration, it is impossible to compare attraction performance with major variables in the wider economic environment (such as currency fluctuations, downturns in tourism etc.).

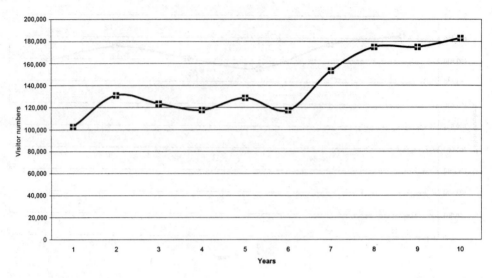

Figure 13.9 Typology C: Constant innovators

Similarly, it is impossible to understand the impact of the competitive environment on attraction operation over the time periods (e.g. the impact of other major attractions opening in the vicinity causing displacement effects on visitation levels).

Performance in terms of visitor numbers must also be seen in the context of differing objectives and backgrounds. Themed commercial attractions are developed with a very different set of operating aims from city museums and galleries. Comparisons and averages are thus computed against a canvas of varying cultural, economic and social environments in which each attraction is placed.

The value such typologies have for performance can only be anticipated at this stage. Yet in the UK context, wherein trade press reports now indicate a difficult and highly competitive trading environment, such initial exploration of life-cycle analysis may be of interest.

Whatever the value of the life-cycles, the environment remains difficult for Scottish attractions. Many of those new attractions hoping to maximise revenue streams from admission prices face increased competition from new museums and galleries, clearly designated as free admission flagships by the UK government. A good example would be the new Tate Modern in London wherein free admission has been catalyzed by additional funding made available by government. Thus the traditional stand-alone attraction faces increased competition from both a 'free admission' museum and gallery sector and a growing private sector investing in mixed family entertainment centres often with an attraction element. Competition will be further heightened by the scale and amount of lottery and Millennium Commission funded attraction development detailed earlier leaving existing operators with much to consider seriously for the next millennium.

REFERENCES AND BIBLIOGRAPHY

British Tourist Authority (1998) *Sightseeing in the UK 1997*. London: British Tourist Authority.
British Tourist Authority (1999) *Sightseeing in the UK 1998*. London: British Tourist Authority.
CBI (1998) *Attracting Attention: Visitor Attractions in the Millennium*. London.
Cooper G., Fletcher, C., Gilbert, G., Sheperd, G. and Wannhill, S. (1998) *Tourism Principles and Practice*. London: Longman.
Davies, S. (1994) 'A sense of purpose: rethinking museum values', in G. Kavanagh (ed.) *Museum Provision and Professionalism*. London: Routledge, pp. 33–40.
DCMS (1998) *The Comprehensive Spending Review: A New Approach to Investment in Culture*. DCMS Statement 24/07/98.
Deloitte and Touche Consulting Group (1998) *UK Visitor Attractions*. Deloitte Touche Thomatsu International.
English Tourism Council (2000) *Visitors to Tourist Attractions 1999*. London: ETC.
Gunn, C. (1979) *Tourism Planning*. Washington: Taylor and Francis.
Inskeep, E. (1991) *Tourism Planning*. New York: Van Nostrand Reinhold.
Leisure Industries Research Centre (1999) *Leisure Forecasts 1999–2003*. London: Leisure Industries Research Centre.
Lew, A. A. (1987) 'A framework of tourist attraction research'. *Annals of Tourism Research*, **14** (4), 553–75.
Middleton, V. (1998) *New Visions for Museums in the 21st Century*. London: Association of Independent Museums.
Moffat Centre for Travel and Tourism Business Development / Scottish Tourist Board (1999) *The Visitor Attraction Monitor 1998*. Glasgow: Moffat Centre.
Moffat Centre for Travel and Tourism Business Development / Scottish Tourist Board (2000) *The Visitor Attraction Monitor 1999*, Glasgow: Moffat Centre.
Museums and Galleries Commission (1994) *By Popular Demand: A Strategic Analysis of the Market Potential for Museums and Galleries Commission in the UK*. London: Museums and Galleries Commission.
Office of Population, Censuses and Surveys (1997) *International Passenger Survey*. London: Department of Culture, Media and Sport.
Office of Population, Censuses and Surveys (1998) *International Passenger Survey*. London: Department of Culture, Media and Sport.
Scottish Enterprise (1997) *Visitor Attraction Development Strategy*. Scottish Enterprise: Glasgow.
Scottish Executive (2000) *A New Strategy For Scottish Tourism*. Edinburgh.
Scottish Tourist Board (1991) *Visitor Attractions: A Development Guide*. Edinburgh: Scottish Tourist Board.
Scottish Tourist Board (1997) *Visitor Attractions Survey*. Edinburgh, Scottish Tourist Board.
Scottish Tourist Board (1999) *Tourism in Scotland*. Edinburgh: Scottish Tourist Board.
Scott Wilson – Resource Consultants (1996) *Scottish Visitor Attraction Development Strategy*. Glasgow: Scottish Enterprise.
Stevens, T. (2000) 'The future of visitor attractions'. *Travel and Tourism Intelligence*, March 2000.
Swarbooke, J. (1998) *The Development and Management of Visitor Attractions*. Oxford: Butterworth Heinemann.

PART 3
SUSTAINABLE TOURISM

14

Defining and Measuring Sustainable Tourism: Building the First Set of UK Indicators

Paul Allin, Joan Bennett and Laurie Newton

ABSTRACT

We describe the process by which the first set of national indicators of sustainable tourism is being derived in the UK. These indicators will apply to England rather than to the whole of the UK. The definition of sustainable tourism emerged as part of the government's sustainable development strategy and became known as 'wise growth', to reflect the need to balance economic growth with the impact on local communities and on the environment. This calls for indicators beyond the 'green' indicators used to assess environmental impact. The indicators have been developed through consultation, within constraints imposed by limited availability of data.

INTRODUCTION

The Department for Culture, Media and Sport (DCMS) is the UK government department responsible for tourism policy. In April 1998, DCMS published a consultation paper *Tourism: Towards Sustainability* (DCMS, 1998). The results of this consultation helped develop a new tourism strategy *Tomorrow's Tourism* (DCMS, 1999), which included a commitment to develop a series of national statistical indicators to help measure progress in achieving sustainable tourism. DCMS commissioned CAG Consultants to assist them to develop the indicators (DCMS, forthcoming).

Sustainable tourism fits within the UK government's overall strategy for sustainable development, which is managed by the Department of the Environment, Transport and the Regions (DETR). The overall strategy, *A Better Quality of Life* (DETR, 1999a), was published only after the start of the tourism project. The subsequent publication of a baseline assessment of the overall strategy (DETR 1999b; UK Round Table 2000) summarized the national set of sustainable development indicators. This recorded that tourism indicators were still under development. The sustainable tourism indicators discussed in this chapter are therefore designed to supplement the set of indicators describing the overall strategy. The tourism indicators have been developed more in parallel with the overall strategy – and interacting with it – rather than taking the broad strategy as the starting point for work in the tourism sector. The development of the tourism indicators did, of course, draw on earlier work on sustainable development indicators (e.g. Department of the Environment, 1996; World Tourism Organization, 1998).

The brief to CAG from the DCMS specified the following mandatory features for the indicators:

- *Consistency* with *Tomorrow's Tourism* and the new national set of sustainable development indicators;
- *Parsimony*: the smallest set of indicators sufficient to demonstrate this compatibility;
- *Pragmatism*: involve minimum (or no) collection of new data; and
- *Peer reviewed*: demonstrate a general degree of acceptance among experts in the fields.

The work on tourism indicators began by asking what topics should ideally be represented by sustainable tourism indicators. We took this approach to avoid defining sustainable tourism as solely those topics for which data are available. Inevitably, the final set of indicators, which relies on existing data sets as required by DCMS, represents a relatively small portion of the original set of topics.

An important component of sustainable development is global commitment ('think global, act local'). One view is, therefore, that sustainable tourism indicators should reflect UK residents' impact overseas and our contribution to global phenomena such as climate change. In contrast, *Tomorrow's Tourism* focuses on tourism within the UK. The decision was made early on to focus on sustainable tourism within the UK, mainly because UK residents' impact overseas is extremely difficult to measure. The final set does not include any direct measure of UK tourists' impact in other countries, but it does include an indicator that relates to climate change.

THE INDICATOR SELECTION PROCESS

Perhaps the most crucial stage in the development of indicators is to define what those indicators should represent, i.e. to define the themes and topics that constitute sustainable tourism. Agreeing the themes and topics effectively determines what we in the UK mean by sustainable tourism. The difference between themes, topics, indicators and data sets is summarized below, and an example is given. For each theme there are likely to be several possible topics, for each topic there may be numerous indicators that could be used, and for each indicator there may be a variety of possible data sources.

- *Themes*   are broad issues.
- *Topics*   are some of the important contributors to a theme.
- *Indicators*   are a time series of data selected to represent the topic.
- *Data sets*   are sets of data which are used to create the time series.

Theme	Topic	Indicator	Data set
Supporting local jobs & economies	Availability of tourism jobs to local people	Percent of tourism jobs filled by local people	Data provided by major tourism facilities

The process by which DCMS and CAG arrived at a set of sustainable tourism indicators was, in effect, to use a 'Delphi group' approach. Questions were posed to a selected panel, who discussed the material in sub-groups and in plenary. The researchers then iterated the outcomes to formulate the next set of questions. The steps were as follows:

1. CAG prepared a discussion paper on sustainable tourism themes and topics and the criteria for indicator selection.
2. Workshop 1 was held to agree the key themes and topics as well as the criteria for indicator selection.
3. CAG prepared a second discussion paper on candidate indicators and data sources.
4. Workshop 2 was held to agree a provisional indicator set.
5. Data were collected, processed and interpreted.
6. A draft final report was prepared.
7. Additional comments were received from DCMS and the English Tourism Council.
8. The final report was completed.

The English Tourism Council (ETC) is a public body funded by DCMS. As part of the tourism strategy (DCMS, 1999) the English Tourist Board was transformed into a strategic body for tourism in England. It was given lead responsibility for developing sustainable tourism in the English domestic market, working closely with other relevant agencies, and for ensuring that action contributes towards the achievement of the government's overall sustainable development strategy. We shall see later that this gave rise to a further phase in the development of indicators.

DEFINING AND RANKING THE TOPICS

A framework for understanding sustainable tourism

At the start of the project CAG prepared a paper on the themes and topics encompassed by sustainable tourism. The initial topic list was derived from a review of relevant literature. The topics were subsequently grouped under the five chapter headings and sub-headings from *A Better Quality of Life,* which form the framework for *Quality of Life Counts.* These five main headings are:

• Sending the right signals;
• A sustainable economy;
• Building sustainable communities;
• Managing the environment and resources;
• International co-operation and development.

Some workshop participants preferred the framework known as VICE (visitors, industry, community and environment) as a way of understanding sustainable tourism. Sustainable tourism encompasses all four components and is very much a two way process. For example, visitors may have a welcome impact on local communities by contributing to local jobs and the diversity of facilities, but also have adverse impacts on tranquillity, safety and congestion. But the process does not stop here. Poor management of the local environment is likely to reduce the quality of visitor experience, discourage visitors and damage the local tourist industry, with consequent repercussion for the local community.

This intricate interdependency sums up the concept of sustainable development, which argues that we live in a complex ecosystem in which it is impossible to separate economy, environment and our quality of life. This is particularly important for tourism, which relies on the maintenance and management of a quality local environment and a welcoming local community. Sustainable tourism is therefore about protecting and managing resources for the future benefit of all.

In the event it was decided for CAG's report to apply the *Quality of Life Counts* framework rather than VICE. This would maintain consistency with the national sustainable development indicators. Also, in the nature of sustainable development, many topics cross several VICE categories. For example, 'resources consumed by tourists' and 'traffic congestion resulting from tourism travel' are the responsibility of both the industry and the visitors and can impact on the environment, which in turn affects the quality of life of the local community.

Ranking the topics

The themes and topics paper was discussed at a workshop in May 1999. Approximately 35 people, representing various sectors of the tourism industry, attended. Many of the topics in the initial list were drawn from publications that took an international perspective. Unsurprisingly, issues of high importance in some parts of the world are less crucial in the UK. The aim of the workshop was to give participants an opportunity to express their views on which topics are most important for the UK.

Nearly 50 possible topics were suggested in CAG's first paper and six additional topics were suggested by workshop participants. Workshop participants were asked to identify the topics that they thought were most important for sustainable tourism in the UK. A voting system was used to allow all participants to have an equal say in the final selection. Table 14.1 presents the top 24 topics. The third column shows the ranking of the topics derived from the votes at the workshop.

A rough idea of the comparative weight given to the overarching themes of sustainable development can be obtained by comparing the number of indicators allocated to each of the *Quality of Life Counts* headings. (see Table 14.2). The headings *Sending the Right Signals* and *International Co-operation and Development* are mainly concerned with the contribution of central government to sustainable development. It is to be expected that these topics are poorly represented within sustainable tourism. Of the remaining three headings, it is noticeable that the impact of tourism on communities has the highest representation while environmental factors appear to be under-represented. But a number of topics which are commonly considered to be environmental, e.g. resources used by tourists and industry, traffic congestion and loss of open space have been allocated to other headings in line with the approach followed in *Quality of Life Counts*. Environmental topics are therefore not as under-represented as might at first appear.

Table 14.1 Topics selected to describe sustainable tourism

DETR headings from *Quality of Life Counts*	Sustainable tourism topic	Rank
Sending the right signals		
Information and involvement	Tourists' awareness of their impacts	17
A sustainable economy		
Doing more with less	Materials used in construction of tourist facilities & supporting infrastructure	= 22
	Resources consumed by tourists	17
Economic stability and competitiveness	Industry profitability / competitiveness	= 3
	Industry investment	13
Developing skills and rewarding work	Quality and quantity of jobs filled by local people	1
Sustainable production and consumption	Provision of more sustainable tourist activities /packages	= 22
	Tourist choices (sustainable or not)	6
	Sustainable practices by tourism facilities	12
Building sustainable communities		
Promoting economic vitality and employment	Links into local economies – retention of tourist spend locally and support for both direct & indirect jobs	2
Meeting social needs	Quality & quantity of tourism provision	= 3
	Tourism support for essential facilities in rural areas	11
	Access to tourism for all	15
	Traffic congestion resulting from tourist travel	8
Shaping our surroundings	Scale & appropriateness of tourism development and supporting infrastructure	10
	Local distinctiveness/diversity/cultural heritage	5
	Loss of open space to tourism developments and supporting infrastructure	21
Bringing it all together – integrated policies	Local management plans and their inclusion in local land use plans and transport strategies	19
Involving everyone	Stakeholder involvement in visitor management plans	7
	Stakeholder involvement in development decisions	14
Managing the environment and resources		
Climate change and energy supply	Contribution to climate change of travel to and within tourist destinations	9
	Contribution to climate change of energy consumption by tourist facilities	20
Freshwater	Demand for water resources by tourist facilities	24
Landscape and wildlife	Conservation, enhancement and damage to habitats and landscape	16
International co-operation and development		
	None	

Table 14.2 Distribution of topics across categories

Quality of Life Counts headings	Topics (%)	
	DETR	Sustainable tourism
Sending the right signals	7	4
A sustainable economy	29	33
Building sustainable communities	28	46
Managing the environment and resources	30	17
International co-operation and development	6	0
	100	100
	(106 topics)	(24 topics)

SELECTING THE INDICATORS

The preparation for and discussion in the first workshop inhabited an ideal world in which sustainable tourism topics were identified regardless of the likelihood of finding plausible indicators. Following that workshop, the project took a more pragmatic turn and investigated potential indicators to represent the top-ranked topics. A second paper on candidate indicators was prepared which described 35 potential indicators. In arriving at this set we considered the suggestions made during the consultation on *Tomorrow's Tourism*.

For all of these indicators a minimum requirement was that there should be at least some likelihood of available data now or in the foreseeable future. In this respect we did not have the luxury of being able to specify the information requirements to meet a full framework, such as that proposed by Radermacher (1999). The paper also considered each indicator against a set of criteria applied by the DETR (Custance and Hillier, 1998; Levett, 1998) to select their headline sustainable development indicators, plus a final two criteria added by CAG. The criteria were:

- resonance to target audience – the tourism industry, central & local government;
- robustness – calculation is transparent and defensible;
- credibility – direction of change reflects public experience;
- sensitivity – responds to changes in the issue it is intended to measure;
- availability of data – trend data is currently available;
- regularity – data is regularly updated – at least every five years;
- cost-effective – data is not prohibitively expensive to purchase or analyse;
- unambiguous – it is clear which direction of change is sustainable.

The first workshop added a further three criteria which were also discussed in the paper:

- internationally comparable;
- payback for data collector;
- threshold or reference value exists.

Some of the candidate indicators appeared to be more viable than others, but we preferred to let the second workshop have the chance to consider 'outsiders'. For some topics we were unable to arrive at any (near) credible indicators and four of the top 24 topics were dropped at this stage. The four were (ranking shown in brackets):

- provision of more sustainable tourism activities ($=22$);
- materials used in construction of tourist facilities & supporting infrastructure ($=22$);
- tourists' awareness of their impacts (17);
- demand for water resources by tourist facilities (24).

The first of these excluded topics was on the grounds that it would be extremely difficult to reach agreement on what qualified as a 'sustainable tourism activity'. Often projects with environmental features have been awarded this title. But as this exercise has shown, there are not only a wide variety of environmental factors to be considered, but also social and economic impacts. The remaining three topics were excluded because they would require costly new surveys. All the topics were relatively low on the ranking list and their loss was not considered to be unduly serious.

The second workshop suggested several alternative indicators and ruled out others as unworkable, misleading or very poor reflections of the topic that they were intended to represent. Following this workshop 26 indicators were selected for further investigation. At this point another four topics were dropped, namely: resources consumed by tourists (22); tourist choices (sustainable or not) (6); tourism support for essential facilities in rural areas (11); and local distinctiveness/diversity/cultural heritage (5), and two stakeholder involvement topics were combined into one. Although several of these topics were highly ranked by the first workshop, our own investigations and the discussions at the second workshop led us to the conclusion that there are no plausible indicators for these topics. CAG suggested that none of these topics should be considered for future indicator sets.

By the end of the second workshop, therefore, the number of topics for which plausible indicators appeared a possibility had been reduce from 24 to 15, and grouped as shown in Table 14.3. The loss of topics occurred across all of the DETR's themes. After the second workshop, two of the *Quality of Life Counts* headings had no tourism topics, although all of the key tourism themes are still represented in this set.

Table 14.3 Comparing the sets of topics

Quality of Life Counts headings	Number of topics DETR	Top 24 tourism	After second workshop
Sending the right signals	7	1	0
A sustainable economy	31	8	4
Building sustainable communities	30	11	8
Managing the environment and resources	32	4	3
International co-operation and development	6	0	0

FINAL CHOICE OF INDICATORS

The final stage of the project with CAG was to deliver precise specifications for each indicator, testing that data were available or likely to become so (details of each indicator are in DCMS, forthcoming). A further round of discussions took place with DCMS and ETC, including to ensure that the indicators made sense: Did we know whether it was good news or bad news if an indicator showed an increase? for example.

A total of 21 indicators are proposed in CAG's final report. The final balance of topics and indicators is shown in Table 14.4. The sustainable communities section has been given higher priority in this set of indicators than in the national sustainable development set. This no doubt reflects the very important impact that tourism has on quality of life, both as an important contributor to general welfare and also as a potential source of both improved facilities and disturbance for local communities.

Table 14.4 The spread of the final set of indicators in the CAG report

Quality of Life Counts headings	Number of topics		Number of indicators
	DETR	Final Set	
Sending the right signals	7	0	0
A sustainable economy	31	3	4
Building sustainable communities	30	6	11
Managing the environment and resources	32	4	6
International co-operation and development	6	0	0

Table 14.5 lists the 21 recommended indicators. Only twelve of these are 'OK', in the sense that we have a back run of data and can continue each time series at regular intervals in future (these are charted in DCMS, forthcoming). Many of the suggested indicators are not amenable for publication at this stage because:

(a) data is expected to become available in the near future (definite in future); and
(b) data could be made available in future if existing data collection is adapted to suit the needs of this indicator set (possible in future).

Table 14.5 Final set of indicators recommended by CAG

Topic	Indicator	Status
A sustainable economy		
Industry profitability/ competitiveness	1. Ratio of holidays taken by UK residents in the UK or overseas	OK
	2. VAT registrations and deregistrations of tourism related businesses	OK
Industry investment	3. Highest qualifications held by workers in tourism-related industries compared with average of all employment sectors	OK
Quality and quantity of jobs filled by local people	4. Average hourly earnings in tourism as per cent of national average	OK
Building sustainable communities		
Quality & quantity of tourism provision	5. Consumer satisfaction with tourism facilities in the UK	Possible in future
	6. Number (proportion) of accommodation registered with harmonized rating scheme	Definite in future
	7. Number of blue flag beach awards in the UK	OK

TOPIC	INDICATOR	STATUS
Access to tourism for all	8. Percentage of elderly and low-income residents not taking a holiday	OK
	9. Number of accommodations recorded as accessible to disabled people	OK
Traffic congestion resulting from tourist travel	10. Per cent UK residents using public transport to reach holiday destinations in the UK	OK
	11. Per cent of all leisure trips taken by UK residents within the UK using public transport (excluding planes)	OK
	12. Traffic congestion caused by visitor journeys	Possible in future
Loss of open space to tourism developments and supporting infrastructure	13. Extent of tourism developments which take place on green-field sites and on previously developed land and buildings	Possible in future
Local management plans and their inclusion in local land use plans and transport strategies	14. Number of local transport plans with visitor management section	Possible in future
Stakeholder involvement in tourism decisions	15. Number of tourism forums including both residents and business as a per cent of all districts	Possible in future
Managing the environment and resources		
Contribution to climate change of travel to and within tourist destinations	16. Carbon dioxide emissions by UK residents' tourist travel in the UK	OK
	17. Carbon dioxide emissions by UK residents' travel overseas	OK
Contribution to climate change of energy consumption by tourist facilities	18. Energy consumption and carbon dioxide emissions by hotels, restaurants, sports and entertainment	OK
Conservation, enhancement and damage to habitats and landscape	19. Number of (large scale) tourism developments on nationally designated sites	Possible in future
	20. Damage and disturbance to SSSIs as a result of recreational activities	Possible in future
Sustainable practices by tourism facilities	21. Number of tourist businesses participating in recognised environmental schemes	Possible in future

POSTSCRIPT: THE TRANSFORMATION INTO 'WISE GROWTH' INDICATORS FOR ENGLAND

As mentioned above, the government has given the new tourism body for England, the English Tourism Council, lead responsibility for developing sustainable tourism in the domestic market. (The three prime objectives of the ETC are quality, competitiveness and wise growth). The Chairman of the ETC is required to report annually, to the

Secretary of State for Culture, Media and Sport, on progress in achieving more sustainable forms of tourism ('wise growth'). So, although the government is committed to developing a series of national statistical indicators to help measure progress in achieving sustainable tourism, it is ETC that is being asked to take ownership of the indicators.

The ETC has reviewed the CAG recommendations and come up with a revised list (Table 14.6), on which it is now consulting. ETC has reverted to the VICE structure discussed above because this is more familiar, to its audience, than is the sustainable development terminology. Details of the final set will be published (ETC, forthcoming). The ETC indicators are for England only. Tourism was one of the functions devolved to administrations in Scotland, Wales and Northern Ireland during 1999 (up to then the national tourist boards were anyway funded by the respective government department, such as the Scottish Office, responsible for certain functions). The government's strategy for tourism is therefore a strategy for England, but one that has clear implications for Scotland, Wales and Northern Ireland. How these implications are resolved in terms of indicators of sustainable tourism has yet to be considered.

CONCLUDING REMARKS

An indicator is there to indicate, it does not tell the whole story. A good set of indicators will pick out a few measures that crystallize key trends, but even this can only tell a partial story. Following widespread consultation, DCMS and CAG arrived at a set of 21 indicators that we believe sum up the key sustainable tourism issues for the UK. Many other important topics have inevitably been excluded. We have seen that there is also a further phase to work through. The English Tourism Council is taking ownership of a set of 'wise growth' indicators for England, on which the Council is to report annually to the Secretary of State for Culture, Media and Sport.

As anticipated, national data are not available for many of the recommended indicators, but most should become feasible in future if relevant organizations can be persuaded to modify their data collection or analysis. In this and other ways, the set of sustainable tourism indicators will no doubt evolve over time.

The tourism strategy also recognises the important contribution to tourism made by local authorities. The strategy commits the government to supplementing the series of national statistical indicators with published guidance on the development of compatible local indicators for sustainable tourism. This guidance is being prepared in association with the British Resorts Association (see Chapter 16). It may be possible in future to aggregate data collected locally, to agreed quality standards, to arrive at national indicators. But this will not, of course, be possible until there has been a wide take up of the local indicator set.

Note

We gratefully acknowledge the substantive contributions made to this project by everyone who took part in the workshops or who made data or advice available. Views expressed in this chapter are those of the authors and do not necessarily represent those of the Department for Culture, Media and Sport or of CAG Consultants.

Table 14.6 Suggested set of national wise growth indicators

SATISFYING FOR VISITORS		
1	Visitor satisfaction	N/a
2	Range of qualifications held by workers in tourism-related industries compared with the average for all workers	OK
3	Percentage of the workforce in the tourism sector participating in professional training	Possible
4	Percentage of accommodation registered with ETC, AA or RAC Quality Assurance Scheme	OK
5	Percentage of accommodation registered as meeting National Accessible Scheme criteria for disabled people	OK
OVERALL HEALTH OF THE INDUSTRY		
6	Net domestic holiday spend	OK
7	Spend per person per night	Possible
8	Composition of tourism sector by business turnover and number of employees	Possible
9	Net change in the VAT registrations and deregistrations of tourism-related businesses, compared to other industries	OK
10	Contribution of holiday tourism to GDP (measured as the ratio of English holiday tourism spend to total UK GDP)	OK
11	Total spend per employee in the tourism sector	OK
12	Low season occupancy vs. high season occupancy	OK
13	Low season spend vs. high season spend	OK
BENEFICIAL TO THE LOCAL COMMUNITY		
14	Percentage of the total workforce employed in the tourism sector	OK
15	Ratio of average hourly earnings in tourism vs. the average national hourly wage	OK
16	Percentage of English adults not taking a holiday	Possible
17	Percentage of destinations with a community planning or LA21 strategy	N/A
18	Tourism spend by region	OK
19	Number of tourism-related planning applications accepted and declined	N/A
20	Audit of community perceptions of tourism	N/A
PROTECTING AND ENHANCING THE ENVIRONMENT		
21	Number of English beaches with a Blue Flag and a Seaside Award	OK
22	Percentage of UK residents using public transport for holiday trips	OK
23	Number of tourist destinations with local transport plans integrating visitor management	N/A
24	Carbon dioxide savings made by the tourism industry	OK
25	Tourism's contribution to the protection of built and natural assets	Possible
26	Number of businesses signed up to recognised environmental management schemes	Possible
27	Biodiversity indicator of natural areas	N/A

Key: OK = baseline data currently available; Possible = data available in next 12 months; N/A – data not available at present

REFERENCES

Custance, J. and Hillier, H. (1998) 'Statistical issues in developing indicators of sustainable development'. *Journal of the Royal Statistical Society,* Series A, 161, 281–90.

DCMS (1998) *Tourism: Towards Sustainability.* London: Department for Culture, Media and Sport.

DCMS (1999) *Tomorrow's Tourism.* London: Department for Culture, Media and Sport.

DCMS (forthcoming) *Sustainable Tourism Indicators: A Report Prepared for the Department of Culture, Media and Sport by CAG Consultants.* London: Department for Culture, Media and Sport.

Department of the Environment (1996) *Indicators of Sustainable Development for the United Kingdom.* London: The Stationery Office.

DETR (1999a) *A Better Quality of Life: A Strategy for Sustainable Development in the United Kingdom,* London: The Stationery Office.

DETR (1999b) *Quality of Life Counts: Indicators for a Strategy for Sustainable Development for the United Kingdom: A Baseline Assessment.* Rotherham: Department of the Environment, Transport and the Regions Publication Sales Centre.

ETC (forthcoming) *Wise Growth Indicators.* London: English Tourism Council.

Levett, R. (1998) 'Sustainability indicators: integrating quality of life and environmental protection'. *Journal of the Royal Statistical Society,* Series A, 161, 291–302.

Radermacher, W. (1999) 'Indicators, green accounting and environmental statistics: information requirements for sustainable development'. *International Statistical Review,* 67, 339–54.

UK Round Table on Sustainable Development (2000) *Indicators of Sustainable Development.* Wetherby: Department of the Environment, Transport and the Regions.

World Tourism Organization (1998) *Guide for Local Authorities on Developing Sustainable Tourism.* Madrid: World Tourism Organization.

15

A Practical Research Framework for Measuring Local Progress Towards More Sustainable Tourism on a Europe-wide Basis

Victor T.C. Middleton and Rebecca Hawkins

SYNOPSIS

This chapter reflects the experience of the authors throughout the 1990s, first as Director and Deputy Director of the World Travel and Tourism Environment Research Centre, established at Oxford Brookes University in 1991, and second, as consultants and authors in this field. It draws in particular on our book, *Sustainable Tourism: A Marketing Perspective* (1998), and work undertaken for the European Environment Agency (EEA) in 1999, in collaboration with Willi Sieber of the Austrian Institute of Applied Ecology. That work set out to provide a new analytical framework through which a series of indicators of more sustainable tourism could be developed and implemented in the short term in the context where it matters the most – the local tourism destination. In the UK context, local destination equates for all working purposes with local authority boundaries – or NUTS level 4/5 as it applies across EU countries.

The chapter questions the validity and practical utility of national indicators of more sustainable tourism. It proposes instead a framework of specific local indicators for the private sector of the tourism industry and for local authorities working together as key players in defining and helping to achieve more sustainable tourism. The focus on local rather than national indicators was endorsed unanimously in the consultation process that accompanied the work for the EEA and strongly endorsed at the UNCSD meeting in New York in April 1999.

Throughout the chapter we use the expression 'more sustainable' rather than 'sustainable' tourism to reflect the fact that many of the measurements we propose are not direct measures of the environmental inputs and outputs of the tourism industry because these cannot be measured at the present time. What they are is carefully chosen surrogate indicators designed to indicate progress (or the lack of it) toward a more sustainable future. We have regard throughout to the social and economic dimensions of environmental impact and management responses as well as to the physical environment. We endorse the World Tourism Organization view that indicators represent 'Information of which decision makers need to be aware to reduce the chances of unknowingly taking poor decisions . . . Selecting the right indicators reduces the wide range of potential information to a set of useable and meaningful measures' (WTO, 1995).

CONTEXT: THE COMPLEXITIES OF TOURISM DEMAND AND SUPPLY THAT UNDERMINE THE VALUE OF NATIONAL INDICATORS OF MORE SUSTAINABLE GROWTH

Over the last decade, since the Rio Summit of 1992 a range of initiatives have emerged to measure progress towards sustainable development in general. Based primarily on the development of indicators of physical environmental impact, these initiatives have drawn on an extensive range of research and assessments of good practice developed since the 1970s. Specifically, there is growing scientific understanding and measurement of the overall causal factors and impacts of global environmental issues, such as atmospheric pollution, global warming, desertification, marine pollution, loss of biodiversity and the contamination/pollution and depletion of fresh water supplies. It is already common practice that such factors and inputs are measured on an international and national basis.

Progress has also been made in measuring the physical and broader environmental impacts of specific sectors of economic activity, for example paper manufacturing, mining and automobile production processes. These global and macro-understandings and the accompanying research processes represent important progress and provide an effective platform for future development of measures and indicators of environmental performance. These measures and indicators in turn help us to understand and begin to monitor the effectiveness of policy responses such as the Kyoto Protocol (global warming) and Agenda 21 (sustainable development).

The range of measures and indicators that have been developed do not yet address the principal issues associated with measuring the overall impact of what many believe is, or will be, the 'World's Largest Industry' – travel and tourism.[1] There is, of course, a mass of circumstantial evidence that tourism activity and businesses providing tourism services contribute directly to global and local environmental and social problems (for example, marine pollution, loss of biodiversity, toxic wastes, wasteful consumption of freshwater and unsustainable use of energy). Tourism is also associated with positive contributions such as provision of infrastructure for wastewater treatment, creation of local employment, protection for fragile environments and support for culture.

Tourism impacts are, however, inseparable from overall impacts, because:

---

[1] Although a small number of initiatives have been established to devise such indicator sets, for example the initiative by the World Tourism Organization that commenced in 1995, many focus on the national level and require the collection/collation of a number of new data sets which do not, as yet, have standardized data collection processes in place.

- Tourism is not a discrete, measurable industry with self-contained demand and supply patterns and separately measurable impacts. Tourism is only partially identified directly in the Standard Industrial Classifications used by economists throughout Europe (NACE Rev. 1).
- As defined by WTO and the UN Statistical Commission (and endorsed by EU countries) tourism includes all who 'travel and stay in places outside their usual environment for leisure, business and other purposes'. The definition includes both stay and day visits, although no country measures both movements systematically, and traditional staying holidays are not always the majority element. Most countries are still unable to measure domestic tourism with any accuracy, although it is increasingly the larger part of all tourism in many European countries.
- As defined, tourism is an expression of the way of life of post-industrial societies, an integral part of the life style for over 90 per cent of the population of developed countries.
- As defined, the bulk of all tourism takes place in locations that are shared with residents with whom visitors inextricably mingle their demand for energy, water, use of transport, cultural, recreational, catering and retail facilities, and their outputs of sewerage and waste disposal. Residents and visitors are part of the same eco-impact system in which the components are mostly inseparable.
- Although holiday destinations are found mainly in coastal, rural, mountain and urban heritage environments, tourism in its multiple forms affects virtually all communities, including visits for business, speciality retailing and social purposes such as families and friends.
- Tourism supply is dominated numerically by SMEs (98 per cent of all enterprises in the sector) with a minimum estimate of 1.46 million businesses in western Europe already employing at least 10 million people. Middleton has elsewhere identified the reasons why it is statistically impossible at present to identify the actual number of such businesses with any statistical accuracy.

Taken together these issues make it evident that, in the light of shrinking public sector budgets for tourism research activity, we are unlikely to be in a position to develop a practical framework through which the relative inputs and subsequent impacts of the tourism industry on the environment or communities in which it operates can be measured effectively at a national level. At national level measurement of the extent of tourism impacts is often not a high priority. At local level, however, the positive and/or negative impacts of the industry on the environment and community can have significant implications for the quality of the tourism experience. They can also have a significant impact on the overall long-term viability of the destination and the industry it supports.

THE NEED FOR A PRACTICAL, LOCAL ANALYTICAL FRAMEWORK

There is growing recognition in all countries that the tourism industry has a vested interest in sustaining and enhancing the quality of the local environment on which it trades. We believe this to be a significant attitude shift over the last decade, which is especially, but not only, true for holiday and leisure tourism. Polluted, eroded, over-built resorts will simply not attract the more demanding customers of the twenty-first century who now have almost infinite destination choices that are literally global.

There is also growing recognition, although the implications are not yet widely pursued, that the tourism industry has a direct responsibility for environmental protection and that tourism activity can, in principle, be managed positively to enhance and protect key aspects of the physical, social and cultural environment. It does so through the revenue and employment it contributes, typically available from no other source, especially not from increasing levels of EU and government subsidy. In 2000, however, indicators are not capable of systematically and reliably measuring and monitoring either the negative or the positive impacts of tourism on the environment.

The principal missing link is effective measurement of tourism volume, impact and response at the destination or local level, where the great bulk of all tourism impacts focus in practice. Although Local Agenda 21 programmes are now being developed across Europe, we are not aware of any systematic framework for measuring and including tourism in that process.

As this chapter is finalized, there is an international proposal currently being processed concerning Local Sustainable Tourism Indicators. This chapter has been submitted for funding under the EU's Fifth Framework Research Programme (Eurostat, 1999–2002). This proposal has been developed by an international consortium (including one of the authors of this chapter) led by David James of Global Tourism Solutions (UK) Ltd who has extensive direct experience of the local methodology for tourism and who also chairs a British Resorts Association Sustainable Tourism Working Group.

A NEW CONCEPTUAL APPROACH FOR MEASURING MORE SUSTAINABLE TOURISM: THE RATIONALE FOR LOCAL INDICATORS

International research into the State of the Environment has led to extensive measurement of key impacts, such as overall outputs of CO_2, CH_4, CFCs, SO_2, NO_x, SO_x, coliform counts in bathing water and loss of biodiversity (WHO data). But it is not possible to calculate reliably at national level the proportion of these impacts due to modern tourism. This is partly because of the ubiquitous nature of tourism. It also partly reflects the fragmented nature of tourism supply (this is an 'industry' identified only by its demand) and the fact that very few countries have yet established continuous measures of all types of tourism at any level. No country has yet established a comprehensive continuous system for measuring all forms of day and staying visits at destination level.

It follows logically that, if it is not possible to measure and monitor the volume of tourism with any accuracy, it is not possible to measure even the physical environmental impacts of an unknown quantity (let alone the more complex social and economic impacts that must also be embraced by sustainable development). Moreover, even in the sectors of tourism where the total volume can be measured with acceptable accuracy, tourism movement is not a homogenous movement in which, say, a 10 per cent increase in volume causes a similar increase in environmental impact.

Impact is a function of the type of visitors and the activities in which they engage. Ten thousand senior citizens in serviced accommodation, travelling by public transport and resting and relaxing around a swimming pool and bar in a purpose-built modern hotel may create only minimal environmental damage. By contrast, just 500 active and regular walkers or skiers may significantly erode fragile environments. By bringing private transport and ski-lifts into fragile areas en route, as well as at the desired location, they may cause long-term damage to the environment they choose. Paradoxically, more tourism may mean proportionally less environmental damage in this case.

In other words, to generate realistic national strategies and programmes for more sustainable tourism and to monitor their success over time – the primary reason for indicators – it would be necessary accurately to measure and monitor the volume of tourism visits by type and purpose. This cannot be done in 2000 and is unlikely to be achieved in an environment of reduced public sector investment in tourism research activity.

RATIONALE FOR LOCAL INDICATORS

If it is not practical at this stage to develop comparable statistical indictors for more sustainable tourism at national level, it is vital to focus on the local or destination level. It is at specific destinations within local government boundaries, where the impact of tourism is most evident and best understood. It is also at destinations where national and international legal and regulatory techniques for planning and visitor management can have the greatest influence. We believe the destination focus is practical and provides the best route to early progress and comparability in Europe.

- By the nature of their work local authorities already know and most co-operate with tourism businesses operating locally, who typically need LA support for planning and development and have to undergo a range of inspections and licensing processes for business operations. Typically, at any well-known visitor destination, there is already an extensive background of co-operation between public and private sector and supportive linkages with representative bodies such as Chambers of Commerce and Tourism Forums. The vital public sector/private sector collaborative links already exist for developing practical local indicators.
- All local authorities in the EU have a duty to reflect the needs and interests of the populations or 'host communities' they serve as part of the normal democratic process. They are required to act as agents of national government for environmental purposes and they also possess extensive environmental data on the activities of local populations, which can assist in unravelling the particular impact of tourism from the general impact of host communities and their leisure/recreation activities. The environmental, planning and regulatory links with national governments and with the EU are already in operation and mostly well developed.
- Although local authorities are the chosen institutions for the exercise of statutory and regulatory powers, there is increasing recognition that forms of self-regulation through voluntary initiatives by commercial enterprises will be a vital element of any successful development and implementation of more sustainable practice. Public sector/private sector collaboration at local level provides the essential forum for the effective development of self-regulation alongside regulatory powers.
- Since 1995/6 Local Agenda 21 initiatives based on national and international legal and regulatory techniques are being actively developed and co-ordinated across Europe and internationally through ICLEI in Europe. Although tourism is generally not yet a standard heading in local Agenda 21 programmes, it is clearly relevant as an important and sometimes a leading sector of the economy in popular

tourist destinations. The local Agenda 21 process provides an internationally recognised, rapidly developing framework of environmental thinking and activity, in which it is possible to develop new ideas and in due course compare them more widely.

CRITERIA FOR AN ANALYTICAL, INTERNATIONALLY ENDORSED FRAMEWORK BASED ON LOCAL INDICATORS

Assuming that local indicators of sustainable tourism are to be endorsed and effectively collected, they must meet the following criteria:

- practical/achievable/measurable in year 2000 (understood by local authorities and by businesses and currently measured/easy to measure with existing procedures/ staff, for example chief engineers in large hotels);
- simple and unambiguous (can be built easily into existing procedures with no/ minimum additional cost);
- relevant to business interests (advantageous to adopt – potential cost saving or facilitation of compliance with existing/anticipated regulation);
- collaborative, recognising that public/private sector partnership is essential to produce effective results with a transparency and involvement of local communities that all will accept. Collaboration extends also to representative bodies for tourism businesses such as Chambers of Commerce and Trade Associations;
- robust/defensible/justifiable/reliable, using carefully tested definitions and data collection methods to ensure that resulting data is accurate, transparent and comparable and is defensible; for example against criticism by environmental pressure groups;
- capable of adaptation for application to small and micro-enterprises in tourism.

CRITERIA FOR THE PRIVATE SECTOR

Reflecting the Agenda adopted for the UNCSD meeting in New York in April 1999, the priorities for the private sector approach to more sustainable development in tourism should embrace:

1. design and management for more sustainable business operations – indicators should also be capable of producing quantified, internationally comparable statistics, based on operational metering and other measurements, that take place routinely. Some highly desirable indicators have to be rejected because they cannot be made operational and comparable on a European basis or because a simple question cannot be phrased to produce a statistically reliable response;
2. management processes to increase awareness and response to environmental issues. The management responses are inevitably less precise and typically have to be based on replies to annual questionnaires;
3. developing partnerships for sustainable development, especially partnerships with local authorities. Information about partnerships is also based on replies to annual questionnaires;

4. developing partnerships for sustainable development within trade associations, chambers of commerce and local tourism forums (as above).

In total, the work developed for the European Environment Agency by the authors proposed detailed lists of indicators of more sustainable tourism that could be applied to three specific types of tourism businesses. These were: tour operators; visitor attractions; and hotels.

These businesses, increasingly, have a significant level of awareness of the range of sustainable development issues that affect their operations. This is especially the case where environmental management processes are perceived to influence the quality of the product businesses are able to offer within the destination. For the larger businesses at least, many already have basic procedures in place to track the level of impact on the environment (and sometimes the community) within which they operate.

In total, the indicators proposed embrace more than 40 measures, many of which are already taken routinely by the larger tourism businesses and which can easily be adapted and transferred to the smaller organizations.

INDICATIVE INDICATORS OF MORE SUSTAINABLE PRACTICE FOR HOTELS

The following eight indicators to measure good management were proposed as relevant to the hotel sector:

1. formal (published) statement of commitment by the hotel to the environment, which can be made available to the public;
2. formal statement of commitment displayed in public area(s) of each hotel (if more than one);
3. named individual with responsibility for environmental matters at corporate level or within each individual hotel;
4. inclusion of environmental information as a standard component in formal training/induction courses for staff;
5. targets and programmes set annually by hotels with agreed system of monitoring for:
    - energy consumption (kWh) per square metre;
    - waste volume (weight/volume sent to landfill/dumped per guest per night);
    - fresh water consumption (volume in cubic metres per guest per night);
    - waste water treatment, retention and re-use (percentage re-used);
    - percentage of sewage waste treated in either a municipal or town plant (BoD at point of discharge);
    - purchase of environmentally friendly chemical products (volume of bleaches and caustic cleaners used/use of bulk dispensers);
    - use and disposal of toxic wastes (total volume disposed of; weight of stored CFCs);
    - programme in place for local community involvement (money, staff time, materials, local purchasing);
    - customer satisfaction monitoring on a regular basis with questions on environmental aspects of stay;
6. membership of an independently certified ecolabel scheme;
7. information/advice about the destination, its wildlife, culture and local crafts included in hotel brochure and distributed to visitors in bedrooms;

8. representation on local tourism forum which includes the municipality and other tourism businesses in the locality.

In general terms, hotels that undertake at least five of these roles, including most of point 5, can be assumed to have a formal environmental programme in place.

DEVELOPMENT AND OPERATION OF THE PRIVATE SECTOR INDICATORS

Each of the eight criteria above are capable of practical definition, understanding and quantification by hoteliers. Such data is already collected and used internally by many of the larger hotel companies. Many medium-sized businesses are rapidly implementing programmes to collect much of this data, especially responding the opportunities to save costs.

In terms of the development of the indicators, it is recommended that the data is collected (in confidence) through a hotel association or tourism association from, say, the ten largest hotels in selected destinations. Assuming an average of 200 bedspaces per establishment, at an occupancy of 70 per cent, this alone will generate important evidence from around half a million visitor nights a year. Totals (averages) only should be made available to the local tourism forum in a way that does not identify the performance of specific businesses. The hotels, selected for inclusion by the tourist association working with the official organizations supporting the destination, will be asked to respond to questionnaires sent direct to the general managers.

Results can provide benchmarks of performance, which help hoteliers to identify the potential they have for both performance improvement and cost savings.

One such initiative that is currently under way, by the International Hotels Environment Initiative (IHEI) and Worldwide Fund for Nature (WWF–UK), with sponsorship from Biffaward, amongst others, has produced a benchmarking tool that effectively operationalizes the indicator set. Available through the internet from October 2000, this tool will be designed to help any hotelier to:

- identify their current level of environmental/social input;
- compare their input to 'industry norms' (relevant to their specific hotel type and climate band);
- calculate the cost savings they could achieve if they reduced their resource consumption to the level of the 'industry norm';
- identify the techniques and technologies that will help them to reduce their level of impact; and
- record their performance year-on-year to ensure they are moving towards sustainability.

For example: consider the case of a five-star luxury hotel that seeks to establish how good or bad it is in environmental management terms and, in this case, as regards water consumption. The hotel may enter the website and enter its current water consumption data from its water bills. The computer is programmed to request answers to a series of questions that reveal as an illustration that it:

- has 200–800 rooms;
- operates at 1.1 to 1.5 guests per occupied room and at 55–90 per cent year-round occupancy;
- operates full HVAC;

- has a heated indoor swimming pool with a surface area of up to 150 m^2 and a health suite;
- has a laundry processing around 7.5 kg per occupied room per day;
- produces 2.5 covers per guest (including employee meals).

Taking all of these factors into account, the system will calculate that the hotel currently consumes 0.86 m^3 of water per guest per night. This compares poorly to other similar hotels recorded in the system with the best consumption level for a similar property being recorded at 0.50 m^3 per guest night.

The computer asks the hotelier to enter the cost of 1 m^3 of water, which is in this case $0.60. It then generates an estimate of the total cost saving that could be achieved if the hotelier used water more efficiently (at the best or satisfactory level) and continued to operate at current occupancy. In this case for a hotel which is open year-round, at the best level, the total saving if it improves its performance in line with the best hotel could sum to $0.23 per guest night or $10,493 over a full year. This figure is an underestimate as it does not take into account the current costs of heating, pumping, storing or treating water.

Techniques that may be relevant to this specific hotelier could include changes in cleaning practices, installation of low-flow shower heads and aerators to taps and installations of timing devices to taps in all public areas.

Tools of this nature have considerable potential to operationalize the indicator sets and to provide private companies with the incentive to improve their sustainability performance.

Other similar initiatives have also been launched for specific aspects of hotels' environmental performance. For example, the government has recently launched a partnership initiative with the Hotel and Catering International Management Association (HCIMA) to recruit 7500 hotels in the UK and provide them with targeted advice to help them reduce their energy consumption (and associated greenhouse gas emissions), while monitoring their performance. The programme is the first voluntary energy efficiency agreement launched by the government as a part of its quest to meet the commitments made at the Kyoto meeting. It has significant potential to help hotels reduce both cost and environmental impacts.

INDICATIVE INDICATORS RELEVANT TO MORE SUSTAINABLE TOURISM FOR LOCAL AUTHORITIES

Twelve indicators to measure impact and good management practice among local authorities are proposed. The potential candidate list of measures that could shed some light on sustainable issues is a long one. The recommended *minimum* practical list of selected indicators for measuring tourism demand and supply and the management responses of local authorities is noted below. The main items below could be used to establish a series of additional indicators such as comparative ratios per head of population, area of land developed for tourism use, expenditure by local authorities on tourism etc.

Tourism supply and demand related indicators (essential estimates to monitor more sustainable development)

1. estimated number of *known* tourist bed spaces available separately in hotels, apartments, holiday villages, campsites (pitches only), marinas and second homes – in total and expressed as ratios of beds per head of residential population and per acre/hectare;
2. estimates of occupancy by month for the main categories of commercially provided accommodation;
3. estimated number and expenditure of staying visitors (tourists) – annual and busiest/lowest months;
4. estimated number and expenditure of day visitors – annual and busiest/lowest months;
5. staying visitors by type – business, holiday, other (following Eurostat/WTO classifications);
6. modal split for transport used to reach the destination – for staying and day visitors separately.

Local authority tourism management response indicators

7. (a) Is research or a formal estimation/model process in operation (annually or less frequently) to monitor the volume of day and staying visitors and the principal segments of tourism?
   (b) Is research or a formal estimation/model process in operation (annually or less frequently) to measure income and employment generation from tourism (direct, indirect and induced)?
   (c) Can measures of tourism jobs per head of local population be compared with other sectors of local employment (full-time and part-time)?
8. Has a Blue Flag/other destination relevant 'ecolabel' been applied for/granted (how many years in last ten has it been achieved?)
9. Is there a Local Agenda 21 programme in place? Does it include tourism? (see also 12 below)
10. Does a local tourism forum exist comprising the main private and public sector interests? Does the forum contribute to agreeing goals, targets and action plans for the local environment and to monitoring positive and negative impacts?
11. (a) Is there a formal Tourism Management Plan available as part of an overall plan for the LA with specific (measurable) goals and a formal monitoring process?
    (b) What are the annual budget and full-time staff numbers allocated to any aspect of tourism planning and environmental control and management by the local authority?
    (c) Which of the following have been in active operation in the last twelve months (illustrations only)?
    – capacity limit set for target number of beds;
    – zoning for tourism development;
    – control of capacity through licensing;
    – restrictions applied to reduce visitor cars;
    – environmental information for local businesses;
    – environmental information for visitors.

12. Are specific environmental design criteria applied for new planning permissions (e.g. for energy, water efficiency, waste control and sewage treatment) ? Are such criteria applied for granting annual licences to tourism businesses and for environmental control inspection purposes?

ROLE FOR NATIONAL AND REGIONAL PARTNERS TO FACILITATE IMPLEMENTATION OF LOCAL INDICATORS

We have been critical of the development and validity of national indicators because we see them as a diversion of energy and resources from the primary focus on the local level. Yet we fully recognize and endorse the role for national, regional and international tourism organizations to promote, facilitate and help co-ordinate the measurement processes established locally. The practical action, on the ground, takes place locally. But there are obvious needs for co-ordination in agreeing what is to be measured, how it is to be measured, how the measures are to be reported and so on. There may also be a need to support the action with seconded expertise and some access to funding. We see this as a bottom-up process, however, based on collaborating local authorities and businesses operating locally, not a top-down process imposed upon them by national bodies.

We stress, in particular, that the willingness of destinations to participate proactively in the indicators process and their desire to make environmental improvements are more important than what is currently known about the volume and value of tourism and the impacts it has on the environment.

CONCLUSIONS

This chapter has highlighted the necessity to target and support the process of collecting information on progress towards more sustainable development at the level at which it is most important – the local destination level. Apart from the validity issue, budget and data resources to measure tourism impacts systematically do not exist at the national level. Even where some data is collected (bearing in mind that few if any countries have a realistic prospect of measuring overall tourism demand as defined by international agreements) the issues of isolating and quantifying the tourism effects separately from the associated effects of resident use, recreation and leisure use etc. appear insuperable. It is difficult to see what practical decisions and action guidance will emerge from it.

At a local level, however, the functional overlap between the quality of the tourism experience and of the natural and cultural environment makes the establishment of such indicators a fundamental priority. Businesses and tourism authorities are already collaborating at this level and have both the incentive and capacity to begin the development of realistic sets of indicators. The understanding of the necessary management processes is sufficiently advanced from the many international *good practice* case studies that are now available to support the process of compiling the practical indicators. They are vital for the future prosperity of private and public sector partners in tourism at the destination level.

This chapter has presented a practical 'bottom-up' analytical framework through which, given the political will, it would be possible to commence the compilation of indicators within a matter of weeks rather than months or years. The authors have no doubt that the process will change and evolve over time with the assistance of tools, such as that currently under development by IHEI and WWF–UK. Such evolution is to be welcomed and will enhance the understanding of sustainable development and contribute to the broader debate, highlighting the real influence that tourism can make in bringing about more sustainable forms of development.

We recognize, of course, that specification of realistic local indicators of more sustainable tourism is certain to call for a range of information, much of which will not actually be available at most destinations in the first year of implementation. Lack of data will especially affect local authorities. But this is a fact of life. The choice of indicators will serve as a statement of information that will be needed over, say, a five-year build-up period, as well as a call for information already available. The first year's responses to indicators will provide information on the current state of the art locally and establish comparable benchmarks for monitoring progress toward more sustainable tourism. Such information will provide vital comparisons for local authorities and for destinations of a broadly comparable type, for example urban, rural and coastal destinations. The rate at which the initially chosen indicators can be implemented in practice will, of itself, be an indicator of progress over time.

Indicators must serve, therefore, both as benchmarks and the means of measuring on a regular, continuing basis:

- the positive and negative environmental impacts made by tourism/tourism businesses;
- the responses made by tourism businesses and local authorities to tackle and ameliorate negative inputs and enhance the positive gains.

We believe that the process of collecting and evaluating local indicators will have marketing, product development and host community development implications through tourism that far transcend the statistical issues. Being committed to an internationally relevant and endorsed process that underpins the future of the 'world's largest industry' should be communicated as a mark of pride, commitment and significant achievement locally.

REFERENCES

The following are sources consulted in the compilation of this chapter.

CEC (1992) *Towards Sustainability: A European Community Programme of Policy and Action in Relation to the Environment and Sustainable Development*, [Com(92)23]. Brussels.

CEC (DG XI) (1993) *Environment and Tourism in the Context of Sustainable Development.* Brussels.

CEC (DG XXIII) (1995) *Tourism and the Environment in Europe.* Brussels.

CEC (Eurostat) (1997) *Community Methodology on Tourism Statistics* (Part 3: Tourism and the Environment). Luxemburg.

DRV (1996) *Environment Recommendations for Tourist Destination Areas: Mediterranean Countries.* Frankfurt.

ECoNett, World Travel and Tourism Council with DGXXIII, website at http://www.wttc.org.

EEA (1994) *Europe's Environment: The DOBRIS Assessment.* Copenhagen: EEA (with UNCE, UNEP, OECD, Council of Europe, WHO, IUCN and Eurostat).

EEA (1997) *Tourism and Environment: Assessment Report (Ingergerd Fangstrom)*. Report commissioned from Statistics Sweden. Copenhagen: EEA.

Environment Strategy Europe: The Way Forward after Maestricht (1996) London: Campden Publishing.

European Union for Coastal Conservation (1997) *The European Coastal Code*. Leiden (Netherlands).

International Federation of Tour Operators (IFTO) (1994) *Planning for Sustainable Tourism: The ECOMOST Project*. Lewes: IFTO.

International Hotels and Restaurants Association and UNEP (1996) *Environmental Good Practice in Hotels*. Paris: UNEP.

International Hotels Environment Initiative (1995) *Environmental Action Pack for Hotels*. London: IHEI.

International Institute for Environment and Development (1993) *Modified EIA and Indicators of Sustainability IIED* (Environmental Planning Issues No.1). London.

IUCN (1991) *Caring for Earth: A Strategy for Sustainable Living*. Geneva: IUCN (with UNEP and WWF).

Mediterranean Commission on Sustainable Development (1998) *Tourism and Sustainable Development in the Mediterranean Region* (MEDPLAN) (Conference at Antalya). See also the Overview report issued in May 1998 with the same title.

McIntyre, G. (1994) *Sustainable Tourism Development: A Guide for Local Planners*. Madrid: World Tourism Organization.

Middleton V. T. C. (1998) 'SMEs in European tourism 'Agenda 2010' '. *Review de Tourisme*, **4**. St Gallen: AIEST.

Middleton, V. T. C. and Hawkins, R. (1998) *Sustainable Tourism: A Marketing Perspective*. Oxford: Butterworth-Heinemann.

Pearce, F. (1995) 'Dead in the water'. *New Scientist*, 4 February.

Plan Bleu (with UNEP) (1998) *A Blue Plan for the Mediterranean Peoples: From Ideas to Action*. Valbonne: Plan Bleu Centre.

Tourism Council for Australia (1997) *Coastal Tourism: Sustainable Development*. Canberra: Department of the Environment, Sport and Territories.

UNCED (1992) *AGENDA 21: A Guide to the United Nations Conference on Environment and Development*. Geneva: UN Publications.

UNEP (1998) *Ecolabels in the Tourism Industry*. Paris: UNEP.

World Commission on Environment and Development (1987) *Our Common Future* (The Brundtland Report). Oxford: OUP.

World Tourism Organization (1995) *Tourism and Environment Indicators*. Madrid: WTO.

World Travel and Tourism Council (1996) *AGENDA 21 for the Travel & Tourism Industry: Towards Environmentally Sustainable Development* (with WTO and the Earth Council). London: WTTC.

WTTC (1996) *The Green Globe* (series of sectoral guidelines for more sustainable travel and tourism businesses). London: WTTC.

16

Local Sustainable Tourism Indicators

David James[1]

INTRODUCTION

At the Fourth International Forum on Sustainable Tourism Statistics, in Copenhagen, 1998, the final plenary session discussed the need for more work on Sustainable Tourism Indicators and discussion of resulting papers at subsequent forums. This chapter is one such contribution and consists of four parts:

1. Local sustainable tourism indicators
2. The issue and principles of sustainability
3. The need for local sustainable tourism indicators
4. The European Local Area Sustainable Tourism Indicators Project

BACKGROUND

In 1997 the British Resorts Association assembled a working group of persons and organizations concerned and engaged in the issues of sustainable development within the tourism sector (The British Resorts Association Sustainable Tourism Working Group (BRASTWG).

Its mission statement is: 'To develop tourism opportunities that leave the visitor, the visited and the environment, (whether natural, built or cultural), enriched by the experience.'

To support this, the BRASTWG has adopted evolving three-year workplans reflecting the following strategy statement:

---

[1] The authorship of this chapter draws on, and presents, the contributions of the many friends and colleagues of the British Resorts Association Sustainable Tourism Working Group, together with its related Indicators Group, and also the European Local Area Sustainable Tourism Indicators Consortium.

'The Working Group, in collaboration with a broad range of partners, will work to develop a synergetic effort between governments, destinations and the travel and tourism industries to identify and encourage good sustainable tourism practice and action.'

The strategy is supported by five strands of action, of which one is: 'To develop appropriate benchmarking programmes locally, nationally and internationally.'

In considering this it became clear that for benchmarking to happen effectively, such a process required to be underpinned by Local Sustainable Tourism Indicators (LSTI) which could demonstrate the relationships and interplay of tourism impacts as measured in respect of the economic effects, environmental effects and social effects for the local community.

This approach was adopted because National/International Sustainable Tourism Indicators would, of necessity, be broad and could not fully inform the myriad of local destination typologies. Because of the wide range of destination typologies, a need for an array of LSTI exists coupled with their linkage to clear, locally developed policies and strategy outcomes.

In June 1999 the attention of BRASTWG was drawn to the Fifth Framework Research Programme of the European Union (FP5). The purpose of this programme is to develop and demonstrate new statistical tasks and methods in application and to develop indicators in the 'New Economy'. Subsequently, the European Local Area Statistics Consortium (ELASTIC) was formed, and in January 2000 a project proposal was submitted within the Fifth Framework Research Programme.

LOCAL SUSTAINABLE TOURISM INDICATORS: WHAT, WHY, WHO, WHERE, WHEN?

The vision

In the tourism sector, tourism indicators have been developed primarily at the macro-level driven by the need of central governments to have quantitative data in respect of the value and volume impacts to drive central policy formulation. At the local level this need has been less well served historically. With the advent of new technology, the needs of the 'New Economy' and the greater ability and need for small to medium-sized enterprises to interface constructively and effectively with governments, agencies and macro-enterprises, greater opportunities exist for innovative programmes to be introduced. Whether by new methods of work, new tools and methods, making old tasks lighter, using old data and methodology differently, the demand for more information is a growing and accelerating imperative.

With the abundance and immediacy of new information becoming available, there are growing needs to use the new technology to simplify tasks, not further complicate them. The transition from an industrial economy to an information-based economy exacts the challenge to examine whether existing statistics and surrounding methodologies remain chained to past thinking or will benefit from new concepts; for example, Can the 'New Economy' itself be the new data source? The project will explore to what extent the new data emanating from the Digital Economy can be exploited.

It is vital to investigate and provide answers and solutions to these changes and needs in an economic sector that is relevant to most economies: tourism – an economic sector which, more than most, demands sustainable development and the means to track such development consistently across political barriers and through time.

BRASTWG, associated with ELASTIC, seek, by virtue of a multi-skilled partnership drawn internationally from government, academia and practitioners, to create new approaches to old and new problems/opportunities in the tourism sector.

The primary objectives adopted for the project are:

1. to create an array of Local Sustainable Tourism Indicators;
2. to ensure that the concepts of Sustainable Tourism Indicators are applicable to a wide range of local environments;
3. to identify the linkage between Local Sustainable Tourism Indicators and those that are applicable regionally, nationally and internationally.

The supporting objectives are:

1. to survey the available literature and experience to decide on the most appropriate themes and the issues emerging from them, and to undertake qualitative interviews with experts in the field;
2. to test the created array of LSTI internationally in a variety of destination types;
3. to create appropriate user-oriented software to ensure effective skills improvement and transfers to the local level;
4. by use of an interactive website, to create an open international forum to engage the expertise of an array of international experts, local destination practitioners, and all levels of government, academia and the tourism industry.

The establishment of the project's primary and supporting objectives derive from a number of unrelated, yet linked, initiatives. These initiatives have had at their heart the need to establish macro-sustainable tourism indicators but, in each case, have concluded in questioning how the development of LSTI might serve the needs of the future and a broader international audience, both simply and affordably.

To do this effectively, senior academics, government officials and senior tourism practitioners of six countries will be working in partnership with a variety of destination types necessary and willing to assist the development and testing of an array of LSTI. Initially, the destination types include at least two examples of each drawn from six countries. They are: major cities; urban tourist destinations; urban non-tourist destinations; rural tourist destinations; rural non-tourist destinations; national parks, seaside and island destinations.

Description of the partnership

The partnership referred to above is made up of the following organizations listed below:

1. Global Tourism Solutions UK Ltd (GTS);
2. Geoff Broom Associates (GB) from the UK;
3. Research Centre of Bornholm (RCB) from Denmark;
4. Centro Internazionale di Studi e richerche sull'Economia Turistica (CISET) from Italy;
5. Central Office of Statistics of Malta (COS);
6. Department for Culture, Media and Sport (DCMS) from the UK.

GTS is a UK company specializing in tourism planning and the modelling of tourism flows at the local authority level. Its directors have both theoretical and applied expertise in tourism development and the operational management of tourism projects. GB is a consultancy partnership which has similar aims and objectives to GTS and has a long track record in local tourism planning. The RCB is a state-funded research institute specializing in regional development with a particular emphasis on tourism in northern European destinations. CISET is part of the University of Venice and is primarily involved with the economics of tourism, but in the broader sense, so as to encompass issues of sustainability.

COS and DCMS are government departments, which have the responsibility for the provision of tourism statistics and have a direct interest in the production of LSTI for managing the development outcomes of the 'New Economy'.

THE ISSUE AND PRINCIPLES OF SUSTAINABILITY

The issue of sustainability

The issue of sustainability[2] is one that is relevant to all economic systems and even more so as our economy moves from an industrial one towards the 'New Economy' in the next millennium. This fact is particularly pertinent to the tourism sector in the European Communities. Much interest and work has started to be addressed to sustainable tourism at the European[3] and International level[4] over the past years. The Amsterdam Treaty puts sustainable development at the core of EU's objectives.

Many countries and local authorities[5] are starting to reflect on the meaning of sustainable tourism and to seek indicators. They investigate how the existing statistical data can be better exploited, and what new data sources are becoming, or will be, available in the future due to the fast developments in the 'New Economy'. Indeed the UK has been particularly active. Various local and regional authorities across Europe and beyond Europe are developing initiatives alone that would better come to fruition if this complementary know-how is shared. Pooling resources and knowledge to develop these indicators at European level will add value to the existing initiatives undertaken in the individual European countries and by taking a harmonized approach will lead to comparable results.

One of the main intentions of the project is to contribute to developing a set of Local Sustainable Tourism Indicators that can be applied across regions and across nations. Because there is a general need to analyse the significance and sustainability of tourism, developing a set of standardized indicators is an important tool to assist the decision-

---

[2] The European Community Fifth Environmental Action Programme defines sustainable development as a harmonious and balanced economic and social development without detriment to the natural resources on the quality of which human activity and further development depend, 1993.

[3] European Commission, *Towards Sustainability*, ISBN 92-827-9471-7.

[4] United Nations, Agenda 21, Chapter 36 'Promoting education, public awareness and training', Paragraph 10: 'Countries should promote, as appropriate, environmentally sound leisure and tourism activities, building on The Hague Declaration of Tourism (1989) and the current programmes of the World Tourism Organization and UNEP'.

[5] Agenda 21 Chapter 28 on Local Authorities paragraph 1: 'As the level of governance closest to the people, Local Authorities play a vital role in educating, mobilising and responding to public to promote sustainable development.'

making process. Such decision-making will be of major concern to policy-makers and enterprises working in a local, regional, national, Community and international context. Among many considerations, LSTI will be useful to:

- community policies related to regional and tourism-related issues (e.g. structural funds, Community tourism initiatives);
- national policies to compare and contrast the development and performance of their regions with other regions of the EEA and other countries such as CECs and Mediterranean countries;
- regional actors concerned with comparing tourism with other regions within their own country and with other regions of the EEA and other countries such as CECs and Mediterranean countries;
- businesses, particularly those related to the tourism sector.

The EU Directive 95/57/EC[6] on tourism statistics provides for basic statistical information that can be used as an input to developing sustainable tourism indicators. Moreover, there exists in most countries a wealth of data on tourism or related to tourism that should be further explored and exploited at European level.

The 1997 report of the Strategic Advisory Group on the Fifth Framework Programme on Information Society applications for transport and associated services on 'Information Society Technologies for Tourism'[7] clearly outlines the importance of tourism for Europe and its R&TD need. The report defines database mining, statistics and analysis as enabling technology and methodology for capacity management (at local and regional level) and for monitoring, planning and forecasting. Moreover, the report recognizes that advanced levels of research and technology required in the tourism sector cannot be afforded by European regions separately and must be supported as well as co-ordinated at European level through European co-operation.

Principles for the sustainable development of tourism

- The environment has an intrinsic value which outweighs its value as a tourism asset. Its enjoyment by future generations and its long-term survival must not be prejudiced by short-term considerations.
- Sustainable Tourism should be recognized as a positive activity with the potential to benefit the community and the place, as well as the visitor.
- The relationship between tourism and the environment must be managed so that it is sustainable in the long term. Tourism must not be allowed to damage the resource, prejudice its future enjoyment or bring unacceptable impacts.
- Tourism activities and developments should respect the scale, nature and character of the place in which they are sited.
- In any location, harmony must be sought between the needs of the visitor, the place and the host community.
- In a dynamic world some change is inevitable, and change can often be beneficial. Adaptation to change, however, should not be at the expense of any of these principles.
- The tourism industry, local authorities and environmental agencies all have a duty

---

[6] OJ L 291, page 32 of 06.12.95
[7] 'Think Tank on IST for Tourism'. V. 5.1 final. 08.12.97

to respect the above principles and to work together to achieve their practical realisation.

THE NEED FOR LOCAL SUSTAINABLE TOURISM INDICATORS

Introduction

The fundamental need for LSTI is to demonstrate change that has occurred over a period of time, whether engineered or by chance. Given that the majority of decision-making in tourism is at the micro- or local level, it is necessary that an array of LSTI are created which have local meaning but wider comparison. For this to happen, multi-disciplined and multi-focus partnerships need to work in a defined structure and their relationship is fundamental to success because no one player has the ability to deliver all the necessary programmes to achieve the necessary sustainability goals and objectives.

The process of policy determination, objective setting, programme delivery and performance evaluation will require a global framework encompassing national, regional and local spheres of influence, so that all stakeholders will have a sense of ownership and greater commitment. Equally it is important that the consumer, however defined, is involved in the process. Applicable to all of the issues is the need to answer a general question: 'What's in it for me?', and for that answer to be given simply and positively with good humour.

It is important to note that, at its meeting, 6–7 June 1995, in Madrid, the WTO Environment Committee considered a paper on 'Tourism and Environment Indicators'. Two sets of indicators were identified: 'Core Indicators of Sustainable Tourism', and 'Destination-Specific Indicators'.

The required Core Indicators of Sustainable Tourism are: site protection; stress; use intensity; social impact; development control; waste management; planning process; critical ecosystems; consumer satisfaction; and tourism contribution to the local economy.

The 'Destination-specific' indices identified were: carrying capacity; site stress; and attractivity.

These indicators were coupled to other 'building blocks' in the process, which included: planning framework for tourism; monitoring; standards accountability; and reporting.

There is widespread agreement that tourism as an activity is unlikely ever to be wholly sustainable in the strict sense of the term. We bear in mind that the total volume of day and staying visits defined as tourism by WTO/UN cannot be measured accurately in any country at the present time and that commitment to tourism growth is typically a government objective for economic and social reasons. There is equally widespread agreement, however, that the activities engaged in by visitors and the businesses and public sector agencies that supply services to them, can be conducted in future in ways that are significantly more sustainable – or less sustainable – than at present.

We adopt the broad view of sustainable development set out in the UK Department for the Environment, Transport and the Regions (DETR) consultation paper which embraces indicators for the economic, social and physical environment and stresses the linkages. Conceptually, we believe that more sustainable tourism – either at a given destination or nationally – means managing the cumulative effect of visitor activities together with the activities of the servicing businesses in ways that can continue into the foreseeable future without damaging the quality of the environment on which the activities are based. Such a definition can accommodate developments in science and technology that will ameliorate negative effects, and in visitor management that will also help harness the beneficial effects.

Background

In tourism terms, the World Tourism Organization defines sustainability in this manner: 'Sustainable tourism development meets the needs of present tourists and host regions while protecting and enhancing opportunities for the future' (WTO, 1995). It is envisaged as leading to the management of all resources in such a way that the economic, social, and aesthetic needs can be fulfilled, while maintaining cultural integrity, essential ecological processes, biological diversity and life-support systems. Much has been written on the concepts of sustainable tourism and interest is now turning towards the practical implementation of the various concepts and ideas.

In general, the practical reaction of governments has been to use legislative controls (which in economic terms correspond to infinite taxes) to manage any negative aspects of tourism development and market incentives to encourage the positive elements. The use of legal regulations necessitates the construction of indicators and the provision of agents to monitor whether codes of practice and the required standards are being met, so that action can be taken to ensure compliance with the ideals of sustainability. The positive side of regulation is the absorption of the ideals of sustainability by the industry and the tourists themselves, so as to generate responsible tourism development. While the former often focuses on restrictions and limits, the latter is about beneficial actions, including developing opportunities for new sustainable tourism products.

The EU Fifth Environmental Action Plan took tourism as one of the key sectors, which it felt was placing pressure on the European environment. Therefore, the European Environment Agency has attempted to include tourism measures in their annual reports, but have had little success in arriving at meaningful indicators, because those that are available simply reflect the size of the activity and do not provide a measure of the impact of tourism on the environment. It proved impossible because of the absence of national data, so they are now looking at the potential for measuring tourism impacts at the local level and aggregating them to arrive at nationally comparable indicators. The thrust of this project is to move this research forward along sustainable tourism lines in order to advance the state of the art, which, by definition, involves much wider considerations than just the environment.

Tourism indicators

Viewed in terms of the environment alone, sustainability can be perceived as a qualitative shift in the nature of the production process to improve resource efficiency, particularly in the case of non-renewable resources, and preservation of the appropriate life-cycle of renewable resources so as to allow recovery. Because the definition of sustainable tourism is much broader than this, the first innovative aspect of the research will be to identify and relate indicators of the actions of tourism as a phenomenon with the impacts of these actions. It might well be suggested that there is no such thing as sustainable tourism; there is less unsustainable or more sustainable, which might be more practical targets.

Broadly speaking the tourist visit involves:

- access: transport to and from the destination and within the destination;
- accommodation: through a variety of establishments;
- activities and attractions: facilitated through the provision of infrastructure;
- social, physical and economic impacts.

These actions can be categorized by the size of the visitor population, the production technology, the size and nature of the industry and environmental and community impacts. What is envisaged at the first stage is the cross-tabulation of tourists' actions by impacts to produce a matrix of indicators which reflect, either by the nature of the data collected or the level of activity, some aspect of sustainability. The cells will also contain indicators that are available at both the national and local level, thus providing a direct link in some instances, while others will be candidates for aggregation from the local to the national and some just of local relevance; for example, the percentage of local employment provided by the tourist industry.

There is a further overlay that can be imposed on the matrix: a standard way of ordering indicators, first introduced by the OECD, is to look at state, pressure and response. Thus a state indicator could be the level of energy consumed by tourist facilities. Pressure indicators reflect activities that contribute to the trend, such as the volume of tourist arrivals. Response indicators indicate action to relieve pressure, such as the take up of 'green' codes of conduct by tourist enterprises. While some of the data required to generate such indicators are not available at present, the potential to exploit digital information generated by new technologies is there.

THE EUROPEAN LOCAL SUSTAINABLE TOURISM INDICATORS PROJECT

Creation of practical LSTI

It is intended to develop and test the broadest array of LSTI possible without loss of comparability and compatibility. To do this, a number of theories must be tested so as to create theorems that may be simply understood and demonstrable. It has long been accepted, if not fully understood, that tourism policies, strategies, programmes, marketing, research and development are driven by the balance of four imperatives: the economy; the environment; the communities; and politics. The ultimate decisions that are made are based upon both quantitative and qualitative inputs regardless of whether evidence exists or is purely theoretical or, worse, 'seat of the pants' based on individual bias. In effect, a series of cost–benefit ratio decisions are made, even if not expressed as such. The project will seek to establish a series of sustainable relationships whereby both quantitative and qualitative ratios can be established. It is vital that, whatever array of LSTI are created, they must be essentially neutral. Having said that, generally when indicators are established it is in the context of proving an output. Therefore, the LSTI must be in their bias, but capable of establishing target outcomes which can, over a period of time, be proved as either a positive or negative achievement. For purposes of compatibility and comparability, it may emerge that a given LSTI may be measured in terms of percentage achievement of a set objective for each ratio adopted.

Given the three main strands of sustainability: economic impacts; environmental impacts; and social impacts, the core LSTI will be devised so as to illustrate selected relationships, e.g. to establish for a given period tourist days vs. population, or, tourist days vs. area; or local employment vs. tourist days; or overseas visitor nights vs. total tourist days, and so on.

The purpose will be to create an array of core LSTI, and the methods for deriving them, where the local destination may select, in each of the three main strands, 3–4 core LSTI out of a selection of, say, 10–15 core LSTI. In addition, secondary LSTI will be provided purely for local circumstances and use. As indicated earlier, a variety of matrices can be established which relate the three key components of access, accommodation and activity, with a range of indicators in respect of production: natural resources, host communities and the visitor.

It is also vital to ensure that the project serves the needs of all of the potential users in the destinations and, also, is able to export both the tools and skill sets to use the LSTI for comparison and benchmarking to establish measures of actual and comparative success. To do this, a thorough issues identification process must be put in place in each destination so as to ensure the LSTI can evolve within a controlled scientific network. The user needs must be the core driving force and the process must encourage local ownership and involvement rather than being part of the imposition of nationally driven research needs. It may not surprise many that the communication between governments, academia and tourism practitioner has been historically poor. With the immediacy of communications and given computer power and literacy at all levels, the opportunity has never been greater to create new exciting and productive linkages whereby internationally the needs of many can be served provided they are prepared to be more open and trusting, without which the challenges of the present and future will remain beyond our reach. The LSTI partnership is persuaded that, by its own example, it will be catalytic in achieving both philosophical and practical acceptance that multi-disciplinary approaches will better serve the growing needs of the New Economy, across sectors and across political borders.

Workplan framework and methodology summary

Workplan framework

The work will take account of and further develop existing national and international concepts set out in existing publications as well as drawing on interviews with experts and practitioners in the field. It will also identify opportunities to take advantage of the developing use by tourism businesses of information and communication technologies to generate additional data for common benefit, as well as exploiting those technologies in collecting, collating, analysing and generating indicator measures.

Phase 1 of the work will conceive, identify, define and field-test an initial array of Local Sustainable Tourism Indicators which:

- measure the actions of tourism as part of the New Economy;
- measure the dynamic impact of these activities on the local economy, communities and environment;
- prioritize themes between core and additional indicators;
- identify existing and potential sources of data;
- develop innovative approaches to capturing and manipulating the data to deliver appropriate measures for each indicator.

Phase 2 will provide an extended demonstration at further destinations in a wider number of countries which have already been approached and agreements to participate obtained in principle. Following the extended demonstration, the Scientific Committee will review the reports from the various destination user groups and create an array of primary and secondary LSTI.

Concurrent with the above, appropriate software packages will be tested and at the conclusion of the project an LSTI software package will be made available on an affordable commercial basis.

Workplan methodology

- review of available scientific papers;
- establishment of themes, topics, indicators, data sets;
- establishment of the initial array of LSTI;
- development of commercial software package to encourage skills transfer;
- field testing of LSTI in pilot areas;
- review of pilot field tests to establish selected LSTI and secondary LSTI;
- field testing for practical evaluation in extended demonstration areas;
- review of demonstration field tests to conclude LSTI and secondary LSTI;
- to prepare a final paper for peer group review and consideration by the EU.

Value-added programme

- development of website for use by partners and as a forum to invite peer group participation;
- to create a European/International debate on LSTI using Fifth International Forum on Tourism Statistics and similar forums created by EU/OECD/WTO, other International/National agencies and academia generally;
- to create a permanent website where a forum can continue beyond the project's completion;
- to have established a network of International LSTI partnerships with a common method, structure and relationship package to ensure benchmarking and the sharing of examples of good practice.

REFERENCES

DCMS (1998) *Tourism: Towards Sustainability: A Consultation Paper on Sustainable Tourism in the UK.*

DCMS (1999) *Tomorrow's Tourism.*

DETR (1998) *Opportunities for Change: Consultation Paper on a Revised UK Strategy for Sustainable Development.*

European Commission (1992) *The State of the Environment in the European Community.*

European Commission (1992) *Towards Sustainability: A European Community Programme of Policy and Action in Relation to the Environment and Sustainable Development* (The Fifth Environmental Action Plan).

European Commission DGXI (1993) *Environment and Tourism in the Context of Sustainable Development.*

LGMB (1999) *Local Agenda 21 Round Table Guidance 17 Sustainable Tourism.*

Middleton, V. T. C. and Siebber, W. (for the European Environment Agency) (1999) *Tourism and the Environment at European Level.*

National Planning Forum (1998) *Planning for Tourism.*

OECD (1993) *OECD Core Set of Indicators for Environmental Performance Reviews.*

Tourism Concern and WWF (1992) *Beyond the Green Horizon: A Discussion Paper on Principles for Sustainable Tourism.*

Tourism Concern and WWF (1996) *Sustainable Tourism: Moving from Theory to Practice.*

UN Commission on Sustainable Development (1996) *Indicators of Sustainable Development: Framework and Methodologies.*

WTO (1995) *Tourism and Environment Indicators.* Report to the World Tourism Organization Environment Committee.

17

Using Tourism Statistics to Measure Demand Maturity

Anne Graham

INTRODUCTION

Over the last few decades the tourism industry has experienced phenomenal growth. At some future stage, however, limits to this tourism growth must occur. These limits may come about because of two key reasons. First, demand factors such as the consumer's ability and willingness to travel may constrain growth. These factors are related to economic and social conditions, such as income, price and leisure time, but also personality traits and attitudes. Second, supply constraints within the tourism industry may also dampen the overall demand. These may occur with the supply of any of the product components (e.g. transport, accommodations, attractions). Lack of sufficient hotel beds is an example. Increasingly supply limits may be imposed on the destination with the aim of developing a more sustainable product, as in Mauritius and Bermuda where a selective number of up-market tourists are being sought (France, 1997). The transport system used to reach the destination may also come under pressure. For example, with air transport there may be a lack of runway or airspace capacity or perhaps environmental measures may reduce the theoretical capacity (Veldhius, 1999; Hartmut-Rudiger, 1999). In addition to these physical limits there may be perceptual constraints. These are when travellers may decide that an airport is too congested to be used or that a tourism resort is too crowded. Thus both physical and perceptual constraints can have the effect of curtailing growth, with the former making it not possible to travel, and with the latter diminishing the desire to travel.

In recent years supply-related issues and the whole area of sustainability have become popular areas of research. By contrast, limits due to demand factors and, in particular, the tourism statistics needed to measure demand maturity, have received far less attention. This discussion will therefore concentrate on the demand factors and so by necessity the complex relationship between demand and supply has been somewhat overlooked. This is considered acceptable since the impact of these supply constraints tends to be greatest at a disaggregate or destination level whilst the emphasis here is very much at the aggregate level. The focus is also on leisure travel since the notions of demand maturity are not so easily applied to non-personal business travel. There are other reasons, such as the increasing sophistication of communication technology (video-conferencing, the internet and so on) which could constrain the growth of business travel by making such travel unnecessary. On the other hand, these technologies may encourage more international and global trade and hence increase the need for further travel.

REASONS FOR LIMITS TO GROWTH OF LEISURE TRAVEL

New travellers

Realistically there will always be sectors of the population who will never travel because of a number of reasons such as family or work circumstances, poor health/mobility or just a lack of interest. Therefore there is likely to be a maximum proportion of the population who will travel. Once this has been reached the proportion of people travelling is likely to stay constant even if incomes rise or prices are reduced. In absolute terms the number could vary because of population changes.

Additional travel

Growth will not only come from new travellers but also from present travellers taking longer or extra holidays. Such growth may be constrained by lack of income or time. These constraints are likely to affect various segments of demand differently. For example, the older persons' market is more likely to be constrained by income, rather than by time. The second-holiday market may also be constrained by time, whereas the short-break market, which primarily relies on weekend time rather than paid holiday time, is likely to be more income sensitive.

Limits on income may occur because of an increase in need to purchase, or an increase in price of, other goods and services, for example health care in the US (Rodgers, 1993; Wheatcroft and Lipman, 1990). Alternatively, limits may occur when there is a lack of motivation or desire to spend more money or time to travel any more. It is quite likely that, as the number of holidays taken by a tourist increases, the desirability to take additional holidays will decrease. Thus the desire to travel may follow the law of diminishing marginal utility with the utility from consuming additional units declining as the rate of consumption increases. If this is the case the tourist will have a greater preference to spend their money or time in other ways, and 'nesting' or staying at home may occur. This is particularly relevant as competition from substitutes appears to be increasing with, for example, expansion of in-home entertainments (cable TV, video, home computers), more local shopping and leisure and recreational facilities. Technology developments in 'virtual reality tourism' may also allow consumers to experience tourism within their home environment (Williams and Hobson, 1995).

The impact of income and time

Consideration must also be given to the situation when two of the key factors allowing tourism to take place, namely income and the availability of time, change. Income levels can be reasonably easily tracked over time by looking at real GDP and consumer-expenditure indicators, but it is much more difficult to assess what has happened to the amount of leisure time in recent years. In the 1960s and 1970s it was generally thought that the improved economic climate would lead to a 'golden age of leisure', or a leisure-based society, by the twenty-first century. Indeed, it is true that people have been retiring earlier and that the average paid holiday entitlement has increased in many countries. There has, however, been contradictory evidence that there is a trend towards more work and less play because of women having to combine the tasks of work and home, ambitious executives spending more time at work, global competition and more job insecurity (Gilbert, 1994; Meurs and Kalfs, 1998; Henley Centre, 1997 and 1998; Martin and Mason, 1998; World Tourism Organization, 1998).

Traditionally, most tourism research has used average paid holiday entitlement plus public holidays as an aggregate measure of 'leisure time'. Such measures can only give a very rough indication of the amount of 'leisure time' available. They assume that the leisure time for the entire population is as for those in employment and that 'official' increases in non-work time result in increases in leisure time, which may not always be the case. Factors such as more part-time, flexi-time and work sharing are also not taken into account. A much more sophisticated measure is needed but calculation of this is beyond the scope of this chapter. Hence by means of illustration most of the analysis which follows has concentrated on the income constraint even though it is recognized that the time constraint may be equally important.

EXISTENCE OF MATURITY IN TOURISM MARKETS

General awareness of the issue

Within the wealth of current tourism research material there appears to have been little empirical research undertaken in the area of demand maturity. This is not to say that it is an issue which is ignored. There are numerous references to 'markets becoming mature' and 'saturation of markets' (Elliot, 1991; Cleverdon, 1990). Referring specifically to the US market, Plog (1991) wrote a book entitled *Leisure Travel: Making it a Growth Market ... Again* in which he discussed why certain people do not travel and what the industry can do to encourage growth. Some literature focuses on net propensity values (i.e. the proportion of the population which is travelling) and the likely existence of an upper ceiling limit. Cooper and Boniface (1994) observed that there were very few examples of net propensity going above 70–80 per cent and thus suggested that this value may be the limit. Schwaninger (1989) did not foresee significant increases in the net travel propensity figures of Switzerland, Sweden and Norway which were already over 75 per cent. Figure 17.1 shows values of net propensity from the latest survey of long holidays undertaken for the European Commission (European Commission, 1998). Net propensity was highest for Denmark, The Netherlands, Sweden and Finland, and lowest for Greece, Austria, Ireland and Portugal – largely reflecting economic factors within the countries.

The use of such data to investigate maturity is rather limited unless gross propensity

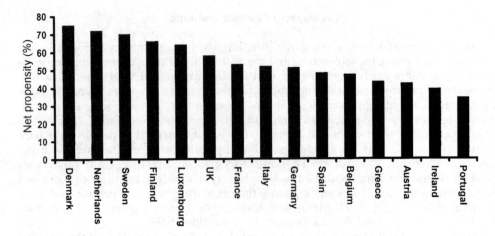

Figure 17.1 Long holiday net propensity values 1997 – European countries
Source: European Commission (1998)

(i.e. the total number of trips per head of population) or travel frequency (i.e. average number of trips) can also be investigated. For example, Pearce (1989) suggested that when net propensity is low (30%), growth in tourist demand will come largely through an increase in the proportion of the population who attain a standard of living enabling them to take a holiday. Where the net propensity is much higher (60–70%), an increase in demand will be mainly from increased frequency. As far back as 1975, Schmidhauser (1975) concluded, in his analysis of travel propensities in the 1960s and 1970s, that there are two decisive changes which occur with a net propensity of about 55–60 per cent and a net propensity of about 75–80 per cent. When these turning points were reached, he stated that there was a tendency for the travel frequency to increase.

Tourism forecasts

Many tourism forecasts are based on some type of econometric model where income and travel costs appear to be the key drivers of demand (Lim, 1997; Athiyaman, 1997; Crouch, 1992; Witt and Witt, 1992*)*. When a selection of origin countries are covered in the forecasts, each model tends to have a different income elasticity which will indirectly infer something about relative maturity of the various countries – although it is rare to find this discussed explicitly in the text (Smeral *et al.*, 1992; Smeral and Witt, 1996).

Some interesting forecasts, looking at the seven major sources of tourists to Australia, were produced by Morley (1998). The estimated income elasticities varied across origins being small for both relatively low-income countries and high-income countries and larger for middle-income countries. From a maturity viewpoint, it could be argued that the high-income countries had reached some kind of maturity because of ample travel opportunities whereas, for the lower-income countries, the travel opportunities were much more limited, hence the smaller elasticity values in both cases. These forecasts are also some of the few to assume changing rather than constant income elasticity values over time with the more 'established' markets of origin, having higher values in earlier than later years. For the other 'newer' markets, there was the reverse situation.

Maturity was also considered in the global tourism forecasts produced every five years by Travel and Tourism Intelligence (Edwards, 1992; Edwards and Graham, 1997). These applied time and income ceiling limits (which slope gently in line with population growth, rising leave periods and real discretionary household incomes) to econometric tourism forecasts of the 30 major origin countries. These limits were estimated by observing the relative amount of spending and time on travel.

Travel by air

Within various different tourism markets perhaps the most extensive coverage of demand maturity can be found when travel by air is considered. Various analysts have investigated past growth trends and assessed whether there is any pattern emerging, such as a S-shaped curve or falling growth rates. For example, annual growth rates of US domestic air traffic dropped from 15 per cent in the 1950s to 5 per cent in the 1980s, which some analysts (e.g. James, 1993; Woolsey, 1993) saw as one sign of market maturity. Others such as Bowles (1994) defined a mature market as one that grows by no more than the rate of economic growth of the country. Airbus (1999) commented on the fact that demand for air travel now lags behind growth in GDP for the US market which they called 'largely matured'. A number of other air transport forecasters make the same assumption (Hanlon, 1999).

Greenslet (1993) compared US passenger revenues rather than numbers with GDP and thus directly took into account the impact of price. Up until the 1980s the travel share of GDP increased steadily but became constant in the 1980s – his definition of a mature market. Airbus (1993) also observed a levelling out of airline revenue as a percentage of GDP in the 1980s in Europe. Rolls-Royce used a similar reasoning in their consideration of maturity (Rolls-Royce, 1994; Miller 1994). They defined a mature market to be one where traffic growth is proportional to GDP and yield growth and went on to define the additional growth above the 'mature market' as 'product' growth. Pilarski and Thomas (1996) considered directly income elasticities in their study of the US domestic and the North Atlantic market – first using sequential elasticity values and, second, using Bayesian statistics. However, they found no evidence of declining elasticity values, which was their definition of a mature market.

DEVELOPING A RESEARCH METHODOLOGY

Behavioural or market demand approach

There are two complementary approaches which can be adopted to investigate maturity. First is a behavioural approach which would involve looking at an individual consumer's travel behaviour and attitudes in order to be able to define and quantify some kind of notion of utility in tourism. Maturity could be associated with factors considered to produce a decline in utility. This type of research would involve building some kind of complex model incorporating economic, psychological and social dimensions of tourism demand. A number of different demographic and social factors would need to be considered, particularly the ageing population, with the 65+ age group generation being more wealthy, healthy and far more likely to travel than past elderly generations. Specialist in-depth consumer surveys or group discussions would generally have be undertaken to obtain such information.

Alternatively, a more aggregate or market demand approach could be adopted. The advantage with this method is that there are already many data sources in existence which can be used, although they all have shortcomings. This is the approach illustrated in this chapter.

Basic methodology

It has become apparent from the above discussion that there are various ways of defining maturity:

1. By considering time series patterns of demand over time. Maturity will then be considered to be setting in if there are declining changes in growth whilst saturation could be considered to exist if there is no growth any more. Time-series curves indicating declining growth patterns, such as log-log or geometric curves (when the coefficients are less than one) and the semi-log curves, could be used to investigate maturity whilst the hyperbola, modified exponential or logistic curve would be more suitable for a 'saturating' situation (Witt and Witt, 1992; Saunders *et al.*, 1987). The key shortcoming here is clearly in ignoring factors which are known to drive demand, such as income and price changes. Both net and gross propensity could be considered to differentiate between growth in new travellers and additional trips taken by existing travellers.
2. By considering demand income elasticity values over time. 'Full' maturity could be defined to occur when the income elasticity is unity or below, or, in effect, when leisure travel starts to be considered more as an essential product rather than as a luxury. Correspondingly 'full' saturation could be defined to occur when the elasticity value is zero. Earlier stages of market maturity could be considered to exist when elasticity values are falling but are still larger than one (Table 17.1).
3. By considering the share of total income spent on travel. if this ratio is constant it will show that changes in income are not producing proportionally larger changes in demand. This is in fact just another way of considering whether the income elasticity is near to the value of one.

The last two definitions could be adapted to relate to the time constraint by looking at 'leisure time' rather than income elasticities.

Table 17.1 The five stages of maturity/saturation

Income elasticity value	Maturity/saturation stage
Constant and substantially greater than 1	Stage 1 (Full immaturity)
Decreasing but still greater than 1	Stage 2
Approaching 1	Stage 3
1 or below	Stage 4 (Full maturity)
0	Stage 5 (Full saturation)

TOURISM DATA ISSUES

Tourist trips

Having defined demand maturity, the next stage involves selecting the most suitable data sources. An obvious source of data is the tourism surveys of residents of different countries. However, major comparability problems exist which make it difficult to undertake meaningful cross-country analyses. These problems occur primarily because of:

- Purpose of Trip – some surveys cover all travel whilst many others may be confined to just holiday trips.
- Duration of Trip – sometimes only trips of over four or five nights are included although increasingly short break data is being collected as well.
- Age Group – the age groups covered can vary considerably with some surveys excluding children.
- Destinations Visited – some surveys classify travel only by destination of longest stay whilst others by first or last country visited.
- Regularity of Surveys – some surveys are undertaken annually whilst others may only be undertaken every 2–3 years.
- Sample Size – the sample size varies considerably.

For comparative research it is more appropriate to use pan-European surveys with a common set of questions, sampling procedures and definitions. By far the most comprehensive survey is the European Travel Monitor (ETM). This is a continuous survey which began in 1988 and uses larger sample sizes than for most of conventional single country holiday surveys. The scope of the survey is also much broader; it covers all travel, business and leisure (although there is very limited information on domestic travel) and all trips of more than one day are included. However, the detailed figures from the ETM are not publicly available and produced solely for subscribers.

Spending data

A more suitable measure to use when considering limits to growth is perhaps travel spending since this directly takes into account the impact of price on demand. For example, if the travel cost is halved, the number of trips may double but the actual amount of income that consumers are prepared to spend on travel may remain the same. International tourist spending data is compiled primarily for balance of payments reasons and should, therefore, be more comparable internationally and over time than other types of tourism data. Problems may occur, however, when banks inaccurately record the spending or misallocate it. Even when such data is obtained directly from interviews, sampling errors may occur or spending may be underestimated (for example, due to omission of credit card spending or pre-paid package holidays).

If spending data is being used to look at demand patterns over time to assess maturity, it will, of course, have to be adjusted for both inflation and exchange rates. More importantly, such data usually excludes spending on fares spent on transport to and from the tourist destinations. This needs to be included if maturity due to income limits is being considered. The data also excludes spending on domestic tourism which needs to be assessed in any analysis because of the potential for substitution between domestic and international travel.

CASE STUDY: THE UK SITUATION

Data sources

The remaining part of this chapter concentrates on the UK as a case study. Various tourism surveys are used. There is the British National Travel Survey (BNTS) which is a home survey that has been undertaken since 1951 – this means that long-term trends can be assessed. It only covers long (i.e. 4 + nights) holidays. The other main home survey is the United Kingdom Tourist Survey (UKTS), which has a broader coverage including both long and short holidays and VFR travel. However, it has only existed in its present form since 1989 and so long-term trends cannot be identified. The air travel data was taken from the International Passenger Survey (IPS) which is based on face to face interviews with a stratified random sample of 260,000 passengers (in 1998) as they enter or leave the UK by the principal air and sea routes, and some from other tourism home surveys, namely Germany (Reiseanalyse RA), The Netherlands (Continuous Vacation Survey CVO) and France (National Holiday Survey funded by INSEE – no longer in existence).

General travel trends

As a starting point, trends in the time series data have been observed. From the BNTS data, it is clear from Figure 17.2 that there has been considerable substitution between international and domestic long holidays and the total market has grown, albeit fairly modestly. The UKTS survey shows that in addition there were 42.5 million VFR trips and 40.5 million short breaks in 1997. The short-break market has grown considerably since 1989 when there were 31.8 million trips, with the small international market more than doubling in size from 1.3 million trips in 1989 to 3.1 million trips in 1997. This highlights the problem, therefore, of excluding short breaks from the main analysis.

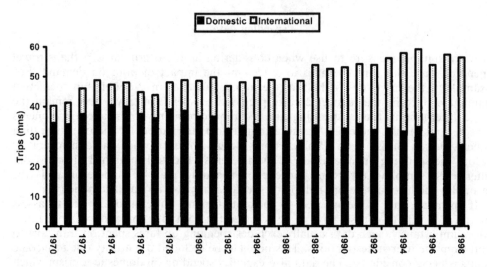

Figure 17.2 British holiday (4 + nights) trips 1970–98
Source: BNTS

'New' growth and 'additional' growth can be investigated by studying the net and gross propensity to travel figures for different markets. It may be seen from Figure 17.3 that in Britain an almost constant proportion of the population (around 60%) has taken at least one holiday (4+ days) in the last 30 years, and so the growth has come from additional holidays. The same seems to be the situation for France (Figure 17.4) (with a lower net propensity value around 55 per cent, although data is not available for the more recent years). Does this mean that the limit on the share of the population who travels for these two countries has been reached? By contrast both net and gross propensity values have been increasing in Germany and The Netherlands (Figure 17.5 and 17.6).

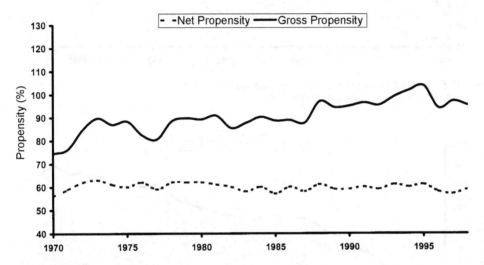

Figure 17.3 Net and gross propensity – British long holidays
Source: BNTS

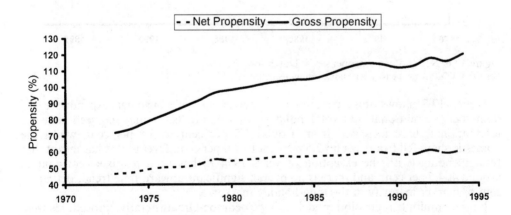

Figure 17.4 Net and gross propensity – French long holidays
Source: INSEE

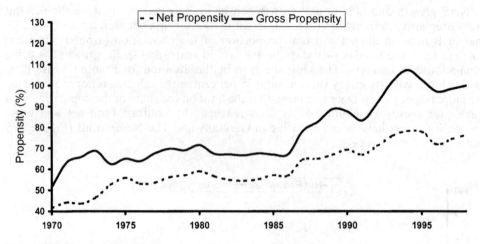

Figure 17.5 Net and gross propensity – German long holidays
Source: RA (West Germany only until 1990)

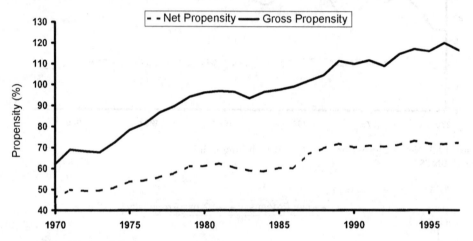

Figure 17.6 Net and gross propensity – Dutch long holidays
Source: CVO (net propensity series discontinuous at 1987)

Figure 17.7 shows this spending as a percentage of consumer expenditure for domestic, international and total holidays of 4+ nights. It may be seen that the international share increased from around 1.5 per cent to 3.5 per cent, whilst the domestic share fell from around 2.5 per cent to 1.0 per cent. Overall this has meant that total spending (with the exception of years 1974–8) has been relatively constant at around 4–4.5 per cent, and there is no overall significant upward time trend, perhaps a sign of market maturity in the long-holiday market.

Log-log multiple regression models using Cochrane-Orcutt iterative procedures were used to calculate income elasticity for this data (Table 17.2). An income elasticity value of 2.06 was obtained for the international market for the whole period 1970–98 and 1.73 period for 1984–98. This shows some early stage of market maturity with the

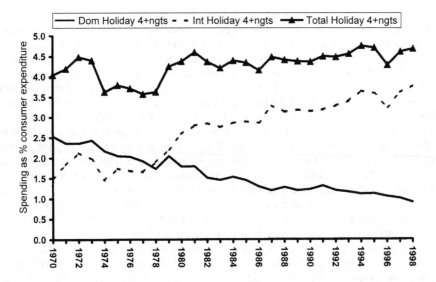

Figure 17.7 Spending on British holidays (4+ nights) as a percentage of consumer expenditure
Source: BNTS

Table 17.2   Income elasticities for UK travel demand models 1970–1998

	1970–1998 Income elasticity	1984–1998 Income elasticity
British long-holiday spend per capita models (BNTS data)		
International	2.23	1.89
Total	1.30	1.28
UK air international trips per capita models (IPS data)		
IT holiday	2.20	1.72
Short-haul holiday	2.22	1.53
Total holiday	2.45	2.00
Short-haul leisure	2.27	1.69
Total leisure	2.42	2.15

declining income elasticities, but full maturity with unit elasticity can still be considered to be a long way off. However, with the overall market the elasticity values were much nearer to one, indicating full maturity, and they appeared to have been this size for some time.

International travel by air

Whilst there has generally been very little research undertaken regarding demand maturity and the UK travel market, there is one segment of this market which has been investigated more fully. This is international air travel by UK residents. One of the earliest discussions can be found in the report by the Roskill Commission (Third London Airport Commission, 1971). The forecasts contained in this report set an upper limit of three leisure air round trips per capita for the end of the century. Since this report, a number of forecasters have continued to assume some kind of limit to growth. The BAA reduces the size of the income elasticities for certain markets, particularly the UK short-haul leisure ones (Maiden, 1995). The Department of Environment, Transport and the Regions (DETR) uses models which give elasticities which decline proportionately with increases in traffic levels and again the elasticities for the short-haul market are estimated to decline more rapidly that the long-haul market (DETR, 1997). Other forecasts, however, for example those produced by the CAA (Abrahams, 1998) and BA (Julius, 1995), have made no explicit assumptions concerning the slowing down of growth. The most comprehensive research to date on UK market maturity was a study by Steer *et al.* (1992). The study concluded that there had been some decline in growth (and hence some evidence of market maturity) of the well-developed mass-European holiday markets, but growth had continued to be strong in the newer markets such as long-haul destinations, winter holidays and short breaks.

Figure 17.8 presents the total air and sea (including Channel Tunnel) international leisure visits by UK residents taken from the International Passenger Survey (IPS) since 1970. Leisure visits are defined as holiday plus Visiting Friends and Relatives (VFR) visits. Overall, it may be seen that there is a very clear upward trend with air travel with an average annual growth rate of 7.4 per cent. The air independent holiday market has grown faster than the inclusive tour market (8.2 per cent compared with 6.8 per cent) and the long-haul market has grown faster than the short-haul market (12.5 per cent compared with 6.5 per cent). These are hardly very surprising observations since they are merely confirming trends which are well known to the industry (Cleverdon, 1997; Cope, 2000; Jones *et al.*, 1997). They could, however, be crudely seen as a sign that these markets are less mature.

It is interesting to observe that income elasticity values in the range of 2.2–2.5 were obtained for the period 1970–98, but for the more recent period (1984–98) the elasticities appeared to be considerably lower, indicating an early stage of market maturity (Table 17.2). For example, for the IT holiday market they had fallen from 2.2

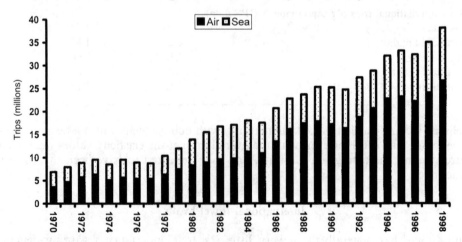

Figure 17.8 UK international leisure trips by UK residents (1970–98)
Source: IPS

to 1.7 and for the short-haul holiday market from 2.2 to 1.5. They were, though, still considerably high than one – the definition of full maturity. However, it was not possible to obtain an overall picture as acceptable models for independent travel and long-haul travel – both markets which are generally considered less mature – could not be constructed. Also VFR travel could not be modelled. In addition it is worth noting that airline liberalization and, particularly, lower-cost air travel could fundamentally change the way that consumers view air travel and the priority which they give to it but this is too recent a development to be picked up in the long time series.

Linking air travel and total travel

Typically, UK air transport demand tends to be modelled in isolation, independent of any other travel markets. In reality, of course, tourists have to make decisions between travelling by air or sea or taking the Channel Tunnel, or taking international or domestic trips, when choosing to use some of their discretionary income and available leisure time for travel purposes. The growth in this air market could, in effect, be due to two alternative factors:

1. market extension: growth in the total leisure market;
2. market penetration: growth caused by a shift in demand from another leisure travel market whilst the total demand remains relatively constant.

If the total demand remains relatively constant, the opportunity for growth in air travel is likely to be limited to the degree of future substitution between different travel markets which can take place. On the other hand, if the scope for future substitution appears limited, then any growth with have to come from growth in the total travel demand.

It may be seen from Figure 17.8 that since 1970 air transport demand increased faster than sea suggesting some substitution from sea to air. Overall, however, the total international market has continued to grow. If this trend were to continue, growth in the air market could still be achieved, even if no further substitution between air and sea or the Channel Tunnel took place. The analysis of the total market, however, suggests that there is less scope for the growth in international travel (especially long holidays) unless there is substitution from domestic travel.

CONCLUSIONS

Limits to growth in tourism is not an issue which will go away. Already much attention in the nineties has been given to supply related limits, with the desire for a truly sustainable product proving to be incompatible with uncontrolled growth. A much less well researched possible development is limits due to demand factors and associated concepts such as market maturity and saturation. The implications of slower growth caused by market maturity could be very significant and could encourage fiercer competition between the large travel organizations which increasingly are dominating the industry as they strive to grow by making gains in market share. This could have consequences for forecasting, marketing, planning, product design and so on – in fact almost every area of operations.

Whilst a simple analysis through time of tourism demand and travel propensities can give valuable insights into travel behaviour, for any thorough analysis of maturity, the key drivers of demand must also be taken into account. Some kind of income elasticity approach is therefore essential as well if a thorough investigation is to be undertaken. For such an analysis, a good consistent time-series data set is needed. Currently this is difficult to find as most of the tourism data which has been collected over a number of years relates only to long holidays, with short-break travel only being considered much more recently. At the moment the ETM database also does not contain data for a long enough period.

In order to assess the impact of the income constraint on travel patterns more fully, a measure of spending which includes both transport costs and domestic and international destination spending is needed but is currently difficult to find in published data. To further the analysis of demand maturity, a realistic indicator of available leisure time over time is also needed. Relating such a measure to tourist-night data, for example, would enable an assessment to be made of the extent to which time constrains or encourages travel. In addition, individual consumer attitudes, behaviour and motivations could be assessed through consumer surveys and discussion groups to add a more qualitative aspect.

Through the UK case study this chapter has tried to show how important it is to adopt an approach which considers the complex substitution effects which may be taking place within the total leisure travel markets, rather than considering any specific travel markets (such as air markets) in total isolation. This may involve using different data sets which can introduce problems of consistency unless greater comparability between the different travel surveys is achieved.

REFERENCES

Abrahams, S. (1998) 'Forecasting demand at regional airports'. University of Westminster Regional Air Transport Seminar, May.

Airbus Industrie (1993) *Market Perspectives for Civil Jet Aircraft*. Toulouse: Airbus Industrie.

Airbus Industrie (1999) *Market Perspectives for Civil Jet Aircraft*. Toulouse: Airbus Industrie.

Athiyaman, A. (1997) 'Knowledge development in tourism: tourism demand research'. *Tourism Management*, **18** (4), 221–8.

Bowles, R. (1994) 'Air travel: a growth or mature industry'. *Canadian Aviation Forecast Conference Proceedings,* Transport Canada, 69–73.

Cleverdon, R. (1990) *Tourism to the Year 2000: Qualitative Aspects affecting Global Growth.* Madrid: World Tourism Organization.

Cleverdon, R. (1997) 'UK outbound'. *Travel and Tourism Intelligence*, **3**, 22–43.

Cooper, C. and Boniface, B. (1994) *The Geography of Travel and Tourism* (second edition). Oxford: Butterworth-Heinemann.

Cope, R. (2000) 'UK outbound'. *Travel and Tourism Intelligence*, **1**, 19–39.

Crouch, G. (1992) 'Effect of income and price on international tourism'. *Annals of Tourism Research*, **19**, 643–64.

DETR (1997) *Air Traffic Forecasts for the United Kingdom 1997*. London: Department of the Environment, Transport and the Regions.

Edwards, A. (1992) *International Tourism Forecasts to 2005*. London: Economist Intelligence Unit.

Edwards, A. and Graham, A. (1997) *International Tourism Forecasts to 2010*. London: Travel and Tourism Intelligence.

Elliot, M. (1991) 'Travel and tourism: the pleasure principle'. *The Economist,* 23 March, 7–20.

European Commission (1998) *The Europeans on Holiday*. Executive Summary. Brussels: EC.

France, L. (ed.) (1997) *Sustainable Tourism*. London: Earthscan.

Gilbert, D. C. (1994) 'The European Community and leisure lifestyles', in C. P. Cooper and A. Lockwood (eds) *Progress in Tourism, Recreation and Hospitality*. Chichester: John Wiley and Sons.

Greenslet, E. (1993) 'Airlines: a declining industry'. *Interavia*, October, 71–3.

Hanlon, P. (1999) *Global Airlines* (second edition). Oxford: Butterworth-Heinemann.

Hartmut-Rudigcr, S. (1999) 'Demand forecasts and airport development needs'. University of Westminster Demand Analysis and Capacity Management Seminar, October.

The Henley Centre (1997) 'The future of the holiday'. *Consumer and Leisure Futures*, Spring, 52–4.

The Henley Centre (1998) 'The evolution of leisure'. *Consumer and Leisure Futures*, Winter, 16–23.

James, G. (1993) 'US commercial aviation: a growth or mature industry. 18th FAA Aviation Forecast Conference Proceeding. FAA – APO, 93–2, 182–202.

Jones, P., Hudson, S. and Costis, P. (1997) 'New product development in the UK tour operating industry'. *Progress in Tourism and Hospitality Research*, **3**, 283–94.

Julius, A. (1995) 'Proof of evidence'. Terminal 5 Heathrow Public Inquiry, BA50.

Lim, C. (1997) 'Review of international tourism demand models'. *Annals of Tourism Research*, **24** (4) 835–49.

Maiden, S. (1995) 'Proof of evidence'. Terminal 5 Heathrow Public Inquiry, BAA31.

Martin, W. and Mason, S. (1998) *Transforming the Future: Rethinking Free Time and Work*. Sudbury: Leisure Consultants.

Meurs, H. and Kalfs, N. (1998) *Transport and Leisure*. ECMT 111th Round Table, Paris, October.

Miller, J. (1994) 'US Domestic Maturity'. Unpublished paper.

Morley, C. (1998) 'A dynamic international demand model'. *Annals of Tourism Research*, **25** (1) 70–84.

Pearce, D. (1989) *Tourist Development* (second edition). Harlow: Longman.

Pilarski, A., Thomas, P. (1996) 'Maturation of air transportation', in D. Jenkins (ed.) *Handbook of Airline Economics*. New York: Aviation Week Group.

Plog, S. C. (1991) *Leisure Travel: Making it a Growth Market . . . Again*. New York: John Wiley & Sons.

Rodgers, J. (1993) FAA Forecast Overview. 18th Annual FAA Aviation Forecast Conference Proceedings, FAA – APO 93–2, 45–76.

Rolls-Royce (1994) *Market Outlook: 1993–2012*. Derby: Rolls-Royce.

Saunders, J., Sharp, J. and Witt, S. (1987) *Practical Business Forecasting*. Aldershot: Gower.

Schmidhauser, H. (1975) 'Travel propensity and travel frequency', in A. J. Burkart and S. Medlik (eds) *The Management of Tourism*. London: Heinemann.

Schwaninger, M. (1989) 'Trends in leisure and tourism for 2000–2010', in S. F. Witt and L. Moutinho (eds) *Tourism Marketing and Management Handbook*. Hemel Hempstead: Prentice-Hall.

Smeral, E., Witt, S. and Witt, C. (1992) 'Econometric forecasts: tourism trends to 2000'. *Annals of Tourism Research*, **19**, 450–66.

Smeral, E. and Witt, S. (1996) 'Econometric forecasts of tourism demand to 2005'. *Annals of Tourism Research*, **23** (4), 891–907.

Steer, L., Davies, G. and Gleave, F. (1992) *Maturity of Demand for Air Travel*. Unpublished report.

Third London Airport Commission (1971) *Report of the Commission on the Third London Airport*. London: HMSO.

Veldhuis, J. (1999) 'Determining the environmental capacity'. University of Westminster Demand Analysis and Capacity Management Seminar, October.

Wheatcroft, S., and Lipman, G. (1990) *European Liberalisation and World Air Transport*. London: Economist Intelligence Unit.

Williams, A. and Hobson, J. (1995) 'Virtual reality: a new horizon for the tourism industry'. *Journal of Vacation Marketing*, no. 2, March 10–20.

Witt, S. and Witt, C. (1992) *Modelling and Forecasting Demand in Tourism*. London: Academic Press.

Woolsey, J. (1993) 'US domestic market: no safe havens'. *Air Transport World*, November, 89–90.
World Tourism Organization (1998) 'Leisure time squeeze will hit tourism'. WTO Press Release,
    16 November.

PART 4
THE INTRODUCTION OF THE EURO

18

The Role of Price Factors for Tourists from the Euro Zone: Hints about the Future of Italy's International Tourism Receipts

Antonello Biagioli, Giovanni Giuseppe Ortolani and Andrea Alivernini

ABSTRACT

It is generally agreed that the long-term trend of international tourism receipts in Italy has been influenced by price factors. Furthermore, it is commonly recognized that international tourism receipts have been boosted by depreciations in the value of domestic currency. Since January 1999, with the advent of Economic and Monetary Union (EMU), the exchange rate of the lira is not varying *vis-à-vis* the currencies of the other euro zone countries. An important portion of the tourist market is affected by this change, as tourism receipts from EMU partner countries account for around a half of the total tourism receipts recorded in Italy.

The aim of this chapter is to provide hints on the impact of the new context of fixed exchange rates on Italy's tourism receipts by analysing past behaviour, both from a short- and long-term perspective. The chapter tries to elicit systematic evidence that could merit further analysis.

The chapter is divided into three parts:

Part 1 describes the impact of international tourism receipts on Italy's balance of payments and the relationship with the general economy, with a focus on the earnings originating from the partner countries of the euro zone.

Part 2 reports the methodology and the outcome of an econometric analysis on a

Note The views expressed in this chapter are those of the authors and do not involve the responsibility of the Ufficio Italiano dei Cambi.

general model in which the country's global international tourism receipts are put into relationship with (a) the relative tourism prices in Italy (*vis-à-vis* the main countries of origin and the main competitor countries); and (b) the aggregate income of origin countries. The analysis utilizes the co-integration approach to highlight long-term interactions along with short-term dynamics.

Part 3 studies the specificities of the influence of price factors for travellers coming from the euro zone compared to travellers coming from outside the zone and the different attitude towards price factors of the range of foreign visitors. Attitude is categorized according to various attributes including country of residence, gender, age and profession of visitors, place of visit, accommodation used etc. The characteristics of the link receipts/prices for the euro zone is carried out through a further econometric analysis of four-year data (1996–9). The subjective judgement of Italy's tourism prices by the different types of visitors is investigated by analysing the responses directly provided by a large representative sample of travellers.

The main findings of the chapter are as follows:

- The analysis of Part 2 shows that there is a significant long-term relationship between international tourism receipts on one side and price factors and income of inbound nationals.
- The analysis of Part 3 indicates that:
  (a) the relationship between price and attitude remains valid restricting the focus on EMU-originated visitors. Moreover, in recent years, the sensitivity of receipts to the changes of price factors appeared even higher.
  (b) travellers seem to be aware of change in prices, as their subjective evaluations reflect to a significant extent the 'real' relative price changes.
  (c) the subjective evaluation of prices is influenced by all the factors considered: the country of origin of the visitors, their socio-demographic characters etc. Nevertheless, it has been possible to identify some visitors' segments that express a more negative evaluation of Italian prices and are therefore more exposed to a loss of competitiveness of the prices of the country's tourist products.

In conclusion, in the past the price factor in Italy has been crucial for travellers from outside and within the euro zone, determining the level of tourism expenditure in the country. It is reasonable to assume that this tendency will continue in the future, in a new context in which a key component of the price factor (i.e. the exchange rate of the domestic currency) is not under national control any more. The future of international tourism receipts from the euro zone is therefore likely to be influenced by the remaining economic factors (namely the domestic price level and the growth of income of the EMU partners) and by non-economic factors.

INTRODUCTION

Italy has always been one of the world's main tourist destinations. Non-economic factors, namely the richness of the country's cultural and historical heritage, the attractiveness and the diversity of the natural resources in the nation's territory, combined with favourable climatic conditions, certainly play a major role in determining the country's competitive advantage.

However, economic factors have also played a significant part in determining the evolution of the country's inflows of foreign visitors. On several occasions, Italy's international tourism receipts, i.e. the aggregated expenditure carried out by non-resident visitors for their stay in the country's territory, have been speeded up or reduced by changes in relatively few economic variables. Price competitiveness is the most frequently cited example of these variables. It indicates the competitiveness of tourism prices *vis-à-vis* the tourism prices of competitor countries. Tourists have proved to be well-informed consumers. Hence, they are more likely to travel to Italy if the cost of the trip is perceived to be attractive in comparison to the cost of a journey in the home country or in a competitor country. In short, given the two countries A and B, a change of price competitiveness of country A against country B is originated by movements of one or both of the following variables:

- a change of domestic prices of country A *vis-à-vis* the domestic prices in country B, and
- a change of the exchange rate of the currency of country A *vis-à-vis* the currency of country B.

In addition to the named price factors, the disposable income of foreign visitors is regarded as another important economic variable influencing the level of international tourism to a country. It is accepted that holidays abroad are superior goods, whose demand, therefore, increases in parallel with income. As a consequence, the changes of aggregate income of the countries of origin of foreign visitors are expected to be positively correlated with the changes in tourism receipts of the destination country. It can be noted that, in the last two decades, the second component of the price factor, i.e. the exchange rate variation, has been more visible in the Italian case. This is because the volatility of the exchange rate of the Italian lira against the other major currencies largely exceeded both the variability of relative prices (denominated in the domestic currency) and the variability of income of origin countries.

The advent of the Economic and Monetary Union in 1999 meant that Italy adopted the common currency with the other ten European Union countries. With respect to the segment of travel within the euro zone, the implication is that one of the sources of variation in the model briefly described above simply disappears. In this new context, the international tourism receipts of the eleven countries of the zone are supposed to depend on the changes of relative internal tourism prices and on the variations of disposable income of origin countries.

This chapter attempts to contribute to the understanding of the implications of the euro introduction on Italy's tourism receipts. The strategy adopted to this end basically consists of analysis of past behaviour in order to identify a systematic pattern that might help to outline the future scenarios. The chapter starts with some notes on the size and the features of Italy's international tourism. This is followed by the core part of the chapter which is divided into two sections. The first part deals with an econometric model whose outcome is the quantification of the impact of two main economic factors, prices and income, on global (from *all* countries) international tourism receipts, over the period 1977-99. The regression analysis used adopts the co-integration approach in order to find out the (possible) long-term relationship between the response variable and the explanatory variables along with the short-term dynamics between them. The aim of this part of the chapter is to assess the features of a model that, although generally accepted, has never been tested with a similar methodology on the Italian case. Hence, this first part of the study provides an analytical understanding of the *general* validity of the model, irrespective of the area of origin of visitors. The second part of the research aims to outline the possible *specificities* of the price effect on the various segment of Italy's international tourism market. In this second part, euro-zone travellers are compared to the travellers coming from the rest of the world. To this end, a second model has been tested, in which the receipts specifically originating from euro-zone countries are the dependent variable. As will be later explained, this exercise can only be carried out analysing a limited period, since a reliable geographical breakdown of tourism balance of payments data has only been compiled in Italy since 1996, via the development of a large sample survey at national borders. Finally, the average subjective evaluation of prices in Italy provided by foreign visitors, in the mentioned sample survey, has been disaggregated according to several attributes: country of origin, gender, age, profession, place of visit, type of accommodation used etc. This allowed the authors to carry out some analysis about the different attitude *vis-à-vis* prices of the various types of visitors.

INTERNATIONAL TOURISM RECEIPTS IN ITALY: EVOLUTION OF THE ECONOMIC IMPACT

The ranking of the top ten international tourism earners compiled by the World Tourism Organization (WTO) shows the outstanding position of Italy in the world tourism market (Table 18.1). In 1998, the most recent year for which comparable figures are available, the country is placed in the third position, with a share of 6.8 per cent of the total world tourism. In the last decade Italy competed with France and Spain to occupy the second position after the United States, by far the world biggest tourist earner.

The aggregate 'international tourism receipts' is conceptually very close to the aggregate represented by the credit side of the Travel item of the balance of

Table 18.1 International tourism receipts by main country of destination, 1998

Rank	Country	Receipts ($m)	% share
1	USA	71,250	16.2%
2	France	29,931	6.8%
3	Italy	29,866	6.8%
4	Spain	29,737	6.8%
5	UK	20,978	4.8%
6	Germany	16,429	3.7%
7	China	12,602	2.9%
8	Austria	11,184	2.5%
9	Canada	9,393	2.1%
10	Mexico	7,897	1.8%
	Other countries	200,686	45.6%
	World total	439,953	100.0%

Source: World Tourism Organization; for Italy, figure revised with UIC data (world total updated accordingly)

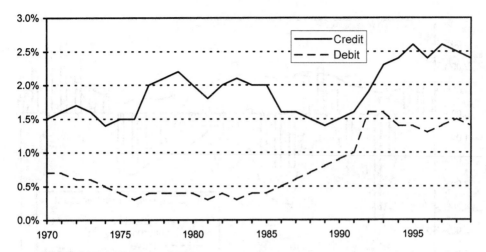

Figure 18.1 Evolution of the ratio between the components of the tourism balance of payments components and the GDP (1970-99)
Source: UIC, Banca d'Italia

payments.[1] Figure 18.1 shows the evolution of the Travel item, or tourism balance of payments as it is often called, as a proportion of the country's GDP. In addition to the credits, the debits (i.e. the expenditures carried out by resident visitors abroad) and the balance between the two components are reported.

The relevant and increasing size of the foreign visitors' expenditures in the country is clearly visible: the ratio credit/GDP, from 1.5 per cent in 1970 reached a record level approximately at 2.5 per cent during the last five years. Moreover, it can be noted that, despite an increased pace of growth of the debit side since the mid-eighties, the Travel balance remained steadily positive.

The structural positive contribution of Travel to the current account of the country's balance of payments is apparent in Figure 18.2. The Travel balance constantly and significantly contributed to the improvement of the current account balance, frequently in deficit over the period under observation.

The significant size of international tourism receipts is reflected by their relevant impact on the country's economy, in terms of value added and generation of jobs (Table 18.2). It has been estimated that inbound tourism, i.e. the inflow of non-resident visitors in the country, contributed in 1998 (directly or indirectly) to 2.2 per cent of the global economy value added. The same segment of tourism generated 3.5 per cent of the total employment. The larger incidence on the employment confirms the typical labour-

---

[1] The content of 'international tourism receipts' was defined by the WTO (see United Nations – World Tourism Organization, 1993), whereas the balance of payments standards were set up by the International Monetary Fund (see International Monetary Fund, 1993). The difference between the two approaches basically concerns the treatment of the expenditure of seasonal and border workers in the country in which they work and the inclusion of the expenditures abroad carried out by students for stays abroad of more than one year. The WTO excludes these items, whereas the IMF includes them. For the purposes of this study, these items can be considered negligible in size. Therefore, the 'international tourism receipts' and 'Travel credits of the balance of payments' are used in the rest of the chapter as equivalent terms.

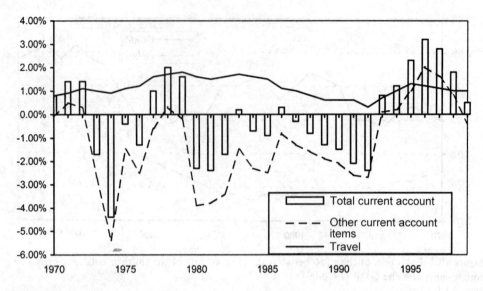

Figure 18.2 Evolution of the ratio 'Travel balance/GDP' and the ratio 'Other current account items balance / GDP' (1970-99)
Source: UIC, Banca d'Italia

Table 18.2 Value added and employment originated by inbound and domestic tourism, direct plus indirect effect, absolute values and incidence on total economy, 1998

Value added		Billion lire	% of total economy
	Inbound tourism	44,558	2.2%
	Domestic tourism	68,265	3.3%
	Total tourism	112,823	5.5%
Employment		Thousand jobs	% of total economy
	Inbound tourism	794	3.5%
	Domestic tourism	1,213	5.3%
	Total tourism	2,007	8.8%

Source: CISET and IRPET (E. Becheri *et al.*, 2000)

intensive features of the tourism industry. In the tourist sector a unit of value added creates more jobs than in other economic sectors. It is also important to notice that the international segment represents nearly 40 per cent of the total internal tourism sector, both for value added and employment.

The composition of inbound flows by country of origin is showed in Table 18.3.[2] In 1999, the euro-zone countries accounted for around a half (49 per cent) of total tourism

---

[2] A more detailed breakdown of receipts by country is in Annex 1, Table A1.1.

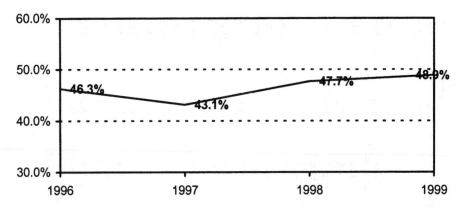

Figure 18.3 Evolution of the share of Travel credits from the euro zone on total Travel credits (1996–99)
Source: UIC

receipts. The travellers from this zone cover a larger share as regards the physical flows, with 57 per cent of the arrivals at borders and 62 per cent of the total night stays. This reflects a lower average daily per capita expenditure (123,000 lire against 209,000) and a higher average length of stay (5.7 nights against 4.6) of euro-zone travellers.

As is well known, German visitors are the most significant tourists in economic terms, accounting for 23 per cent of total earnings. The other six countries have a share over 6 per cent of the total. The USA, Austria and France, each with a share between 9 and 10 per cent, form a first group of countries. The second group is composed of the UK, Switzerland and Japan, each with around 7 per cent. A strong concentration on a few partners is therefore apparent. These seven countries account for some 72 per cent of the total receipts.

The share of the euro zone has been relatively stable over the last four years (Figure 18.3), with a slight tendency to increase. Longer time series analysis on the geographical breakdown of receipts would have been useful to test the stability of the geographical composition of the inflows, but a reliable allocation of Travel transactions by partner country is only available from 1996, when the sample survey on international tourism was started.[3] This lack of data is significant for its implications for the subsequent part of the analysis.

---

[3] The survey is carried out by the UIC on a continuous basis through around 140,000 annual face-to-face interviews at borders of a representative sample of both residents travelling abroad and non-residents travelling in Italy. It replaced the previous collection system based on bank reports, which involved a significant bias in the geographical distribution because of the allocation of a relevant part of the transactions on the basis of the currency used. The survey was also meant as a preparation to the advent of the single currency, which was supposed to hinder the usability of bank reports of the euro-zone countries for Travel compiling. For details on the survey methodology, see Biagioli (1997), Mirto and Ortolani (1998) and World Tourism Organization (1999). On the bias involved by the old collection system see Ortolani (1998). On the need for revision of collection systems for Travel in the light of the single currency, see Eurostat (1997, 2000a and 2000b).

Table 18.3 Travel credits, number of visitors and number of night stays by area and country of origin of the visitors (absolute values and percentage composition, 1999)

Area of origin	Country of origin	Travel credits (billion lire)	% share	Visitors (× 1000)	% share	Night stays (× 1000)	% share	Average length of stay (nights)	Average daily per capita expenditure (1000 lire)
Euro zone	Austria	4,910	9.5	6,814	10.8	34,515	10.4	5.1	142
	Belgium	773	1.5	779	1.2	5,952	1.8	7.6	130
	Finland	174	0.3	96	0.2	921	0.3	9.6	189
	France	4,585	8.9	11,254	17.8	40,815	12.3	3.6	112
	Germany	11,974	23.1	14,461	22.9	100,730	30.4	7.0	119
	Ireland	156	0.3	76	0.1	781	0.2	10.2	200
	Luxembourg	49	0.1	60	0.1	312	0.1	5.2	156
	Netherlands	1,505	2.9	1,436	2.3	12,180	3.7	8.5	124
	Portugal	131	0.3	75	0.1	665	0.2	8.8	196
	Spain	1,044	2.0	854	1.4	8,180	2.5	9.6	128
	Total Euro Zone	25,300	48.9	35,906	56.8	205,052	61.9	5.7	123
Extra-EMU	UK	3,696	7.1	2,154	3.4	17,551	5.3	8.1	211
	Switzerland	3,496	6.8	12,003	19.0	22,607	6.8	1.9	155
	USA	5,162	10.0	1,515	2.4	18,428	5.6	12.2	280
	Canada	485	0.9	190	0.3	2,549	0.8	13.4	190
	Japan	3,432	6.6	888	1.4	9,136	2.8	10.3	376
	Other countries	10,173	19.7	10,516	16.6	55,988	16.9	5.3	182
	Total Extra-EMU	26,445	51.1	27,266	43.2	126,258	38.1	4.6	209
World		51,745	100.0	63,172	100.0	331,309	100.0	5.2	156

Source: UIC

TOURISM RECEIPTS, PRICES AND INCOME: AN ECONOMETRIC ANALYSIS OF LONG-TERM AND SHORT-TERM TRENDS THROUGH THE CO-INTEGRATION APPROACH

Framework

This section describes the influence that the changes of relative tourism prices and aggregated income of the countries of origin have on Italy's global international tourism receipts. Specifically, this section focuses on decisive factors affecting tourism receipts and an econometric model is built connecting Italian receipts from tourism (as a dependent variable) with:

a)   the income of countries of origin of travellers visiting Italy;

b)   the (tourism) price levels in Italy relative to (i) the price levels in origin countries and (ii) the price levels in countries representing potential alternative destinations for foreign travellers (competitor countries).

This introduces the second section of the research, which will attempt to test the validity of the model found here in relation to the euro-zone partners. This strategy is in line with the chapter objective, i.e. finding the influence of price factors on tourism receipts originating from the single currency area.

In the choice of the explanatory variables the approach is quite 'traditional', since it follows the suggestion commonly formulated in the literature.[4] The 'innovative' aspect of the research can be found in the attempt to ascertain the presence, and the features, of long-term interactions between the variables of the model in the Italian case, through the conceptual framework of the co-integration theory. This approach has been inspired by Raminhos (1997), who first implemented this strategy in relation to Portuguese international tourism receipts.

It is necessary to notice initially that the dependent variable of the model should be more correctly the international tourism receipts of visitors coming to Italy only for holiday reasons. Business travellers' expenditures – as well as the expenditures of students, medical patients, people visiting relatives, etc. – which are, in principle, influenced by different factors, should therefore be excluded. The exclusion is not carried out because a reliable split of receipts by purpose of travel is only available from 1996, and this involves an insufficient length for the time-series analysis. However, the authors follow Raminhos (1997) in assuming that, for the aims of this study, the total receipts are a satisfying substitute of the receipts for holiday reasons. The rationale is that:

a)   the receipts related to holiday trips represent the most important part of the total receipts[5]; and

b)   holiday reasons are often an important secondary motivation for business trips and for trips with other purposes.[6]

---

[4] Artus (1970, 1972), Loeb (1982) and, more recently, Syriopoulos and Sinclair (1993) have applied this approach in various national contexts. Chiesa and Castaldo (1984) developed an econometric model for Italy's tourism balance of payments for the period 1962–83. Carraro and Pesce (1995) illustrated an integrated econometric model for the forecasting of Italy's international tourism flows.

[5] Receipts from trips motivated by personal reasons represented 74.3 per cent of the total in 1999.

[6] The authors adopt the hypothesis formulated in this sense by Artus (1972).

The first section below deals with the description of the model and the methodology used for the construction of the variables. The second analyses the series stationarity and assesses whether a long-term relationship (co-integration) exists. In the third section a model with an Error Correction Mechanism (ECM) is estimated and, in the fourth, conclusions are drawn.

Specification of the model

As mentioned, the authors apply to the Italian case (with some adaptations) the econometric approach implemented by Raminhos (1997) in relation to the Portuguese context. The dependent variable – the Italian tourism receipts (referred to as TR) – is supposed to be influenced by income and price factors. The income factor (GDP) is introduced to take into account the fact that the variations of disposable income of travellers influence the travellers' attitude towards taking holidays abroad and, consequently, their level of expenditure.

The price factor indicates the relative advantage or disadvantage that Italy presents as a tourism destination for foreign travellers. Origin countries' and competitor countries' price levels are added to exchange-rate indicators to build a competitiveness index. This index is compared with an Italian price index to obtain a measure of the relative prices of origin countries (OCP) and competitor countries (CCP) *vis-à-vis* Italian prices. Economic theory suggests an inverse relationship between receipts and both CCP and OCP. In fact, an increase of the latter indexes means, respectively, a loss of competitiveness of Italy's tourism supply compared to other countries of destination or compared to destinations in the country of origin itself (domestic tourism from the travellers' standpoint).

Thus, the demand model can be set out as

$$TR = f\,(Y^\circ,\, P,\, P^\circ TC^\circ,\, P^c TC^c)$$

where:

TR = Italy's international tourism receipts at constant prices
Y° = aggregate disposable income in travellers' origin countries
P = level of prices of tourism goods and services in Italy
P° = level of prices of tourism goods and services in travellers' origin countries
P^c = level of prices of tourism goods and services in competitor countries
TC° = exchange rate of the currency of origin countries *vis-à-vis* the Italian lira
TC^c = exchange rate of the currency of competitor countries *vis-à-vis* the Italian lira

(The exchange rates are calculated as the number of Italian lira needed to buy a unit of foreign currency.)

Quarterly data for the period 1977–99 (92 observations) are used in the model. All the variables have been logarithmized, in order to make clear the meaning of the coefficient of the estimated relationships, as in this way they approximate elasticities, and to avoid problems of heteroscedasticity of the variables during the estimation phase.

Dependent variable

TR is represented by the series of Italy's Travel credits of the balance of payments, which is transformed at constant prices using the consumer price index (CPI) as a deflator. Theoretically, a tourism price index should have been considered, but such an index is at the moment unavailable. The approximation involved by the use of the CPI is, however, considered negligible for the aims of the study.

The typical strong seasonality of the series is eliminated by a deseasonalization procedure.[7] The use of seasonal dummies has been avoided because of the difficulties that it would have caused in performing the series stationarity tests.

Independent variables

Relative prices of the origin countries vis-à-vis Italian prices (OCP)

An index of the aggregate price level of origin countries has been developed. The set of origin countries has been restricted to the seven major contributors to Italian tourism receipts: Austria, France, Germany, Japan, Switzerland, United Kingdom and United States.[8]

The index (base 1995 = 100) is calculated as follows:

$$OCP_t = 100 \times \sum_{i=1}^{7} \frac{CPI_t}{CPI_{it} \times CER_{it}} \times \omega_{it}$$

where:

CPI_t =   Italy's consumer price index at period t
CPI_{it} =   consumer price index of the origin country i in period t
CER_{it} =   exchange rate of the Italian lira *vis-à-vis* the currency of origin country i in period t

and:

$$\omega_{it} = \frac{PRES_{it}}{\sum_{i=1}^{7} PRES_{it}}$$

where $PRES_{it}$ is the number of night stays in Italy of travellers of country i in period t. Since the number of night stays disaggregated geographically were only available with an annual frequency, the weights ω_{it} are brought to the quarterly frequency simply assigning to the four quarters composing of a given year, the annual value of the corresponding year.

Relative prices of the competitor countries vis-à-vis Italian prices (CCP)

Ten competitor countries are considered: Austria, France, Germany, Greece, Portugal, Spain, Switzerland, Turkey, United Kingdom and United States. They were chosen on the basis of a question asked in the 1997 to foreign travellers in Italy, in the framework

---

[7] The procedure is the SABL (Seasonal Adjustment, Bell Labs) of the FAME software package.
[8] As mentioned earlier, these countries adequately approximate the global context, since they represent around 92 per cent of the total of Italy's tourism receipts.

of the frontier survey. The question was, 'If you hadn't come to Italy, which other country would have you chosen for your trip?' The first ten countries in the rank of the frequencies of the replies have been included.[9] The index of the aggregate price level of competitor countries (base 1995 = 100) is developed as follows:

$$CCP_t = 100 \times \sum_{i=1}^{10} \frac{CPI_t}{CPI_{it} \times CER_{it}} \times \omega_{it}$$

with:

CPI_t =   Italy's consumer price index at period t
CPI_{it} =   consumer price index of country i in period t
CER_{it} =   exchange rate of the Italian lira *vis-à-vis* the currency of competitor country i in period t

and:

$$\omega_{it} = \frac{TR_{it} \times CCF_{it}}{\sum_{i=1}^{10} TR_{it} \times CCF_{it}}$$

where TR_{it} are the Travel credits of the balance of payments of the competitor country i in period t, expressed in millions of US dollars (source WTO) and CCF_{it} are the percentage frequencies of the first ten countries in the rank of the replies to the question mentioned above. This approach attempts to take into account in the weights of competitor countries both the general (TR_{it}) and the Italy-specific tourism attractiveness of these countries (CCF_{it}).

Aggregate income of origin countries

The income factor is represented by an index of the aggregate income of origin countries. The same set of origin countries considered for the variable OCP is adopted. The index (base 1995 = 100) is developed as a weighted average of origin countries' GDP:

$$GDP_t = \sum_{i=t}^{7} GDP_{it} \times \omega_{it}$$

where:

GDP_{it} =   index of gross domestic product (at constant prices – 1995 = 100 – and seasonally adjusted) of origin country i in period t
ω_{it} =   same weight used for the OCP variable (see above)

---

[9] The percentage frequencies were the following: France = 31.4, Spain = 22.8, Greece = 12.6, Austria = 7.7; Switzerland = 5.9, UK = 5.9, USA = 5.8, Germany = 3.5, Turkey = 2.2, Portugal = 2.2.

Stationarity and co-integration

Before estimating the regression model, the degree of integrability of the series must be studied. If the series are non-stationary the standard tests for the assessment of the significance of the model and of the parameters of the equation are strongly biased; moreover, the hypothesis of a relationship between the variables might be accepted even if it is only of a spurious nature.

The Augmented Dickey-Fuller (ADF) test[10] is used to check the existence of a unit root in the series. It consists in checking the significance of the estimated coefficient of y_{t-1} in the regression:

$$\Delta y_t = \lambda y_{t-1} + \beta_1 \Delta y_{t-1} + \ldots + \beta_p \Delta y_{t-p} + \varepsilon_t$$

where the autoregressive order p is chosen to make $\varepsilon_t \cong N(0, \sigma^2)$.

The results (Appendix 3) are consistent with the graphic analysis of the series (Appendix 2): all the series have a unit root, i.e. are integrated of order $1 - I(1)$, so they need to be differentiated to be included in a meaningful regression equation.

Moreover, the existence of co-integration indicates the presence of a long-term interaction between the series. So, the regression equation has not to be estimated in the first differences, since in this case only the short-term dynamics would be taken into account. The presence of co-integration allows for the estimation of a formulation of the model in which the long-term effect (called Error Correction Mechanism (ECM)) is combined with the short-term dynamics, expressed by the differentiation of the non-stationary variables.

In order to test the presence of co-integration it is necessary to estimate the following static regression, representing the long-term solution, under the hypothesis that all the series are I(1):

$$LTR_t = \alpha + \beta_1 LOCP_{t-1} + \beta_2 LCCP_{t-1} + \beta_3 LGDP_{t-1} + \varepsilon_t$$

Since it can be reasonably assumed that the decision to make a trip is made a quarter in advance of the date of the visitor's departure, one-period lags are considered for the regressors.

In case of co-integration, the residuals of this regression are usually autocorrelated but stationary. Hence the test for the checking of the co-integration can be reduced to an ADF test on the residuals of the static regression, following Bodo, Parigi and Urga (1990). The estimation of this model gives:

$$LTR_t = \quad 3.19 - 1.55 \ LOCP_{t-1} + 0.19 \ LCCP_{t-1} + 1.70 \ LGDP_{t-1}$$
$$(t) \quad (3.86) \ (-4.44) \qquad (0.43) \qquad\qquad (26.61)$$

with:

$$R^2 = 0.90; \ F(3,87) = 256.94; \ DW = 1.04$$

Therefore, the coefficients of the variables LOCP and LGDP have the expected signs: negative for the price factor and positive for the income factor. The sign of LCCP is instead not correct but the coefficient of this variable is not significant and will therefore be eliminated from the model, as is explained below.

---

[10] Said and Dickey (1984). It is a generalization of the Dickey-Fuller test (Dickey and Fuller, 1979). The ADF test, as most of the subsequent analysis, has been carried out through the PCGIVE 9.2 package (Doornik and Hendry, 1994).

Since the graphic analysis of the residuals shows that they are stationary, with zero mean and no trend, an ADF test without constant and trend on the residuals can be used. The ADF test value is -3.43, while the critical value at a significance level of 1 per cent is -2.59. As a result, the nil hypothesis of one unit root can be rejected and it can be assumed (a) that the residuals are stationary and (b) that the variables of the static regression are cointegrated.

The LOCP and LCCP series show a correlation of 0.92. This appears to be to a large extent the consequence of the fact that the set of countries of origin of the tourists is almost identical to the set of the competitor countries. Moreover, LCCP is not significant in the static equation, so it can be removed from the model. Re-estimating, the result is:

$$LTR_t = 3.45 - 1.41 \ LOCP_{t-1} + 1.70 \ LGDP_{t-1}$$
$$(\ t)\quad (6.15)\ (-12.13) \qquad\qquad (27.13)$$

with:

$$R^2 = 0.90; \ F(2,88) = 388.94; \ DW = 1.05$$

The loss of information deriving from the removal of LCCP seems, therefore, negligible, with an unchanged value of R^2 and an increased F. In addition, the ADF test without constant and trend on the residuals is -3.34. Given that the critical value is the same as the previous analysis, the residuals are still stationary and the series of the model remain cointegrated.

Then the approach of Bodo, Parigi and Urga (1990) is followed. These authors worked out an empirical procedure for testing the existence of a single co-integration vector on the basis of a work by Johansen (1988).[11] As the existence of a single co-integration vector is established at the 1 per cent level, a model in which it is possible to distinguish long and short-term effects can be showed. Then, a variable, the mentioned ECM, is introduced as long-term solution of the model.

---

[11] The procedure described by Bodo, Parigi and Urga (1990) consists of estimating three regressions between the first difference of the three variables of the reduced model and their lagged values, and the other three regressions between the two-period lagged values of the levels of the three variables and their lagged values. The residuals of these six regressions are respectively included as columns in two matrices 3×87, U_0 and U_3. Let:

$$S_{33} = U'_3 U_3$$
$$S_{03} = U'_3 U_0 = S_{30}$$
$$S_{00} = U'_0 U_0$$

that are matrices 3×3. The solutions λ_i of the equation: $|\lambda S_{33} - S_{30} \ S_{00}^{-1} \ S_{03}| = 0$ represent the squared canonical correlations and can be used to build the test:

$W = -t \log (1-\lambda_r)$, $r = 1,2,3$, distributed as a $\chi^2(1)$. The hypotheses are checked in a sequential way:

H_0^3: at most two co-integration vectors

H_1^3: two co-integration vectors

H_0^1: no co-integration vectors

H_1^1: one co-integration vector

If H_0^3 is not rejected, H_0^2 vs. H_1^2 is considered, and then H_0^1 vs. H_1^1. If H_0^1 is rejected, there is one co-integration vector, otherwise no co-integration vector between the variables of the model exists.

The final model

A model taking into account the ECM is specified, including four lags of the differentiated variables, that allows us to consider the effects of the lagged variables for a one-year period, the equilibrium relationship and four dummies D_i, which are added in order to sterilize the effects of some outliers. The general specification of the model is as follows:

$$\Delta LTR_t = \alpha + \sum_{j=0}^{4} \beta_j \Delta LOCP_{t-j} + \sum_{j=0}^{4} \gamma_j \Delta LGDP_{t-j} + \sum_{j=1}^{4} \delta_j \Delta LTR_{t-j}$$

$$+ \delta_5 LTR_{t-1} + \beta_5 LOCP_{t-2} + \gamma_5 LGDP_{t-2} + \lambda_i D_i + \varepsilon_t$$

where the long-term solution, corresponding to the ECM, is represented by:

$$LTR_{t-1} + \frac{\beta_5}{\delta_5} LOCP_{t-2} + \frac{\gamma}{\delta_5} LGDP_{t-2}$$

and $\delta_5 < 0$ is the condition for the admissibility of a representation of the model in the form of an ECM.

This model is progressively reduced, eliminating non-significant variables and lags, up to the following final specification:

$$\Delta LTR_t = 1.96 - 1.53 \ \Delta LOCP_t - 1.02 \ \Delta LOCP_{t-1} + 1.05 \ \Delta LOCP_{t-2}$$
$$(6.15) \ (-5.40) \qquad (-3.21) \qquad\qquad (3.74)$$

$$+ 3.29 \ \Delta LGDP_t - 2.60 \ \Delta LGDP_{t-2} - 0.45 \ ECM + 0.18 \ D84Q2$$
$$(-3.53) \qquad\quad (-2.81) \qquad\quad (-6.14) \qquad\quad (2.77)$$

$$+ 0.19 \ D91Q4 - 0.16 \ D98Q1 - 0.19 \ D99Q1$$
$$(3.09) \qquad\quad (-2.62) \qquad\quad (-3.11)$$

where:

$$ECM = LTR_{t-1} + 2.95 \ LOCP_{t-2} - 1.74 \ LGDP_{t-2}$$

represents the long-run effect and D84Q2, D91Q4, D98Q1, D99Q1 the dummies for the quarters indicated in their names. The long-term solution of the model is therefore:

$$LTR = c - 2.95 \ LOCP + 1.74 \ LGDP$$

where c is a constant that depends on the assumptions made about the trend of the independent variables in an equilibrium situation.

The diagnostic tests, whose results are summarized in Table 18.4, indicate that the model overcomes any autocorrelation, heteroscedasticity and mis-specification problem.[12]

---

[12] R^2 is the coefficient of determination. F tests the hypothesis that all the coefficients, apart from constant, are zero. *AR(1–5)* tests the autocorrelation of residuals up to the fifth order. *ARCH(1–4)* tests the heteroscedasticity of residuals. *Normality* tests the normality of the distribution of the residuals. X^2 and $X_i * X_j$ test if it is necessary to introduce in the model, respectively, squares or cross-products of the variables already present in the model. *RESET* test if there are omitted variables. The values in brackets are the probability of getting values of the tests higher than the values observed: they show how likely it is to get at least such a test outcome if H_0 were true.

Table 18.4 Values of the diagnostic tests for the final model

Coefficient/test	Value	Probability
R^2	0.62	
F(10,76)	12.447	[0.0000]
AR(1–5)	0.44613	[0.8147]
ARCH(4)	1.0672	[0.3796]
Normality	0.32203	[0.8513]
X^2	0.68561	[0.7963]
Xi*Xj	0.72709	[0.8225]
RESET	2.2955	[0.1340]

The coefficient of ECM (–0.45) has the correct sign. According to the co-integration theory the value of the coefficient of ECM converges towards the real parameter's value at a higher rate than the one based on the static regression estimated above. This coefficient can be interpreted as the average rate of adjustment of the short-run values of the model towards the long-term equilibrium.

Summary of the results of the analysis

In the short-term, Italy's tourism receipts depend on the current, one-period and two-period lagged values of prices in the origin countries and on present and two-period lagged values of the aggregate income of the countries of origin. As prices in competitor and origin countries are highly correlated, mainly due to the inclusion of nearly the same countries in the two groups, the dependence of tourism receipts on origin-country prices can be extended to competitor-country prices.

A long-term interaction between the variables exists. The coefficients of the long-run solution are highly significant. The ECM parameter, estimated as –0.45, reflects the adjustment towards the long-term equilibrium arising in a given period from the previous-period short-run specification.

The long-run coefficients, representing the elasticities of tourism receipts with respect to origin-country prices and their gross domestic product, have a sign that is consistent with the prevailing economic theory, i.e. negative for prices and positive for income. The absolute values of the coefficients are higher than the unit, in accordance with the results obtained in other studies:[13]

- a 1 per cent increase of the aggregate income of origin countries causes an average increase of 1.7 per cent in tourism receipts;
- a 1 per cent decrease of Italy's prices *vis-à-vis* the prices of origin countries causes an average increase of nearly 3 per cent in tourism receipts.

The elasticity of the income factor is also consistent with the economic theory, which considers international tourism as a superior or luxury good.

---

[13] The Portuguese case, from the study of Raminhos (1997) resulted in elasticities of –2.23 for the relative prices of Portugal *vis-à-vis* the prices of competitor countries and +2.86 *vis-à-vis* the aggregate income of origin countries.

RECEIPTS AND PRICE FACTORS: SPECIFICITIES FOR EURO-ZONE COUNTRIES AND FOR VISITORS' SEGMENTS

Framework

It has emerged from the econometric model described in the previous section that, with reference to the *aggregate* tourism receipts (that is the receipts originated from *all* countries) a clear and stable relationship between international tourism receipts and price factors exists. In this section, the second part of the study is illustrated. It aims at providing further details of the influence of price factors on *specific segments* of Italy's international tourism market. Most particularly, the purpose of this section is to describe:

a) the specific features of the interaction between the receipts originated from the two areas under study, the euro zone and the Extra-EMU area, and the respective relative prices and income;

b) the characteristics of the evaluation of Italian prices in the various types of visitors, classified according to their socio-demographic features, their country of origin, the accommodation used, and so on.

Model of Italy's international tourism receipts originated from the euro zone

This element of the chapter aims to identify the specificities of the influence of price and income factors on Italy's tourism receipts originated from the euro zone. In other words, in line with the objective of the chapter, the authors want to test the validity of the general model illustrated in the first part of the research in relation to this specific area of origin of the visitors.

   To this end, specific regression models are estimated. The first model (model E) puts into relationship the country's receipts originated from the euro zone (LTRE)[14] with the one-period lagged values of (a) the relative tourism prices of Italy *vis-à-vis* the euro zone countries (LOCPE) and (b) the aggregate income of the euro zone (LGDPE), as follows:

$$\text{Model E:} \quad \text{LTRE}_t = \alpha_E + \beta_1 \text{LOCPE}_{t-1} + \beta_2 \text{LGDPE}_{t-1} + \varepsilon_t$$

The second model (model X), analyses the same phenomena in relation to the country not belonging to the euro zone or Extra-EMU countries:

$$\text{Model X:} \quad \text{LTRX}_t = \alpha_X + \gamma_1 \text{LOCPX}_{t-1} + \gamma_2 \text{LGDPX}_{t-1} + \varepsilon_t$$

As mentioned, a reliable geographical breakdown of Italy's receipts is only available since 1996, when the UIC frontier survey was started. For this reason the analysis will be limited to the quarterly figures from 1996 to 1999. The restricted length of the time series does not allow for a comprehensive econometric analysis through the adoption of the co-integration approach. A simple static linear regression model will therefore be estimated.

---

[14] The names of the variables are similar to those used in the first part of the research. Logarithmized variables are considered.

The change of the reference time period (starting from 1996 instead of from 1977 as it was in the first part of the study) involves the need to complete the analysis by estimating also a third model (model W) in relation to the receipts, prices and income of all countries:

$$\text{Model W:} \quad LTRW_t = \alpha_W + \delta_1 LOCPW_{t-1} + \delta_2 LGDPW_{t-1} + \varepsilon_t$$

The specificities of the euro zone *vis-à-vis* the Extra-EMU area will be then identified by the comparison between β_1 and γ_1, in order to assess the possible different elasticity of the price factor, and between β_2 and γ_2, in order to assess the possible different elasticity of the income factor. Moreover, the parameters relevant for the two areas will be compared with the parameters related to the world (δ_1 and δ_2).

The analysis covered all the ten euro-zone partners (Austria, Belgium, Finland, France, Germany, Ireland, Luxembourg, Netherlands, Portugal, Spain) and the main extra-EMU countries of origin, i.e. Canada, Japan, Switzerland, the United Kingdom and the United States. The receipts from these countries have been aggregated to form the receipts originated from the respective areas (EMU, extra-EMU, world) and they have been subsequently seasonally adjusted. The aggregate indexes of relative tourism prices (LOCPE, LOCPX and LOCPW) have been developed with the same approach as used in the previous section of the chapter. The only difference is that the country weights, instead of the number of night stays of the travellers from the corresponding country, are in this case the receipts originated from the same country.[15] The same weighting methodology is adopted for the income variables (LGDPE, LGDPX, LGDPW).

The evolution of the time series, all transformed in the form of an index base 1996 = 100, is visible in Appendix 4 (Figure A4.1). The receipts from the two zones (EMU and extra-EMU) remained nearly stationary during the four-year period of observation, with the exception of a strong drop for the euro zone in the third quarter of 1999, mainly because of the effect of the Kosovo crisis, which took place in the first half of 1999 and discouraged the advance bookings of holidays in Italy for the subsequent summer.

The relative price index remained practically constant *vis-à-vis* the euro zone, due to the ongoing process of convergence of the EMU area. In relation to the extra-EMU area, the wider variability of the index reflects the higher volatility of the exchange rate of the lira against the currencies of the area. The US dollar, the Canadian dollar and the pound moved jointly, increasing their value during the period, with the exception of the year 1998. The Japanese yen, after a drop between the summer of 1997 and the summer of 1998, showed a strong increase. The Swiss franc sharply decreased in 1996 and remained stable afterwards. The overall effect is therefore a tendency to increase the competitiveness of Italy's prices *vis-à-vis* the prices of the extra-EMU area.

Table 18.5 shows the final specification of the three models and the respective diagnostic tests. Three dummy variables are included to remove the effect of some outliers in the first three quarters of 1999.[16] The diagnostic tests indicate a good fit of the model, particularly for the euro zone and the total receipts, with no problems of

---

[15] In the previous section of the chapter it was necessary to use the number of night stays as a proxy of the receipts geographically disaggregated, because the latter were not available for the years before 1996.

[16] The outliers, in the second and third quarter for the extra-EMU area and in the third quarter for the EMU area, are likely to be connected to a drop in the expected inflows in relation to the mentioned tensions in Kosovo.

autocorrelation of the residuals. The parameters' signs are in line with the expectations: negative for the price factor and – with the exception of model X for which the coefficient (γ_2) is not present because it is not significant – positive for the income factor. The comparison of the elasticities of the price factor shows a higher absolute value for the euro zone: 2.12 against 0.71 for the extra-EMU area and 1.01 for the world. The elasticity of the income factor is also higher for the euro zone (3.12) than for the world (0.97). Therefore, the results substantially confirm the validity of the model described in the previous section, that can be consequently extended, in a long-term perspective, to both the EMU and the extra-EMU area. Particularly, price factors appear to be relevant in explaining the evolution of Italy's tourism receipts. Moreover, with the necessary caution suggested by the short length of the time series used for this second econometric exercise, it might be inferred that in recent years the sensitivity to price factors has been for the euro zone not smaller but greater than that for the rest of the world.

Table 18.5 Model of Italy's tourism receipts by area of origin (1996-99). Parameters and diagnostic tests

Model for Italy's receipts from EMU countries (model E)

$$LTRE_t = -2.12\ LOCPE_{t-1} + 3.12\ LGDPE_{t-1} + 0.13\ D99Q2 - 0.40\ D99Q3$$
$$(t)\quad\quad (2.62)\quad\quad\quad\quad (3.85)\quad\quad\quad\quad (1.98)\quad\quad\quad (-6.19)$$

$R^2 = 0.83$; Adjusted $R^2 = 0.78$; $F(4,11) = 22,467.77$; DW $= 1.78$; AR(1–4) $= 1.06$ (see note 17 below)

Model for Italy's receipts from extra-EMU countries (model X)

$$LTRX_t = 7.86 - 0.71\ LOCPX_{t-1} - 0.12\ D99Q2 - 0.12\ D99Q3$$
$$(t)\quad (5.55)\ (-2.29)\quad\quad\quad (-2.76)\quad\quad (-2.54)$$

$R^2 = 0.56$; Adjusted $R^2 = 0.44$; $F(3,11) = 4.60$; DW $= 1.66$; AR(1–4) $= 0.29$

Model for Italy's receipts from all countries (model W)

$$LTRW_t = 4.80 - 1.01\ LOCPW_{t-1} + 0.97\ LGDPW_{t-1} + 0.11\ D99Q1 - 0.26\ D99Q3$$
$$(t)\quad (2.66)\ (-2.79)\quad\quad\quad (3.78)\quad\quad\quad\quad (4.18)\quad\quad (-9.68)$$

$R^2 = 0.93$; Adjusted $R^2 = 0.90$; $F(4,10) = 31.96$; DW $= 1.97$; AR(1–4) $= 0.90$

The subjective evaluation of Italian tourist prices: analysis by type of visitor

In this section, after having investigated the role of price factors for the Italian international tourism market from a macro-economic perspective, an attempt is made to point out the role of the same factors from a micro-economic standpoint. The objective is to outline the specific judgement of prices of the various categories of visitors, classified according to several attributes, such as the visitors' gender, age and profession, the place of visit and the accommodation used. Having in mind the framework of the analysis illustrated in this chapter, attention will be also paid to the need to point out the possible differences in the attitude toward prices between the

---

[17] AR(1-4) tests the autocorrelation of the residuals up to the fourth order.

visitors originated from the two 'currency areas', i.e. the euro zone and the rest of the world.

The main source used for this part of the analysis is the mentioned UIC survey. Among other information (number and characteristics of visitors, tourist behaviour, pattern of expenditure), it collects scores assigned by visitors, in a scale from 1 (minimum satisfaction) to 10 (maximum), to Italian prices and several other aspects of their stay in Italy. The list of aspects investigated by the survey are the following (the abbreviations used further on are indicated in brackets):

1. courtesy and character of local people (courtesy)
2. cities and works of art (art)
3. scenery, natural environment (environment)
4. hotels (and other available accommodation) (hotels)
5. food, cuisine (food)
6. prices, cost of living (prices)
7. quality and choice of goods in shops (shopping)
8. tourist services and information (information)
9. safety of tourists (safety)
10. overall opinion (overall)[17]

The size of the source database, composed by hundred thousands of face-to-face interviews, allows for accurate and fairly disaggregated analysis. The analysis has been restricted to the visitors who travelled in Italy for holiday reasons, spending at least one night in the country. The restriction by purpose of visit aimed at the exclusion of business travellers and visitors travelling for particular personal reasons (study, healthcare etc.), whose 'attitude' to price factors is considered of a peculiar nature, for the reason mentioned above. The exclusion of same-day visitors is, instead, motivated by the need to balance the sample composition, by sterilizing the very strong concentration of this segment in a few bordering countries: same-day visitors from France, Switzerland and Austria represent 80 per cent of the total. Finally, in order to simplify the analysis (without a relevant loss of precision) only the following seven main countries of origin are taken into account: Austria, France and Germany for the euro zone and Japan, Switzerland, the UK and the USA for the extra-EMU area.

Table 18.6 shows the annual average score given by the visitors during the whole period in which the survey was operated, disaggregated by individual aspect. The overall score is always around 8.4, indicating the very positive evaluation given by the visitors to their stay in Italy. Environment, art, courtesy and food are the items that receive the highest appreciation (above 8), whereas prices – although they receive a substantially good judgement (6.9 is the average of the four-year period) – are the aspect for which the visitors are less enthusiastic.

Starting to focus on the key aspect, the prices in Italy, a preliminary analysis has been carried out to test whether the changes of the subjective judgement of prices, collected from visitors by the UIC survey, adequately reflects the evolution of the 'real' economic conditions. To this end, for each country of origin the correlation between (a) the average score assigned to prices by the visitors coming from that country and (b) the

---

[18] The 'overall' score represents the global assessment of the satisfaction for the trip given by the visitors. See Touring Club Italiano – Ufficio Italiano dei Cambi (1998), and Ufficio Italiano dei Cambi (1998) for a regression study in which the analysis of the weights of the various aspects in 'explaining' the general satisfaction is carried out.

Table 18.6 Average scores assigned by non-resident visitors to various aspects of their stay in Italy – visitors travelling for personal reasons, 1996–9

Aspect	1996	1997	1998	1999	All years
Courtesy	8.61	8.57	8.53	8.49	8.55
Art	8.73	8.72	8.84	8.59	8.72
Environment	8.81	8.78	8.73	8.69	8.75
Accommodation	7.78	7.97	7.92	7.91	7.90
Food	8.44	8.59	8.63	8.52	8.54
Prices	6.62	6.94	6.98	6.90	6.86
Shopping	7.91	8.04	7.96	7.85	7.94
Information	7.62	7.67	7.67	7.71	7.67
Safety	7.77	7.89	7.86	7.90	7.85
Overall	8.44	8.42	8.47	8.43	8.44

Source: UIC

relative price index of Italian prices *vis-à-vis* the prices in the same country of origin. The relative price index (base 1996 = 100) was developed, for each country of origin and for the world, with the same methodology used in previous part of the research.[18]

Figure A5.1 in Appendix 5 shows the evolution of the two variables for each country. The visual analysis confirms that a significant correlation exists between them, for almost all countries, even if not always to the same extent. Visitors from the USA and from the UK appeared able to evaluate 'correctly' the changes of relative prices, thus adequately assessing, mainly, the proportions of the relatively sharp shifts of their currency against the lira. On the contrary, the average score for Italian prices of Austrian visitors was highly variable during the period, despite the fact that the relative price index remained practically constant.

Table 18.7 synthesizes the behaviour for the different countries of origin by indicating the linear correlation coefficient between the two variables under study. With the exception of Austria, a substantial correlation – correctly negative given that a higher relative price index means a less competitive level of Italian prices – is found for all countries and for the world (–0.41).

As a conclusion, visitors are generally aware of the level of relative tourism prices. This result legitimates the continuation of the descriptive analysis through the investigation of the different attitudes toward prices of the different visitors' segments. The investigation has been carried through the analysis of the differences of the average scores assigned to Italian prices by the various types of visitors, during the period 1996–9. This is categorized according to the following nine attributes, which classifies the visitors in a set of modalities:[19]

[19] For the period t, the relative price index for an individual country i (OCP_{it}) is calculated transforming into an index base 1996 = 100 the indicators $OCPA_{it} = CPI_t/(CPI_{it}*CER_{it})$, where CPI_t is the consumer price index of Italy in period t, CPI_{it} is the consumer price index of country i in period t and CER_{it} is the exchange rate of the currency of the country i *vis-à-vis* the Italian lira in period t. For the aggregate 'world', a weighted average is calculated, using the receipts from each country as the weights.

[20] Table A6.1 in Appendix 6 lists the modalities for each attribute.

Table 18.7 Correlation between the average score assigned to Italian prices and the index of relative prices of the country of origin *vis-à-vis* Italy's prices (visitors travelling for holidays, with at least one overnight stay in Italy) 1996–9

Country of origin	Linear correlation
Austria	0.08
France	–0.34
UK	–0.89
USA	–0.92
Switzerland	–0.61
Japan	–0.75
Germany	–0.30
World	–0.41

Source: UIC

- zone of origin of the visitor (EMU/extra-EMU);
- country of origin of the visitor;
- age of the visitor;
- sex of the visitor;
- profession of the visitor;
- accommodation used by the visitor;
- area of destination in Italy;
- year and quarter in which the trip was undertaken.

Table 18.8 Results of the ANOVA on the influence of visitors' attributes on the score assigned to Italian tourism prices (visitors travelling for holidays, with at least one overnight stay in Italy) 1996–9

Source	Degrees of freedom	Sum of squares	Mean square	F value	Pr > F
Model	30	8369333.466	278977.8	91.18	0.0001
Error	84159	257508286.3	3059.783		
Corrected total	84189	265877619.7			
	C.V.	Root MSE		VPRE Mean	
	775.8756	53.55825601		6.90294372	

Attributes	Degrees of freedom	Type I SS	Mean square	F value	Pr > F
Zone	1	561,409.7633	561,409.7633	183.48	0.0001
Country	5	3,795,667.872	759,133.5743	248.1	0.0001
Age	4	191,250.5987	47,812.64968	15.63	0.0001
Sex	1	94,831.01222	94,831.01222	30.99	0.0001
Profession	4	780,608.4262	195,152.1066	63.78	0.0001
Accommodation	6	660,296.9511	110,049.4919	35.97	0.0001
Area	3	812,496.4686	270,832.1562	88.51	0.0001
Year	3	1,093,680.639	364,560.2132	119.15	0.0001
Quarter	3	379,091.7344	126,363.9115	41.3	0.0001

(Number of observations in data set = 86,481 (84,190 excluding observations with missing values))

The classic ANOVA (analysis of variance) approach has been adopted to test the influence of each attribute on the level of the score attached to Italian prices. The results of the ANOVA (Table 18.8) show that all the attributes are extremely significant, also thanks to the large number of available non-missing observations (n = 84,190). It can be concluded, therefore, that each combination of modalities brings a significant change to the average score for prices. Although all the modalities are therefore relevant to explain the perception of prices, it is interesting to synthesize the information from the visitors' replies by looking at the modalities that involve the larger deviation from the global average of the sample.

Tables A6.2, A6.3 and A6.4 in Appendix 6 show the annual average scores for each visitors' group in relation to the world and the two areas of origin, i.e. the EMU area and the extra-EMU area. Table 18.9 below reports, for each group, the differences from the global average, again disaggregated by area of origin. Looking at the differences from the global average whose absolute value is larger, it appears that:

- Austrian visitors evidence a very positive consideration of Italian prices. Their average score for prices is in fact 0.40 higher than the global mean for all countries of origin. On the contrary, the visitors from the USA are less satisfied (–0.59), followed by the French (–0.40). In general, visitors from outside the euro zone are less satisfied with Italian prices (–0.17).
- As regards the tourists' profession, the students constitute a category particularly critical of price levels (–0.36).
- People staying in youth hostels provide a much more negative perception of Italy's prices (–0.69) than the visitors using other types of accommodation. This evidence, in the light of the previous remark concerning students, suggests a tendency to a negative evaluation of Italian prices by young people. This is, in fact, confirmed by the fairly negative difference for visitors aged up to 24 years (–0.12 for the euro zone and –0.07 for the rest of the world). The appreciation of visitors staying at rented dwellings is also negative if they come from the euro zone (–0.23) but becomes clearly positive (+0.32) if the visitors come from the extra-EMU area.
- An opposition between euro and non-euro zone is also apparent with respect of the area of destination: non-euro visitors give a positive evaluation of the prices in Southern Italy (+0.33), whereas euro-zone tourists evaluate them negatively (–0.19). The negative judgement of the prices in the Centre is stronger for the euro-zone travellers (–0.33) than for the extra-EMU residents (–0.15).

Focusing on visitors from the euro zone, it is then possible to summarize the segments that showed the more negative attitude toward prices and that might, consequently, be more affected by a possible loss of competitiveness of the Italian tourist products (the negative differences below –0.1 are selected):

- country of origin: France (–0.45)
- age: up to 24 years (–0.12)
- profession: students (–0.37)
- accommodation: youth hostel (–0.77)
                  rented dwelling (–0.23)
                  other (–0.16)
- area of destination: centre (–0.33)
                  south and isles (–0.19)
                  north-west (–0.11)
- period of the year: fourth quarter (–0.19)

Table 18.9 Average scores assigned by non-resident visitors to Italian prices – disaggregation by various attributes of the visitor and of the trip (visitors travelling for holidays, with at least one overnight stay in Italy), 1996–9. (Differences from global averages)

	EMU countries	extra-EMU countries	All countries
Zone of origin			
EMU	–	–	0.05
Extra-EMU	–	–	−0.17
Country of origin			
Austria	0.35	–	0.40
France	−0.45	–	−0.40
UK	–	0.23	0.06
USA	–	−0.42	−0.59
Switzerland	–	0.15	−0.02
Japan	–	0.01	−0.16
Germany	−0.01	–	0.04
Age of visitor			
0-24 years	−0.12	−0.07	−0.13
25-34 years	−0.02	−0.03	−0.03
35-44 years	0.06	0.07	0.08
45-64 years	−0.02	0.05	0
65 years and more	−0.02	−0.12	−0.05
Sex of visitor			
Male	−0.02	−0.01	−0.01
Female	0.05	0.02	0.02
Profession			
Employed (subordinate)	0	0.09	0.02
Self-employed	0.07	−0.09	0.04
Student	−0.37	−0.26	−0.36
Housewife	0.14	0.12	0.13
Retired	0.08	−0.02	0.07
Accommodation			
Rented dwelling	−0.23	0.32	−0.14
Owned dwelling	0.22	0.12	0.2
Guest of relatives/friends	0.01	0.13	0.03
Tent, caravan	0	0	0.03
Other	−0.16	−0.04	−0.12
Youth hostel	−0.77	−0.5	−0.69
Hotel, tourist village	0.03	−0.02	0.01
Destination area			
North-west	−0.11	0.18	−0.04
North-east	0.15	−0.02	0.16
Centre	−0.33	−0.15	−0.3
South and isles	−0.19	0.33	−0.06

	EMU countries	extra-EMU countries	All countries
Quarter			
QTR1	0.1	0.03	0.06
QTR2	0.07	−0.05	0.05
QTR3	−0.02	0.05	0
QTR4	−0.19	−0.05	−0.16
Global	0	0	0

Source: UIC

As a conclusion, the subjective evaluation of Italian prices cannot be easily explained by a relatively small set of visitors' attributes. However, the analysis has shown that some segments have a stronger tendency to orient their evaluation in the positive or in the negative sense.

CONCLUSIONS

In accordance with prevailing economic theory and with the results of studies referred to in other national contexts, the authors have found that Italy's tourism receipts have a clear long-term relationship with the aggregate income of the visitors' home countries and the relative prices of Italy *vis-à-vis* the origin and competitor countries. The exposition to price competitiveness during the period 1977–99 was relevant, given that a 1 per cent loss of this indicator caused a 3 per cent decrease of tourism receipts. The authors have also found that this relationship is not only valid for the aggregated receipts, i.e. originated from all countries, but also in relation to the receipts specifically originated from visitors resident in the euro zone, although this result requires further confirmation because of the lack of sufficiently long time series.

Exploiting the database originated by the UIC frontier survey, the subjective evaluation of Italian prices provided by a large sample of non-resident visitors has been analysed. It has emerged that the visitors are generally able to assess adequately the real changes of relative prices. The visitors' evaluation of prices is significantly influenced by all the attributes considered: the tourists' socio-demographic characteristics (sex, age, profession), the country of origin, the area of destination, the accommodation used and the time of the year in which the trip is undertaken. Among the visitors coming from the euro zone, the analysis allowed identification of some visitors' groups that express the more negative evaluation of prices and are therefore likely to be particularly exposed to a loss of price competitiveness of the country's tourism industry. They are, above all, the French tourists, the youngest visitors (particularly the students), those staying at youth hostels and the tourists visiting the Centre of Italy.

BIBLIOGRAPHY

Artus, J. R. (1970) 'The effect of revaluation on the foreign travel balance of payments of Germany'. *International Monetary Fund Staff Papers*, **17**.

Artus, J. R. (1972) 'An econometric analysis of international travel', *International Monetary Fund Staff Papers*, **19**.

Biagioli, A. (1997) 'Sample survey on Italian international tourism'. Third International Forum on Tourism Statistics. Paris: OECD.

Becheri, E. *et al.* (2000) *Nono Rapporto sul Turismo Italiano 2000.*

Bodo, G., Parigi, E. and Urga, G. (1990) 'Test d'integrazione ed analisi di cointegrazione: una rassegna della letteratura ed un'applicazione'. Temi di Discussione del Servizio Studi, Banca d'Italia, n. 139.

Carraro, C. and Pesce, C. (1995) 'La domanda internazionale di turismo: un'analisi ecnometrica basata sui panel data', Gruppi di Ricerca Eonomica Teorica ed Applicata: Working paper, no. 6.

Chiesa, C. and Castaldo, P. (1984) 'Il turismo con l'estero dell'Italia'. *Rivista Internazionale di Scienze Economiche e Commerciali,* **7**, 639–48.

Dickey, D. A. and Fuller, W. A. (1979) 'Distribution of the estimators for autoregressive time series with a unit root'. *Journal of the American Statistical Association,* **47**, 427–31.

Doornik, J. A. and Hendry, D. F. (1994) *PCGIVE 8.0 Manual.* Institute of Economics and Statistics, University of Oxford.

Eurostat (1997) 'Measuring the travel item of the balance of payments of EU member states.' *Travel Task Force Report.* Proposals for Stage 3 of EMU.

Eurostat (2000a) Revision of the Collection Systems for the Travel Item of the Balance of Payments of EU Member States Following Stage Three of the EMU. Technical Group Travel Report (draft).

Eurostat (2000b) Papers on Collection Plans and Methodologies for Travel. Technical Group Travel Report (draft).

International Monetary Fund (1993) *Balance of Payments Manual* (fifth edition).

Johansen, S. (1988) 'Statistical analysis of cointegration vectors'. *Journal of Economic Dynamics and Control,* **12**, 231–54.

Loeb, P. D. (1982) 'International travel to the United States: an econometric evaluation'. *Annals of Tourism Research,* **9**, 7–20.

Mirto, A. P. and Ortolani, G. G. (1998) 'Methodology for the collection of statistics on tourist movements at land frontiers'. Seminar on Frontier Statistics in European Countries. Madrid: World Tourism Organization.

Ortolani, G. G. (1998) 'Frontier survey and bank reporting system: comparison of results' (mimeo).

Raminhos, M. M. C. (1997) 'Models of receipts from tourism in Portugal: cointegration dynamic specification and forecast' (mimeo).

Said, S. E. and Dickey, D. A. (1984) 'Testing for unit roots in autoregressive: moving average models of unknown order', *Biometrika,* **71**, 599–608.

Syriopoulos, T. C. and Sinclair, M. T. (1993) 'An econometric study of tourism demand: the AIDS model of US and European tourism in Mediterranean countries', *Applied Economics,* **25**, 1541–52.

Touring Club Italiano – Ufficio Italiano dei Cambi (1998) 'Turismo estero al Sud: una occasione di sviluppo'.

Ufficio Italiano dei Cambi (1998) *The Geography of International Tourism Demand in Italy.*

United Nations – World Tourism Organization (1993) *Recommendations on Tourism Statistics.*

World Tourism Organization (1999) *Seminar on Frontier Statistics in European Countries* (Surveys on Inbound and Outbound Tourism). Madrid.

APPENDIX 1: DETAILED GEOGRAPHICAL DISAGGREGATION OF ITALY'S INTERNATIONAL TOURISM RECEIPTS

Table A1.1 Italy's international tourism receipts by region, subregion and country of origin (million $US) 1996–9.

Region	Subregion	Country	1996	1997	1998	1999
Africa	*Eastern Africa*	*Eastern Africa (Total)*	*53*	*25*	*32*	*30*
	Middle Africa	*Middle Africa (Total)*	*10*	*10*	*7*	*16*
	Northern Africa	Algeria	50	51	27	36
		Morocco	35	32	28	26
		Tunisia	54	64	71	76
		Northern Africa (Other)	0	1	3	1
	Total Northern Africa		*140*	*148*	*129*	*138*
	Southern Africa	South Africa	45	99	48	53
		Southern Africa (Other)	3	1	2	3
	Total Southern Africa		*48*	*100*	*50*	*56*
	Western Africa	*Western Africa (Total)*	*62*	*57*	*59*	*46*
Total Africa			**312**	**340**	**277**	**285**
Americas	*Caribbean*	*Caribbean (Total)*	*54*	*21*	*24*	*24*
	Central America	Panama	3	1	2	0
		Central America (Other)	8	8	10	9
	Total Central America		*11*	*9*	*12*	*9*
	Northern America	Canada	243	351	297	265
		Mexico	60	102	122	92
		USA	2,620	3,319	3,262	2,826
		Northern America (Other)	0	0	1	
	Total Northern America		*2,923*	*3,771*	*3,682*	*3,183*
	Southern America	Argentina	161	218	184	158
		Brazil	339	463	375	210
		Chile	21	44	55	36
		Venezuela	26	27	17	41
		Southern America (Other)	71	73	51	36
	Total Southern America		*618*	*825*	*681*	*482*
Total Americas			**3,606**	**4,625**	**4,399**	**3,697**
East Asia & Pacific	Northeastern Asia	China	149	153	205	203
		HK,China	62	66	31	40
		Japan	3,209	2,818	2,275	1,894
		Korean Republic	378	262	51	70
		Taiwan	74	112	35	69
		Northeastern Asia (Other)	3			
	Total Northeastern Asia		*3,875*	*3,411*	*2,596*	*2,276*
	Southeastern Asia	Indonesia	24	31	3	19
		Malaysia	28	37	6	22
		Thailand	36	26	21	33
		Southeastern Asia (Other)	113	132	124	109
	Total Southeastern Asia		*201*	*227*	*153*	*183*

Region	Subregion	Country	1996	1997	1998	1999
	Australasia	Australia	467	557	335	259
		New Zealand	53	71	44	65
	Total Australasia		*520*	*629*	*379*	*324*
	Melanesia	*Melanesia (Total)*	*0*	*1*	*3*	*3*
	Micronesia	*Micronesia (Total)*	*1*	*0*		*1*
	Polynesia	*Polynesia (Total)*	*1*		*0*	*0*
Total East Asia & Pacific			**4,598**	**4,267**	**3,131**	**2,788**
Europe	Central/East Europe	Hungary	144	82	78	115
		Poland	118	163	206	204
		Romania	38	37	40	46
		Russian Federation	665	920	795	577
		Central/East Europe (Other)	146	137	150	228
	Total Central/East Europe		*1,111*	*1,338*	*1,269*	*1,170*
	Northern Europe	Denmark	163	148	180	218
		Finland	92	96	73	95
		Ireland	65	103	100	86
		Norway	82	109	99	107
		Sweden	196	235	207	203
		UK	1,565	1,732	2,014	2,028
		Northern Europe (Other)	6	6	5	21
	Total Northern Europe		*2,168*	*2,430*	*2,677*	*2,757*
	Southern Europe	Croatia	877	592	527	432
		Greece	561	539	552	536
		Portugal	109	78	67	72
		Slovenia	435	294	345	309
		Spain	532	565	766	572
		Yugoslavia	146	61	38	21
		Southern Europe (Other)	140	283	146	98
	Total Southern Europe		*2,801*	*2,411*	*2,441*	*2,040*
	Western Europe	Austria	1,417	1,616	2,027	2,691
		Belgium	529	493	440	424
		France	2,117	2,001	2,292	2,509
		Germany	8,241	7,194	7,752	6,561
		Luxembourg	25	69	26	27
		Netherlands	758	578	686	822
		Switzerland	1,720	1,606	1,807	1,911
		Western Europe (Other)	72	97	57	124
	Total Western Europe		*14,879*	*13,655*	*15,088*	*15,070*
	East Mediter Europe	Israel	102	133	110	82
		Turkey	89	128	109	81
		East Mediter Europe (Other)	17	12	13	7
	Total East Mediter Europe		*208*	*272*	*232*	*170*
Total Europe			**21,168**	**20,107**	**21,706**	**21,207**

Region	Subregion	Country	1996	1997	1998	1999
Middle	Middle East	Egypt	74	92	63	81
East		Kuwait	10	16	8	6
		Libya	15	25	7	33
		Saudi Arabia	31	30	50	49
		Middle East (Other)	96	77	78	66
	Total Middle East		*226*	*239*	*205*	*236*
Total Middle East			**226**	**239**	**205**	**236**
Southern	Southern Asia	India	79	83	93	104
Asia		Iran	9	23	14	15
		Southern Asia (Other)	19	29	40	26
	Total Southern Asia		*107*	*135*	*148*	*145*
Total Southern Asia			**107**	**135**	**148**	**145**
Not classified	*Not classified*	*Not classified*	*0*	*0*	*0*	
WORLD TOTAL			**30,017**	**29,714**	**29,866**	**28,359**

Source: UIC

APPENDIX 2: GRAPHS OF THE TIME SERIES (MODEL OF STATIONARITY AND CO-INTEGRATION)

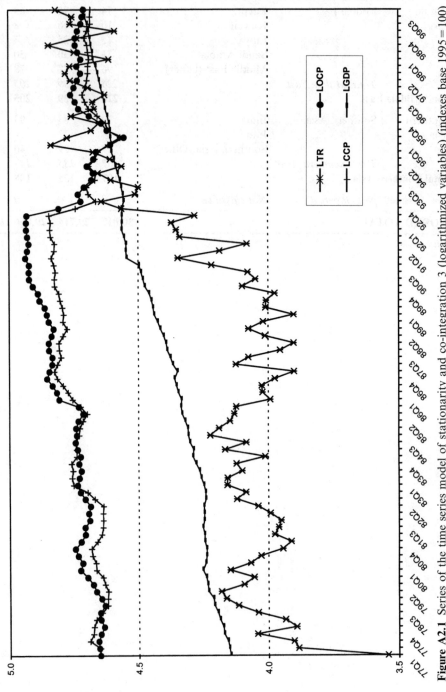

Figure A2.1 Series of the time series model of stationarity and co-integration 3 (logarithmized variables) (indexes base 1995=100)

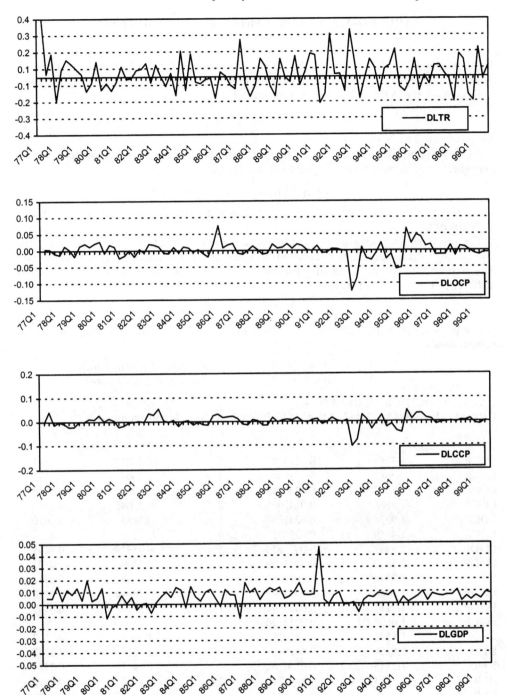

Figure A2.2 Series of the time series model of independent variables (first differences of logarithmized variables)

APPENDIX 3: STATIONARITY TESTS (ADF TEST)

The test adopted in this chapter is the Augmented Dickey-Fuller (ADF): the test derives from the Dickey-Fuller test, whose validity is sound if the residuals ε_t of the series y_t generated by the AR(1) data generation model:

$$y_t = \rho y_{t-1} + \varepsilon_t$$

are distributed as N $(0, \sigma^2)$.

As this hypothesis can not be verified for any series, the ADF test checks the nil hypothesis of one unit root adopting the model:

$$\Delta y_t = \lambda y_{t-1} + \beta_1 \Delta y_{t-1} + \ldots + \beta_p \Delta y_{t-p} + \varepsilon_t \tag{1}$$

where the autoregressive scheme order p is chosen as to make the residuals distributed as N $(0, \sigma^2)$.

The test consists in estimating regressions of type (1); selecting the model having the highest lag with a significant coefficient, looking at the λ coefficient. If λ is significant (the hypothesis can be checked with the usual t-test) λ measures the value of ρ-1 (difference from unity of ρ) in:

$$y_t = \rho y_{t-1} + \beta_1 \Delta y_{t-1} + \ldots + \beta_p \Delta y_{t-p} + \varepsilon_t$$

where $\rho = 1$ is the hypothesis of a unit root in the series. So the following hypothesis system holds:

$$H_0 : \lambda = 0 \Longleftrightarrow \rho = 1 \qquad \text{(presence of a unit root)}$$
$$H_1 : \lambda < 0 \Longleftrightarrow \rho < 1 \qquad \text{(absence of a unit root).}$$

Unit root tests 1978 (3) to 1999 (4)
Critical values: 5% = −3.462; 1% = −4.067; constant and Trend included

	t-adf	å lag	t-lag		t-prob
LOCP	−1.7794	0.024129	5	0.28017	0.7801
LOCP	−1.7681	0.023988	4	−1.2604	0.2112
LOCP	−2.0812	0.024076	3	1.5960	0.1144
LOCP	−1.8006	0.024305	2	−0.43045	0.6680
LOCP	−1.9338	0.024184	1	3.3985	0.0010
LOCP	−1.4319	0.025675	0		
LGDP	−2.4447	0.0071554	5	0.038396	0.9695
LGDP	−2.5322	0.0071100	4	2.6300	0.0103
LGDP	−1.9849	0.0073682	3	1.1400	0.2577
LGDP	−1.8080	0.0073819	2	0.78940	0.4322
LGDP	−1.7111	0.0073649	1	0.51073	0.6109
LGDP	−1.6606	0.0073320	0		
LTR	−1.8552	0.082026	5	1.5864	0.1167
LTR	−1.5706	0.082809	4	2.3062	0.0237
LTR	−1.2543	0.085015	3	−2.1401	0.0354
LTR	−1.5874	0.086874	2	−3.3603	0.0012
LTR	−2.3213	0.092164	1	−0.85553	0.3948
LTR	−2.6766	0.092015	0		
LCCP	−1.0616	0.032877	5	−1.4152	0.1610
LCCP	−1.3679	0.033085	4	−1.1555	0.2514

LCCP	−1.6308	0.033154	3	0.86442	0.3899
LCCP	−1.4907	0.033103	2	−0.29572	0.7682
LCCP	−1.5956	0.032918	1	3.0805	0.0028
LCCP	−0.9928	0.034560	0		

Conclusions: no value is lower than the thresholds; the nil hypothesis of one unit root can not be rejected for any series.

APPENDIX 4: GRAPHS OF THE EVOLUTION OF THE TIME SERIES (FINAL MODEL, pp. 231–2)

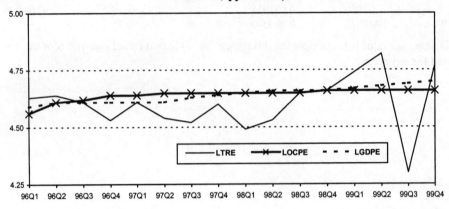

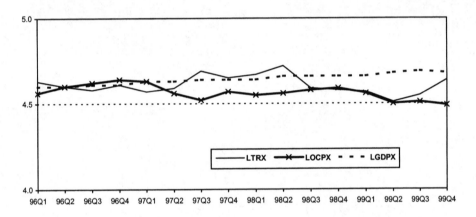

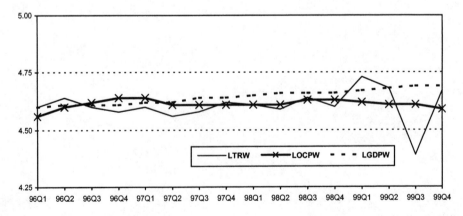

Figure A4.1 Series of the evolution of the time series model, final model (Logarithmized variables) (indexes base 1996 = 100)

APPENDIX 5: GRAPHS OF THE EVALUATION OF PRICES VS. THE ACTUAL PRICES

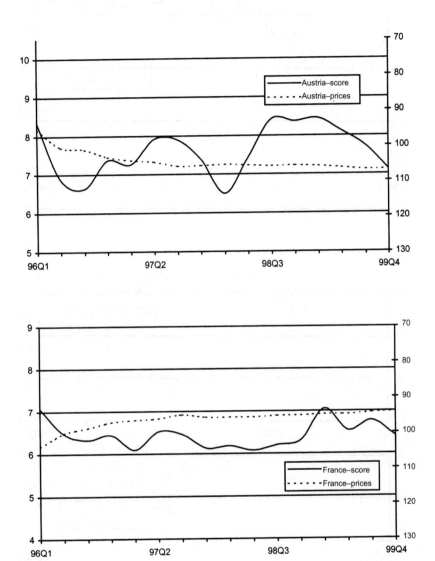

KEY:
Country-score = Average score assigned to Italian prices (on a scale from 1 to 10) by the visitors resident in the country (scale on the left). Only visitors travelling for holiday reasons and spending at least one night in Italy are considered.
Country-prices = Index (base 1996 = 100) of relative tourist prices of the country *vis-à-vis* Italy. A decrease of the index value means an increase of price competitiveness of Italian tourist prices. (Scale on the right, inverted to improve readability)

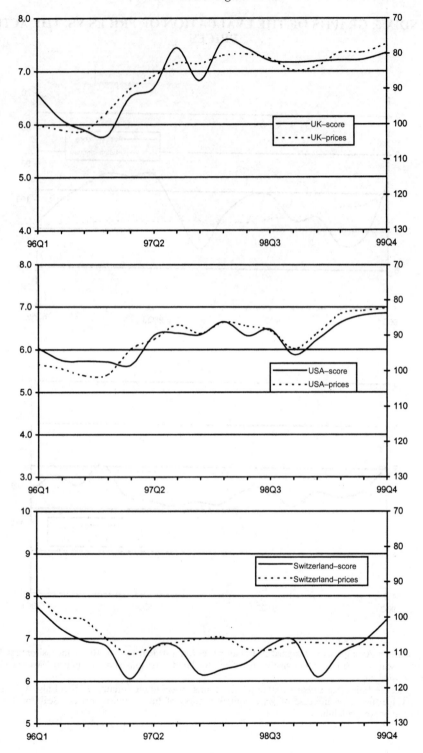

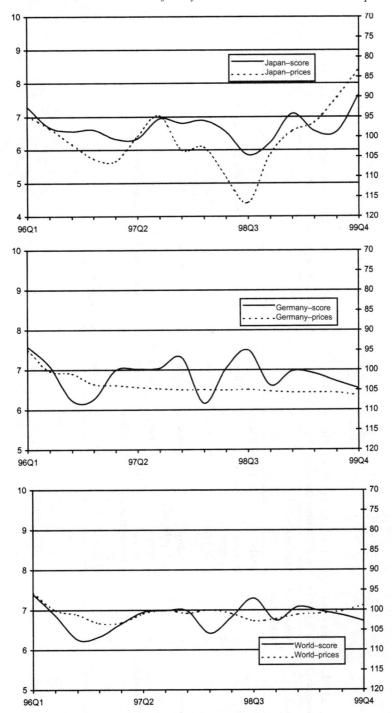

Figure A5.1 Subjective evaluation of prices and actual relative prices (1996–9)

APPENDIX 6: ANALYSIS OF THE EVALUATION OF ITALIAN TOURISM PRICES BY TYPE OF VISITOR

Table A6.1 List of the attributes and the respective modalities considered for the ANOVA on the influence of visitors' attributes on the score assigned to Italian tourism prices (visitors travelling for holidays, with at least one overnight stay in Italy), 1996–9

Attribute	Number of modalities	Modalities						
Zone	2	EMU	Extra-EMU					
Country	7	Austria	France	Germany	Japan	Switzerland	UK	USA
Sex	2	Female	Male					
Age	5	0–24 years	25–34 years	35–44 years	45–64 years	65 years and more		
Profession	5	Employed (subordinate)	Housewife	Retired	Self-employed	Student		
Area	4	Centre	North-East	North-West	South and Isles			
Accommodation	7	Guest of relatives/friends	Hotel, tourist village	Other	Owned dwelling	Rented dwelling	Tent, caravan	Youth hostel
Year	4	1996	1997	1998	1999			
Quarter	4	QTR1	QTR2	QTR3	QTR4			

Table A6.2 Average scores assigned by non-resident visitors to Italian prices – disaggregation according to various attributes of the visitor and of the trip (visitors travelling for holidays, with at least one overnight stay in Italy), 1996–9. All countries of origin

	1996	1997	1998	1999	All years
ZONE OF ORIGIN					
EMU	6.66	7.03	7.07	6.89	6.91
extra-EMU	6.50	6.61	6.71	6.96	6.69
COUNTRY OF ORIGIN					
Austria	6.46	7.30	7.60	7.33	7.26
France	6.45	6.40	6.17	6.68	6.46
UK	6.06	7.01	7.32	7.23	6.92
USA	5.77	6.28	6.32	6.70	6.27
Switzerland	7.11	6.62	6.69	6.89	6.84
Japan	6.85	6.58	6.39	7.00	6.70
Germany	6.72	7.07	7.08	6.78	6.90
AGE OF VISITOR					
0–24 years	6.66	6.80	6.67	6.78	6.73
25–34 years	6.48	6.79	7.21	6.82	6.83
35–44 years	6.79	7.09	6.99	6.89	6.94
45–64 years	6.59	6.95	6.93	7.00	6.86
65 years and more	6.52	6.99	6.60	7.12	6.81
SEX OF VISITOR					
Male	6.63	6.97	6.95	6.85	6.85
Female	6.58	6.81	7.04	7.01	6.88
PROFESSION					
Employed (subordinate)	6.59	6.96	7.06	6.95	6.88
Self-employed	6.85	7.07	6.86	6.80	6.90
Student	6.37	6.50	6.50	6.61	6.50
Housewife	6.76	6.75	7.24	6.96	6.99
Retired	6.48	6.94	7.05	7.16	6.93
ACCOMMODATION					
Rented dwelling	6.40	6.86	6.81	6.82	6.72
Owned dwelling	6.82	7.29	7.12	6.98	7.06
Guest of relatives/friends	6.85	6.95	6.70	7.05	6.89
Tent, caravan	6.42	7.01	7.44	6.66	6.89
Other	6.65	6.76	6.87	7.12	6.74
Youth hostel	6.22	6.22	5.94	6.27	6.17
Hotel, tourist village	6.65	6.91	6.97	6.93	6.87
DESTINATION AREA					
North-west	6.83	7.04	6.66	6.73	6.82
North-east	6.67	7.08	7.31	7.02	7.02
Centre	6.34	6.54	6.61	6.74	6.56
South and Isles	6.50	6.83	6.75	7.10	6.80

	1996	1997	1998	1999	All years
QUARTER					
QTR1	7.40	6.66	6.41	7.08	6.92
QTR2	6.87	6.95	6.82	6.98	6.91
QTR3	6.26	6.99	7.29	6.87	6.86
QTR4	6.33	6.98	6.74	6.72	6.70
GLOBAL	**6.62**	**6.94**	**6.98**	**6.90**	**6.86**

Source: UIC

Table A6.3 Average scores assigned by non-resident visitors to Italian prices – disaggregation according to various attributes of the visitor and of the trip (visitors travelling for holidays, with at least one overnight stay in Italy), 1996–9. Countries of origin = EMU

	1996	1997	1998	1999	All years
COUNTRY OF ORIGIN					
Austria	6.46	7.30	7.60	7.33	7.26
France	6.45	6.40	6.17	6.68	6.46
Germany	6.72	7.07	7.08	6.78	6.90
AGE OF VISITOR					
0–24 years	6.71	7.02	6.70	6.75	6.79
25–34 years	6.47	6.90	7.38	6.77	6.89
35–44 years	6.82	7.17	7.02	6.89	6.97
45–64 years	6.63	6.99	7.01	6.99	6.89
65 years and more	6.74	7.06	6.64	7.13	6.89
SEX OF VISITOR					
Male	6.67	7.06	7.01	6.83	6.89
Female	6.61	6.87	7.20	7.02	6.96
PROFESSION					
Employed (subordinate)	6.61	7.02	7.17	6.89	6.91
Self-employed	6.94	7.16	6.90	6.86	6.98
Student	6.28	6.73	6.46	6.64	6.54
Housewife	6.73	6.81	7.38	6.93	7.05
Retired	6.64	6.96	7.12	7.15	6.99
ACCOMMODATION					
Rented dwelling	6.38	6.85	6.76	6.77	6.68
Owned dwelling	6.68	7.39	7.18	7.14	7.13
Guest of relatives/friends	6.92	6.99	6.78	6.99	6.92
Tent, caravan	6.38	7.07	7.45	6.67	6.91
Other	6.66	6.77	7.04	7.10	6.75
Youth hostel	6.43	6.65	5.81	5.99	6.14
Hotel, tourist village	6.75	7.02	7.06	6.92	6.94
DESTINATION AREA					
North-west	6.81	7.17	6.59	6.62	6.80
North-east	6.69	7.13	7.37	7.05	7.06
Centre	6.38	6.58	6.65	6.68	6.58
South and Isles	6.50	6.79	6.65	6.93	6.72

	1996	1997	1998	1999	All years
QUARTER					
QTR1	7.55	6.86	6.14	7.23	7.01
QTR2	6.95	7.05	6.87	7.02	6.98
QTR3	6.24	7.02	7.43	6.85	6.89
QTR4	6.37	7.15	6.81	6.53	6.72
GLOBAL	**6.66**	**7.03**	**7.07**	**6.89**	**6.91**

Source: UIC

Table A6.4 Average scores assigned by non-resident visitors to Italian prices – disaggregation according to various attributes of the visitor and of the trip (visitors travelling for holidays, with at least one overnight stay in Italy), 1996–9. Countries of origin = Extra-EMU

	1996	1997	1998	1999	All years
COUNTRY OF ORIGIN					
UK	6.06	7.01	7.32	7.23	6.92
USA	5.77	6.28	6.32	6.70	6.27
Switzerland	7.11	6.62	6.69	6.89	6.84
Japan	6.85	6.58	6.39	7.00	6.70
AGE OF VISITOR					
0–24 years	6.58	6.45	6.63	6.84	6.62
25–34 years	6.52	6.50	6.68	6.98	6.66
35–44 years	6.63	6.60	6.88	6.89	6.76
45–64 years	6.46	6.78	6.69	7.04	6.74
65 years and more	5.99	6.81	6.44	7.07	6.57
SEX OF VISITOR					
Male	6.47	6.53	6.74	6.94	6.68
Female	6.54	6.71	6.66	6.98	6.71
PROFESSION					
Employed (subordinate)	6.54	6.70	6.73	7.14	6.78
Self-employed	6.52	6.60	6.74	6.52	6.60
Student	6.53	6.19	6.57	6.52	6.43
Housewife	6.81	6.66	6.72	7.11	6.81
Retired	5.96	6.86	6.68	7.20	6.67
ACCOMMODATION					
Rented dwelling	6.68	6.96	7.11	7.20	7.01
Owned dwelling	7.21	6.70	6.86	6.50	6.81
Guest of relatives/friends	6.72	6.82	6.52	7.19	6.82
Tent, caravan	6.79	6.39	7.17	6.52	6.69
Other	6.61	6.71	5.96	7.19	6.65
Youth hostel	5.96	6.04	6.13	6.48	6.19
Hotel, tourist village	6.39	6.59	6.72	6.98	6.67
DESTINATION AREA					
North-west	6.88	6.69	6.79	7.15	6.87
North-east	6.42	6.60	6.80	6.79	6.67

	1996	1997	1998	1999	All years
Centre	6.29	6.50	6.56	6.82	6.54
South and Isles	6.51	6.96	6.99	7.48	7.02
QUARTER					
QTR1	7.02	6.19	6.89	6.74	6.72
QTR2	6.54	6.54	6.66	6.81	6.64
QTR3	6.35	6.88	6.74	6.97	6.74
QTR4	6.23	6.49	6.52	7.32	6.64
GLOBAL	**6.50**	**6.61**	**6.71**	**6.96**	**6.69**

Source: UIC

19

The Single Currency and the New Tourism Expenditure Survey in Spain (EGATUR)

Antonio Martínez Serrano

PREVIOUS EXPERIENCE IN MEASURING TOURISM EXPENDITURE

Frontur survey: Movimientos turísticos en fronteras

Movimientos turísticos en fronteras – Frontur (Tourism movements in frontiers), a survey of the Instituto de Estudios Turísticos, set up in May 1996, includes some questions on the expenditure made on the journey to Spain by inbound tourists, such as the total expenditure during the stay in Spain, average expenditure per person per day, breakdown by country of residence, cost of package-tour bookings made before in the country of residence, and other variables. These questions were included with the aim of obtaining estimates and, as an additional aspect, characterizing tourism behaviour.

It should be pointed out that the way this information is collected in the field allows for the application of on-line validation tests of data collected; this operation greatly improves the quality of information by reducing to a minimum the need for corrections and imputations in the subsequent data-processing.

The expenditure data currently included in the Frontur survey does not respond exclusively to the aim of obtaining aggregate estimates of revenue from inbound tourism and payments by outbound tourism. The sample distribution design incorporates a certain under-representation of arrivals by road as compared with arrivals by air, and also for some countries with sizeable shares of arrivals by road (e.g. France and Portugal).

The current design of Frontur, however, incorporating information from administrative registers and questionnaires, allows for a quantification of visitor inflows into Spain and a highly accurate assessment of their behaviour.

These are some of the problems to consider in a new approach that will allow data checking and correction methods to be fined-tuned, bearing in mind the degree of dispersion of the key variables for tourist segments defined by characteristics that are currently not taken into consideration.

Familitur survey: Movimientos turísticos de los españoles

Movimientos turísticos de los españoles – Familitur (Tourism movements of Spanish residents), also run by the Instituto de Estudios Turísticos, is basically a response to the information requirements laid down in Directive 95/57/EC.

As from 1999 the configuration will provide a satisfactory response to the information needs of the Autonomous Communities on interregional tourism flows of Spanish residents and a detailed study of short trips to second residences.

Since June 2000, the new questionnaire has included a more detailed study of domestic and outbound expenditure, although in terms of the estimation of expenditure there are at least two aspects worth stressing in methodological terms:

- Familitur is a household survey whose target population is the whole Spanish population; by its very nature therefore, and due to the size of its travelling population sample, and specially the population travelling abroad, it is by no means ideal for the estimation of tourism expenditure aggregates with the necessary level of information breakdown.
- Data is collected on trips made in the previous four months, which is not ideal for obtaining aggregates of the total volume of expenditure, although it offers reliability in terms of estimates of the volume of tourism, analysis of tourist behaviour and a good approximation of the expenditure breakdown by goods and services.

Other sources for measuring tourism expenditure

The *Encuesta Continua de Presupuestos Familiares*, (Continuous Household Budget Survey) carried out by the Instituto Nacional de Estadística (National Statistical Office) includes a specific module to analyse the expenditure made inside and outside the usual environment and a brief expenditure breakdown.

In the interest of setting up an integrated system of indicators and tourism information sources the Instituto de Estudios Turísticos has suggested that the module be extended by a more detailed expenditure breakdown and an estimation of the structure of tourism consumption of residents involved in both domestic tourism (a critical element for implementing tourism satellite accounts and obtaining a weighting-factor vector for drawing up a tourism price index) and outbound tourism.

THE INTRODUCTION OF THE EURO AND ITS IMPLICATIONS

Introduction

The single-currency policy affects the financial system of the member states, both at central bank level and the banks that participate in its application. But the main tasks carried out by the European System of Central Banks are channelled through the Eurosystem. This takes in the Central European Bank and the central banks of the member states that have adopted the euro in the third phase of monetary union. There are, therefore, currently eleven national central banks in the Eurosystem.

For statistical purposes the eleven states using the single currency will lose all information as from 2002 on transactions carried out in their old currencies. This will have a direct effect on the traditional system used by the Bank of Spain for estimating the balance of payments entries. Specifically, the Bank of Spain will lose a large part of the information furnished by the various banks on the payments made by Spanish residents in foreign countries and the payments made by non-residents in Spain. This information is essential for the journeys entry in the services sub-balance of the current account of the balance of payments.

The measurement of tourism expenditure by traditional methods

The experience in drawing up statistics on tourism expenditure at a national level in Europe has traditionally been linked to the estimation of a set of aggregates and concepts such as:

- tourism receipts and payments in the balance of payments (transactions between residents and non-residents of the compiling economy for travel and tourism purposes);
- aggregate consumption of non-residents in Spain and the consumption of residents abroad, in the context of national accounts;
- the compiling of the Tourism Satellite Account, which can be characterized as an integration of the demand-and-supply side to measure the economic impact of tourism, to be drawn up in accordance with the common methodological guidelines laid down by the World Tourism Organization, OECD and Eurostat and presented recently to the United Nations Committee.

In 1995 the Balance of Payments Working Party set up by the Task Force 'Travel' began its work on compiling and finding solutions for the problems that the introduction of the single currency would pose for the traditional data-collection system based, in a large majority of the European Union member states, on banks' reports and credit card data. Following this method the resident banks give information on tourism transactions such as hotels, travel agencies, sales levels and cashing of cheques, credit card payments, sales and purchases of notes etc.

The measurement of tourism by means of payment is the most frequently used method in countries in which the central bank is responsible for the balance of payments and is hence used in Spain. Under this method resident banks give information on tourism-related fund transfers carried out by resident or non-resident holders of accounts in their offices (the transaction has to be communicated by the resident party thereof). Most tourism receipts and payments are included in this group, for example, payments for hotels and travel agencies with foreign operators or payments of travellers cheques and credit-card expenditure. Given the payment systems for these last two transactions, their correct treatment sometimes calls for direct information from the payment agencies.

Banks also give information on the buying and selling of coins and notes to non-residents and also on interbank sales of national currency when non-resident banks demand such for their clients. The information thus obtained is rounded out by an estimation of the transactions below the 500,000 peseta threshold.

The system as described above has a number of limitations. The most important are the following:

- lack of reliability in the geographical distribution, since, when the originating country is unknown, the transaction is imputed to the country associated with the currency;

- lack of information on payments by residents in other countries with national currency, and also of the revenue when non-residents pay with pesetas in Spain;
- the fact that notes bought from and sold to non-residents are included as a tourism transaction means that transactions related to services, goods or even return on capital might be included under this heading.

In the Spanish case the traditional estimation procedure includes the estimation of credits:

(+):   receipts of travel goods and service providers from non-residents through all means of payments;

(+) (–): over-the-counter sales to non-residents of peseta notes against foreign notes, less purchases of peseta notes against foreign notes;

(+) (–): dispatch/return delivery of peseta notes to non-resident banks;

(+) (–): sales/purchases of peseta notes against drawings/deposits on bank accounts or travellers and personal cheques;

(+):   over-the-counter sales to residents of peseta notes against foreign notes, for amounts below 500,000 pesetas;

(+):   percentage of the remaining lump sum below the threshold;

and debits:

(+):   payments to non-residents for travel goods and service providers though all means of payments (including credit card gross flows);

(+):   purchases from residents of peseta notes against foreign notes for amounts below 500,000 pesetas;

(+):   percentage of remaining lump sum below the threshold.

The euro and the setting up of the new tourism-expenditure survey

The main sources for collection of travel statistics are the frontier surveys, bank reports, credit card data, surveys carried out at accommodation establishments, partner country data, administrative sources and surveys of tourist intermediaries.

The three main options considered by the Task Force Travel for combining the various potential sources in a suitable collection system were the frontier survey-based system, the household survey-based system and the hybrid system – a mix between the first two procedures.

All these sources are used in Spain but the estimation of tourism expenditure is mainly focused on a new frontier survey. The design and implementation of this new statistical survey for measuring tourism expenditure result from the acknowledgement of the effects that will ensue from the forthcoming introduction of the single currency of the European Union.

The definitive introduction of the euro as official currency in January 2002 means that many of the registers currently used for estimates of tourism expenditure will disappear. This information system will thus have to be replaced by another, which will not only be more costly but also particularly difficult to design and run. According to the Eurostat document 'Community Methodology on Tourism Statistics' (1998), the introduction of the single currency will make it impossible to obtain information on cash receipts and payments between the countries of the European Union, so there is a need to replace the current systems with new methods.

From the first half of 2002 only euro-denominated bank notes will be in circulation. In the Spanish case the implications of this will include the following:

- the disappearance of bank notes denominated in national currencies;
- the loss of a considerable part of the data records (around 60 per cent) used by the Bank of Spain for estimating the travel and tourism items of the balance of payments;
- the loss of the information used by the Instituto Nacional de Estadística for determining the aggregate consumption of non-residents in Spain and the consumption of residents abroad.

In light of this situation a think-tank was set up in September 1997 with representatives from the Bank of Spain, the Instituto Nacional de Estadística and the Secretaría de Comercio y Turismo (State Secretariat for Trade and Tourism), represented by the Instituto de Estudios Turísticos. The aim was to set up a working party chaired by the Instituto Nacional de Estadística to design a new statistical survey for estimating tourism expenditure and drawing up the first tourism satellite account in Spain.

THE NEW SURVEY ON TOURISM EXPENDITURE

A pilot study on tourism expenditure

Throughout 1998 the Instituto de Estudios Turísticos carried out a pilot study to test a questionnaire designed for the collection of tourism-expenditure information. The specific aim was to ascertain:

- the appropriateness of the questions and envisaged answer states in relation to each type of interviewee;
- the interviewees' comprehension of the questions, detecting any problems that may crop up due to:
  - the wording of the questions;
  - communication in different languages;
  - the duration of the interviews;
- obtained productivity.

Other aspects tested were the place and form of interviewing resident journey-makers in Spain and, in particular, the results of a telephone-interviewing method for overcoming the problems of interviewing journey-makers in their destination point.

The pilot study involved personal questionnaires in the airports of Madrid and Tenerife Sur, the former being representative of the tourism of business and international traffic and the second of leisure and holiday tourism.

The interviews were conducted in the departure lounges for non-resident passengers and the baggage-collection hall, passenger-arrival areas and taxi queues for resident passengers. Personal interviews were also carried out in La Jonquera, a border point between Spain and France.

These pilot studies led to small revisions in the questionnaires, affecting mainly the design of the questionnaire layout and alterations in some questions that caused certain confusion. The aggregate figures obtained from the pilot study have been cross-checked against those coming from the bank register system (Bank of Spain) and Frontur and no major differences have come to light.

Information needs

Apart from the enormous interest of the information generated in terms of the economic analysis of tourism, the new survey meets a set of information needs of the balance of payments and national accounts, in addition to providing key inputs to the future elaboration of the Tourism Satellite Accounts (under the responsibility of the Instituto Nacional de Estadística, available at the end of 2000). These needs are outlined below:

Balance of payments needs

- aggregate data on tourism expenditure with a monthly frequency and a breakdown into the European Monetary Union area and elsewhere;
- aggregate quarterly data with a more detailed geographic breakdown plus professional/personal purpose of the journey, with a breakdown of the latter by health, education and others. Information is also required on the expenditure of border-crossing and temporary workers, at least with an annual frequency;
- breakdown of the part of tourism expenditure that corresponds to international transport, including package tours. This item, representing a divergence from WTO recommendations, is included in balance-of-payments statistics as international passenger transport;
- detailed information on means of payment used.

National accounts needs

- data concerning expenditure on package tours: information on services included as a guideline for estimating the cost structure or net valuation of package tours. In this matter the Egatur survey will be complementary to the information obtained from surveys to tour operators;
- breakdown of expenditure by purpose of trip, with the objective of allocating it either to final demand or to intermediate demand, covering expenditure on package tours, bookings made before starting the trip and expenditure during the stay in Spain;
- breakdown of the expenditure of non-residents and residents on trips abroad, by products or services. Two approaches are possible here:
  - a breakdown according to Tourism Satellite Accounts recommendations;
  - other possible breakdown according to National Accounts needs.

Methodological references

The Encuesta de Gasto Turístico, Egatur (Tourism Expenditure Survey), carried out by the Instituto de Estudios Turísticos since the end of May 2000, is a new frontier survey that collects information on tourism expenditure made by residents and non-residents.

Egatur is directly linked with the Frontur survey as its basic framework in terms of results (Frontur will provide the gross-up factors for the sample results) and methodology (Frontur will provide the operational support for fieldwork organization control).

The Egatur expenditure survey is divided into four sub-surveys:

- expenditure of travellers by road (border posts):
  - journey-makers resident in Spain;
  - journey-makers non resident in Spain;
- expenditure of air travellers (airports):
  - journey-makers resident in Spain;
  - journey-makers non resident in Spain.

The differences accounting for the setting up of four sub-surveys reside fundamentally in the sample design and the method of contacting the informant for carrying out the interview. Information-collection arrangements, the processing, management and control thereof and the actual contents of the corresponding questionnaires are methodologically comparable in the four sub-surveys.

The questionnaires are structured in several blocks, referring to information on the journey, expenditure in the home country, in the destination country, a specific block for same-day visitors and transit visitors, a block on means of payment and a block on the distribution of the tourism group.

The differences between the blocks of one questionnaire and another refer, basically, to the wording of the questions to do with the purpose of the trip. These questions hence lend themselves easily to the generation of a single, unified questionnaire.

The questionnaires have been designed according to the test-graph methodology and hand computers are used for the recording, validation, registering and telematic transmission of field information, thus ensuring top quality in the data collected and a swift dissemination of the information obtained.

Data collection began in May 2000 (starting with airport surveys, interviews in the road sub-survey to be incorporated later with the collaboration of the police) and, initially, a hybrid system will overlap for at least one year, so the data is collected by both systems; by the current one (based on bank reports and credit card data) and by the new survey. The main reason for adopting this hybrid system is to achieve at least a full year in which information from both systems is available, for purposes of cross-checking consistency between both sources.

The sample is grouped in nineteen strata: nine in the road modality, nine by air and the remaining one to be constituted by the ferry of Algeciras. The stratification of border-crossing points has been done with the following study variables in mind (transport mode – road and airports):

- in the case of roads: bordering country;
- number of foreign visitors and Spanish residents that entered (or returned) in 1998, at each border-crossing point;
- seasonal nature of the entries;
- nationality of the foreign visitors;
- typology of the journey-makers (tourist, same-day visitor, transit visitor);
- geographical proximity between land border-crossing points and airports.

Each month has a different sample allocation, depending on the tourism movements observed during 1998 and making a distinction between the population of residents and foreigners. The sample size for each one of the populations is shared out between road and airport in accordance with the number of entries in each mode but weighting airports to the detriment of roads due to their greater heterogeneity in terms of home countries.

The overall size of the sample is 86,028 journey-makers, of which 61,023 are non-residents and 25,005 residents in Spain. Broken down by mode, 39,520 are by road and 46,508 by air.

A specific approach has been adopted for some aspects requiring special treatment:

- partition of visitors into segments according to types, allowing for a differentiated treatment;
- approach to organized tours that include visits to other countries;
- recording of travel-party expenditure, or personal expenditure when the informant is not in possession of information relating to the group;
- approach to the total expenditure of the trip by means of pre-journey expenditure and/or expenditure during the stay at the destination, according to the type of organization in each case;
- recording of monetary amounts in the currency chosen by the informant for each expenditure item;
- treatment of package tours: total cost and services included.

The Instituto de Estudios Turísticos is backed up by the institutional co-operation of the Instituto Nacional de Estadística and the Bank of Spain, channelled through a technical working group. The Instituto de Estudios Turísticos is directly responsible for running the survey and carrying out the fieldwork, while the Instituto Nacional de Estadística plans to take on responsibility for the elevation of the primary data and the Bank of Spain will be responsible for the dissemination of the tourism entry in the current account of the balance of payments.

BIBLIOGRAPHY

Araldi-Mecsa. (2000) *Propuesta sobre el gasto turístico*. February.

Calvo, A., Cuervo, A., Parejo, J. A. and Rodriguez, L. (1999) *Manual de Sistema financiero español* (12th edn), *Capítulo,* **5**, 130.

Eurostat (1998) *Community Methodology on Tourism Statistics*. Brussels: Eurostat.

Eurostat and Banco de España (1998) *Gentleman's agreement between Eurostat and Banco de España: The Estimation Procedure*.

Guerreiro S. (1999) *Statistics on Tourism Expenditure*. April.

Instituto de Estudios Turísticos (1999) *Encuesta piloto sobre el gasto turístico*. June.

Instituto de Estudios Turísticos (2000) *Statistics on Tourism Expenditure: The Spanish Experience*. April.

Martínez, A. (2000) *El SEC 1995 como sistema: Las unidades estadísticas y su agrupación*. Enero 2000.

Martínez A. (2000) *El turismo desde la óptica de la demanda (presentación)*. II Seminario sobre estadísticas Turísticas para la elaboración de la Cuenta. Satélite del Turismo. May.

Morales, R. (1998) 'La estimación de las transacciones de bienes y servicios en la balanza de pagos'. *Capítulo,* **4**, 21, May.

Technical Group Travel Report. Revision of the collection systems for the travel item of the balance of payments of EU member states following states three of the EMU. February 2000.

PART 5
RESEARCH AND METHODOLOGY

20

Practical Solutions to Impossible Problems? Lessons from Ten Years of Managing the United Kingdom Tourism Survey

Brian Hay and Mic Rogers

INTRODUCTION AND BACKGROUND

The main aim of this chapter is to outline the methodology adopted by the four UK Tourist Boards in measuring the volume and value of tourism in the UK, and to discuss the challenges we faced in running the survey and the practical solutions we adopted to overcome these challenges. In 1988 the four UK statutory tourism boards awarded NOP the contract for managing and running the United Kingdom Tourism Survey (UKTS), and NOP has been responsible for running this survey from 1989 through to 1999.

The main objective of the UKTS is to provide measurements of tourism by residents of the United Kingdom, in terms of both volume (trips taken, nights spent away from home) and value (expenditure on those trips and nights). The second objective is to collect details of the trips taken and of the people taking them.

These objectives extend to:

- tourism by people of any age: the survey includes a count of children accompanying adults on trips, and separately of children making tourist trips unaccompanied by adults;
- tourism for any purpose: although the survey naturally lays great emphasis on the important holiday sector, this is not just a holiday survey; also covered is tourism for the purpose of visiting friends or relatives, for work or business purposes, conferences and exhibitions or indeed almost any other purpose. The trips not covered by the survey are for reasons such as temporary removal, hospital admission or school visits;
- tourism in the sense of trips away from home which last for one night or more up to a maximum of 60 nights. Day excursion trips are not covered by the survey at

all; trips of more than 60 nights' duration cannot be adequately and representatively covered by the method of survey adopted, and are therefore excluded;

- tourism to any destination in any country of the world, using any accommodation type.

Each month, continuously, interviews are conducted face-to-face, in the homes of a fresh representative sample of UK adults aged 15 or more. The sample used is a two-stage stratified probability sample – more commonly called a random sample. This entails drawing 'first-stage sampling units' (sampling points) – 540 separate parliamentary constituencies in Great Britain and 24 wards in Northern Ireland – proportionate to the population throughout the UK.

Within each of those points 'second-stage sampling units' (that is, individual adults) are selected by using the current electoral registers. From a random start point in each of the 564 sampling points, every fifteenth name on the register is selected and passed to local interviewers, whose task it is to contact the named person, and only the named person, for interview. Up to four recalls are made at different times and on different days of the week, in order to obtain an interview with these selected electors; no substitutes are used in the sample.

In order to convert this sample of electors into a sample representative of adults, it is necessary to supplement the basic sample with non-electors wherever they are encountered at addresses of the selected electors. By this method a total of 70,413 interviews were conducted with adults aged 15 or over in the course of fieldwork for the UKTS 1999, which led to the reporting of 33,828 trips. Over the course of the last eleven years we have interviewed some 700,000 UK residents, who reported on 250,000 trips.

In each interview a questionnaire is used which was developed for the UKTS through a combination of experience of earlier surveys conducted by the boards, pilot work, and extensive experimental work, to overcome problems of over-reporting and under-reporting of the incidence and value of tourism trips. The same questionnaire was used in UKTS throughout the survey's eleven years to date (1989–99) changing only in points of minor detail.

The questionnaire asks, each calendar month, about trips taken away from home, which began in the month prior to interview, and the month before that. This two-month memory period was adopted in the survey in order to obtain the most cost-effective use of the interview – by achieving reports of two months from each survey respondent – while minimizing the risk of poor reporting due to failing memory (some trips are relatively insignificant for the respondent and would be badly reported with longer recall periods).

For each month in turn, throughout each year of the UKTS, samples of adults interviewed are computer-weighted to a constant profile, in order to remove the possibility of change being made falsely apparent by periodic fluctuations in the characteristics of samples interviewed. The weights adopted for this purpose set the profile of adults in the UK, in terms of sex, age, region and socio-economic grade, to a mid-year fixed estimate.

Some of the major changes in the trend data we have seen over the 1990s include:

- the UKTS began by measuring a decline in tourism undertaken by the British during 1990 compared to the 1989;
- in 1991 there was no further significant change overall, despite continuing economic recession throughout the year;

- in 1992 it seemed that the recession might be over, as a small increase in tourism volumes was measured;
- in 1993 this recovery was only temporary, and tourism volumes (although not values) fell again;
- in 1994, even with allowances due to the effect of switching data collection to 'CAPI', possibly meaning that survey respondents would be prompted to recall more trips than they previously reported, we did see a sharp upturn. Tourism by the British really did come out of recession, and volumes and values for the first time surpassed the 1989 levels;
- in 1995 tourism volumes surged further ahead, but spending on tourism was slightly reduced;
- in 1996 tourism trips increased a little, but tourist nights declined slightly, and spending stood still in real terms;
- in 1997, with only a very small allowance needed for further methodology changes (the adoption of CAPI in Northern Ireland), all three measures (trips, nights, spending) again moved ahead substantially to new records;
- in 1998, with no further methodology changes the record levels in 1997 were not quite repeated, but trips, nights and spend were greater than in other years apart from 1997;
- in 1999 there were further modest increases in all three measures.

Some of the basic data trend from the UKTS for UK tourism trips in the UK is noted below.

Table 20.1   Volume and value of UK residents tourism in the UK (millions)

	1990	1991	1992	1993	1994	1995	1996	1997	1998	1999	% change 1990/99
Trips	95.3	94.4	95.6	90.9	109.8	121.0	127.0	133.6	122.3	146.1	+53.3%
Nights	399.1	395.6	399.7	375.9	416.5	449.8	454.6	473.6	437.6	495.3	+24.1%
Spend (£)	10,460	10,470	10,665	12,430	13,215	12,775	13,895	15,075	14030	16,252	+55.4%
Spend (£) at 1999 prices	14,298	13,129	12,851	14,730	15,277	14,295	15,104	15,950	14,366	16,252	+13.7%

Sources: UKTS 1990/99

METHODOLOGICAL ISSUES IN MANAGING THE UKTS

Throughout the period of the survey a number of methodological issues arose and the major ones facing the boards and their solutions are discussed below.

Market penetration of the 4+ night holiday market

The EU directive on tourism statistics required the UK government to supply data on the incidence of 4+ holiday nights taken by UK residents both in the UK and to overseas destinations. In order to generate this data for the EU the method chosen was to ask a complex question in the January fieldwork each year of the UKTS. The question sought to establish the proportions of adults who have taken a holiday of 4+ night within the UK, to any destination outside the UK, and both within the UK and abroad. The agreed pilot method was to ask in two out the three weekly samples interviewed in mainland Great Britain (GB) and all adults interviewed in Northern Ireland (NI) as part of the January fieldwork, which lead to reporting in January 1997 of 4158 adults aged 15 or over. The question used was worded as follows using a showcard.

Q1: 'During the whole of last year, 1996, did you go away from home on any kind of holiday lasting four or more nights?' If YES:

Q2 (Showcard) 'Which one of these phrases described the sort of holiday or holidays of four or more nights you took in 1996?'

In the whole of last year, from January to December 1996, I took a holiday of four or more nights away from home:

- *just in the United Kingdom (that is England, Northern Ireland, Scotland, Wales, the Channel Islands or the Isle of Man);*
- *just abroad outside the United Kingdom;*
- *Both within the UK and Abroad.*

From this question we estimated that some 26 per cent of all adults (12.4m) took a holiday or holidays of four or more nights within the UK, but did not go on holiday anywhere abroad outside the UK, in that year. Some other results indicated that:

- 23 per cent (10.6m) took at least one holiday of four or more night outside the UK that year, but took no such holiday within the UK;
- 10 per cent of all adults (4.9m) took such holidays both within and outside the UK;
- 40 per cent of all adults (19.2m) took no holiday of four or more nights away from home.

The results are highly correlated with social class; 81 per cent of ABs to 42 per cent of DEs took a holiday of four or more nights, but the EU does not require us to comment on such interesting tropics, rather they just require us to report the data.

The survey method did highlight the difference between the GB and NI data, with NI residents being less likely than others in the UK to have taken a holiday solely in the UK, or in the UK at all, and conversely they are more likely than others to have a holiday solely to destinations abroad. The difference could be due to a fundamental difference governing the will and ability of those in NI to venture beyond the British Isles. Or it could be due to a mis-match between the design and execution of the samples in the two parts of the UK, rendering comparison invalid. Both hypotheses were rejected and the differences were explained by the geographical context of the residents of NI, namely the sharing as they do uniquely among UK residents a land boundary with another country, which produced these observed differences. Those residents of NI perceive a holiday in the Republic of Ireland as a 'domestic holiday' rather than a trip abroad. The question was subsequently modified to add the words 'The Channel Islands, the Isle of Man, the Republic of Ireland' as separate responses so that we could add these destinations to our definition of abroad, rather than just relying on the respondent to define the meaning of 'abroad'.

Recall of type of accommodation used

At the beginning of the survey it was agreed that, in practice, hotels/motels would be grouped with guesthouses as though they were one type of accommodation. This was a conscious decision by the Boards and NOP based on previous experience of respondents' inability to differentiate between the two accommodation types. To test this assumption it was agreed to ask a sample of respondents the exact name and address of the establishment they stayed in during their trip, which also satisfied the following criteria:

- the trip destination was within the UK;
- that only or first mentioned place of stay on the trip included the use of hotel/guest house accommodation;
- within that place of stay, hotel/guest house accommodation was used solely or for the greatest number of nights.

The accommodation name and address details would therefore be collected for up to seven trips taken by one respondent, and for just one destination for each trip in the accommodation type. The wording of the question tested was:

Q: 'We are trying to check how easy it is for people to give us completely accurate information about which particular map region they visited. So that place you stayed at on this trip to _____ can be plotted on a map, would you tell me ...'

- *if you stayed in a hotel/guest house ... the exact name and address of the hotel/guest house where you stayed?*
- *if you stayed in any other accommodation type ... the exact street name and place you stayed?'*

Given that we operate a two-month recall, the best month for the largest sample would have been September for trips taken in July and August, however, because of delays in agreeing to the work we ask the questions in October for trips taken in August/ September 1991. From interviewing some 5603 adults in the UK and 241 in NI, we collected data on 1973 trips in the UK. The scripts bearing the records of the trips spent in hotels/guesthouses in the UK were sent to the four UK boards, and then they, or via their own regional boards, classified these records to their own definition for each name and address provided by the respondents. The contractor then cross-checked each of the board's coded accommodation type given by the respondent.

Almost all (98 per cent) of the respondents stayed in one place in one map region, and of the small number of trips that involved two or more regions there was no consistent pattern, therefore there is no reason to believe that selecting only the first mentioned place of stay for inclusion in the study will bias the results.

Of the 1973 UK trips, 499 (25 per cent) satisfied the criteria outlined above, and these were as follows:

- Total number of trips   499
- Full address provided   154 (31%)
- Partial address provided   68 (14%)
- No address provided   277 (56%)

The majority of trips had no address, with obvious implications for this experiment. Therefore analysis of those trips where details were provided, without regard to the high proportion of trips where details were absent, may lead to misinterpretation in the measurement of accuracy of responses. The reason for the lack of address details could be due to either:

- respondent unwilling to disclose the details;
- respondent unable to recall the address details (assuming they knew in the first place);
- the way the question was worded/method used to collect the address details was inadequate.

It is difficult to know the degree each of these factors played in causing the lack of address details, but it is best to assume that all of them played some part. The fact that so many trips lacked address details is an important finding in itself. If the respondent is unable to recall the name and address of the establishment they stayed in, are they able to distinguish whether it was hotel or a guesthouse? From the addresses sent to boards it was possible to identify the accommodation used in 222 trips.

Table 20.2 Accuracy of recall of UK accommodation used

| | Respondent classified accommodation as: | |
	Hotel	Guesthouse
Verified as such	116 – 59%	5 – 21%
Actually a guesthouse	26 – 13%	
Actually a hotel		4 – 17%
Other accommodation	12 – 6%	3 – 13%
Cannot be verified	44 – 22%	12 – 50%

Of the respondent-classified trips taken in hotel accommodation, almost three out of five (59 per cent) were verified as correctly classified as a hotel by the boards, another 13 per cent were found to be in guesthouses, while another 6 per cent were in some other type of accommodation. In all, 19 per cent of hotel trips were incorrectly classified. The boards were unable to verify the accommodation type for a further 22 per cent of the hotel trips. In addition, the boards could not classify some 50 per cent of the guesthouse trips.

Table 20.3 Correctness of accommodation classified

	Total responses (N = 222) (%)	All verified responses (N = 166) (%)
Correctly classified as a hotel	52	70
Correctly classified as a guesthouse	2	3
Wrongly classified as a hotel when actually a guesthouse	12	16
Wrongly classified as guesthouse when actually a hotel	2	2
Wrongly classified hotel/guesthouse when actually another type of accommodation	7	9
Cannot be verified	25	N/A

While in the majority (54 per cent) of instances respondents were able to distinguish correctly between hotel and guesthouse, there is no doubt that a large proportion of respondents did find it difficult to distinguish between the two accommodation categories. In most instances the two categories are mistaken for each other, although sometimes they are both mistaken for some other type of accommodation altogether. This conclusion is based on respondents being able to provide the name and address details of the established they stayed in, but most residents in this experiment were unable/unwilling to provide this level of information. There is no reason to believe that this (unable/unwilling) group of respondents would be any better at correctly classifying the accommodation stayed in than those able to provide address details, indeed they may be somewhat worse.

From this experiment it was concluded that a further breakdown of this accommodation category, by splitting the hotel/guesthouse category into two categories, would lead to greater error associated with the data. The hotel/guesthouse combined category would produce more accurate data than the suggested split categories.

Accuracy of UKTS data at the local district level

Since its inception in 1989 the UKTS has asked respondents to identify from a map their region of tourism destination and the name of the place in which they stayed. From these details all domestic (GB) trips are then clerically coded, down to the level of district council areas, the smallest municipal area in the UK with powers. The census of place names is used both as a code frame for this clerical operation, and at the same time to check that the respondent has in each case correctly allocated the place mentioned into the correct map region (county or unitary authority) during the interview. There was concern expressed about the accuracy of the information given by the respondents, which is then used to identify the trip destination. The place name provided by the respondent may be a guess or just wrong, possibly given with helpful intentions, or a name which although accurate cannot be traced. There was also an unproven theory that small places may be under-reported, and larger places over-reported as a result of a tendency to name recognised centres of population, rather than unheard fringe names. The objective of this experiment was to investigate the degree of non-sampling error associated with district council-level data.

As no previous investigation had been conducted on the accuracy of such local data, the method chosen for this study was untried. Once again we added an additional question to the UKTS, and we asked for details of the address stayed at during the trip on the September 1991 UKTS. This led to the reporting of 2228 trips of which 1973 were in the UK. Of these trips, full address details were provided for 455, partial addresses for 585 trips and no address details for 943 trips. So the largest group of trips (943 (48 per cent)) under investigation provided no address details, and this has obvious implications for this experiment. Analysis of those trips for which addresses were provided, without regard to the high proportion of trips where details were absent, may lead to misinterpretation in the accuracy of the destination place names. Given the high number of trips excluded from the investigation, it was deemed inappropriate to conduct a large test on the accuracy of district data based solely on a select group of trips for which addresses had been provided, as the results may contain an unknown degree of bias. Instead two small-scale experiments were undertaken, namely by use of geodemographic database (Pinpoint) and by personal checking by the fieldforce supervisors.

As Pinpoint contains all the district boundaries in GB, it should be possible to allocate any given address (providing it has a postcode) to the correct district council. As a test, 27 addresses were sampled from the full address category and were given to Pinpoint. The selection procedure was not meant to be systematic; it was, rather, a matter of looking at the completed questionnaires and choosing which ones looked complete and could lead to a definite result. They were selected from different parts of the country, and referred to different types of accommodation, but none contained any postcodes. Of the 27 addresses, Pinpoint found postcodes for eighteen, and of these eighteen addresses six postcodes were easily found, but four were matched to more than one postcode. These addresses tended to belong to holiday-camps and centres, which can be spread over large areas, and could contain more than one postcode. A further eight addresses were considered poor matches with the postcodes. Once the postcodes were identified for each of the addressees the district council was identified, and in seventeen out of the eighteen cases the district council was correctly matched. The fact that Pinpoint was only able to match postcodes for two-thirds of the addresses taken from the 'full address' category meant it was unlikely to be a successful method in identifying district councils on any large scale.

The contractor also sent to each of its twelve regional fieldforce supervisors, addresses taken from the 'full address' category where the named address by the respondent fell within the supervisor's region. The supervisors' job was to find out the identity of the district council in which each address they had been allocated was located. They either did this themselves or made use of the local interviewers, or contacted the appropriate district council. Of the total 43 addresses sent out for personal checking, 34 (79 per cent) were correctly allocated to the district council, four (9 per cent) where incorrectly allocated to the district, three did not allow the district council to be identified, and in two cases (5 per cent) the address was not traceable. In all four instances where the incorrect district was allocated, the respondent always allocated the place to the adjacent district council area.

The personal checking exercise showed the correct district council had been identified from the place name given by the respondent, in the majority of instances. However, although the sample size is small, the results of the personal checking do indicate there is a degree of non-sampling error (in addition to sampling error) attached to the district-level data. Overall therefore, the evidence suggests that identifying the district council from respondents' answers is an imprecise way of capturing district councils as a destination. While it is possible that improvements could be made to capturing data from the UKTS at the district level, by asking for the full address for each destination for each trip as this would allow for more accurate coding for the half of the sample able to provide the address details, it would be very expensive to administer. Also it could lead the respondent feeling that too much detail was being asked. It could be possible that a better form of wording could be used to gather the precise name of the location than that used in the survey, by for example asking about parts of London, rather than London as a whole as the survey does at present. As a result of this experiment no change was made to the wording of the UKTS.

Multi-purpose business trips

There was a perception that leisure trips were being added to business trips, therefore it was questioned if the data produced by the UKTS was sufficiently robust to measure this trend. For example, if a respondent goes on a trip because of the their duties as an employee, but then chooses to stays extra nights at the destination for social reasons, then the UKTS probably mistakenly captures all these trips and their associated expenditure as business trips. Similarly, if the respondent's partner chooses to go along on the same trip entirely for social reasons, the partner's trip could also be recorded as a business trip, as this was the main reason for the (respondent's) trip. In order to test the extent of such multi-purpose trips, the following question was asked after the current question about trip purpose:

Q: *'Do any of the descriptions on this list apply to this particular trip or not?*
If YES, which, any others?

- *The trip was extended for more nights than was strictly necessary for its main purpose, to include time spent on purely social/pleasure/leisure purposes*
- *Someone else on the trip was the person who had to travel; I just went along with them for social/pleasure/leisure purposes*
- *I/we took the opportunity of staying overnight in other destinations for social/ pleasure/leisure/purposes, rather than staying solely in the place or places that had to be visited to begin with*
- *The day and date of the trip was decided at least partly so as to be pleasant or convenient for social/pleasure/leisure considerations during the trip; the date was not chosen solely to fit in with business*
- *The place that I/we travelled to was at least partly decided so as to be pleasant or convenient for social/pleasure/leisure purposes; the choice was not solely to meet business/work/conferences requirements*
- *No, none of these descriptions applies to this trip'.*

In an ideal world this type of question would be asked for a long period of time, in order to overcome any seasonal bias. In might easily be imagined, for example, that 'bolt-on' optional parts of primarily business trips within the UK are more attractive at times of the year when there is good weather or during school holidays. However, costs and timing dictated that the questions were run from February 1997 through to July 1997. The results indicate that the majority of trips, over 90 per cent, were driven entirely by business/work consideration, but that a substantial minority of them involved other intentions.

In some 4 per cent of all business trips, the trip was lengthened for more nights than was strictly necessary; this increased to 6 per cent of overseas business trips. In 2 per cent of the trips the UKTS respondent did not personally need to travel at all, but simply accompanied from choice someone else who had to travel. One per cent of business trips visited at least one extra overnight destination. With 2 per cent of business trips the timing of the trip was decided on the basis of social considerations, rather than solely on business needs. Finally, for 2 per cent of all business trips the destination was chosen for non-business reasons.

From these estimates some 1.45 million business trips were entirely discretionary rather than obligatory out of the 39.1 million recorded in 1997. The results of this experiment did not support the suggestion that this market segment should be subject to any special marketing activity, as it only accounts for a small part of the current leisure market. As a result of this experiment, no action was taken to change the wording of the survey questions.

Recording activities as a main or secondary activity

For about one in seven of the trips recorded by the UKTS each year the respondents claim that one of the reasons for the trip is for a series of activities listed on a showcard, with swimming being claimed as second in popularity to hill-walking, even in the winter months! Although the intention of this experiment was to investigate the robustness of just the swimming data, to set the experiment in context, it was expanded to include golf and cycling, as these activities could easily be undertaken and viewed by some respondents as a casual pastime, yet by others as a serious and dedicated pursuit. Therefore a question was added to the list of activities:

Q: 'You say that (swimming/golfing/cycling) was the main purpose for taking this trip. Is it really the case that this trip was planned as a (name of activity) trip, or is it just that (name of activity) was one item on the list of activities that you and your party mostly did, while you were away on this trip?

- *was really planned as (swimming/golfing/cycling) trip*
- *(swimming/golfing/cycling) was just the thing I/we did the most, while away'*

The experiment was intended to run for a whole year, to overcome any seasonal bias, because many of even the most popular activities were reported to be the cause of only a small minority of all trips. Of the 36,115 trips record during 1997, 14 per cent were classified as being a 'main purpose activity trip'. Details of the weighed estimates recorded were as follows.

Table 20.4 Estimates of trips taken mainly for the following activities

	Number of trips (million)	Proportion of all trips to the UK (%)
Hiking/hill-walking	3.49	3
Visiting heritage sites	1.46	1
Sailing/boating	1.14	1
Indoor swimming	10.8	1
Visiting theme parks	1.08	1
Watching live performing arts	1.02	1
Taking part in any other sport	0.97	1
Watching any sporting event	0.76	1
Visiting artistic/heritage exhibits	0.65	*
Golfing	0.63	*
Outdoor swimming	0.62	*

* Less than 0.5%

The only observations on the data that were possible were the higher incidence of swimming as the main purpose of the trip in overseas trips, but this is not unexpected. There was however a much higher level of swimming-related tourism, particularly indoor swimming in Northern Ireland in 1997, and this was also reported in the 1995 data at 8 per cent, and 6 per cent in 1996. It was also noted that in trips taken from Northern Ireland the incidence of activity trips was also much higher: 17 per cent in 1995, 15 per cent in 1996 and 12 per cent in 1997. This could either be explained by an activity particularly associated with Northern Ireland, or by the coding by the Irish fieldforce.

Table 20.5 Swimming, golfing and cycling trips

	Indoor swimming	Outdoor swimming	Total swimming	Golfing	Cycling	Golfing and cycling combined
Identified as main purpose by core UKTS questionnaire	1.262m	1.676m	2.938m	0.857m	0.765m	1.622m
Found by experiment question to be 'Really planned for that purpose'	0.262m (21%)	0.280m (17%)	0.542m (18%)	0.592m (69%)	0.338m (44%)	0.930m (57%)
Just what I/we mostly did on the trip	0.999m (79%)	1.396m (83%)	2.396m (82%)	0.265m (31%)	0.426m (56%)	0.691m (43%)

The above table provides the weighted estimates for swimming, golfing and cycling trips in the UK, and from this table it was concluded that, swimming as an activity was named from the showcard list of options as the main purpose of five times more trips than were really planned for that purpose. Golfing and cycling, other popular activities which might be taken, like swimming, with different degrees of seriousness, are proportionally much more likely to be the real causes of trips, when named as the main purpose. Nevertheless, this still leaves a large proportion of these golfing and cycling trips that were not really designated for that specific purpose, it just turned out that these were activities undertaken more than anything else during the course of the trip.

It was concluded that the UKTS probably over-reports the importance of activities as the main purpose of trip, as respondents associated high participation as the main reason for the trip. As a result of this experimental work, it was decided to reverse the order of the activity questions in the questionnaire, and to modify slightly their wording. The expectation (supported by the as yet unpublished 1999 UKTS results) was that the number of claims for activity trips would be reduced slightly to a more realistic level by allowing respondents an opportunity to say which activities they had undertook during a trip, before asking whether such activities were the main purpose for taking the trip.

Missing data

The convention in the late 1980s and first adopted at the start of the UKTS in 1989 was that when respondents were unable or unwilling to supply expenditure data, that average spending values from the complete records for that same month of the survey were inserted as substituted data. It was always acknowledged that this had advantages as well as disadvantages. The chief advantage was the contractors could provide for every trip, data in a consistent and comprehensive fashion throughout the survey, so enabling grossed up estimates to be provided for each month. The disadvantage was that as the monthly data was already circulated it was not possible to produced revised monthly data in light of the full year's data. But in practice, the advantages outweighed the disadvantages.

From 1989 to 1992 the cumulative monthly data were no more than a few percentage

points different from the estimates that would have been produced if the reporting of
the data had been delayed until the whole year's data were accumulated, and used
instead of the monthly data.

In 1994, the survey changed over to CAPI from a paper and pencil survey, and
because of this no action was taken to re-examine the data, as the two data collection
methods were so different. However, when the full year's 1995 data was produced it
contained expenditure estimates which were substantially different from those in the
previous year. What we did find was that by inserting the same average estimate for all
trips that:

- the UKTS spending estimate in the UK could have been overestimated by 9 per
  cent and overseas spending underestimated by 7 per cent;
- if the UK average per blank UK trip was inserted in the year-end total of UK,
  spending would be 6 per cent more than in 1993, not the 17 per cent as estimated;
- if the abroad average had been used the year end total for overseas spending would
  have increased by 30 per cent, instead of the 21 per cent estimated.

In practice, the problem of inserting average values only works well if those respondents
who fail to give an expenditure amount are perfectly representative of, and identical to,
those who do give such an answer. It would be wrong to provide average data to the
blanks when we know these respondents are different. One possible hypothesis to
explain the increase is that with the introduction of CAPI at the beginning of 1994 trip
year, this produced a yield of trips that was substantially different from the samples
previously achieved by the previous pen-and-paper questionnaire. Also the types of
trips now recorded by CAPI were atypical both in their propensity to produce
incomplete data, and in their true expenditures. However, when applied to the data in
1995 by both the old and new systems, this hardly produced any difference.

On further investigation what we did find was that the 1994 survey did for some still
unaccountable reason, identify more UK trips rather than abroad trips, and these trips
were more likely to have been cheaper trips rather than the more expensive trips. The
adoption of a single bland average for these trips meant that we overestimated the total
amount of expenditure. The new method for filling in missing data that we
subsequently adopted was that instead of using the same monthly survey average for
all the missing data from the current survey month, we now used the average amount
spent for different types of trips for the whole of the previous year. On test running the
old and new method we are satisfied that by using the previous year's averages by type
of trip this produces a much more reasonable substitute that just the current month's
average. It should be recalled that only about 1 per cent of respondents are unable to
provide expenditure data.

UKTS recall period

In the UKTS we use a two-month recall period, that is in March we ask about trips
taken in both January and February, and in April we ask about trips taken in February
and March. The advantage of this recall period is that we effectively double the sample
for any single month, but the disadvantage is that it takes an additional month to
produce the monthly data. One of the possible advantages of increasing the recall
period to three months could be that it may be possible to reduce the sample by one
third, thereby reducing survey costs; however, it would take longer to produce the
monthly results.

An experiment was therefore undertaken which would be at a minimum scale but would still adequately meet the experimental objectives, and cause a minimum disruption to the standard UKTS. The experiment entailed that each month 10 per cent of the sample would be asked about trips in the three months prior to the interview, rather than the two moths as in the rest of the sample. In order to provide the largest available sample sizes and, consequently, the best statistical confidence in the findings, the items selected for reporting were restricted to the volume and value of tourism undertaken to all destinations, and the main purpose of all trips, their nights and expenditure. The questions were also only asked in GB and not in NI. In order to implement any change it was recognized that it would not possible to run the experiment for a full twelve months. The experiment asked about trips in the period August–December 1994 for fieldwork conducted in November 1994 to March 1995. Before the results were known, it was agreed that the full experiment should ultimately be capable of determining whether or not a relative difference of 3 per cent between the test and control data was statistically significant.

Table 20.6 Volume of trips generated by test (3 month recall) and control (2 months recall)

	Test 3-month recall Trips (millions)	Control 2-month recall Trips (millions)	Maximum difference accounted by sampling error	% Points difference
Total	50.5	62.6	16	**–19%**
Destination				
UK	41.1	50.9	18	**–19%**
England	31.3	42.6	20	**–27%**
N. Ireland	–	0.2	37	–
Scotland	5.0	3.9	45	+28%
Wales	5.1	4.5	57	+13%
Non-UK	9.5	11.9	41	–20%
Trip Purpose				
Holiday (non-VFR)	24.1	31.7	23	**–24%**
Holiday VFR	4.8	8.2	49	–41%
All Holidays	29.0	39.7	24	**–27%**
VFR	12.7	14.4	38	–12%
Business	5.6	6.0	50	–7%

Bold in last column indicates statistical significance at the 95 per cent level of confidence

The experiment successfully produced a conclusion, that is the extension of the period of recall from two months to three months failed to reach its required action standard, in that the results collected from a three-month recall period were shown to be statistically different from those collected contemporaneously using a two-month recall period, all other design and execution details remaining otherwise as constant as was practically possible. At the lower levels of data disaggregation when no statistically valid differences were noted, the direction of nominal difference in the results varied; sometimes the experimental results were higher, sometimes they were lower than the control results. That is in keeping with normal expectation that individual survey observation will scatter both above and below the mean. In the case of statistically significant differences, though, the experimental three-month recall were consistently lower than those from the two-month control data.

The clear implication of the results of this experiment is that the longer three-month recall period encourages the survey respondents to forget about some trips which in reality were taken, and which would have been reported if a two-month recall period were used. As a result of the experiment no changes wee made to the length of recall.

CONCLUSIONS

Throughout the UKTS we have tried to strike a balance between the need to maintain consistency to ensure that the survey results can measure real change over time, yet to understand the need for, and the effect of, any proposed changes to the survey methodology. Through some major experiments with the survey we have been able to provide clear evidence to show that many requested changes, while possible, were not desirable when looking at the bigger picture, that of data consistency. Where changes were incorporated into the data, we have tried to ensure we were fully aware of the effect of these changes.

21

The Future of the United Kingdom Tourism Survey

Helen Ford and Ian Wright

BACKGROUND

Since January 1989 statistics of tourism by residents of the United Kingdom have been provided by the United Kingdom Tourism Survey (UKTS). The survey is sponsored by the four national tourist boards of the UK (The English Tourism Council, The Northern Ireland Tourist Board, The Scottish Tourist Board and the Wales Tourist Board).

The UKTS is designed to measure the volume and value of tourism trips taken by UK residents, and to identify the types of trip and the types of people taking trips. This includes *all* trips, no matter what their purpose or destination, as long as they involve an overnight stay away from home.

The design of the survey from its inception to the end of 1999 has been described in some detail in chapter 20 and so we do not enter into such detail here. However, a brief recap will aid understanding of how UKTS 2000 differs from the old survey.

Up until the end of fieldwork covering trips made in 1999, the survey was administered via a face-to-face omnibus, which utilized a two-stage probability sample design. The omnibus approach naturally brought the sponsors certain cost benefits over an ad hoc survey. UKTS questions were always placed at the start of the omnibus questionnaire, in order to avoid any questionnaire order effects. However, it had been known for some time that the omnibus survey was to be discontinued from early 2000. Therefore, an alternative vehicle for the UKTS would have to be found. This provided an ideal opportunity to review the survey in its entirety.

The sponsoring boards, therefore, commissioned Peter Lynn of what was then Social and Community Planning Research (SCPR, now the National Centre for Social Research), and Roberts-Miller Associates to conduct a multi-stage review of the UKTS.

Stage A of the review assessed the data and information needs of the sponsors and other relevant parties. Stage B assessed relevant survey and research methods. Stage C drew upon stages A and B to recommend cost-effective methods for meeting the sponsors' objectives.

No survey sponsor undertakes lightly, or even contemplates, changes to a survey which has been running continuously for eleven years. However, some design effect was almost inevitable, given that even if the survey had remained with the same agency, the vehicle would have changed from omnibus to probably some form of ad hoc design. Thus, acting on the recommendations of the survey review, the sponsors decided to bite the bullet and make changes to the survey, but with the provisos that every effort was made to ensure consistency over time in the data delivered, and that every care was taken to assess, understand and quantify any inconsistencies that did arise.

Thus from March 2000 (and thus covering trip data from January 2000) the survey has been conducted by BMRB International utilizing a new research methodology, which we now go on to detail. We should stress that this is very early days for the new survey. Data from initial waves have only recently become available, and so what we present here are our preliminary findings, on the understanding there is still much exploratory work to be done. However, we hope these preliminary findings are of interest, and may provide useful guidance for anyone contemplating similar surveys.

UKTS 2000

As to be expected, many features of the old survey were retained for UKTS 2000. The most fundamental change was a switch from face-to-face data collection to a telephone interview. The reasons for this and other changes are discussed below.

Sample design

The probability design of the old survey was retained. Information collected by the survey is used routinely by the sponsors and other interested parties in government and industry. The survey is also published annually as *The UK Tourist*. It is therefore critical that the survey's measurements are based on the soundest of foundations in order to maintain its standing as an industry currency, and to instil confidence in both current and potential users of the data. Benefits of a probability design include:

- no sample selection bias;
- permits estimation of confidence intervals (even though these are routinely and erroneously calculated for quota samples);
- tends to produce higher response rates;
- enables quantitative assessment of non-response biases, and development of correction procedures if necessary.

In the case of the UKTS in particular, a rigorous approach to sampling is essential because availability for interview and thus chance of selection is inherently linked to what the survey is attempting to measure (i.e. trips away from home). Thus the temptation of the cost benefits associated with quota sampling was resisted.

Sample size

The following target for survey precision was adopted by the sponsors, in the light of intended use of the data: '95% confidence intervals of no greater than $+/-$ 5% for estimates of annual volumes of trips and nights to England, Scotland and Wales and other regions of the UK receiving at least 10 million trips per annum.'

It was evident from the review that sample clustering was to have a great bearing on the ability of the survey to deliver sample estimates with the required precision in a cost-effective manner. The level and nature of geographical clustering of the sample has a number of very important implications for an in-home, face-to-face survey.

Reducing the distance between addresses within a cluster has the effects of:

- reducing fieldwork costs;
- increasing the speed with which the field work can be completed for each cluster;
- increasing the design effect, thereby reducing the precision of estimates.

Reducing the number of clusters, for any given sample size, has the effects of:

- reducing the fixed costs of interviewer briefing and deployment;
- increasing the design effect, thereby reducing the precision of estimates.

It was therefore important to strike a balance between the need for cost-efficient fieldwork and the need for precise estimates.

The old UKTS design involved an annual sample of 564 clusters (540 in Great Britain and 24 in Northern Ireland) of 264 sampled names. In 1998 an average of 135 interviews was achieved from each cluster. Each cluster is split into twelve tranches or 22 names each, one tranche being covered each month of the year. The clustering units in Great Britain were constituencies, but the sample of names is selected at a fixed interval of one in fifteen. Thus, in practice, the sample was drawn from a set of 3960 consecutive names on the register (264×15) and was therefore limited to just one or two wards within the constituency. The clustering units in Northern Ireland were single wards.

Calculations showed that the design factor from this design was around three, which clearly has a large impact on the precision of estimates taken from the survey. Table 21.1 below shows the approximate minimum sample sizes required to deliver confidence intervals of $+/-$ 5 per cent on trip volumes to the main countries and regions of the UK.

It can be seen that the old sample design, based as it was on c. 80,000 interviews per annum, delivered adequate precision for annual estimates for all countries other than Northern Ireland and for all regions of England, but not for sub-divisions of Scotland or Wales. Indeed this sample size and design was able to deliver the same level of precision for commonly used sub-annual estimates (e.g. Jan–April) for the majority of regions, and would have done so on a slightly reduced sample of 70,000.

However, if it were possible to reduce the design factor significantly, possibly as low as one for a totally unclustered design, then the required sample size would be much smaller. The equivalent sample sizes required for such a design are given in Table 21.2.

The differences between Tables 21.1 and 21.2 are striking, and demonstrate the precision gains that can be achieved through efficient sample design. An unclustered design (with an associated design factor of one) would mean that the total number of interviews achieved per annum need only be around 12,000 in order to deliver adequate precision for annual estimates for all the constituent countries of the UK (including

Table 21.1 Required sample sizes to deliver confidence intervals of $+/-5$ per cent, assuming old UKTS design

Destination	Annual sample size required
UK	5,400
N. Ireland	100,000
England	6,300
Scotland	29,000
Wales	29,000
Cumbria	65,000
Northumbria	59,000
N. West	31,000
Yorks. and Humber.	31,000
Heart of England	29,000
E. Midlands	37,000
E. Anglia	29,000
London	31,000
West Country	22,000
Southern	27,000
South East	33,000
HIE area of Scotland	535,000
SE/Rest of Scotland	140,000
N. Wales	350,000
M. Wales	630,000
S. Wales	240,000

Table 21.2 Required sample sizes to deliver confidence intervals of $+/-5$ per cent, assuming a design factor of one

Destination	Annual sample size required
UK	650
N. Ireland	12,000
England	750
Scotland	3,500
Wales	3,500
Cumbria	7,700
Northumbria	7,000
N. West	3,700
Yorks. and Humber.	3,700
Heart of England	3,500
E. Midlands	4,500
E. Anglia	3,500
London	3,500
West Country	2,500
Southern	3,200
South East	3,900
HIE area of Scotland	64,000
SE/Rest of Scotland	17,000
N. Wales	41,000
M. Wales	75,000
S. Wales	28,000

Northern Ireland) and regions of England. A sample of 25,000 would further provide adequate precision for all commonly used sub-annual estimates for the same countries/regions, apart from January–April estimates.

Thus the attraction of a high-quality design delivering a design factor of one was compelling, given the cost–precision ratio. In the end the sponsors decided on a sample of 50,000 per annum, to achieve the highest level of precision available for the given budget.

But how was this to be achieved? We consider this issue shortly, but first we address another facet of sample design.

Sampling over time

Continuous fieldwork has been necessary for the UKTS to provide comparable data for each period in time. Historically the survey adopted a design which involves interviewing equal-sized representative samples each month. However, as we all know, the distribution of trips over time has a seasonal element. Therefore, it could be possible, by over-sampling those months which show the largest number of trips, to obtain a greater level of precision for any given sample size.

However, close examination of the distribution of trips showed that whilst seasonality did indeed exist, it was insufficiently marked to allow an efficient over-sampling design. Therefore sample sizes have remained equally distributed across the twelve months of the year.

Data collection

Face-to-face interviewing is generally accepted to be the most flexible form of data collection for survey data, both in terms of the data that can be collected and the demands that can be put on the respondent. Self-completion or postal questionnaires are limited in both the complexity and amount of the information they can collect. Telephone interviews cannot make use of visual aids. The interview length is also limited since the lack of rapport between interviewer and respondent relative to a face-to-face interview makes it easier for a respondent to cut short an interview.

However, face-to-face interviewing is by far the most expensive data collection mode, and requires samples to be clustered for fieldwork to run efficiently. This is a requirement for neither telephone nor postal surveys, and so each was considered as possible alternatives to the face-to-face approach historically adopted by the UKTS.

Postal survey

The possibility of adopting a postal data collection mode for the UKTS was quickly dismissed due to the complex nature of the questionnaire.

Telephone interviewing

One of the main obstacles to the widespread adoption of telephone interviewing for probability sample surveys has been the difficulties of sampling. Historically, one of the major concerns has been that not all households have a telephone. As recently as 1990, only 88 per cent of UK households had a telephone in their home. This would not have been a great issue if those with phones did not differ from those without (although one may still have had reservations about representing only 88 per cent of the population). However, there are differences, of course, with those without phones being a relatively polarized group.

However, much has changed over recent years. Telephone penetration has now reached almost 97 per cent of households. This makes it comparable, if not slightly superior, to the coverage provided by the electoral register, the sampling frame used historically by the UKTS. (The electoral register omits c. 5–6 per cent of residential addresses, although some degree of compensation was achieved on the UKTS by attempting to interview those not on the register.) Therefore, telephone, in terms of population coverage, is a viable data collection mode for surveys such as the UKTS.

Another barrier to telephone interviewing has been the fact that not all numbers in the UK have been of a standard length, which means that numbers generated by a Random Digit Dialling (RDD) technique do not all have equal chance of selection. Furthermore, there has been a dearth of information about which blocks of numbers were in use. However, telephone numbers are now of a standard length, and OFTEL (the UK telecommunication watchdog) publishes lists of all the blocks of numbers that have been issued to a service provider.

Traditional approaches to telephone sampling have included sampling from phone-books, which has the obvious, and increasing, shortcoming that ex-directory numbers are not sampled. The proportion of ex-directory households is now approaching 40 per cent. The fact that those with new lines have to opt in to the directory, amongst other deterrents, can only encourage this figure to increase. More importantly, those households that are listed are distinctly different from those that are not. One attempt to solve this problem has been the use of list-assisted RDD, whereby numbers are sampled from phone-books, and the last digit (or digits) randomly altered, in order to represent unlisted numbers. Although this works to an extent, it still under-represents ex-directory households.

BMRB International uses a variant of this approach for many of its commercial consumer surveys. Instead of taking sample numbers from phone-books, seed numbers are taken from its face-to-face omnibus. The omnibus uses random location sampling, sampling some 10,000 enumeration districts (the smallest area for which census data are released, typically 150–200 households) a year. All enumeration districts (EDs) have equal chance of inclusion (no restricted master sampling frame is used), and some 6 per cent of all EDs are used each year.

Thus, the seed numbers include some ex-directory numbers, which increases the chance of an ex-directory number being generated (on the basis that there is some degree of clustering for ex-directory households). However, while an improvement, this method still under-represents ex-directory households to some degree. This is because ex-directory numbers are still not present in their true proportion in the original seed sample (such households are more reluctant to give out their number, even to a market research interviewer!), and because the degree of clustering mentioned above is only partial.

Therefore, if telephone interviewing was to be adopted for UKTS 2000, a more satisfactory form of sampling was needed. In the end, BMRB International approached a sample provider in the United States, whom we had often used for list-assisted, regional telephone samples. The company, Sample Surveys Incorporated (SSI), is dedicated to the provision of telephone samples, having been in this business for over 20 years. They number several UK research agencies among their customers, together with academic and other institutions. SSI can provide truly random samples of telephone numbers, where each working number has equal chance of inclusion. A brief synopsis of their approach follows.

There are some 13,000 STDs (or blocks) allocated to residential service in the UK. A number of these are drawn at random, in proportion to the number of contact numbers eventually required. Four random digits are then added to the end of each of these numbers to create a full telephone number. These numbers are then dialled to screen out unassigned numbers. As a result each block will be represented in proportion to the number of working numbers within it. Business numbers are also screened out.

Respondent selection

The old UKTS identified named respondents from the electoral register. The adoption of a telephone methodology requires a means of identifying respondents for interview such that within a household all eligible residents are given an equal chance of selection. The two most commonly used methods are the Kish grid and the last birthday rule. The former, involving as it does an initial listing of all members of the household by name, was felt to be too intrusive for a telephone interview. It could easily hinder an interviewer at the crucial rapport-building stage, and thus harm response rates by encouraging refusal. Therefore, the last birthday rule has been adopted.

Weighting is applied at the analysis stage to equalize the probability of selection between households of different sizes (i.e. a person who lives alone has three times the probability of selection of someone in a three-person household).

A small change to the sample definition was made as a result of the switch to telephone interviewing. The UKTS sample definition was changed from all adults resident in the UK aged 15 or more, to all adults resident in the UK aged 16 or more. This was in order to bring the survey into line with ESOMAR guidelines on interviewing those aged 15 or under by telephone. It is now advised that parental permission should be obtained for such interviews. It was felt that the negligible impact of such a change, certainly in the context of other more substantial changes, did not warrant the cost and logistical implications required to avoid it.

Response rates

The response rate achieved by a probability sample survey is a good indicator of its quality. The higher the response rate, the more confident one can be about the impact of non-response bias, and thus the credibility of the results. Several steps have been taken to help maximize the response rate. However, there are also several factors pertinent to the survey which have the potential to harm the response rate.

As the survey works to a monthly fieldwork and reporting cycle, the relatively short fieldwork period for such a large sample (now some 4200 interviews per month) is potentially detrimental to attempting a large number of contacts on different days/times. However, the ad hoc survey in place now gives more flexibility on this matter than the previous omnibus approach. The latter involved issuing a sample replicate in each of the first three weeks of each month, with five or six days' field work available for each replicate, with the inherent danger of under-representing people who make more trips than average.

Telephone data-collection also gives more control and flexibility. When the UKTS was run on the face-to-face omnibus, up to four visits were made to a household to establish contact, spread over different times and different days. This may have been restricted to some extent by the omnibus vehicle, but this number of call-backs is not atypical of face-to-face probability surveys, due to cost.

On UKTS 2000 nearly all useable numbers where no contact has been made are called a minimum of ten times. There are specific rules for when the first of these contacts may be made, controlled by the computer from a custom-built sample management system and so guaranteed beyond the influence of the interviewer. These rules ensure contact is attempted over a good spread of days and times. Once contact has been made, a minimum of a further two attempts are made to get an interview, with up to five attempts made in total. (In fact, since the first wave of fieldwork further improvements have been made to the sample management system such that the timing of all of the first ten calls is computer controlled, via seven versions of the programme, dependent on which day of the week fieldwork starts (fieldwork always starts on the first day of the month).)

The interview is also very variable in length, which may be contributing to higher levels of abandoned interviews than usually obtained. Although the interview is currently averaging about twelve minutes (although we can expect this to rise when summer holidays are reported), no interview is actually of this length. The interview is either very short or very long, depending on how many trips the respondent has made in the last two months. In the case of a short interview the respondent almost immediately skips to the classification section, in an interview lasting six to seven minutes, which may seem a little odd and intrusive to the respondent, who may refuse to finish the interview. This was observed during piloting of the new survey, and further reassurances were added to the interview to stop this, but drop-out has not been stopped completely. This clearly would not have been an issue in the past when the UKTS formed part of an omnibus survey. Even if a respondent did not have any trips to report, there would be other sections of the omnibus to complete prior to classification, which we surmise would then appear less intrusive. We also felt that this effect may be impacting on the actual data collected (see below).

At the other extreme, somebody who has taken a lot of trips may have an interview of 40 minutes or more, which can also cause drop-out.

The little evidence we have from March fieldwork suggests there may be some substance to this hypothesis. Seventeen per cent of abandoned interviews were with people who had made four or more trips.

A further measure taken to improve response rates was to attempt to convert initial refusals. Initial refusals are divided into two categories: hard and soft refusals. Hard refusals are where the correct respondent has been identified by the last birthday rule, and has refused quite categorically to participate, perhaps even exhibiting signs of annoyance or rudeness. Soft refusals are where the selected respondent is perhaps uninterested, or does not have the time, or where a refusal has been made on their behalf (proxy refusal). To a large extent, this distinction is subjective and down to the interviewer's judgement – would I, or someone else, be able to get an interview with this person if I called back at another time?

Refusals are re-contacted by experienced interviewers, who are adept at encouraging participation. This small team is briefed for the task, a special introduction is used, and the team as a whole receives a small incentive for a good conversion rate. Interviewers working on the main survey are monitored to ensure they do not regard the refusal outcome as an easy option.

Initially, attempts were made to convert both hard and soft refusals, but the pilot study showed that attempts to convert hard refusals were very unproductive, and could even cause complaint and harm the sponsors' image. Therefore, it was decided that only soft refusals should be re-contacted.

Conversion of refusals has proved to be very successful at improving the response rate. Nonetheless, we believe that both the refusal and response rates can still be improved, and we will continue to address this.

Table 21.3 Response and refusal rate, March 2000 fieldwork

	%
Response rate	37
Refusals	39

Questionnaire issues

There will inevitably be questionnaire issues when moving from face-to-face to telephone data-collection. The most obvious of these issues is the use of prompt material, usually in the form of showcards, of which the old UKTS had several. However, it appeared that all such questions would translate well to the phone, lists being relatively straightforward and short, with one exception. The exception concerned a showcard (appended) used to capture activities undertaken whilst on a trip. The card listed some 26 activities. Clearly, it would be impractical to read out such a long list during a telephone interview and expect the respondent to comprehend and remember the list. Therefore, the list was broken down into sub-categories of types of activity, each asked as a separate question with a short answer list.

However, the major questionnaire issue was that of location coding. On the face-to-face questionnaire the location of trip destinations was coded by showing the respondent a set of maps (example appended) and asking them to identify the relevant map segment. Our solution for telephone data-collection was to incorporate an electronic database of place names into the CATI programme. This has several advantages. It allows the interviewer to check with the respondent at the time any ambiguities (e.g. Richmond, Yorkshire or Richmond, Surrey). Another advantage is that data are collected at a much higher level of geographical precision than was possible from simply coding map segments. This gives the flexibility to aggregate places into any reference areas used currently, or that may be used in the future, rather than be restricted to the areas predefined on maps. A further enhancement is that other data can be held in the database of place names, such as population and type of resort. This could have several potential variable uses in the future, and I am sure we have not thought of all of them. For example, during the interview, the respondent is asked whether their trip destination is best described as the seaside, large city/town, small town or countryside/village. It could be interesting to compare respondent perceptions of their destination with more official classifications (for example, is Southampton the seaside, do suburbs of London count as small towns in their own right?).

One further change to the questionnaire necessitated by the change in data collection has been to reduce the number of trips for which full details are collected; full details were recorded for only the first seven of these trips. However, given that only a tiny proportion of people take more than seven trips in any two-month period, this was not an issue. Due to the constraints placed on interview length by telephone interviewing (some interviews still take 40 minutes or more), the number of trips for which full details are collected has been reduced to three (although key data on purpose and destination are collected for up to ten trips). However, the proportion of people taking more than three trips in a two-month period is also very small.

Preliminary findings

An initial pilot study was run in November 1999. This comprised 400 interviews and was run over the entire month, in order to replicate as far as possible a normal month's interviewing. These data were then compared with data taken from the face-to-face survey still being conducted by NOP, from the same fieldwork period. This comparison indicated that while, pleasingly (for the sake of trend analysis), the two data sets were very similar, there were one or two crucial differences. The most marked of these was undoubtedly the increased incidence of trip taking observed in the BMRB sample. However, despite its relatively large size, the pilot study was still small compared to the main survey. It was not until data for trips undertaken in January 2000 became available that we would have the closest thing to a parallel run. It would not be a true parallel run because data for January trips would come from the last wave of NOP fieldwork in February and the first wave of BMRB fieldwork in March. Thus for January trips the NOP data would be referencing the previous month, and the BMRB data referencing the month before last. Nonetheless, both data sets would be substantial (c. 4000–4500 interviews) and so would permit thorough investigation.

In the meantime, eager to understand any discrepancies between the two survey designs, BMRB ran a few key questions regarding incidence of trip taking on both its face-to-face and telephone ACCESS omnibus services. A smaller second pilot was also run, primarily to test further procedures for improving response rates.

The ACCESS face-to-face omnibus interviews a representative sample of adults in Great Britain aged 15 or over each week. It is a Random Location design, typically sampling 195 EDs each week. Although not a strict probability design, nonetheless it is of high quality, and would provide useful diagnostic data. The questions used were taken directly from the UKTS questionnaire still running on the NOP Random omnibus. Just over 1000 interviews were conducted 3–9 February 2000.

The ACCESS telephone omnibus runs every weekend, interviewing a representative sample of adults aged 16+ living in Great Britain. A form of RDD sampling known as number propagation is used (which takes seed numbers from our face-to-face omnibus and adds or subtracts a fixed number to the seed). Just over 1000 interviews were conducted 4–6 February. The only difference between the face-to-face and telephone questionnaires was that the former used a showcard to remind respondents of the reference time period for trip taking, and that any trip involving an overnight stay away from home counted.

Table 21.4 shows the incidence of trip taking for both samples. The figures quoted relate to any trip taken in the two-month reference period. The table also shows the proportion of trip takers from NOP's February fieldwork.

The BMRB ACCESS figures suggest that the telephone approach leads to a 26 per cent increase in reported trip incidence. There is some discrepancy between the BMRB

Table 21.4 Incidence of trip taking, ACCESS Omnibus February 2000

	% trip takers January 2000/ December 1999
NOP February fieldwork	32
ACCESS face-to-face omnibus	35
ACCESS telephone omnibus	44

and NOP face-to-face surveys, but at less than 10 per cent this is far lower than between the two data-collection modes, and could readily be ascribed to differences in sampling and timing of fieldwork.

This raised a number of interesting hypotheses regarding sampling effects, questionnaire effects and even whether people were more willing to mention what they regarded as insignificant trips over the phone, or felt more secure admitting they spent nights away from home via this medium.

In May of this year we were finally able to compare two substantial data sets derived from the two different designs. Naturally, we began by looking at the incidence of trip taking, firstly in the unweighted data sets. This was 18 per cent from the BMRB data, 12 per cent from the NOP data set, an increase of 50 per cent, which was clearly a more substantial difference than we were expecting, or hoping for. However, the demographic profiles of the two unweighted data sets were different, as Table 21.5 shows.

The BMRB sample is a younger one than the NOP sample, also tending more towards the higher social grades. It is also younger and of a higher social grade than it should be (whereas the NOP sample tends to be older and have more people in the lower social grades than it should). These are differences we might expect from the two different methodologies. These differences also fed through into working status, whereby the BMRB sample had too many people working whereas the NOP sample had too few. All of these characteristics can clearly impact on the incidence of trip taking and so these profiles were adjusted with corrective weighting (there are several other stages of weighting which we do not have space to detail here, but which do not impact on the incidence of trip taking).

However, overall the number of trips taken by trip takers is very similar between the two samples, as shown in Table 21.6.

Table 21.5 Demographic profile of BMRB (March fieldwork) and NOP (February fieldwork) data sets; Sex/Age/Social Grade

	BMRB – telephone(%)	NOP – face-to-face(%)	TGI (NRS)(%)*
Male	43	43	49
Female	57	57	51
16–24	12	12	15
25–34	23	15	19
35–44	21	19	18
45–54	16	17	16
55–64	13	15	12
65+	15	22	20
AB	21	16	21
C1	35	28	27
C2	19	21	22
DE	25	35	29

*These profiles are taken from BMRB International's TGI survey, which itself is weighted to the National Readership Survey (NRS), a large-scale probability survey of the population.

Table 21.6 Number of trips taken by demographics

	BMRB (%)	BMRB no. trips	NOP (%)	NOP no. trips
Total	18	1.63	12	1.59
Male	21	1.83	13	1.69
Female	16	1.43	12	1.51
16–24	24	1.81	19	2.35
25–34	20	1.81	16	1.50
35–44	18	1.67	11	1.48
45–54	20	1.53	14	1.53
55–64	15	1.28	12	1.35
65+	11	1.37	7	1.14
AB	29	1.64	23	1.60
C1	19	1.42	15	1.47
C2	12	2.14	10	1.71
DE	12	1.74	6	1.67
England	18	1.69	13	1.62
Scotland	20	1.70	13	1.53
Wales	17	1.21	10	1.29
Northern Ireland	14	2.08	5	1.09
Working	21	1.66	16	1.67
Not Working	14	1.57	9	1.48

When the demographic profiles are corrected the BMRB incidence of trip taking is reduced to 17 per cent and the NOP incidence increased to 14 per cent (we would have expected it to have less impact on the BMRB incidence as the BMRB demographic profile required less correction). This equates to a 27 per cent increase in the incidence of trip taking due to change in methodology, which is what our pilot study has led us to expect.

We have explored a number of hypotheses as to why this difference exists. First, we wondered if the increased number of call-backs possible with telephone data-collection led to more trip takers being interviewed. If one looks at the number of trip takers in the BMRB sample by the number of contacts made, the figures suggest this makes very little difference. Six per cent more trip takers are picked up with three or more contacts as opposed to one or two contacts, but this hardly explains the 27 per cent divergence we have seen.

We then considered the geographical spread of the two interviewed samples. Perhaps the unclustered nature of the telephone sample led to more trip takers being interviewed. The difference in clustering between the two samples is amply demonstrated by the fact that on average BMRB interviewed 1.26 people per postcode sector whereas the corresponding figure for the NOP sample is fifteen. We looked at the population density of these sectors, to ascertain whether the BMRB sample contained more interviews in rural areas, which may lead to a greater incidence of trip taking.

However, the average population density of sectors between the samples was almost identical, and although there were small differences in the distribution of household densities, these were insufficient to explain the differences observed.

We also considered whether people who had not taken a trip were discouraged from completing the BMRB interview because it was the only topic in the interview, whereas when UKTS had been part of an omnibus there would have been other topics on which they felt could contribute meaningfully. However, BMRB's experiment on its omnibus services (see above) appears to discount this theory. We shall continue to explore this issue. However, to date we have no reason to doubt the accuracy of the new survey. In order to look at trend data in a meaningful way we shall need to adjust data from previous years.

The other, expected, and far less serious divergence was in the proportion undertaking activities whilst on a trip (Table 21.7). The greater degree of prompting on the telephone leads to higher reporting of most activities, which we think can legitimately take to be a more accurate figure.

Table 21.7   Activities undertaken whilst on a trip (January)

	BMRB (%)	NOP (%)
Any activity undertaken	65	37
No activity undertaken	35	63
Motor boat cruising	1	*
Other boating	3	1
Water-skiing/power-boating	*	*
Indoor swimming	10	7
Outdoor swimming	5	3
Any swimming	14	9
Fishing (sea angling)	1	1
Fishing (coarse or game)	1	*
Shooting/stalking/hunting	1	*
Horse riding/pony-trekking	2	*
Tennis	1	1
Golfing	3	1
Cycling	4	1
Mountaineering, etc.	1	*
Snow skiing	1	2
Field studies, etc.	7	1
Participation in any other sport	5	2
Multi-activity package	2	*
Watching sport	4	6
Watching performing arts	7	3
Cinema	9	2
Theme/activity park	4	
Heritage sites	15	8
Other hobby/special interest	16	7

* = less than 0.5%
(Base: BMRB: 746, NOP 836)

The future

There are already a number of plans for the future of the UKTS. First and foremost, we shall continue to monitor and assess key measures from the survey, in order to understand how current data relates to the post.

It is hoped that after the first year of the new survey, we shall be able to refine the design yet further, and remove a minor flaw, which can also be found in many similar surveys. Currently, the survey asks about trips started in the previous two months. Logically, this limits the maximum length of trip that can be reported to c. 90 days, as for longer trips the respondent would not yet have returned. This method is also likely to under-represent trips started late in the previous month. Therefore, the intention is to switch to trips ended in the previous two months. Currently questions probe the start and finish date of trips taken to assess the potential impact of changing this aspect of the survey. Indications are that this will have only a marginal effect, as one would hope and expect, but will improve the rigour of the design nonetheless.

There are also plans to register the survey as a National Statistic. National Statistics is the UK government's plan for improving the accountability and integrity of official statistics. This means that the survey will be assessed for its methodological rigour, and certain parameters will have to be observed regarding access to and reporting of the data. It is hoped this process will be complete by early 2001.

Finally, there are proposals to fuse BMRB International's TGI data to the UKTS. TGI is an annual survey of c. 27,000 UK adults, collecting a vast breadth of data on people's activities, purchases and media consumption, at brand and category levels. Data fusion is a paper in itself, and so we cannot go into detail here. However, a fused UKTS/TGI data set would allow powerful market segmentation and targeting.

CARD 8

ACTIVITIES
DOING / PLAYING / GOING

A. Motor-boat cruising	Q. Multi-activity package
B. Other sailing/yachting/boating/ canoeing/windsurfing	R. Watching any sport/sporting event (please state which sport/event)
C. Water-skiing or power-boating	S. Field study/nature study/bird or
D. Indoor swimming	wildlife watching
E. Outdoor swimming	T. Watching performing arts –
F. Fishing – sea angling	theatre/concert/opera/ballet
G. Fishing – coarse or game	U. Visiting (cinema)
H. Shooting/stalking/hunting	V. Visiting (theme park or activity
I. Horse-riding/pony-trekking	park)
J. Tennis	W. Visiting 'heritage' sites/castles/
K. Golfing (*not* 'mini-golf')	monuments/churches etc.
L. Cycling	X. Visiting artistic or heritage
M. Hiking/hill-walking/rambling/ orienteering	exhibits (museums/art galleries/ heritage centres etc.)
N. Mountaineering/rock-climbing/ abseiling/caving/potholing	Y. Some other particular hobby/ special interest holiday (please
O. Snow skiing	state which one)
P. Taking part in any other single particular sport (please state which sport)	Z. Some other particular activity not on the list (please state which)

SCOTLAND

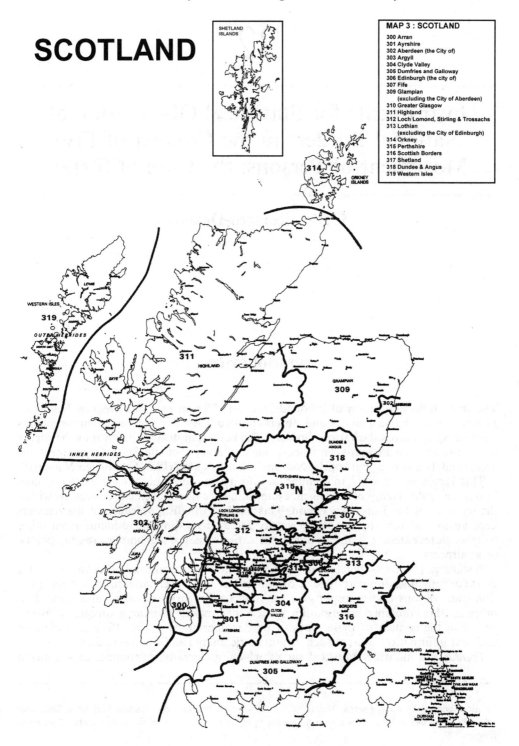

MAP 3 : SCOTLAND

300 Arran
301 Ayrshire
302 Aberdeen (the City of)
303 Argyll
304 Clyde Valley
305 Dumfries and Galloway
306 Edinburgh (the city of)
307 Fife
309 Glampian
   (excluding the City of Aberdeen)
310 Greater Glasgow
311 Highland
312 Loch Lomond, Stirling & Trossachs
313 Lothian
   (excluding the City of Edinburgh)
314 Orkney
315 Perthshire
316 Scottish Borders
317 Shetland
318 Dundee & Angus
319 Western Isles

22

Instruments for Statistical Observation at National Borders in the Context of Free Movement of Persons: the Case of Spain[1]

Carlos Romero-Dexeus

INTRODUCTION

The Spanish Border Survey of Inbound Tourism (*Movimientos Turísticos en Fronteras: Frontur*) is the basic analysis and observation tool for the tourism of non-residents entering Spain across the various borders. The body that draws up and runs the survey is the Instituto de Estudios Turísticos, under the aegis of the State Department for Trade and Tourism, as part of the National Statistics Plan (Plan Estadístico Nacional).

This survey was devised to counter an information loophole caused by the coming into force of the Treaty of Schengen, establishing the free movement of persons within the territory of the European Union. This marked the disappearance of the registers kept up to that time by the state security forces, recording all residents from other member states entering Spain via any of the various road or rail border-crossing points, or at airports.

A statistical tool was therefore devised, different from the normal procedure in that it used not only questionnaire-type information but also purely administrative information from various bodies responsible for road traffic, airports, trains and ships. It is precisely this combined information source that makes *Frontur* a unique statistical survey in the context of these types of border operations, in its efficient pooling of different information sources such as automatic counts and questionnaires.

Frontur is a monthly statistical survey which, as already mentioned, uses a mixed

---

[1] Basic Bibliography used: *Frontur Methodological References*, Instituto de Estudios Turísticos, December 1999; *Work Document No 3: Obtaining typologies at road frontier crossings*, Instituto de Estudios Turísticos, January 1997.

system to obtain its results; based upon the relevant administrative records (concerning each one of the transportation modes); both vehicle counts at road border crossings (1,500,000 vehicles were counted in 1999) and sample interviewing (at road and airport border points) are carried out on a continuous basis. Each one of the four transportation modes involves the collaboration of the corresponding official body: the road traffic authority (Dirección General de Tráfico), airport authority (Aena), seaport authority (Puertos del Estado) and the national railway operator (RENFE).

As far as sample interviewing is concerned, *Frontur* actually consists of two different surveys, one being carried out on visitors leaving the country, the other one on those entering it. The entry survey is currently being carried out at 22 road border crossings as well as seventeen airports, using a brief questionnaire that records general aspects of the trip, through a set of questions that vary according to the typology of the traveller being interviewed. Travellers are classified into tourists (foreign residents intending to stay overnight in Spain), excursionists or same-day visitors (those staying less than 24 hours) and Spanish residents returning home after a trip abroad.

In the exit sample survey, which is also carried out at both road borders and airports, a longer questionnaire is used, which, in addition to the questions contained in the entry questionnaire, includes personal data as well as quantitative and subjective questions regarding the planning of the trip and characteristics of the stay.

Throughout 1999, 70,000 entry interviews were made at road borders, along with those corresponding to all passengers on a total of 2500 flights. As for the exit survey, a total of 20,000 interviews were conducted at road borders and 20,000 at airports.

SOME METHODOLOGICAL ASPECTS RELATED TO THE COLLECTION OF INFORMATION ON INFLOWS OF PERSONS AND VEHICLES ENTERING THE COUNTRY THROUGH THE ROAD BORDERS

Frontur can be said to consist of four basic sub-surveys, one for each way of entering Spain, be it road, air, sea or rail. The two most important, however, are roads and airports. It should not be forgotten that 94 per cent of the tourists coming to Spain during the last year did so by road or air. It is, therefore, these two sub-surveys that call for the most elaborate treatment and take up the most human and financial resources.

On this occasion we will deal exclusively with the road sub-survey, i.e. the monthly collection of information on the flow of vehicles and persons across the various border points of Spain, ignoring for the time being the fact that this information then has to be pooled at the end with that obtained from the other transport modes.

The ultimate aim of the processes described below is none other than the most accurate estimation possible of the number of persons entering Spain across each of the 22 border posts that have been taken into account for conducting the study, plus their breakdown by basic characteristics of interest from the point of view of tourism analysis.

Estimating the number of travellers

The process of estimating the number of persons entering Spain through the road borders can be divided into three stages.

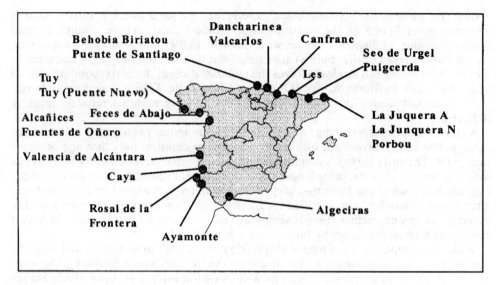

Figure 22.1 Spanish road border crossings map under the control of Frontur survey

First stage

In this first stage we need to know the total number of vehicles that cross the road borders. This information is furnished by the Dirección General de Tráfico (DGT), a body whose responsibilities include that of finding out the volume of traffic on the various roads of Spain's national network. This information is obtained from innumerable automatic counting devices fitted at all road borders, working 24 hours a day, 365 days a year. The importance of this type of administrative information in the following estimation process lies in the fact that it is the only information with a universal character; i.e. it offers an ideal reference framework for estimating the total number of visitors crossing the borders.

The information furnished by DGT has some limitations. The most important for carrying out the survey are:

- the impossibility of distinguishing more than three vehicle sizes: light, medium or large;
- no information is given on the number of vehicle occupants, much less on their nationality or the length of their stay;
- it cannot distinguish between lorries and coaches/buses;
- on some occasions the automatic counters may break down for a longer period than is desirable, whereupon it becomes necessary to resort to information from similar days of previous months or the same month of the previous year.

To overcome these limitations *Frontur* has set up a manual counting system and a vehicle-entry questionnaire.

Second stage

Once we understand the total numbers of vehicles entering Spain across the various road borders, with the above-mentioned limitations, we will then stand in need of some type of sample information for ascertaining, on the one hand, the type of vehicle in question, mainly to distinguish between lorries and coaches/buses and, on the other, the vehicle occupation and the basic characteristics of the persons travelling within.

Agents are therefore posted at a sample of the same border-crossing points as those that contain the automatic counters of DGT, working in eight-hour shifts and in a sample of days from each month of the year. Portable computers of an enormous versatility enable them simply to key in all passing vehicles, identifying clearly not only the type of vehicle but also the number of occupants and the nationality of the licence plate. The information thus obtained at the end of each month gives a more detailed breakdown of vehicle flows across a given border than that furnished by DGT. This information within each eight-hour working day is census based, i.e. it registers each and every one of the cars crossing a road border on a given day of a given week of the month. Furthermore, the portable computers are perfectly synchronized with the clocks of DGT's automatic counters so that each of the manually recorded registers, with the time at which it was recorded, can be easily cross-checked against the information from this same time-band from DGT.

Sometimes, on roads with the heaviest traffic, or in months of the year with the greatest tourism movements such as August, it is necessary to post two agents, manually counting the vehicles on each carriageway of a motorway. This is the case of the two motorways with heaviest traffic between France and Spain: Biriatou and La Junquera.

The information obtained from the manual counts is as follows:

1. The type of vehicle entering the country, distinguishing between: light vehicles (car, car towing a caravan or trailer, motor caravan, van or minibus, motorbike, others) and heavy (microbus, coach, bus, lorry, large van or pickup).
2. The number of persons travelling in the vehicle. In the case of buses, microbuses and coaches a note is made of the number of passengers by the following classification: empty, fewer than 10 passengers, 10–30 passengers, more than 30 passengers.
3. Nationality of the licence plate of the entering vehicles, according to the following closed list of countries: Spain, Portugal, France, Germany, Great Britain, Belgium, Holland, Italy, Switzerland, Andorra and others.

Given that these manual counts and sample information can be obtained without stopping the vehicles, the number of counts made throughout the year is very high. In the last year a total of 1.5 million vehicles of different types were counted; in the months of greatest traffic up to 300,000 vehicles can be registered.

The procedures described above tell us the number of vehicles and the average occupation, and hence the number of persons that have entered in each type of vehicle and licence plate nationality. All this assumes that the selected vehicle sample for manual counts is representative of the total numbers of vehicles afforded by DGT.

Third stage

Once we know the total number of persons by type of vehicle and nationality that have entered across the road borders, it is then necessary, for tourism purposes, to find out some essential characteristics of these persons, to be able to give a detailed tabulation of the previously obtained total of persons, breaking them down by variables such as home country, type of visit (resident in Spain, tourist, same-day visitor, passer-through), motive of the trip, type of accommodation, number of overnight stays etc.

The variables included in the questionnaire and their possible states are:

1. means of transport used, in accordance with the above-mentioned classification;
2. nationality;
3. home country – Spain, France, Portugal, Morocco, Germany, Italy, others;
4. duration of stay;
5. destination;
6. motive of the trip;
7. total occupants in the vehicle.

Besides these variables there is another variable of enormous importance for tourism purposes; the type of visitor which is generated from the characteristics 'home country' and 'duration of stay'. This is a characteristic of the journey-maker that is not directly asked for but it is deduced from whether or not the person is resident in Spain and, if not, whether he/she plans to make any overnight stays (then it is possible to classify them as tourists or same-day visitors) or whether he/she is passing through en route to another country.

Groups of travellers identified by the investigation:

● people resident in Spain who are returning from or leaving for a foreign country;
● foreigners who are entering or leaving the country who are travelling by day without staying overnight in Spain but returning to sleep in their place of residence;
● foreigners who are passing through Spain but whose destination (if they are entering the country) or their place of origin (if they are leaving) is another country;[2]
● foreigners who come to Spain for whatever reason and stay for at least one night. This is the main group to be surveyed and the one that is most interesting for the investigation.

The best way of finding out all these characteristics is an entry questionnaire of the vehicles previously selected by type of border post and time-band. In this case, although the questionnaire is very short, it will be necessary to stop the vehicles. Refusals occur, either because the vehicle fails to stop or refuses to answer; in this case a note is made of the type of vehicle, the nationality of the licence plate and the number of occupants. This allows a control to be kept at all times over any possible deviations or biases in the selected sample.[3]

The small size of the road-entry questionnaire means that a huge amount of information can be collected throughout the year.

After the third and last stage we are in a position to be able to ascertain the total

---

[2] In the case of Spain there are two examples of this type of group very common: emigrants in other European countries who are going on holiday or returning from Portugal or countries in the area of the Magreb (mainly Morocco) and who are using Spain as a transit country, and the case of people who are just passing through Spain on the way to Portugal or to any of the African countries.

[3] See Appendix I: *Frontur* Road Entry Questionnaire.

number of tourists, same-day visitors and residents who enter Spain across the various road borders, together with some of their main characteristics. This information is forthcoming within two weeks, thanks to the automatic modem system of sending data collected in the most distant parts of Spain from the agents' personal computers to the central office where all the information is processed. The information sent includes both manual counts and entry questionnaires.

Lastly, another benefit of the information obtained from administrative registers, manual counts and entry questionnaires is the greater coverage of exit surveys in terms of the population 'universe' furnished by entries. The exit survey provides the bulk of tourism-related information that proves highly useful for the sector when analysing trends by nationalities, dates, destinations, expenditure etc. The questionnaire includes not only the basic breakdown values of the expenditure survey, in the interests of a perfect correspondence with the universe, but also questions of a personal nature together with others of a quantitative character, to do with the identification of the visitor and aspects concerning the design of the trip and their stay in Spain (see attached exit questionnaire of *Frontur*).[4]

Sample design

The road border samples have been designed with three factors in mind: the objective of the study, the auxiliary or complementary information available and the human and economic resources to be used. The first factor prompted us to distribute the overall annual sample in both space and time, so as to cover exhaustively all border crossings and, at least partially, the different times of the year. The second factor to bear in mind is the information regularly furnished by DGT on the vehicles passing through the various border crossings. Finally, the cost of the survey determines some important aspects thereof. Mention should be made here of the material impossibility of studying adequately all the months of the year and all the border crossings.

In view of the countries bordering on Spain and the traffic towards Africa, four groups of border-crossing points have been established, each one corresponding to a type of traveller flow. One is made up by the border crossing points with Portugal, another by the border crossing points with France, another only by Seo de Urgel and another in Algeciras to take in Africa traffic. The inclusion of Seo de Urgel among the crossing points corresponding to France stems from the fact that many visitors from France enter Spain via the Andorra road.

Typologies of border-cossing points

To back up the sample design use is made of a previous study that was carried out when initiating the *Frontur* survey: *Typologies in each border crossing point*. This study allowed a precise typology to be obtained of days in each border post, so that a classification can be made of the 365 days for each post of the reference period in search of groups of days with a similar traffic throughout the 24 hours.

The variables to be used to ascertain the typology are the 24 hours of the day and the vehicle flows provided by DGT. Although the latter data comes in three categories

---

[4] See Appendix II: *Frontur* Road Exit Questionnaire.

(light, medium and heavy) it had been grouped into two light categories and the rest. In statistical terms, therefore, we now have 365 cases or days to classify in terms of 48 variables (24 hours for light vehicles and 24 hours for the rest).

These quantitative-type typologies have been obtained from the known historical data of DGT, but in order to be of use they need to be extrapolated to the following year. In other words, a prediction is made of the type of day for each of the 365 days of the sample period running from May 1999 to April 2000. To this end different statistical breakdown techniques are used.

The following factors are taken into account when selecting the months for manual counts or questionnaires in each post:

- Which are the most important posts in terms of their heavy traffic? These posts will be surveyed every month of the year.
- Which are the most important holiday months? In these months all or most border-crossing points will also be surveyed, e.g. July, August and March.
- Alternate months in which counts or questionnaires are effected in remaining points, so that if one month has not been included in the sample, the previous one was or the next one or an adjacent one will be.
- Survey posts and months that were left out the previous year.

This strategy means that after two years of obtaining samples, we now have sample information for all posts in all months.

From all this information various typologies can be obtained. These will tell us the structure and variability of vehicle and person flows at the borders and allow us to optimize and reduce the number of sample months selected.

APPENDIX I: *FRONTUR* ENTRY QUESTIONNAIRE: QUESTIONS ASKED

Date:

Time frame:

Point of survey:

Code:

1. Language used to address the informant and his/her nationality

2. Can you answer a few questions?

3. Means of transport used

4. Usual place of residence

5. Province and Town of residence

6. Countries in which you have spent the night during your trip abroad

7. Do you intend returning to France today?

8. Are you in transit to another country?

9. Country destination

10. Overnight stays you intend making during transit through Spain

11. Overnight stays you intend making in Spain

12. Indicate main area and place of destination

13. Purpose of your trip

14. Total passengers in the vehicle and how many of them form a homogeneous tourist group

15. Size of tourist group by number of persons

16. Distribution of tourist group by age and sex

17. Sex, age, studies and activities of each member of the homogeneous tourist group

18. Number of passengers

19. Sex of the informant

20. Age of the informant

APPENDIX II: *FRONTUR* EXIT QUESTIONNAIRE: QUESTIONS ASKED

Date:

Time frame:

Point of survey:

Code:

1. Language used to address the informant and his/her nationality

2. Can you answer a few questions?

3. Means of transport used

4. Usual place of residence

5. Province and town of residence

6. Do you intend making an overnight stay abroad?

7. Indicate countries where you intend making an overnight stay and number of nights in each

8. Have you crossed Spain in transit to another country?

9. Indicate country of origin of this trip and overnight stays in Spain

10. Overnight stays in Spain

11. Purpose of trip

12. Main reason

13. Frequency of your visits to Spain

14. Reasons for trip

15. Approximate date of entry into Spain and number of days stay

16. Areas and places where you have spent the night, and number of nights during your stay in Spain

17. Indicate the activities carried out during your stay

18. Degree of satisfaction in relation to the following items

19. Is this your first visit to Spain?

20. Have you visited Spain during the last three years?

21. How many times have you visited Spain, apart from this time?

22. Do you expect to choose Spain for holidays during the next 12 months?

23. Organisation of visit to Spain

24. Price of individual package tour

25. Concepts included in the package tour

26. Main type of accommodation used (where most nights were spent)

27. Name of accommodation and category

28. Total passengers in the vehicle and how many of them form a tourist group

29. Size of tourist group by number of persons

30. Sex, age, studies and professional status of each member of the tourist group

31. Distribution of members of the tourist group by age and sex

32. The information you provide on expenses refers to yourself only or to the group.

33. Travelling expenses in Spain, not including those disbursed in your country in order to make this trip (amount and currency)

34. Number of passengers

35. Sex of the informant

36. Age of the informant

23

A Case Analysis: Spanish Domestic and Outbound Tourism Survey (*Familitur*)

Eva Aranda Palmero

INTRODUCTION

This chapter aims to give an account of Spain's experience of research into the tourism behaviour of Spanish residents by using a panel-type statistical survey. Spain is one of the few countries that use this information-collection method for studying national tourism. We therefore believe it to be of interest to share our experience and describe the advantages of this system for obtaining useful, reliable and up-to-date information.

The statistical survey upon which this study is based is called *Familitur* (Movimientos turísticos de los Españoles: Tourism Movements of the Spanish), and it is drawn up by the Tourism Studies Institute (Instituto de Estudios Turísticos: IET).[1] Its main objective is to collect information on all trips made by the Spanish (national tourism), both inside Spain (domestic tourism) and abroad (outbound tourism), providing they involve at least one overnight stay outside the usual environment.

A Short History of *Familitur*

The choice of a panel-type modality over other sample-design alternatives has followed upon a whole process of reflection being carried out by the Instituto de Estudios Turísticos since 1996, the first year of setting up the previous survey, at which time, albeit only experimentally, the choice had already been made to panelise a small fraction of the total of the selected census sections.

---

[1] El Instituto de Estudios Turísticos depends on the State Department for Trade and Tourism, which in turn depends on the Economics Ministry. It is a statistical survey included in the Plan Estadístico Nacional (National Statistics Plan).

The results of the partial panelisation in the first year of the sample prompted IET to opt for a completely panelised sample in the two following years, 1997 and 1998. This modality was then continued in the new statistical survey *Familitur* begun in 1999, on the basis of a totally renewed household panel.

In 1999 a series of survey improvements was also made, with an increase of the sample (rising from 3800 households in each data-collection to 10,800) plus a series of modifications in the questionnaire. The main advantages of these changes were the obtaining of figures at a regional level and the study of a phenomenon not hitherto dealt with: short-duration trips to second residences.

METHODOLOGICAL REFERENCES OF *FAMILITUR*

Since 1996 the Instituto de Estudios Turísticos has been the body responsible for running the *Familitur* statistical survey, in fulfilment of the statistics commitments taken on by Spain in section C of Council Directive 95/57/EC on the collection of statistical information in the field of tourism.

A brief explanation will now be given of the methodological process of the *Familitur* statistical survey; any readers who desire more information on the matter should refer to the working document 23: 'Movimientos Turísticos de los Españoles (*Familitur*): Referencias metodológicas (methodological references)', available in the Instituto de Estudios Turísticos and on the organization's web page: www.iet.tourspain.es.

Sample type and units

To carry out the survey a selection is made of a panel of households by using a two-stage cluster sample with subsample and stratification of the first-stage units. The first-stage units are the census sections of the Instituto Nacional de Estadística (National Statistical Office). The second-stage units are the main family dwellings. Thus the working sample universe excludes collective establishments, the latter concept embracing all hotel-type establishments.

The sample consists of 1200 sections distributed between the seventeen Autonomous Communities making up the whole national territory, in accordance with criteria other than those of the strict proportionality of their respective populations, with a non-proportional allocation. Thus, the distribution chosen for the sample stratification is representative in the smaller communities, population-wise, increasing in all of them the number of sections that would otherwise correspond to them in terms of strict proportionality. Nine households are chosen randomly in each of the 1200 census sections, the final sample resulting in a panel of 10,800 households.

Reference period: four-monthly versus three-monthly

The survey is effected in three data-collections throughout the year, each involving questions on the trips made during the four months running up to the interview month. In 1997 and 1998 the data was collected on a three-monthly basis, dividing the sample each time into three groups. This made it difficult to obtain information during interviews scheduled for holiday months such as July or August, when the families were on holiday.

Another problem posed by this three-monthly method was the splitting up of holiday periods. The inclusion of different data-collections in the same holiday period (such as the summer season) meant that a complete analysis of holiday seasons had to wait for the following data-collection to be carried out.

These factors led to a rethink of the reference periods in the methodological change of 1999, the conclusion being drawn that the best data-collection period would be four months. The following three reference periods were thus established: the first to record trips made from February to May in a June interview: this meant that this reference period would always include trips made at Easter, whether this fell in March or April – a crucial factor for making year by year comparisons; the second period covers the four months of the summer season (June to September) in an October interview, when most people have returned from their summer holidays; and the October to January period records all Christmas trips, the interview to be conducted in February.

This data-collection method is not incompatible with the three-monthly information requirements of the Council Directive since, although the survey's reference period is four-monthly, three-monthly information can still be furnished.

IET would like to take this chance to suggest the need to harmonize somewhat the consideration of the various holiday seasons in the various tourism statistical surveys produced, both by the different bodies and by the distinct countries, thus ensuring that the figures would always be comparable.

Collection of the information

As for the information-collection system, it is a mixed system combining personal interviews in the homes of the panellists and telephone interviews. During the first operation the information is collected in a personal interview in the home of the members of each household under study, selecting one household member as the main informant. In subsequent data-collections, once the household panel has been set up, the method is characterized by the flexible use of two systems combined in the most efficient manner: telephone collection of the information (CATI) and personal home interviews when the interviewee prefers or when the household cannot be contacted by telephone. Telephone calls to households for carrying out the telephone interview are made on different days of the week and at different times of the day with the paramount objective of locating the main informant.

Validation and imputation

When all the information is available from the 10,800 questionnaires of each campaign, the first step is to subject all this information to a series of logical controls designed to ensure its quality, before processing. All data is thus subjected to consistency programmes to correct all wrong information, following validation rules that may be consulted in the various methodological documents published by IET.

Once the information has been debugged, the next step is to carry out lack-of-response imputation tasks, insofar as this has not been corrected in the validation phase.

Elevation

In broad terms the *Familitur* survey could be considered as three surveys in one, for there are three analysis units each with a different treatment. First comes the analysis of the household, involving a study of its characteristics and access to, or possession of, certain durable consumer goods such as a second residence or tourism equipment. Second comes the investigation of the household members, including information on their socio-economic characteristics. Last comes the study of the trips made by these household members, in which an analysis is made of their basic characteristics such as the type of accommodation used, the means of transport, how the trip was organized etc. Each of these analysis units is related directly to an area of the questionnaire. It should be stressed that, although they could be considered as three different operations, the interrelationship between each one and the cross-checking of data between them is of paramount importance.

As already mentioned, they could be considered as three different operations, insofar as the elevation framework of each one is different. Thus, household data is elevated to the total of Spanish households; the elevation framework of the sample data of household members is the total number of people living in Spain, while the trips made are elevated in terms of the calculated weights of each one, based on the weight of each person who made the trip. As might be expected, the balancing matrices used for households and household members are also different. Furthermore, the processing of the data obtained for each of the analysis units is very different.

Obtaining the results

In the tabulation plan the information is structured into three basic blocks, to tie in with the aforementioned analysis units: households, household members and trips. Thus, the first block includes a study of the households, with details, for example, on whether or not the household is a traveller one, i.e. whether or not it has access to a second residence. The second block concentrates on the analysis of the household members, offering information of the type: travellers or non-travellers, by age group, level of education etc. Lastly, the third block, studying the trips made, concentrates on the study of the characteristics thereof, such as type of accommodation, means of transport, how the trip was organized etc.

The concept 'traveller', to be explained herein, is linked to the household members and is obtained in this information block.

Although the tabulation plan has not included it this year, information can also be offered on trips correlated with the information on the household members, since the socio-economic characteristics of each traveller are known. A study can thus be made of the academic qualifications of persons using the hotel, or the occupation of persons making business trips, to give only two examples.

Analysis tool: Pulsar

It has already been mentioned that certain variables can be correlated with others even though this is not included in the tabulation plan. On certain occasions it is also necessary to effect special operations for comparing certain results with those offered by other sources. It should be pointed out that this type of cross-check and operation can be effected simply and immediately, since all survey information is loaded into a user-friendly programme (Pulsar) which carries out all these investigations in a few minutes and without any need for handling complex computing systems.

Dissemination of results

IET publishes annually all tables of the tabulation plan, both as hard copy and in computer format. It also draws up reports for each season. All this information is available on the Institute's web page.

There is also a series of agreements with regional statistics institutes for furnishing the primary files, so that the latter may use them for ad hoc purposes.

SPANISH TOURISM BEHAVIOUR: THE IDEAL NATURE OF A PANEL

We are first of all going to sketch in some of the characteristics of the tourism behaviour of Spanish residents. It was precisely these features that prompted IET to opt for a panel-type statistical survey to study this matter.

From the point of view of inbound tourism, Spain ranks second worldwide in the number of tourist arrivals. From the point of view of national tourism, however, an analysis of the tourism activity of Spanish residents shows that half of the total Spanish population make trips.

One of the characteristics of these trips is that they are principally (82 per cent) domestic trips. Another of the particular features of tourism in Spain, in comparison with tourism elsewhere, is the phenomenon of the second residence. The Household Panel of the European Union allows for a study of access to such properties in the various countries of the EU, showing the relative importance of such residences in Spain. In 1999, trips to a second residence accounted for over 63 per cent of the total of trips made by the Spanish residents.

The explanation for this phenomenon lies, perhaps, in the fact that migration within Spain has led to a situation where 50 per cent of the Spanish population live in a different place to where they were born. *Prima facie*, this could well lead to a great number of trips to visit family or friends. The figures for 1999 seem to bear out this hypothesis, since 32 per cent of the total trips made by the Spanish were for this purpose.

It can be seen that Spanish tourism behaviour differs from the typical picture in other countries, distinguished by the low percentage of the traveller population, the use of the second residence and the low rate of outbound trips.

These factors motivated a thoroughgoing research into both the traveller and non-traveller population, as well as an investigation of the socio-economic characteristics lying behind the tourism behaviour of the Spanish residents.

MAIN CONTRIBUTION OF *FAMILITUR*: THE STUDY OF THE TRAVELLER

Definition and concept of traveller

A Commission Decision[2] defined 'traveller' as 'any person on a trip between two or

---

[2] Commission Decision of 9 December 1998 on procedures for implementing Council Directive 95/57/EC on the collection of statistical information in the field of tourism.

more countries or between two or more places within his/her country of residence'. The interpretation of this definition by the Instituto de Estudios Turísticos understands the concept 'traveller' to be associated with a person, so that an individual is to be considered a traveller when he/she has made at least one trip, regardless of whether more than one was made. According to this interpretation, the analysis unit 'traveller' requires a special treatment, very different from the 'trip' unit. Indeed, a trip is not associated with a person but rather with a displacement. Delving a little deeper into both definitions, we can say that displacements can straightforwardly be aggregated, whereas 'travellers' need to be aggregated in a special way to ensure the same individual is not counted as a 'traveller' twice. The calculation of the number of 'travellers', therefore, requires a longitudinal analysis of each individual.

To help clear up both concepts we are going to give a brief example: if an individual makes two trips during January and three in February, he/she will be counted as one 'traveller' in January, one 'traveller' in February and one 'traveller' in the cumulative period January–February. For the purposes of counting trips, however, this person will have made two trips in January, three in February: a total of five in the aggregate period January–February.

Surveys conducted at border crossings or destination points use the 'trip' as analysis unit. The main advantage of these surveys is that the informants are always the people actually making the trip, so they can offer much more information on the associated characteristics of the trips. As is logical, however, these surveys are not addressed to non-travellers, so no information can be obtained on this group, nor can the results be brought into relation with them.

It can safely be claimed that the best way of obtaining the 'traveller' variable is by a panel-type survey. In surveys with independent samples it is difficult to monitor the same individual over time, so it is impossible to find out whether or not the same person is being counted as a 'traveller' twice. If, for example, the same German citizen should visit Spain on repeated occasions during the same reference period, all the trips made to Spain with an overnight stay will be counted as 'trips'. Furthermore, in surveys carried out, for example, in hotels, the same person staying in different hotels will be counted under different trips, since it is impossible to follow each individual over time.

Calculation of the 'traveller' variable, therefore, allows us to offer results relative to the whole population; for example, that 49.7 per cent of the Spanish population made some sort of trip in 1999. There might well be other means of obtaining this information besides the panel method, such as taking an independent sample at a given moment of time and asking individuals whether they have made a trip during this year. But this method would suffer greatly from the memory effect, and it would also be impossible to establish a trend of the proportion of travellers in different periods of time. For all these reasons, it is thought that the best method of obtaining this variable is the use of household panels.

It should be stressed here that the *Familitur* survey complies with the information requirements of the Council Directive since, as well as investigating the 'traveller' variable, it also offers the results of 'trips', which is the analysis unit required by the Directive. The social reality of Spain and the particular tourism behaviour of its inhabitants prompted IET to opt for a panel-type study that could offer not only trip information but also a sociological study over time of the trip behaviour of the inhabitants of Spain.

Behaviour as a function of socio-economic characteristics

The *Familitur* questionnaire records the socio-economic characteristics of each member of the households forming part of the panel, so that each 'traveller' and 'non-traveller' is totally identified by a series of characteristics such as sex, age, level of study, employment situation etc. As might be expected, this information has been duly exploited for analysing the variables 'traveller' and 'non-traveller' in terms of their socio-economic characteristics.

As well as breaking down the Spanish population into travellers and non-travellers, therefore, various social aspects can be brought into the picture. Valuable data can thus be obtained; for example that 53 per cent of the employed Spanish population made a trip, whereas only 38 per cent of the unemployed population did so.

The reasons that dissuaded non-travellers from travelling can also be recorded, thus building up a complete picture of why 'travellers' travelled and why 'non-travellers' did not.

'Non-travellers' can be considered as potential travellers, so information obtained on their characteristics and motives can be highly useful for designing promotion campaigns.

Longitudinal analysis

The longitudinal analysis of travellers' and non-travellers' behaviour is the main advantage of using a household panel. Repeated information on the same households over time allows us to see how certain social changes might influence tourism behaviour. In each data-collection, a revision is made of the socio-economic data of each household member, thus recording any changes that may have come about. A detailed analysis of this information will then show the impact of certain social changes on tourism behaviour, such as a change in employment or marital status.

The annual number of 'travellers'

The *Familitur* survey is conducted in three data-collections throughout the year, each one giving information on the number of 'travellers' and the number of 'trips', both cumulative and month-by-month. The number of 'travellers' in each data-collection is relatively easily obtained, since all individuals making up the panel are common to all data-collections, so it is easy to monitor them over time.

For longer time periods, however, in which there are, logically, additions and drop-outs, the most accurate estimator for obtaining the number of travellers for a longer period than the reference period was considered to be the result of the common sample. A sub-sample is thus taken of the total sample including only individuals common to all data-collections. This sub-sample, thanks to the excellent collaboration of the families and the excellent acceptance of the survey, amounted to 89 per cent of the effective sample. In other words, more than 89 per cent of the households making up the panel in the first data-collection continued to collaborate throughout. The household sub-sample was adjusted to the total population by using the same balancing matrices as those used from data-collection to data-collection.

The households

Up to now, little reference has been made to the study of the households, as we have been concentrating on the study of the members. It should be pointed out, however, that the information obtained from the study of the individuals is extendable to the households. The household characteristics studied include their make up (number of members, occupancy status of the main dwelling) and other, more specific, tourism factors such as access to a second residence and ownership of certain durable consumer goods of tourism use. The households' tourism behaviour can thus be analysed on the basis of these characteristics and an assessment can be made for each period of time of whether or not they are traveller households[3] and how changes in their characteristics affect their tourism behaviour.

Access to a second residence deserves special mention. As previously pointed out, short-stay trips to second residences were studied for the first time in 1999. It has been shown that this type of trip is of the utmost importance in Spain, representing 63 per cent of total trips made by the Spanish residents during the year. The concept of second residence is broader in *Familitur* than in other statistical sources,[4] since it includes houses of families or friends as well as owned or rented property. But the information-collection method allows results, suitably processed, to be compared with those offered by other sources.

OTHER ADVANTAGES OF USING A HOUSEHOLD PANEL

The memory effect

A key problem in statistical surveys for measuring tourism behaviour is the memory effect. This matter was raised in a meeting held in Rome from 24 to 26 November 1999,[5] and it soon became obvious that it was indeed a problem for many countries. In *Familitur*, families are asked about trips made in the four months running up to the interview month, so it often happens that the interviewee has forgotten some aspects thereof, such as exact dates or expenditure. *Familitur* therefore issues all families with a trip notebook in the initial interview, in which they can jot down all the characteristics of the trips just after making them, while the information is still fresh in their memory. This type of tool would not be possible in other types of surveys but in a panel the family know beforehand that they are going to be asked about specific matters in a certain period of time. This, together with the trip notebook, helps to offset the memory effect.

Results also show that the survey has been very positively accepted, with fewer than 5 per cent of households dropping out between data-collections.

---

[3] A *traveller household* is defined as one in which at least one of its members has made at least one trip in the reference period.

[4] Censo de Población y Vivienda (Population and Housing Census), Encuesta Sociodemográfica (Socio-economic Survey) and Household Panel of the European Union, drawn up by the Spanish National Statistical Office.

[5] Methodological workshop on the implementation of the Council Directive 95/57/EC on tourism statistics, 24–6 November 1999, Rome, Italy.

Typological analyses and predictions

The wealth of socio-economic information obtained in connection with tourism behaviour and on the population's tourism habits will allow typological analyses to be carried out, from which it may be possible to derive prediction models of future tourism activity of residents. These typological analyses will then also make it possible to conduct surveys with different reference periods for different households depending on the traveller type by which they are characterized. IET plans to introduce a methodological change in *Familitur* to weight the surveying effort in favour of households characterized as making many trips.

CONCLUSIONS

The use of a household panel for studying tourism affords a series of innovations. Taking as an example the survey Movimientos Turísticos de los Españoles (*Familitur*), run by the Instituto de Estudios Turísticos, an analysis has been made of the advantages of using this type of survey.

Thus, a study has been made of the concept of traveller, thereby making it possible to calculate the traveller percentage of the population. Mention has also been made of the rich possibilities offered by the socio-economic analysis of the population, both for carrying out one-off social studies and for making predictions.

Lastly, an explanation has been given of what is considered to be the main advantage of using a panel; namely how it serves for analysing changes in the tourism behaviour of individuals brought about by changes in their socio-economic characteristics.

BIBLIOGRAPHY

Applying the Eurostat Methodological Guidelines in Basic Tourism and Travel Statistics. A Practical Manual. Eurostat, March 1996.

Commission Decision of 9 December 1998 on procedures for implementing Council Directive 95/57/EC on the collection of statistical information in the field of tourism. Official Journal of the European Communities, 15 January 1999.

Community Methodology on Tourism Statistics. European Commission, 1998.

Council Directive 95/57/EC of 23 November 1995 on the collection of statistical information in the field of tourism. Official Journal of the European Communities, 6 December 1995.

Kasprzyk, D., Duncan, G., Kalton, M. and Singh, M. P. (1989) Panel surveys. Wiley series in probability and mathematical statistics. Chichester: John Wiley.

Movimientos Turísticos de los Españoles (Familitur): Referencias Metodológicas. Documento de trabajo 23, Instituto de Estudios Turísticos. Secretaría de Estado de Comercio y Turismo, Ministerio de Economía.

Recommendations on Tourism Statistics. World Tourism Organization/United Nations.

24

A Methodology to Measure Tourism Expenditure and Total Tourism Production at the Regional Level

Luis Valdés Pelaez, Javier de la Ballina, Rosa Aza Conejo, Enrique Loredo Fernandez, Emilio Torres Manzaneda, José M. Estébanez, José Santos Domínguez Menchero and Eduardo A. De Valle Tuero

The analysis of tourism at a regional level has traditionally been neglected in Spain. With respect to tourism expenditure, those methodologies usually employed to quantify it ignore the importance of excursionists and tourists lodged at private accommodation establishments. As a consequence, when making decisions supported on reports relative to the social impact of tourism, it is increasingly necessary to improve the information systems. In this chapter we propose a new model for measuring regional tourism expenditure as well as total tourism production, through the expenditure made by visitors lodged at public or private accommodation establishments, as well as the expenditure incurred by excursionists. As an example, we present the results obtained in Asturias in 1999.

Key words: statistic; tourism expenditure; tourism production; region.

INTRODUCTION

The amount of tourist expenditure and total tourism production observed over a particular period of time are essential pieces of information for planning economic policies. The difficulty involved in determining these macroeconomic figures is further

---

[1] Rütter, H. and Berwert, A. (1999) 'A regional approach for tourism satellite accounts and links to the National Account'. *Tourism Economics*, **5** (4), December, 353–81.

accentuated when we seek to get them in a regional context,[1] where there is a considerable lack of specific data due to the limitations that the central government and its statistical institutions have in obtaining reliable sub-national results.

At the regional level, as in the case of the Principality of Asturias, a region situated in the north of Spain, the estimation of the volume of business activity generated by tourism and its corresponding economic impact was hampered by the following problems:

- the fact that Asturias is traditionally an industrial region where tourism only really began to develop in relatively recent times, in comparison with the established 'tourist' regions of Spain, such as the Canary Islands, the Balearic Islands and Andalusia;
- the absence of an official regional statistics institute;
- the wide variety of accommodation typologies, from hotels to rural establishments; and
- the lack of systematic information regarding the activities in which visitors engage. Most statistical data available was of a very varied nature and had been carried out in specific time periods, mainly during the summer season.
- existing statistical reports, both at national and local levels, only provided partial data (the number of overnight stays, visits, tourists etc.) of one segment of the tourism market, namely, hotels. However, no information was available regarding other types of accommodation or markets.

In 1997, the System of Tourism Information in Asturias[2] (hereafter, SITA project) was launched. It was headed up by a research team from the University of Oviedo and, with the support of the Regional Administration, developed a permanent mechanism for the compilation, processing, analysis and dissemination of tourism information that is necessary for both public and private institutions. With an aim to carry out a comprehensive analysis of the tourism sector in the Principality of Asturias, four complementary research areas were considered (Figure 24.1)

- *analysis of tourism demand*: the study and follow-up of the characteristics of visitors coming to Asturias;
- *analysis of tourism supply*: the study of tourism firms in Asturias, with particular attention to accommodation establishments;
- *analysis of occupancy rates*: the study of the occupancy rates in the different accommodation establishments in Asturias; and
- *macroeconomic analysis*: the acquisition of the main aggregate tourism indicators in the Asturian economy.

In this chapter, we present the methodology applied by SITA in order to quantify tourism expenditure by visitors to our region, as well as the application of the results to the analysis of the economic impact of tourism in the region. This methodology is based on two fundamental features. On the one hand, the determination of the occupancy rate in the public accommodation establishments surveyed. On the other, the analysis of tourism demand, categorizing visitors as excursionists and tourists; if the latter then they are classified according to the kinds of establishments in which they stay (public versus

---

[2] A more detailed explanation can be found in Valdés, L., Ballina, F. J., Aza, R., Díaz, A. M., Domínguez, J. S., Iglesias, V., Menéndez, J. M., Torres, E. and Del Valle, E. A. (1998) *El Turismo en Asturias en 1997.* Sistema de Información Turística de Asturias. Oviedo: Consejería de Economía del Principado de Asturias y Universidad de Oviedo.

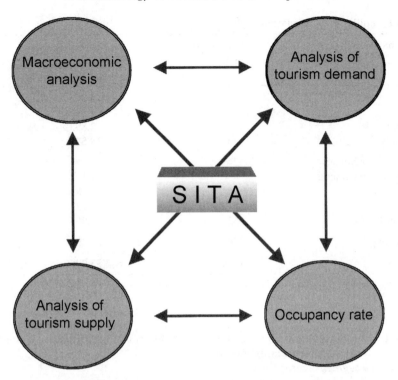

Figure 24.1 The structure of SITA project

private accommodations), the length of the stay and the economic expenditure made over that period. In the following sections we present briefly the main actions undertaken in both procedures.

CALCULATION OF THE OCCUPANCY RATES IN ACCOMMODATION ESTABLISHMENTS

Accommodation establishments exist in these officially regulated categories in Asturias: hotels, hostels, hostelries, rural houses, boarding houses, rural apartments, hotel apartments and campsites. Given the broad range of accommodations available to tourists in Asturias (Table 24.1), one recognizes the need to analyse the occupancy rates in a reduced number of homogeneous segments. Consequently, the different types of establishments identified as public accommodations are grouped into three differentiated segments of analysis, according to their characteristics and location:

- *hotels segment*: all hotels except Asturian manor houses, hostels, hostelries and hotel apartments;
- *rural tourism segment*: the construct of rural tourism deserves an explanation; it comprises those establishments that are situated in a rural environment and are

Table 24.1 Public accommodation 1999

Establishments	Number of units	Place	% Beds over the total
Hotels*	327	14,398	27.1
Hostelries	53	1,235	2.3
Boarding houses	253	2,893	5.5
Total hotels	**633**	**18,526**	**34.9**
Asturian manor houses	24	453	0.9
Rural tourist apartments	97	1,182	2.2
Rural houses	374	2,189	4.1
Hostels	57	3,132	5.9
Total rural tourism	**552**	**6,956**	**13.1**
Total camping	**58**	**27,554**	**52.0**
Total units	**1.243**	**53,036**	**100.0**

* within this category we include hotel apartments: 12 establishments with 837 beds
Source: SITA

specifically regulated. This segment includes rural apartments, hostels, rural houses,[3] and Asturian manor houses;[4]

- *campsites segment*: campsites.

Once we have outlined the different segments of accommodation to consider, we can turn to the method for calculating the occupancy rate. It can be defined as the variable that relates the capacity of available accommodation every month and its effective use – measured by the people whose names appear in the establishment's daily register. The population to be sampled is the number of beds available in tourist establishments, since what is recorded is the presence or absence of the occupant for each overnight stay. Each type of establishment was surveyed along the following lines:

- *procedure for data collection* by means of questionnaires made face-to-face to public accommodation establishment managers;
- *period of data collection*: the survey was designed to significantly cover the period of time throughout which we sought to determine occupancy rates. It should be specifically possible to evaluate the differences between 'weekend' and 'weekday'

---

[3] The rural houses are a network of rural accommodation establishments regulated by Decreto 26/91, de 20 de febrero, de la Consejería de Industria, Comercio y Turismo, por el que se regula la modalidad de Alojamiento Turístico denominado 'Casa de Aldea' (Boletín Oficial del Principado de Asturias de 16 abril 1991), modified by the Resolución de 26 de abril de 1993, de la Consejería de Industria, Turismo y Empleo, por la que se desarrolla el Decreto 26/91 (Boletín Oficial del Principado de Asturias de 3 de mayo de 1993).

[4] A quality mark established by the Principality of Asturias composed by establishments that observe quality requirements regulated in the 69/94 Decree of 1 September. It defines Asturian manor houses as a type of tourist accommodation located in exclusively natural and/or rural settings, of a traditional construction which boasts the typical architectural features associated with the Principality of Asturias, and in which all the comforts of modern home living are combined with a quality service designed to meet the client's every need, in peaceful and relaxed surroundings.

occupancy. Therefore, data was collected twice a month; once during the first fortnight and again during the second. Every time the interviewer paid a visit to the establishment, he requested the number of places occupied during one of the two weeks (from Monday to Sunday) of the corresponding fortnight. Accordingly, we were able to cover reliably the period under scrutiny (we ended up with data relating to fourteen days in any given month) and obtained occupancy statistics relating both to weekend and weekday occupancy;

- *area of data collection*: the survey covered the entire geographic extension of the Principality of Asturias, which was divided territorially into the western, central and eastern zones.

This survey method permits a systematic collection and a relatively rapid calculation of the 'global', 'weekend' and 'weekday' occupancy rates, as well as the corresponding statistics for the different geographic areas and types of establishments. Accordingly, it is possible to ensure that the maximum error in the global estimate of monthly occupancy rates for each kind of establishment will be lower than 5 per cent, with a 95 per cent confidence level (Appendix 1).

The survey plan was slightly modified in order to adapt it to the specificity of campsites, because certain inaccuracies were detected in their real occupancy rate. This imbalance was principally attributable to the following circumstances:

- First, the opening period for campsites is greatly influenced by the seasonal nature of their activity. For the great majority of Asturian campsites the opening season runs from the Easter-holiday period, either in March or April, to around the third week of September. Only a very reduced number of establishments remain open throughout the entire year.
- Second, they represent more than half the region's accommodation capacity. Even though there are only 58 campsites in all, the number of accommodation places they provide over the summer period by far exceeds the capacity of all other accommodation options in Asturias. This is an essential factor when it comes to analysing the number of tourists that visit Asturias during the high season: if the true level of campsite occupancy is not computed accurately, it will significantly distort the estimate of tourist numbers.
- The occupancy data provided by campsites does not include, to any reliable extent, tourists who stay in permanent caravans on campsites,[5] given that arrival and departure registers kept by campsites do not normally account for the movements of those people who holiday in caravans on a semi-permanent basis.

Given these peculiarities, a two-part analysis is performed in order to determine overnight stays and the number of tourists on campsites. On the one hand, we apply to 'pure' campers the same methodology employed for hotels and rural tourism. On the

---

[5] On the problem of permanent caravans on campsites, legally speaking it is unlawful to contract accommodation for a period in excess of eleven months in any given year. However, almost all campsites rent out a considerable extension of land on a permanent basis, which is mainly occupied by caravans that remain parked there throughout the whole year. Normally, owners make use of their caravans over the entire opening season on payment of an agreed annual fee, and they avail of free access to the campsite and to their caravans, regardless of whether the establishment is open to the public or not. Consequently, the campsite register does not reflect either the length of stay or the number of times permanent caravan owners visit the campsite throughout the year, simply because a number of available places are hired out on a permanent basis.

other hand, we carry out annually a survey to estimate the number and size of permanent caravans, as well as the proportion of campsite clients that use this type of accommodation (Appendix 2).

ANALYSIS OF TOURISM DEMAND

The second feature of this methodology is the analysis of tourism demand. We compile, by means of a personal survey, a variety of data concerning the characteristics of visitors to Asturias, taking into consideration tourists staying at public accommodation establishments, in private accommodations and also excursionists. Within public accommodation establishments, we separate tourists using identical segments to those applied for the determination of occupancy rate:

- *hotel tourists*: those tourists who stay in the establishments classified as hotels in the broadest sense of the term;
- *rural tourism tourists*: those individuals who overnight in establishments situated in a rural environment; and
- *campers*: those who stay at registered campsites.

This survey is carried out in a stratified way with proportional allocation according to the number of places available, type of establishment, occupancy rate, geographic area and period being surveyed. It is configured in such a way that it obtains, with 95 per cent confidence level, a maximum error of no more than 5 per cent (Appendix 3).

In order to obtain information about excursionists and tourists who stay in private accommodations, a random survey of street-side interviews was designed in accordance with the estimated number of visitors for each geographical zone (Appendix 4). Consequently, we were able to establish the proportion of tourists and excursionists.

In the analysis of tourism demand, it also carried out a detailed study of factors such as the duration of the stay, reasons for the visit, geographic zone chosen, kind of holiday, season of stay, expenditure made both inside and outside the place of accommodation etc. In this way, we are able to provide a more complete picture of the habits of visitors that come to Asturias (Figure 24.2).

APPLICATION AND RESULTS

Quantification of visitor numbers

Given that our objective is the determination of the economic activity of tourism in Asturias, we also need to consider the expenditure made by visitors both by those who opt to stay at public and private establishments, and the financial outlay made by excursionists in the principality. This is known as domestic tourism in Asturias and includes both internal and receptor tourism.

Once the units we wish to analyse have been defined, we proceed to quantify them, taking into account the difficulty that such a task entails as Asturias lacks border-control points and, therefore, does not avail of data concerning visitor transit patterns. We will begin by looking at those visitors who overnight at public accommodation establishments.

122. – What kind of accommodation are you going to stay at? (Pregunta ablerta. Anótese la respuesta màs adecyda: sólo UNA)

23. Tipo de alojamiento	24. What will be your daily expenditure?	25. For many people?	26. Nutritious regime $(SA_1/AD_2/MP_3/PC_4)$	27. Quality/price
	Ptas.	*Personas*		

Concepto	Distribución	Gasto
Hostelry: Breakfasts/Eaten/Dinners	In your accommodation In restaurants	Ptas./person/day Ptas./person/day
Several Expenses in Hostelry	In bars/cafes In pubs y discoteques	Ptas./person/day

33. – How much money have you budgeted for the following concepts? (Se refiere al gasto global en estas actividades en el viaje).

Concepto	Distribución	Gasto	¿Para cuantas personas?
Activities	Sports, museums, cinema …	Ptas.	Persons
Transport	Petrol, bus …	Ptas.	Persons
Purchases	Gifts, food, fairs, craftsmanship …	Ptas.	Persons

Figure 24.2 Expenditure questions in the demand questionnaire

In Asturias we can consider this variable thanks to data obtained from the survey carried out on public establishments, which form part of a series of operations aimed at shedding light on tourist accommodation facilities through the analysis of the occupancy rates in the establishments (Table 24.2).

As of 31 December 1999, there are 51,341 accommodation places available in the Principality of Asturias which can be considered as public according to the classification of the WTO.[6]

The research data facilitate the determination and quantification of the number of overnight stays and tourists who stay at public accommodation establishments, from the analysis of occupancy rates, the number of accommodation places available and the average stay of this category of tourists, and according to the type of establishment chosen.

With these two values we obtain the number of overnight stays by multiplying the average occupancy rate by the number of accommodation places and by the number of days of the chosen period according to each segment of analysis (hotels, rural tourism and campsites). This figure of overnight stays allows us to determine the number of tourists accommodated in establishments, which in 1999 amounted to 1,535,330 paying guests.

---

[6] World Tourism Organization (1994) *Concepts, Definitions and Classifications for Tourism Statistics.* Madrid: WTO.

Table 24.2   Level of annual occupation 1999 (%)

Annual occupancy rate	%
Global (hotels and rural tourism)	43.1
Western area	37.4
Central area	47.3
Eastern area	38.9
Hotels	46.4
Rural tourism	33.8
Rural tourism (hostels excluded)	39.1
Camping	23.9

Source: SITA

The determination of the number of private accommodations beds is fraught with difficulty. In order to achieve this task, we had recourse to a previous national study[7] that, even though it may be somewhat dated, is a most suitable reference given its assertion that the behaviour of the population, in this regard, does not vary excessively. Considering that from 1993 to the present day the number of rooms provided in public accommodation establishments has increased considerably (although we could consider that the number of rooms in private establishments has also shown the same tendency), we have preferred to take a more conservative position, correcting the proportion of tourists accommodated according to the kind of establishment, public or private, provided by the aforementioned study, which undervalues the latter. Previous research put the proportion of tourists accommodated in public establishments at 40 per cent while the percentage of those overnighting in private tourist accommodation (PTA) was estimated at 60 per cent. For 1999 we adjusted the proportion to 56 per cent and 44 per cent respectively, because of the tendency detected by the demand survey of higher occupancy levels in public establishments in comparison with private ones.

On the other hand, the previously mentioned study (IET, 1997a) only refers to the behaviour of Spanish visitors, without taking account of foreign tourists. Available figures indicate a small proportion of the latter in comparison with the overall total, a mere 8.4 per cent of foreign tourists in public establishments and 9.6 per cent in PTA. Applying the 44 per cent–56 per cent proportion to the whole tourist population will not alter the results substantially. The proportion of tourists according to the kind of accommodation chosen, in line with the aforementioned considerations, can be seen in Table 24.3.

Table 24.3   Tourists proportion

Tourists	%
Public establishments	44.0
Private establishments	56.0
Total tourists	100.0

Source: SITA

---

[7] Instituto de Estudios Turísticos (1994): *El turismo de los españoles 1993*. Madrid: Secretaría de Estado de Comercio Turismo y Pymes.

Table 24.4   Proportion of tourists/excursionists

Visitors	%
Tourists	70.0
Excursionists	30.0
Total	100.0

Source: SITA

Table 24.5   Visitors to Asturias in 1999

Visitors to Asturias		Total 1999
Tourists	Public lodging	1,535,330
	Private lodging	1,954,057
Total		**3,489,387**
Excursionists		1,495,452
Total Visitors		**4,984,839**

Source: SITA

Table 24.6   Total expenditure per visitor and trip

Total Expenditure per visitor and trip	Pesetas	Euro
In public establishments	53,286	320.26
In private tourist lodging	47,554	285.81
Excursionists	3,937	23.66

Source: SITA

The determination of the number of visitors who do not overnight – namely excursionists – always introduces an additional difficulty. The data obtained in the demand analysis, which corresponds to the interviews carried out at tourist locations, established the proportion of tourists and excursionists at 70 per cent and 30 per cent respectively. (Table 24.4).

Since we have determined the number of tourists that overnight in public accommodations, 1,535,330, we can obtain the number of tourists in PTA and the number of excursionist with the previously mentioned proportions (Table 24.5).

Estimate of tourist expenditure

The demand survey facilitates the quantification of average expenditure made by each kind of visitor (Table 24.6). Following this criterion, expenditure has been broken down into: 'hotel and restaurant services', 'purchases of food products', 'sundry purchases', 'sundry activities' and 'transport', trying to keep a correspondence with the classification of industrial activities put forward by input–output tables of Asturias.

The expenditure carried out by all tourists on accommodation is regarded as hotel and restaurant expenditure. In the case of food expenditure, the same consideration cannot be made.

Tourists accommodated in establishments, with the exception of campsites, generally take their meals in their place of accommodation, in bars or restaurants, which leads us to consider that they declared this expenditure on food in the same category as accommodation, and both were included under the hotel and restaurant services heading. In order to determine the expenditure on food by tourists who overnight in private accommodation, and, similarly, in the case of those who stay at campsites, we assume that they sometimes take their meals in restaurants and bars, and at other times in their place of accommodation (with the exception of those who stay in rented rooms). As a result, declared expenditure on food has been divided into two parts, the first being added to the cost of accommodation – which corresponds to restaurant expenditures – and the other representing expenditure on purchases of food products.

In the case of excursionists, accommodation expenditure does not exist and we consider that all food expenditure is made in restaurants or bars. This expenditure is, therefore, classified under hotel and restaurant services.

It is assumed that expenditure related to sundry purchases, in each of the three visitor types, is carried out in commercial establishments.

Having determined the proportion of expenditure per visit, according to the type of visitor and type of expenditure (obtained from the demand survey), the following findings resulted (Table 24.7).

Table 24.7 Percentage distribution of expenditures

Distribution of expenditure	Public lodgings (%)	Private tourist lodgings (%)	Excursionists (%)
Lodging	81.6	62.2	61.5
Food	4.2	16.5	–
Shopping	7.9	13.5	17.3
Transport	5.6	6.7	17.5
Leisure activities	0.7	1.1	3.7
Total	100.0	100.0	100.0

In this case, because of campers, the hotel and restaurant section is overvalued, but it is compensated by the category corresponding to the tourists accommodated in rented rooms, who we consider to take their meals – like the rest of the tourists in private accommodation – in their places of accommodation. This circumstance is unlikely to occur and gives rise to an overvaluation of this category that, as we were saying, can compensate the previous overvaluation. This consideration can be validated with the sales made by campsite food stores.

We proceed, therefore, to multiply the travel expenditure for each kind of visitor by the number of visitors and apply the corresponding percentage to the breakdown considered in order to obtain the expenditure carried out in the different sections. Consequently, the tourism expenditure will be found by multiplying the number of visitors by the total expenditure per visit and by applying the percentage corresponding to hotel and restaurant services to that figure. We then add the data obtained relating to the three types of visitors in order to obtain the results for 'tourism expenditure in hotel and restaurant services' (Table 24.8).

Table 24.8 Tourism expenditure in hotel and restaurant services

Expenditure in hotel and restaurant services		Euro (pesetas)
Tourists lodged in public establishments Hotel and restaurant expenditure	$E_i \times Nt_i \times D_i$	400,994,531.90 (66,719,876,185)
Tourists lodged in private establishments Hotel and restaurant expenditure	$E_i \times Nt_i \times D_i$	57,771,218.609 (96,073,535,110)

E_i: Total expenditure per visitor and trip
Nt_i: Number of tourists
Ne_i: Number of excursionists
D_i: Distribution of expenditure
Source: SITA

Table 24.9 Total expenditure

Expenditure concept	Pesetas	Euro
Total expenditure in hotel and restaurant services	128,111,493,404	769,965,582.46
Total expenditure in purchases of food products	18,228,457,582	109,555,236.51
Total expenditure in sundry purchases	20,646,109,957	124,085,619.93
Total expenditure in transport	11,784,860,773	70,828,439.73
Total expenditure in sundry activities	1,849,466,122	11,115,515.26
Total expenditure	**180,620,387,837**	**1,085,550,393.89**

Source: SITA

In the same way we will proceed with the other sections considered obtaining the 'Tourism expenditure' (Table 24.9).

Tourism production by activities

It is necessary to determine direct tourism production in a different way depending on each individual activity.

Taking into consideration that 'tourism expenditure in hotel and restaurants = hotel tourism production', we can estimate the direct production in hotel and restaurants which comes to €769,965,582.46 (128,111,493,404 pesetas) (Table 24.9).

With regard to purchases, different criteria should be applied to both those referring to 'food products' and those referring to 'sundry purchases'.

Production, in business, does not correspond to the total number of sales as in hotel and restaurant services, but to the commercial margins of these activities. Determining commercial margins is usually a complicated task. However, we have a regional study[8] that quantifies these margins at 25 per cent corresponding to food stores and at 40 per cent in the case of shops where visitors make their sundry purchases. By applying these

---

[8] Ballina, F. J., Vazquez R., and Trespalacios J. (1997) Análisis y Diagnostico del Comercio de Gijón. Gijón: Unión de Comerciantes de Gijón.

Table 24.10   Tourism production of commercial services

Commercial services	Margin	Expenditure Euro (pesetas)	Production Euro (pesetas)
Total expenditure in sundry purchases	40%	124,085,619.93 (20,646,109,957)	48,293,901.03 (8,035,429,016)
Total expenditure in purchases of food products	25%	109,555,236.51 (18,228,457,582)	28,226,525.97 (4,696,498,750)
Tourism production of commercial services			76,520,427.00 (12,731,927,766)

Source: SITA

Table 24.11   Internal production of purchases

	%	Expenditure Euro (pesetas)	Production Euro (pesetas)
Sundry purchases	60.0	120,734,752.57 (20,088,572,541)	72,440,851.54 (12,053,143,524)
Purchases of food products	75.0	112,906,103.87 (18,785,994,998)	84,679,577.90 (14,089,496,249)
Total			157,120,429.44 (26,142,639,773)
Internal production of purchases (commercial margins discounted)			70.31%
Internal production of purchases		110,471,373.94 (18,380,890,024)	

Source: SITA

percentages to the corresponding expenditure categories, we obtain the direct production in purchases, both with regard to food and to the rest, 'tourism production of commercial services' (Table 24.10).

Once the commercial margins have been discounted, we cannot reduce the value of the rest of the expenditure in purchases, but rather it is necessary to determine what proportion of these purchases is satisfied by internal production.

We assume that the total expenditure under these concepts, less the commercial margins, is satisfied by internal production in the same proportion that it is for the total family consumption in Asturias. For this reason we find the ratio of the total family consumption in Asturias divided by the consumption satisfied in Asturias (subtracting from it, consequently, family consumer demand satisfied by the rest of Spain and abroad). We obtain a value of 70.31 per cent that corresponds to the data provided by the input–output tables for Asturias in 1995 (Table 24.11).

With regard to transport, given that 80.8 per cent of public accommodation tourists travel in private vehicles and 8.5 per cent by coach, whether they be rented or regular services, it can be considered that the entire expenditure related to this concept is satisfied by the 'sales and repair of vehicles; filling stations' category, that we named transport. A similar circumstance is found in PTA, with 76.6 per cent travelling in private vehicles and 9.6 per cent by coach, and excursionists present a similar behaviour, with 70.7 per cent travelling in private vehicles and 25.1 per cent by coach. Accordingly, we arrive at the total production for Section 39, transport.

Total tourism production

The input–output model permits the quantification of the direct and indirect effects that produce an increase in tourism demand, in each section of activity. This is achieved by feedback which, through intermediate demand, is produced in the economic system, recognizing that the effects of demand are not met simply by direct satisfaction, but are transmitted to the rest of the activity thanks to the network of dominant interrelations.

An increase in demand, on being satisfied, generates an increase in activity (direct effect) for the first providers of the demand (hotels, restaurants etc.) who should adjust their orders to their suppliers (foodstuffs, drinks etc.). These suppliers, in order to satisfy the additional demand, will generate a second cycle of transactions since, they will have to increase purchase orders from their suppliers (indirect effects) and so on.

The effects of the final demand are not limited to direct and indirect effects, but rather they generate an increase in company profits and family incomes. This in turn means greater consumption and investment, thereby initiating a new cycle of effects known as induced effects.

The indirect effects can be evaluated by applying the appropriate technical coefficients. A technical coefficient a_{ij} indicates the value of a good or service belonging to i sector, which is necessary to consume in order to be able to produce a monetary unit of a product of the j sector. This coefficient indicates, therefore, the reactions of the economic system in the face of increased production in a sector of activity that is destined for final demand. The inverse of Leontief of regional coefficients is defined from the matrix of technical coefficients. The multiplier of regional vertical output expresses the increase which domestic production has to undergo as a consequence of the increase of a monetary unit in the production (of the named sector) in the column that is destined for the final demand.

To determine the indirect effects of tourism we use the values of the corresponding regional coefficients to account for the impact of activity on the regional economy.

Total tourism productions, both direct and indirect, can be found with the regional multipliers provided by the TIOA (Tablas Imput-Output Asturias) in 1995.[9] The multiplier used in the Internal Production of Purchases category corresponds to a synthetic multiplier found from the corresponding regional multipliers of activities that contribute most to tourism consumption.

Multiplying the direct tourism production (corresponding to this activity) by its multiplier, we obtain the total tourism production of each sector. Adding the total tourism production of each activity, we will obtain the total tourism production (direct and indirect), see Table 24.12.

The methodology applied gives rise to a problem in that it generates an undervaluing of the economic effects of tourism given that it only considers current tourism expenditure. It fails to take account of the gross formation of capital as a consequence of tourism demand. For example, it would be necessary to consider in this regard, the building activity that is directly attributable to tourism demand, differentiating the

---

[9] Sociedad Asturiana de Estudios Económicos e Industriales (SADEI) (1998) Tablas Imput–Output 1995. Contabilidad regional. Servicio de Publicaciones del Principado de Asturias, Consejería de Economía. Oviedo.

Table 24.12 Total tourism production (direct and indirect)

	Regional multiplier	Production Euro (pesetas)	Total production (direct and indirect) Euro (pesetas)
Hotel and restaurant services	1.378257	769,965,582.46 (128,111,493,404)	1,061,210,453.79 (176,570,562,564)
Commercial services	1.189247	76,520,427.00 (12,731,927,766)	91,001,688.24 (15,141,406,900)
Internal production of purchases	1.265	110,471,373.94 (18,380,890,024)	139,746,288.04 (23,251,825,881)
Transport	1.186	70,828,439.73 (11,784,860,773)	84,002,529.52 (13,976,844,877)
Sundry activities	1.258179	11,115,515.26 (1,849,466,122)	13,985,307.87 (2,326,959,436)
Total			**1,389,946,267.46 (231,267,599,657)**

Source: SITA

production from building activity to that destined towards second homes for tourism by non-residents or residents. But if we consider one part of the production in the building sector as tourism production, then we would similarly have to consider the income of the corresponding property.

The reason for not taking into account these elements and the costs of undervaluing of tourism that it involves, is derived, on the one hand, from the difficulty of its determination and, on the other hand, from the recommendations of the WTO. Indeed, WTO, in several publications[10] (see, for example, *Collection of Tourism Expenditure Statistics* (WTO, 1994), specifies that purchase by a visitor of a second home along with the profits attributed to this should not be considered as tourism expenditure, justifying this argument on the basis of the practical difficulties of their quantification. Some writers, e.g. Bull,[11] refer to the possible relationship of this decision with the notion that Tourism is merely a temporary or transient phenomenon.

Notably, we cannot quantify the induced effects since the input–output Tables do not take them into consideration. Once the total tourism production has been found, in order to obtain the Gross Value-Added to the factor costs, we will use the coefficients about the production of the different branches of the activity (Table 24.13).

From the 1998 figure of the Gross Value-Added at current price[12] and the estimates of real growth and of prices with a discount rate of 4.5 per cent, we estimate that the Gross Value-Added in 1999 is €11,000,693,507.87 (pesetas 1,830,361,390,000). In this case, the contribution of tourism to the Gross Value-Added of the Principality of Asturias can be estimated at 7.35 per cent.

---

[10] Organización Mundial de Turismo (OMT) (1992) Manual para el estudio de la economía turística en el ámbito macroeconómico. Madrid: OMT.

[11] Bull, A. (1994) La economía del sector turístico. Madrid: Alianza Editorial.

[12] Sociedad Asturiana de Estudios Económicos e Industriales (SADEI) (1999) Datos y cifras de la economía asturiana 1998. Oviedo: Cajastur.

Table 24.13 Gross Value Added to current price, GVA cp

	Coefficient (%)	Total production (direct and indirect) Euro (pesetas)	GVAcp Euro (pesetas)
Hotel and restaurant services	56.10	1,061,210,453.79 (176,570,562,564)	595,339,064.57 (99,056,085,598)
Commercial services	79.40	91,001,688.24 (15,141,406,900)	72,255,340.46 (12,022,277,078)
Internal production of purchases	57.60*	139,746,288.04 (23,251,825,881)	80,493,861.91 (13,393,051,707)
Transport	59.80	84,002,529.52 (13,976,844,877)	50,233,512.65 (8,358,153,236)
Sundry activities	72.20	13,985,307.87 (2,326,959,436)	10,097,392.29 (1,680,064,713)
Total			**808,419,171.88 (134,509,632,333)**

* The 57.6 % ratio used corresponds to the Global Spanish Production
Source: SITA

The procedure also allows us to obtain the number of jobs created by tourism. For this, the same source we mentioned earlier, (i.e. the TIOA, 1995) is used which will provide us with the Gross Value-Added figure per job for each activity (Figure 2.12).

CONCLUSIONS

The absence of regional tourism statistics triggered the creation of the SITA project, as an instrument for the elaboration and analysis of tourism information in Asturias. The final aims of this initiative are to assist the different tourism agents in the making of decisions and to collaborate in the design and follow-up of the regional tourism policy.

The SITA project has developed a methodology coherent with the recommendations of international tourism institutions (WTO and OECD). It allows us to obtain the number of visitors and occupancy rates, as well as an estimate of tourism expenditure and total tourism production in the region.

It is undeniably true that there remain some limitations in our approach, mainly derived from the uncertainty of some parameters used in the model (e.g. the proportion of tourists lodged in private and public establishments, or the proportion of excursionists over the total of visitors). It would also be advisable to get a greater segregation of expenditure components and a more detailed knowledge of tourism supply.

Overcoming these limitations is the challenge that the SITA team will be facing in the near future, in order to improve our knowledge of regional tourism. Anyhow, we believe that with the such a methodology, we have laid the foundations to proceed towards the elaboration of a tourism satellite account at the regional level. Surely this is one of the most ambitious objectives in the field of tourism statistics, as stated at the 1999 Niza World Conference on the Measurement of the Economic Impact of Tourism.

BIBLIOGRAPHY

Banco Bilbao Vizcaya (BBV) (1997) *Renta nacional de España y su distribución provincial 1993. Avance 1994–95.* Madrid: Banco Bilbao Vizcaya.

Instituto de Estudios Turísticos (IET) (1996) *Tabla Intersectorial de la Economía Turística TIOT 92.* Madrid: IET.

Instituto de Estudios Turísticos (IET) (1997a) *Dimensión regional de los impactos macroeconómicos del turismo. Documento de trabajo nº9.* Madrid: IET.

Instituto de Estudios Turísticos (IET) (1997b) *Guía de fuentes estadísticas para el análisis de la economía del turismo.* Madrid: IET.

Menéndez, J.M., Torres, E., Domínguez, J. S.(1998) *Diseño de un plan de muestreo para obtener el grado de ocupación hotelera en Asturias.* XXIV Congreso Nacional de Estadística e Investigación Operativa. Almería, pp. 181–2.

Menéndez, J. M., Torres, E., Domínguez, J. S. (1998): *Metodología para determinar el número de turistas en Asturias.* XXIV Congreso Nacional de Estadística e Investigación Operativa, Almería, pp. 183–4.

Menéndez, J. M. Torres, E., Domínguez, J. S. (1999) *Metodología para determinar el número de turistas en los campings asturianos.* I Congreso Nacional Turismo y Tecnologías de la Información y las Comunicaciones: nuevas tecnologías y calidad. Turitec '99, Málaga, pp. 375–82.

Paci, E. (1996) 'El papel del turismo en el sistema económico', in Instituto de Estudios Turísticos (IET) *Tablas Intersectorial de la Economía Turística TIOT 92.* Madrid: IET.

Quevedo, J. (1999) 'La información estadística para el análisis del turismo'. *Estudios Turísticos* **140**. Madrid: Instituto de Estudios Turísticos (IET).

Sinclair, M. T. and Stabler, M. (1997) *The Economics of Tourism.* London: Routledge.

Unión Europea (1995) *Directiva 95/57/CE del Consejo de 23 de Noviembre de 1995 sobre recogida de información estadística en el ámbito del turismo.* DO Nº L 291 de 6.12.1995, p.32.

Unión Europea (1999) *Decisión (1999/34/CE) de la Comisión de 9 de Diciembre 1998 sobre los procedimientos de aplicación de la Directiva 95/57/CE del Consejo sobre la recogida de información estadística en el ámbito del turismo.* DO Nº L 9 de 15.1.1999, p.23.

Valdés, L., Ballina, F. J., Aza, R., Díaz, A. M., Domínguez, J. S., Iglesias, V., Menéndez, J. M., Torres, E., Del Valle, E. A. (1999): *El Turismo en Asturias en 1998.* Sistema de Información Turística de Asturias. Consejería de Economía del Principado de Asturias y Universidad de Oviedo.

World Tourism Organization (WTO) (1994) *Recommendation about tourism statistics.* Madrid: WTO.

World Tourism Organization (WTO) (1994) *Collection of tourism expenditure statistics.* Madrid: WTO.

World Tourism Organization (WTO) (1995) *Collection of domestic tourism statistics.* Madrid: WTO.

World Tourism Organization (WTO) (1995) *Collection and compilation of tourism statistics.* Madrid: WTO.

APPENDIX I: TECHNIQUE SPECIFICATIONS OF THE SAMPLING TO DETERMINE THE OCCUPANCY RATE IN PUBLIC ACCOMMODATION

AREA	PRINCIPALITY OF ASTURIAS
TARGET POPULATION	Units of lodging establishments within the area.
DATA COLLECTION	Personal questionnaire carried out by phone or fax.
POPULATION SIZE	Variable, depending on the number of units available, due to seasonal reasons (it ranges from 25,482 to 53,036 units).
SAMPLE SIZE	Variable, depending on the size of the population (ranging from 1,681 to 29,235 units). Due to seasonal nature, the sampled number varies between 112 and 173.
DATE OF DATA COLLECTION	Two alternative weeks every month, from Monday to Sunday. Occupancy of all establishments was checked fourteen times per month.
SAMPLE ERROR	Maximum error less than 2%.
CONFIDENCE LEVEL	95.5% Z = 1.96 p = q = 0.5
SAMPLING PROCEDURE	Cluster sampling according to the number of units in the establishments. Stratifications are contemplated with proportional allocations according to type of establishment, area and day of the week.
DATE OF THE FIELDWORK	Year 1999.

Source: SITA

APPENDIX II: TECHNIQUE SPECIFICATIONS OF THE TOURISM SUPPLY

AREA:	Principality of Asturias
DATE OF COLLECTION:	June 1999 to December 1999
SAMPLING PROCEDURE:	Personal questionnaire
UNIVERSE:	Lodging establishments

ESTABLISHMENTS	POPULATION SIZE	SAMPLE SIZE	RELIABILITY*
Hostels	58	37	± 9.78%
Tourist apartments	77	57	± 6.66%
Rural houses	321	284	± 1.98%
Asturian manor houses	60	53	± 4.64%
Campsites	24	24	± 0.00%
3–4–5 star hotels	69	67	± 2.05%
1–2 star hotels	234	196	± 2.83%
Boarding houses	314	131	± 6.55%
Total	1,157	849	± 1.74%

* With 95% confidence level, the maximum error in estimates of percentages
Source: SITA

APPENDIX III: TECHNIQUE SPECIFICATIONS OF THE DEMAND SURVEY IN PUBLIC ACCOMMODATION

AREA	PRINCIPALITY OF ASTURIAS
TARGET POPULATION	Tourists lodged in establishments
DATA COLLECTION	Personal questionnaires to tourists in Asturias
	Language: Spanish, English and French
POPULATION SIZE	Infinite population
SAMPLE SIZE	2,558 interviews in lodging establishments
DATE OF DATA COLLECTION	Along the whole month all over the year
SAMPLING ERROR	1.75%
CONFIDENCE LEVEL	95.5% $Z = 1.96$ $p = q = 0.5$
SAMPLING PROCEDURE	Stratified random with proportional allocation according to number of units available, occupancy rate, type of establishment, area and period of interest
DATE OF FIELDWORK	January to December 1999

Source: SITA

APPENDIX IV: TECHNIQUE SPECIFICATIONS OF THE DEMAND SURVEY IN TOURISM PLACES

AREA	PRINCIPALITY OF ASTURIAS
TARGET POPULATION	Visitors to Asturias
DATA COLLECTION	Personal questionnaires to visitors in Asturias
	Language: Spanish, English and French
POPULATION SIZE	Infinite population
SAMPLE SIZE	1,190
DATE OF DATA COLLECTION	Along the whole month all over the year
SAMPLING ERROR	3.98%
CONFIDENCE LEVEL	95.5% $Z = 1.96$ $p = q = 0.5$
SAMPLING PROCEDURE	Systematic selection of destination points with a control of quota according to tourist volume in each area
DATE OF FIELDWORK	January to December 1999

Source: SITA

25

Second Homes and Rented Accommodation: Dimension and Role – Methodology and the Case of the Province of Venice

Mara Manente and Isabella Scaramuzzi

1. INTRODUCTION

This chapter discusses the evaluation of private non-rented accommodation as part of the NACE Group 70.20, and of dwellings rented from private individuals or professional agencies, as part of the NACE Group 55.23, according to the EU Community Methodology, in terms of:

- their quantification;
- their specification (typology and main characteristics); and
- their role in the economic system of tourist destinations.

This is, in fact, an important phenomenon for many European countries, and, in particular, for specific destinations where this typology of accommodation may become a fundamental, or a unique, choice for tourists. Furthermore, staying in private accommodation implies different spending patterns and travel characteristics, and has a different impact on the local economy.

Methodology, problems and results concerning private tourist accommodation estimates, are discussed by carrying out an analysis for the seaside resorts of the province of Venice (Caorle, Chioggia, Eraclea, Jesolo, Bibione, Cavallino, Lido di Venezia). This study is part of a project promoted by the Province of Venice with the aim of defining the economic (tourism consumption and turnover) and physical (nights and arrivals) scenario generated by private tourist accommodation, and of analysing their typologies and their structural characteristics such as dimensions, services, prices etc. The preliminary results of this study have been taken into account by Eurostat in the section 'Some examples of national practices for data collection on private tourist accommodation' in the *Technical Manual on Data Collection on Private Tourist Accommodation* (Eurostat, 2000, draft).

The developed methodology allowed us to estimate:

- the number of houses potentially used as private tourist accommodation units;
- the average size of houses in square metres;
- the number of rooms;
- the number of bed places;
- the number of overnight stays in second homes and rented accommodation; and
- the economic role in terms of expenditure and turnover generated by tourists choosing this typology of accommodation.

Part 2 of the chapter specifies the analysed aggregate on the basis of the community methodology. Parts 3 and 4 discuss the pros and cons of the explored data sources and the adopted approach. Parts 5 and 6 present the main results from the number of units to the economic role of this sub-system.

2. DEFINING AND COUNTING THE PHENOMENON

As is well known, the community methodology on tourism statistics (Eurostat, 1998; UE, 1999) subdivides the group 'Private tourist accommodation' as follows:

A. Private rental accommodation
    A1 Rented rooms in family houses
    A2 Dwelling rented from private individuals or professional agencies
B. Private non-rented accommodation
    B1 Owned dwellings
    B2 Accommodation provided without charge by relatives or friends
    B3 Other private accommodation (tents, caravans, and any type of mobile accommodation).

The phenomenon here discussed and measured includes:

A. Private rental accommodation
    A2 Dwelling rented from private individuals or professional agencies
B. Private non-rented accommodation
    B1 Owned dwellings
    B2 Accommodation provided without charge by relatives or friends (if classified as dwellings not permanently occupied).

The two components, the first as part of the NACE Group 70.20 and the second as part of the NACE Group 55.23, are here analysed separately.

Once the phenomenon has been delimited, the number of both private rental accommodation and non-rented ones has to be counted. The second step implies the passage from the accommodation units to the number of potential bed places, and the third step to the estimate of total nights spent. This approach can correct official data on private tourist accommodation which, according to Italian classification, represent a residual item including those units not inscribed in any Business Register (REC), and completely excluding part B of the defined aggregate.

3. SOURCES OF INFORMATION: ADVANTAGES, DISADVANTAGES AND COST-BENEFITS

A concise analysis of the available data sources in terms of advantages and disadvantages and cost-benefits arising from their systematic use is presented in this session: the final goal being to suggest some methodological guidelines in order to reach harmonized and compatible results which could be compared both over time and in different places. Furthermore, data sources require an analysis for each step of the adopted approach in order to provide specific and consistent results at any level.

It is well known that it is statistically difficult to cover this phenomenon as it is difficult to delimit and is greatly variable in nature. This is also why official statistics do not include such typologies of accommodation, and the development of adequate local monitoring systems is limited to just a small number of realities in Europe.

However, the growing importance of the phenomenon mainly at a destination level requires a large effort in order to overcome such limits and reach consistent results through the use of secondary data sources. From the study here discussed it emerges clearly that for each step of the adopted approach it is necessary to use more than one source, since each one frequently gives information on some aspects of the phenomenon. Furthermore, because of the difficulty of comparing data coming from different databases, the conjoint analysis frequently cannot answer the need of a complete set of quantitative information.

The number of private houses potentially used as tourist accommodation units

In order to estimate the sub-system of private tourist accommodation units according to the definition used in this study, it is crucial:

- to quantify the universe of 'non-permanently occupied dwellings';
- to classify the different uses of such a sub-system; and
- to carry out the analysis at least for each municipality.

The need to define and interpret this universe by typology and by site is crucial for a detailed and comprehensive analysis of the characteristics both of supply and demand, as well as for a reliable estimate of the number of nights and of the economic role of this system.

The main data sources which could be used in order to study the private tourist accommodation system in Italy are here discussed in terms of the pros and cons.

The Italian Census of the Population and Houses (ISTAT, 1993) represents the main source of information. It allows for a basic distinction between two categories of houses, 'occupied' and 'non-occupied' houses, by municipality. Private tourist accommodation is part of the latter category and it is possible to estimate since the census provides this additional information:

- number of houses and bedrooms according to the reason for the non-occupancy: use for holiday, use for work/study, use for other reasons, non-use;
- for each 'non-occupancy' category, the number of houses and bedrooms according to the availability declared by the owner: only for sale, only for rent, for both sale and rent, neither for sale nor for rent.

The possibility of having direct access to the whole databank of the census, and to individual records, is crucial in order to elaborate individual data and to quantify the number of private tourist accommodation for specific zones inside each municipality. In fact, as the objective of this study is to estimate the phenomenon in the coastal area of the province of Venice, it is necessary for some municipalities, for example Venice, to isolate the zones of the municipality which could really be considered seaside destinations.

The census is the only data source permitting such a territorial detail of information, this is why other available sources which could be used in order to achieve a proxy of the stock of private tourist accommodation have been explored but not used:

- ENEL (National Electricity Board): the number of contracts drawn up for electrical connections concerning non-residents could be used as a proxy of the private tourist accommodation. Since electricity can be considered as a primary good, this data source is commonly considered highly reliable and consistent.
- TELECOM: the telephone cannot be considered an essential utility in the same way as electricity, and the number of contracts cannot be used as being representative of the phenomenon. Furthermore, the diffusion of mobile phones limits its reliability even more. Previous studies estimated that only 12 per cent of the non-occupied houses of the seaside district of the province of Venice is provided with telephone services.
- Conservatoria Registri Immobiliari di Venezia (Office of the real estate register of Venice): register of the transfer of title deeds, which includes information on buyers and sellers, on the typologies of sold and bought dwellings and on their location. This data source could be very useful in order to analyse the main features of local, regional and extra-regional owners according to the number of units owned, their typology and their location. The major limits are:
  - the archives are not yet computerized;
  - the registration takes into account the date of presentation of the deed to be registered, without any other criterion of classification.
- Municipal Cadastre and ICI (municipal real estate tax): these two data sources do not distinguish the dwellings according to their use, and give information only on the total stock.

Finally, the choice of one or more of the listed data sources for the estimate of the number of private tourist accommodation should not only be linked to the reliability and consistency of the data bank but also to a cost-benefit analysis in terms of: (a) additional elements which would be useful for the analysis and related to the effort required to find and homogenize them; (b) possible costs for computerization or for changing computer systems, software and database.

From the number of private tourist accommodation to the number of bed places

For the quantification of the number of bed places the same data sources can be used. Starting from the census and from the estimates of the units and the surface area, the study indicates two possible methods of evaluation of the bed places.

The first adopts a theoretical average index of capacity, to be calculated for each site using the official local data on the private tourist accommodation. The assumption is that the average capacity of the officially counted private accommodation is representative of the capacity of the whole system. This value may be compared with existing literature on this topic: Gardavsky, in Pearce (1989), and Lawson and Baud-Bovy (1977) suggest a standard of 4–5 bed places per unit.

The second introduces a theoretical standard of surface area per bed place, starting from the information on the surface area of each rental accommodation unit and taking into account specific quality indicators.

From the number of bed places to the number of nights

The data sources used here are mainly those discussed above.

Electricity consumption for the contracts signed with non-residents is the most commonly used information to both estimate the number of nights in the tourist private accommodation and control the official data. It is well known that this approach overestimates the phenomenon since the same pattern of consumption of the residents is adopted also for potential tourists. This assumption cannot be considered as being consistent, since summertime and holiday behaviour is largely different from wintertime and usual habits. Moreover, holiday homes frequently do not have a complete set of domestic electric appliances such as washing machines, tumble driers etc., and it is also possible that the cleaning would be done by professional services. So only individual data on daily consumption by non-residents might allow for a reliable estimate of the number of nights. The production of such a database requires expensive procedures.

The use of the telephone, on the contrary, can be considered less reliable as indicators of the number of nights in private accommodation because of both the growing use of mobiles and the very different pattern of use and consumption which characterizes residents and non-residents.

Water consumption could represent, in principle, a good proxy of additional use due to holiday-makers. Actually, this source can become unreliable and produce overestimated results. This is the case with some destinations (for example, the seaside district of the province of Venice) where, during the summer period, the supply of water includes consumption for sprinkling gardens and for agriculture. Furthermore, asking suppliers for homogeneous and computerized data according to standard procedures is a very difficult task.

Information on waste disposal could be considered an additional source. Also, in this case, results in terms of nights could be overestimated; in fact, in peak periods the increase in quantity is due not only to the growing number of people staying in the destination but also to the increased production of activities such as restaurants, shops etc. Furthermore, in the Italian case, data on waste disposal are available only on a yearly basis, and monthly details (which experts of the sector claim are unreliable estimates) would require very complex and expensive procedures.

4. THE ADOPTED APPROACH

On the basis of the previous overview on the possible data sources, census information on 'non-occupied units' has been considered as the most adequate in order both to quantify the stock of private tourist accommodation and to describe its main structural and qualitative characteristics. In fact, the census gives details about the most important aspects of the buildings and of each unit, such as age, number of storeys, existing lift, as well as the availability of services such as central heating, telephone, kitchen, number of bathrooms etc. Such information is crucial in assessing strategies and actions which could be carried out for the improvement of the range of supply as well as the quality of the system of private accommodation and of its competitiveness.

The number of non-occupied units has been adopted as a proxy of the sub-system of private tourist accommodation. The private non-rented accommodation has been calculated by deducting from the total number of non-occupied units used for holiday, those declared available for sale and/or for rent. Finally, the private rental accommodation is the difference between total private tourist accommodation and private non-rented accommodation.

The estimate obtained at the time of the last census (1991) could be updated on a yearly basis: the Italian Statistics on Building Activity (ISTAT, various years), giving each year the number of new houses and rooms (for which the distinction between residential and non-residential buildings is available), represents a fundamental source in order to improve the database.

The estimate of the number of bed places has been obtained following the second approach as described earlier, i.e. the use of a surface theoretical standard per bed place. This standard has been determined on the basis of some consistent assumptions:

1. The minimum building standard for hotel rooms (according to the Veneto Region regulation) is 12 sq.m. per double room and 9 sq.m. per single room. This value does not include the per capita availability of facilities such as kitchens, bathrooms, dining-rooms and shared terraces, porches and spaces in common use (staircases, lift, hall etc.).

2. The use of the average size of dwellings in Venetian seaside resorts, according to the census database and the average number of rooms per dwelling. This value takes into account the spaces in common use too. The range of values is between 32 and 16 sq.m. per room: e.g. with two beds per room the standard ranges from 16 to 8 sq.m. per person. Data is consistent with the following:

3. International literature indicates for seaside regions a standard ranging from 11 to 15 sq.m. per bed place including per capita availability of common-use facilities (Lawson and Baud-Bovy, 1977). Similar results (range from 8 sq.m. to 16 sq.m. per bed place, including common-use facilities) have been obtained by analysing the brochures of some relevant European seaside regions (i.e. *Catalogues Cléconfort* for Aquitaine Coast Resorts: Archachon, Lacanau, Pyla etc.) which indicate the surface area of each unit available for rent as well as the number of bed places. This information is not available in the brochures for the Venetian seaside district.

To conclude, there is reason to believe that the result of this crossing evaluation can determine a standard of surface area per bed place which could be consistently applied to the Venetian region. A satisfying proxy taking into account the present situation of the district and the need to achieve an improved standard of quality has been estimated as 11 sq.m. per bed place.

To verify our assumption we have applied the standard 11 sq.m. per bed to the 1300 apartments listed for Bibione in the agency brochures: they show the number of bed places, but not the surface area (see above). The result (number of beds × 11 sq.m.) is absolutely consistent with the average surface area of apartments in the census data (58.7 sq.m. per unit).

Finally, the estimate of the number of nights has been arrived at by adopting the yearly average rate of use as it results from the official data on private accommodation of each resort of the district, given by the local tourist boards. Problems of over-estimation and unequal distribution of the effects generated by the use of data on water and electricity consumption or on waste disposal could be overcome in that way.

5. MAIN RESULTS: PRIVATE TOURIST ACCOMMODATION, BED PLACES, NIGHTS

Using the number of 'non-occupied houses' as the best proxy of the private tourist accommodation units in the seaside resorts of the province of Venice, the impressive dimension of the phenomenon becomes clear: 55,000 units counted in the 1991 census compared to 47,000 units declared as 'occupied'. According to this hypothesis, 54 per cent of the dwellings in the seaside resorts of the province potentially might be considered as part of the local tourism economy: 3.2 million sq.m., corresponding to a 59 sq.m. average surface per tourist accommodation unit, compared to 4.3 million sq.m. for dwellings occupied by residents (92 sq.m of surface per unit).

According to the method described in Part 4, private non-rented accommodation is 37 per cent of this stock (20,000 units) and rental accommodation the remaining 63 per cent (35,000 units) (Table 26.1): these estimates should be interpreted in a flexible way in the sense that units declared as owned dwellings come in and out from the subset of the rental units (individually or through professional agencies) without the possibility of being controlled and monitored.

Starting from the surface area of the 'non-occupied' units and assuming 11 sq.m. per bed place, the estimated number of potential bed places for tourist use is 292,000, 109,000 of which are in private non-rented accommodation and 183,000 in the rental accommodation units.[1] When compared with the official data of the Local Tourist Board (APT) these results stress how underestimated these latter are: the 292,000 estimated bed places are twice the official count of 144,000 (Table 26.1).

According to the approach described in Part 4, the number of estimated nights in private tourist accommodation is twice the official sources:[2] 13 million in 1991, 5 million in owned dwellings and 8 million in rental units (Table 26.2).

Besides measuring the stock of private tourist accommodation in each seaside resort of the province of Venice and evaluating in terms of nights the tourist demand choosing this typology of accommodation, this study aims at assessing the economic role of this form of tourism. The availability of daily tourist expenditure estimates for 1996[3] by typology of accommodation, and by item of expenditure and by seasonality, has allowed us to perform this analysis. In order to reach these results, the number of nights for 1991 has been updated to 1996 using the average rate of growth of the nights in private tourist accommodation officially counted by the local tourist boards. A total of 13.9 million nights have been calculated for 1996, 5.2 million of which are owned dwellings and 8.7 million rental accommodation units. Furthermore, the number of nights in tourist private accommodation during the high season (July and August) has been assessed by using the ratio of monthly official nights in private accommodation over yearly official nights in private accommodation. In order to take into account the characteristics of each resort, the ratio has been calculated and used separately for each

---

[1] By following the first method (Part 3), the number of bed places per unit would be 4.6 and the total number of beds about 252,000 (93,000 in private non-rented accommodation and 159,000 in rented accommodation).

[2] The estimate by using electricity consumption gives a result of about 17 million nights.

[3] These estimates are the result of the survey on tourist expenditure in the Veneto Region carried out by CISET in 1995 and updated to 1996 (CISET, 1996a, 1998).

Table 25.1 Private tourist accommodation in the Venetian seaside region (1991)

	Caorle	Chioggia	Eraclea	Jesolo	Bibione	Cavallino	Lido di Venezia	Total
Units								
Total	10,136	5,928	2,406	13,729	19,132	1,965	1,602	54,898
Private non-rented accommodation (a)	6,363	2,606	86	4,529	4,850	1,024	893	20,351
Private rental accommodation (b)	3,773	3,322	2,320	9,200	14,282	941	709	34,547
Surface area (sq.m.)								
Total	623,692	319,410	126,937	775,172	1,122,108	123,519	125,687	3,216,525
Private non-rented accommodation (a)	394,061	120,176	8,706	263,008	279,963	65,832	67,363	1,199,109
Private rental accommodation (b)	229,631	199,234	118,231	512,164	842,145	57,687	58,324	2,017,416
Bedplaces								
Total	56,699	29,037	11,540	70,470	102,010	11,229	11,426	292,411
Private non-rented accommodation (a)	35,824	10,925	791	23,910	25,451	5,985	6,124	109,010
Private rental accommodation (b)	20,876	18,112	10,748	46,560	76,559	5,244	5,302	183,401
Official data (APT)								
Private accommodation	3,368	1,700	1,552	5,247	18,735	218	28	30,848
Bed places	18,615	12,000	5,436	34,302	69,340	4,426	223	144,342

(a) Owned dwellings plus accommodation provided without charge by relatives or friends (if classified as dwellings non-permanently occupied).
(b) Dwellings rented from private individuals or professional agencies.

Table 25.2 Number of nights in the private tourist accommodation sub-system of the Venetian seaside region (1991)

	Caorle	Chioggia	Eraclea	Jesolo	Bibione	Cavallino	Lido di Venezia	Total
Nights								
Total:	3,053,000	1,653,000	904,000	1,979,000	4,640,000	479,000	567,000	13,275,000
in private non-rented accommodation (a)	1,929,000	622,000	62,000	672,000	1,158,000	255,000	304,000	5,002,000
in private rental accommodation (b)	1,124,000	1,031,000	842,000	1,308,000	3,482,000	223,000	263,000	8,273,000
Official data (APT)								
Nights in private accommodation	1,002,218	683,298	425,800	963,516	3,153,782	188,615	11,067	6,428,296
Days of use per year	54	57	78	28	45	43	50	45
Rate of use	14.8	15.6	21.5	7.7	12.5	11.7	13.6	12.2

(a) Owned dwellings plus accommodation provided without charge by relatives or friends (if classified as dwellings non-permanently occupied).
(b) Dwellings rented from private individuals or professional agencies.

site.[4] The result for the whole tourist region indicates that 64 per cent of the nights in private tourist accommodation are concentrated in the high season, the same period when average tourist expenditure is higher too.

Because of the lack of specific information on the seasonal characteristics of tourism demand in private rental and non-rented accommodation, the same behaviour seen from official data (the seasonality ratio) has been adopted. It is well known that among the improvements of the approach used, one of the priorities should be the definition of parameters both of use and seasonality representing the specificity of the two subsets. In fact, while the use of coefficients calculated on the basis of official data can be considered a good proxy of the dynamics and characteristics of the private rental system, the same coefficients could be inconsistent if adopted in order to describe the structure and the evolution of the non-rented system. Ad hoc surveys aiming at exploring level, length and seasonality of use should be carried out in order to overcome such limits.

6. THE PHYSICAL AND ECONOMIC DIMENSION OF TOURISM IN THE SEASIDE RESORTS OF THE PROVINCE OF VENICE

Tourism in the seaside resorts of the province of Venice follows, for the most part, the traditional pattern of holidays: medium–long-stay tourists , holidaying with the family frequently in private tourist accommodation, coming from Italy or from German-speaking countries (Germany and Austria cover 60% of total international nights), preferring short- to medium-haul trips by private car, and avoiding package solutions (only 8% apply to a travel agency). Furthermore, this behaviour goes hand in hand with a lower propensity to consume when compared to other tourist regions (art cities, spa resorts etc.) of the province: in fact, the average expenditure per night is the lowest in seaside resorts and the highest in art cities. As a final result, by comparing the weight of the seaside district in terms of nights (the physical dimension) and in economic terms (the economic dimension) the loss for the area becomes clear: counting 48.6% of the nights, it explains only 33% of the gross revenue.

The daily average expenditure of tourists choosing a seaside holiday in the province of Venice amounts to 80,000 lire (€40): 43% concerns accommodation, 27% food, 10% transport (prevailing, and at the same time limited, local excursions by private car can explain this modest amount, nearly 80% of which is due to petrol costs), 14% shopping activities and 3% recreational activities, inclusive of deckchair, beach umbrella and bathing-hut hire costs.

Tables 25.3a and 25.3b summarize the estimates of the physical (nights) and economic (gross revenue) dimensions of the seaside district of the province of Venice. Furthermore, the role of each segment of tourism demand choosing different typologies of accommodation can be pointed out. As far as data on collective accommodation (hotels and other means of accommodation) they do not differ from one table to the other, while the tables differentiate themselves in the last column, showing official data (Table. 25.3a) and estimates (Table. 25.3b) of tourist private accommodation.

---

[4] The seasonality index has been calculated as the average of the monthly trends officially registered in the private tourist accommodation in the period from 1991 to 1995.

Table 25.3a Physical and economic dimension of tourism by means of accommodation in the Venetian seaside region (official data, 1996)

	1–2 star hotels	3 star hotels	4–5 star hotels	Campsites	Other collective establishments	Private accommodation	Total
Nights	2,327,456	3,576,934	1,066,428	8,580,478	457,078	6,667,874	22,676,248
% nights	10.3	15.8	4.7	37.8	2.0	29.4	100.0
Gross revenue (billion lire)	256	480	181	525	37	429	1.909
% gross revenue	13.4	25.2	9.5	27.5	1.9	22.5	100.0
Per capita daily tourist expenditure (lire) (a)	110,122	134,236	169,705	61,229	81,259	64,281	

(a) CISET estimates (1996a, 1996b, 1998); UIC (1997)

Table 25.3b Physical and economic dimension of tourism by means of accommodation in the Venetian seaside region (estimates,1996)

	1–2 star hotels	3 star hotels	4–5 star hotels	Campsites	Other collective establishments	Private accommodation (b)	Total
Nights	2,327,456	3,576,934	1,066,428	8,580,478	457,078	13,938,750	29,947,124
% nights	7.8	11.9	3.6	28.7	1.5	46.5	100.0
Gross revenue (billion lire)	256	480	181	525	37	742	2.222
% gross revenue	11.5	21.6	8.1	23.6	1.7	33.4	100.0
Per capita daily tourist expenditure (lire) (a)	110,122	134,236	169,705	61,229	81,259	64,112	

(a) CISET estimates (1996a, 1996b, 1998); UIC (1997)
(b) COSES–CISET estimates

Estimated nights in private accommodation are nearly 14 million (37.7% in non-rented accommodation and 62.3% in rental accommodation), while official ones are 6.7 million; in terms of gross revenue, the estimate is 742.1 billion lire, while the gross revenue corresponding to official nights is 429 billion lire.

Furthermore, Table 25.3b demonstrates that tourists in hotels represent 23.3% of total nights in the district (7.8% 1- and 2-star hotels, 11.9% 3-star hotels and 3.6% 4- and 5-star hotels), while their weight in terms of gross revenue is 41.2%. On the contrary, tourism in campsites and in private accommodation contributes in terms of nights (75.2% of the total) more than in terms of gross revenue (57% of the total). This can be easily understood by reporting the different levels of daily average tourist expenditure: tourists who overnight in hotels spend from a maximum of 170,000 lire (4- and 5-star hotels) to a minimum of 110,000 lire (1- and 2-star hotels), while tourists in campsites and private accommodation spend no more than 65,000 lire. This latter daily amount includes accommodation (26,700 lire), food (21,500 lire), transport (5,800 lire), recreation activities (2,300 lire), shopping activities (7,000 lire) and other expenses (732 lire). In the high season (July and August) the daily average expenditure in private tourist accommodation rises to 74,600 lire, while in the low season it falls to 58,600 lire. The difference between the two levels is clearly due to the cost of the rent which represents respectively 48% (high season) and 42% (low season) of the daily average expenditure.[5]

Gross revenue generated by tourism in private accommodation: estimates by resort

Using the estimates of nights and of the daily average expenditure by resort it is possible to calculate the gross revenue generated by this important typology of tourism for each seaside resort and to analyse its role in the local economy.

As already discussed, the total gross revenue linked to tourism in private accommodation is 742.1 billion lire, 196.3 (26.5%) of which is due to non-rented accommodation and 545.8 (73.5%) to rental accommodation. In terms of the role of each resort, Table 25.4 shows that Bibione produces 35.4% of the total gross revenue (262.5 billion lire); this percentage rises to 39.8% (217 billion lire) for the rental component. Caorle follows with 148 billion lire (19.9% of the total gross revenue), then Jesolo with 126.8 billion lire (17.1% of the total gross revenue) and Chioggia with 92.7 billion lire (12.5% of total gross revenue). As was expected, the gross revenue produced by tourism in non-rented accommodation is lower than that linked to the rental accommodation system: but it is important to note that this gap is particularly relevant in the case of Chioggia, Eraclea, Jesolo and Bibione. Only in the case of Caorle is there equilibrium between the two components. The database and procedure used to reach these results can explain this diversity:[6] furthermore, in the case of Caorle the difference is due to the strong predominance of second homes in two well-known sites of the municipality: Duna Verde and Porto S. Margherita.

---

[5] These results have been elaborated on the basis of the tourist expenditure estimates by item of consumption (CISET, 1996a, 1996b, 1998), apart from the accommodation item, for which a survey on rental fares in the seaside district of the province of Venice has been carried out for the period 1996–7.

[6] It is important to point out that other elements could influence the estimates, e.g. recent units for which the use has not yet been completely defined, or units which have been defined as non-occupied because of their status of decay, and not available for rent or sale, but at the same time not usable for holidays.

Table 25.4 Gross revenue produced by tourists in private accommodation by resort (estimates in billion lire) (1996)

	Total		Private non-rented accommodation (a)		Private rental accommodation (b)	
	v.a.	%	v.a.	%	v.a.	%
Caorle	148.0	19.9	75.7	38.7	72.3	13.2
Chioggia	92.7	12.5	24.4	12.4	68.3	12.5
Eraclea	56.9	7.7	2.4	1.2	54.5	10.0
Jesolo	126.8	17.1	26.4	13.5	100.4	18.5
Bibione	262.5	35.4	45.5	23.2	217.0	39.8
Cavallino	25.5	3.4	10.0	5.1	15.5	2.8
Lido di Venezia	29.6	4.0	11.9	5.9	17.7	3.2
Total expenditure	742.1	100.0	196.3	100.0	545.8	100.0

(a) CISET estimates (1996a, 1996b, 1998)
(b) COSES–CISET estimates

Table 25.5 Gross revenue produced by tourists in private accommodation by item of expenditure (estimates in billion lire) (1996)

	Total		Private non-rented accommodation (a)		Private rental accommodation (b)	
	v.a.	%	v.a.	%	v.a.	%
Accommodation	221.1	29.8	-	-	221.1	40.5
Food	299.1	40.3	112.7	57.4	186.4	34.2
Transport	81.4	11.0	30.7	15.6	50.8	9.3
Recreation activities	31.8	4.3	12.0	6.1	19.8	3.6
Shopping	98.5	13.3	37.1	18.9	61.4	11.2
Other expenses	10.2	1.4	3.8	2.0	6.4	1.2
Total expenditure	742.1	100.0	196.3	100.0	545.8	100.0

(a) CISET estimates (1996a, 1996b, 1998)
(b) COSES–CISET estimates

Figures 25.1 and 25.2 conclude the analysis by resort, showing the estimate of the weight of each typology of tourism, including that in hotels and in campsites. This is only a preliminary evaluation which simply distributes the total gross revenue as showed in Table 25.3a per typology of accommodation among the resorts, according to the weight of each site in terms of nights. One of the main objectives of this study, in fact, is to stress the importance of developing a methodology in order to analyse the physical and economic dimension of tourism in private accommodation, while the other means of accommodation play a marginal role. A careful and accurate analysis of the role of the registered accommodation (REC) should start from reliable information on the daily average tourist expenditure made by tourists overnighting in the different means of accommodation of each resort.[7]

---

[7] This information would require the conjoint elaboration of the results of the Survey of tourists in the Veneto region (CISET, 1996a, 1996b, 1998) and the estimates by municipality of the Italian border survey carried out annually by the Italian Office of Exchange.

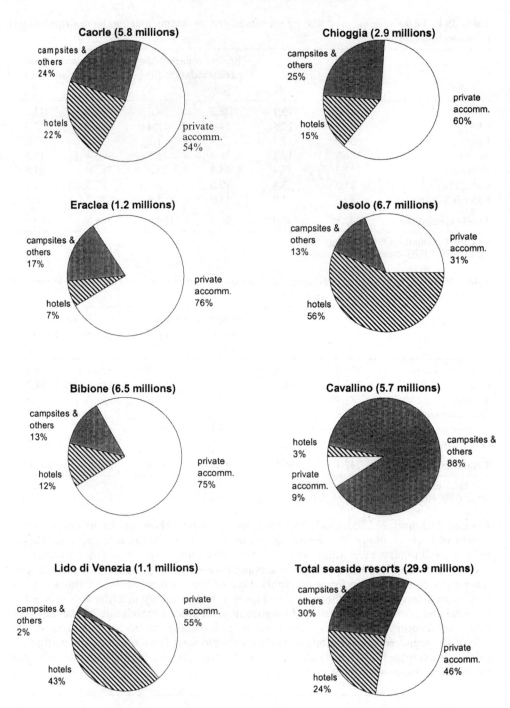

Figure 25.1 Number of nights by means of accommodation

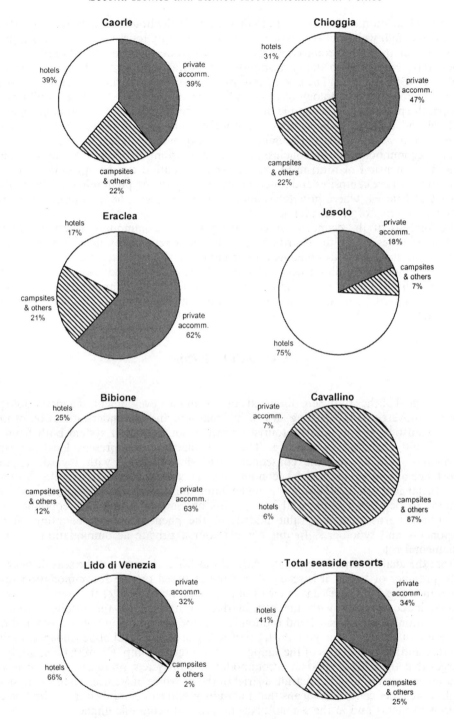

Figure 25.2 Gross revenue generated by tourists by means of accommodation

The specialization of Jesolo and Lido di Venezia in the hotel accommodation system explains the high weight of the gross revenue produced by tourism overnighting in this category over the total produced in each of the two destinations: 74.2% and 66.1%, respectively, compared to the corresponding importance in terms of night: 56% for Jesolo and 43% for Lido. The role of campsites justifies the crucial impact of the gross revenue linked to this typology of tourism for Cavallino (86.8%) and the equilibrium between the physical and economic dimension of the system (88% in terms of nights): the level and pattern of consumption of tourists choosing campsites are lower than those of tourists in hotels, and similar to the expenditure behaviour of tourists in private accommodation. In conclusion, the equilibrium between the physical and economic dimension of tourism in private accommodation can be appreciated in the destinations where campsites and hotels of lower category are predominant. This is also the case of Eraclea, where private accommodation represents 68% in terms of nights and 62% in terms of gross revenue.

The analysis of the economic role of the private accommodation system can be concluded by describing the distribution of the gross revenue by item of expenditure (Table 25.5): food generates the highest percentage (40% of the total and 299.1 billion lire), accommodation follows with 221.1 billion lire (29.8%) and then shopping with 98.5 billion lire (13.3%). The composition changes if the two components are analysed separately: in particular, accommodation becomes the first item (40.5%) for tourism in rental units.

7. CONCLUSIONS

The main goal of the study here discussed consists in the development of a methodology in order to overcome the existing lack of information, and the under-estimation of the official statistics, concerning the tourist private accommodation system both from a physical and economic perspective. The inadequacy of the present local tourism information systems and the consequent loss of knowledge with regards to the importance of tourism in the local economy are well known: this analysis seeks to stress how crucial it is for destinations to understand the dimensions of tourism and the relationship between the physical role (nights and arrivals) and the economic role (expenditure, gross revenue, value added) of the phenomenon by counting all its components and typologies. In this context tourist private accommodation plays a fundamental role.

From the analysis and the estimates carried out for each resort of the seaside district of the province of Venice it is revealed that the analysed private accommodation sub-system increases by 32 per cent in terms of nights, and by 16 per cent in terms of gross revenue in comparison with the official data. Furthermore, the results permit a confrontation of the physical and economic roles of each typology of tourists and an evaluation of the local tourism industry performance and its level of dependence on the structure and characteristics of the supply–demand relationship. From the case study it emerges that the private tourism accommodation sub-system produces 33 per cent of the total gross revenue of the seaside district of the province of Venice, while its physical weight is 46.5 per cent. This means that this sub-system can be ranked in the first place in terms of nights and in the second place in terms of economic impact.

Note: This chapter summarizes the results presented in M. Manente and I. Scaramuzzi (1999) *Le case dei turisti, Il Mulino*. The authors would like to thank Dr Cristiana Pedenzini who elaborated the main results and followed each step of the methodology, from the analysis of the available sources to the management of the census records.

REFERENCES

CISET (1996a) *Tourism Expenditure in the Veneto Region* (M. Manente and V. Minghetti, Quaderni CISET) n. 16.1/96, n.16.3/96, Venice: Libreria Editrice Cafoscarina.

CISET (1996b) *Tourism Demand Segmentation and Consumption Behaviour: An Economic Analysis* (P. Costa, M. Manente and V. Minghetti, Quaderni CISET), n. 14/96. Venice: Libreria Editrice Cafoscarina.

CISET (1998) *Il fatturato del turismo nel Centro Storico di Venezia* (M. Manente and L. Andreatta, Quaderni CISET), n. 19/98. Venice: Libreria Editrice Cafoscarina.

Eurostat (1998) *The Community Methodology on Tourism Statistics*. Luxemburg.

Eurostat (2000) *Technical Manual on Data Collection on Private Tourist Accommodation* (A. Griguolo, M. Redaelli and G. Vaccaro), Final Draft, Luxemburg, March.

ISTAT (1993) *Censimento generale della popolazione e delle abitazioni*, 1991. Rome.

ISTAT (various years) *Statistiche dell'attività edilizia*. Rome.

Lawson F. and Baud-Bovy M. (1977) *Tourism and Recreation development*. London: Architectural Press.

Manente M. and Scaramuzzi I. (1999) *Le case dei turisti*. Bologna: Il Mulino.

Pearce D. G. (1989) *Tourism Development*. New York: Longman Scientific and Technical.

UE (1999) Commission Decision of December 1999 on the procedures for implementing Council Directive 95/57/EC on the collection of statistical information in the field of tourism.

UIC–Italian Office of Exchange (1997) 'Border surveys on International Tourism to Italy'.

26

Scottish Leisure Travel 1972–1997: Utilizing the National Travel Survey

Geoff Riddington and Colin Sinclair

INTRODUCTION

The response of many researchers when faced with questions about how people behave in their leisure time is to collect primary data on a relatively small sample and then infer general behaviour from the sample. Over the years, however, governments have conducted a number of surveys such as the General Household Survey and Household Expenditure Survey that throw light on leisure behaviour. These have the significant advantages that they are both large enough to give a statistically valid picture, and have been running long enough to provide an accurate picture of how things are changing and developing. This chapter is concerned with describing the less-well-known National Travel Survey, explaining how it can be utilized and, as a means of illustration, looking at the way leisure travel in Scotland has been evolving.

THE NATIONAL TRAVEL SURVEY

The National Travel Survey is a survey of the actual travel by individuals for one week as recorded by them in a logbook. It was first conducted in 1965/6 as a one-off survey, and no raw data from that period has survived. In 1972 the survey was revived and continued, initially every two years until 1988, when it became continuous. The survey covers some 10,000 households on a two-year cycle selected from within 740 Postal Survey Units (PSUs) that ensure accurate geographical and socio-economic representation of the UK as a whole. At this PSU level there are details of the location, density and concessionary fare schemes that operate in the area.

Data on each household is collected, covering factors such as house type, household composition, socio-economic characteristics, vehicle access, and access and attitudes to public transport. There are some 40 variable fields in each household record.

Data on the vehicles in each household are also collected. The 29 fields, for each of the 1000-plus vehicles, include details of the vehicle, usage, fuel consumption and support for costs (i.e. company cars).

Within each household there are, on average, 2.3 individuals. Data in each individual's record include sex, age and position in household; job description and income; handicaps; season tickets and passes; and details of the travel to work. The details of each journey made by the individual in the week, on average around sixteen, form a record in the journeys file. These details include purpose, mode, distance, speed, origin and destination, and, finally, the number of stages.

Whilst most journeys consist of a single stage, some 10 per cent of journeys involve 'changes' of mode, which constitute separate stages. Thus, there are some 300,000 stages for the corresponding 280,000 recorded journeys. Details on the stage-file record distance, number in car (or group), ticket prices/types for public transport, and car owner/parking for private transport.

Finally, since 1992, respondents have also been asked about long distance (over 50 miles) journeys in the previous three weeks, and these, together with the journeys over 50 miles, recorded in the current week, form the Long Distance Journey File. Data here cover purpose, origin/destination, distance and mode. It should be noted, however, that journeys outside the UK are excluded and, consequently, the survey cannot be used as a record of foreign holidays.

In total, details of some 2.66 million journeys are available, these details amounting to some 150 characteristics. Some 30 per cent or 800,000 of these journeys are for leisure purposes, an incredibly rich data source for researchers.

EXTRACTING AND MANIPULATING DATA

The original base data (minus identifying characteristics such as names and addresses) is available from the Data Archive at Essex University. Full information on the archive and ordering the NTS data is available at www.data-archive.ac.uk. The data, which can be ordered on-line, is distributed on CD-ROM in SPSS format. It consists of a series of linked files structured as in Fig 26.1.

Links are provided by a single common variable: PSU identifier in the households file; household identifier in individual data files and individual identifier in journey and stage files. As a result, in order to select, say, journeys made by Scots, we have to merge

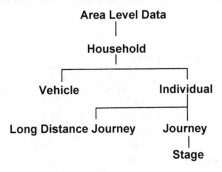

Figure 26.1   Linked file structure of NTS data

journey, individual, household and PSU files and then extract only the Scottish data. Because of the size of the data files, this can produce problems.

With the latest released data sets, and using SPSS V9, processing problems were relatively small. This contrasts with the earlier data sets which were extremely difficult to use. The problems ranged from an SPSS syntax file which bore no relationship to any version of SPSS we are aware of, and had to be deconstructed and then rebuilt; files without a common variable; and major problems with space when undertaking necessary sorting. All these problems were, however, eventually overcome.

One important note for the unwary when using the latest data is the change of coding. Instead of starting at 1, all the codes now start at zero, and the corresponding number is less 1 throughout the series. This change is not noted in the documentation and is masked, because the variable description in the output contains the old code. As a result, for example, a variable in the journey-purpose data set coded 12 will be described in output as '13 – Participation in Sport'. If extracting data on the basis of the old codes the results will be incorrect.

Finally, it must be recognized that the sheer number of data items can make processing quite slow. For example, the latest journey file contains some 6 million pieces of data.

THE RESULTS

In this section we summarize some key indicators of leisure travel behaviour by Scots in 1997, compared both to the British as a whole in 1997 and to Scots from 1972 onwards. Clearly, the geography of Scotland is very different from the rest of the UK, with 70 per cent of the population in an industrialized central belt, concentrated in about 15 per cent of the land area, with the rest of the population thinly spread over 85 per cent of the land mass. In addition the 40 per cent of the population in the Strathclyde Region, in the west of Scotland, have, probably, the best public transport system in the UK. This may either be the result or cause of one of the most striking differences between Scotland and the rest of the UK: the large numbers of people without access to a car (see Table 26.1).

The most significant feature here is that Scots tend to make fewer journeys for leisure purposes than south of the border. As will become clear later, availability of a car significantly increases the likelihood of leisure travel.

Table 26.2 compares the types of leisure activities undertaken as extracted from the latest 1995/7 complete survey

Table 26.1 Number of cars per household in 1997

	Scotland (%)	UK (%)
None	34.82	29.50
One	46.96	45.27
Two	16.19	22.01
Three	1.62	2.90
Four or more	0.40	0.32

UK

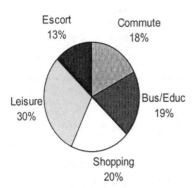

Scotland

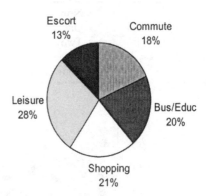

Figure 26.2 Distribution of journeys by purpose

Table 26.2 Comparison of leisure journey purpose 1995/7: Scotland vs UK (%)

	UK 95–7	Scotland 95–7
Visit friends	14.0	14.0
Eat/drink at friends	2.5	2.3
Other social	1.5	1.2
Public entertainment	4.0	4.1
Sport: participate	2.4	2.6
Holiday base	1.1	1.0
Day trip	2.4	2.1
Just walk	1.9	1.9
	29.8	29.2

Both groups are remarkably similar, with Scots slightly more active (sport participation) but less likely to take day trips. Again, the reason relates to the difficulties in such trips if a family does not have access to a car.

We now turn to the changes that have occurred in Scotland over the last 25 years. A word of warning however: as with all surveys, there have been, over the years, a number of changes. Some of these are definitional, often to clarify problem areas – such as when one counts a walk as a journey stage – and sometimes they reflect different needs; for example, to identify parents driving children to school. In this context, journey-purpose classification may be slightly problematic.

Table 26.3 shows the pattern of car ownership in Scotland in 1972 and 1997. Although there has been a significant increase, particularly in two-car families, it should be noted that over one third of the population of Scotland are still dependent upon public transport.

Figure 26.3 shows changes in household size and journeys per individuals over the period.

This data confirms what has been happening throughout the UK; household size has been falling as younger people move out earlier, and divorce has created more single-

Table 26.3 Number of cars in household

	1972 (%)	1997 (%)
None	37.4	34.8
One	51.6	50.0
Two	8.8	16.2
Three	1.4	1.6
Four or more	0.8	0.4

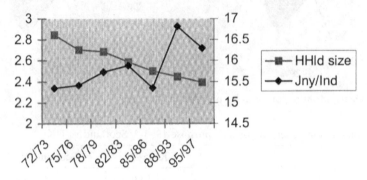

Figure 26.3 Changes in household size and journeys/week: Scotland 1972–7

parent households. In contrast, mobility, as identified by the number of journeys made by individuals, has been increasing as more people gain access to the car.

Table 26.4 shows the growth in length of journey, particularly for leisure purposes, and Table 26.5 identifies the substantial increase in the number of leisure trips per individual. The composition of leisure trips is given in Table 26.6.

Table 26. 4 Average journey length (miles) Scotland 1972/7

	1972	1997	Increase (%)
Leisure	9.4	11.2	19.15
Other	6.6	7.5	13.64
Total	7.4	8.5	14.86

Table 26.5 Leisure trips per individual (per week)

1972	1997	Increase (%)
4.06	4.76	17.13

Table 26.6   Types of leisure trips 1972/7

	1972 (%)	1997 (%)	Change (%)
Social	60.70	58.61	−3.44
Eat/drink	6.99	7.98	14.23
Entertainment	23.91	13.91	−41.83
Sport (participant)	4.88	8.89	82.24
Holidays/trips	3.52	10.60	201.18

This table (and those following) must be treated with care because of definitional problems, however, it is clear that there has been a move away from going out for entertainment and general social purposes towards meals out, sport and holiday trips. One imagines this reflects the decrease in leisure time associated with the growth in women in work and the increases in income that allow for eating out and holiday trips. The gratifying growth in participation in sport is the result of a combination of factors; new facilities, increase in female participants, decrease in physical work and, just possibly, health-based advertising.

Table 26.7 shows the mode of transport used for leisure trips.

Table 26.7   Mode of travel by type of leisure activity 1972/7

	Car/Van (%)	Bus (%)	Train (%)	Walk/Cycle (%)
Social	46.69	35.97	1.40	15.93
Eat/drink	58.81	18.03	0.00	23.16
Entertain	45.27	31.32	2.29	21.12
Sport	54.85	21.48	4.20	19.48
Holidays	57.10	20.50	22.40	0.00

1972

	Car/Van (%)	Bus (%)	Train (%)	Walk/Cycle (%)
Social	84.22	5.16	0.48	10.15
Eat/drink	78.82	5.88	0.00	15.29
Entertain	81.08	9.73	0.00	9.19
Sport	84.32	4.66	0.00	11.02
Holidays	78.06	11.45	2.06	8.43

1997

The obvious feature is the total dominance in 1997 of the car. Those without a car – the poor and elderly – either stay at home or use the bus. Use of the train to get to a holiday destination has virtually disappeared with the growth of the car and air charters to foreign climes.

Table 26.8 shows the length of journeys undertaken by Scots for their leisure.

Table 26.8   Average journey lengths by leisure type

	1972	1997	Change (%)
Social	7.02	11.42	62.9
Eat/drink	3.53	6.64	88.1
Entertain	4.43	8.58	93.6
Sport	8.62	6.87	−20.3

The general increase in journey length is marked, with the notable exception of sport. Given the increase in participation, this would tend to confirm the impact and success of new local facilities.

Finally, Table 26.9 looks at gender differences:

Table 26.9   Gender participation in leisure activities

	1972		1997	
	Male (%)	Female (%)	Male (%)	Female (%)
Social	45.8	54.2	42.9	57.1
Eat/drink	64.4	35.6	63.5	36.5
Entertain	55.6	44.4	51.4	48.6
Sport	83.6	16.4	64.8	35.2
Hols/trips	52.4	47.6	54.4	45.6

Some notable features are the extent to which men go away without women, the extent to which the male dominance in sport is being eradicated and the continuing tradition of males going out for a drink and females going out for a chat. The surprising extent that these differences have been maintained is illustrated by the fact that when going on holiday 88 per cent of the drivers are male, going to a restauraunt 84 per cent are male, and going to the cinema, an activity dominated by the young, 76 per cent are male.

CONCLUSIONS

This chapter is merely illustrative of the type of information that can be obtained from the NTS. The data set is large enough to look at county-by-county differences, differences by age, differences by income, effects of prices, differences in number of company cars between regions or over time, etc. The list is almost endless.

With the growth of computer power and the means to transmit large volumes of data, inquisition of these huge government surveys is a real possibility. Skills need to be developed to exploit their potential but, as this chapter shows, the results can be illuminating.

27

Getting the Measure of Tourism: Research Developments in Monitoring Destination Marketing Performance

A. V. Seaton

ABSTRACT

This chapter looks at the uses of research in destination marketing, and explores its dual role as a measure of destination performance and destination agency performance, and the relationship between these two distinct functions. The chapter identifies two main performance indicators in tourism research – those measuring behaviour and those measuring communication effects – and appraises the techniques associated with each, using a number of international case histories. The chapter emphasizes the central issue of measuring performance in relation to defined and specified goals.

The analysis suggests how destination marketing evaluation has improved in the last decade through adopting research techniques first developed in the marketing of fast-moving consumer goods, and that there is scope for studying other fmcg procedures that can be utilized in tourism. The chapter concludes by suggesting a number of future agendas for evaluation research including: the development of longitudinal, destination-choice models and the analysis of visitation cycles; regional disaggregation analyses; the measurement of the host impact of VFR tourism at destinations; and measures of media impact on destination image and visitor behaviour.

INTRODUCTION

The practices of destination and destination-agency monitoring are still emerging fields, and ones that greatly vary between international NTOs (national tourist organizations) and ATBs (area tourist boards). Until the 1980s, most tourism organizations devoted little effort to measuring their own performances in influencing tourism movements, or tracking destination movements except in broad trends. They tended to rely, in the main, on selective, impressionistic data supported by PR publicizing inputs rather than outputs. Many still do. It is still possible to read annual reports for NTOs or ATBs that provide accounts of what has been done, with much less attention to what they achieved – inputs, not outputs.

In the late 1980s and 1990s a growing climate, in the west, of scrutiny of public sector institutions, and pressures for accountability, stimulated a number of new initiatives. International agencies began to adopt a broader range of performance indicators, including measures of tourism promotion. An observable trend in the UK has been the growing adaptation of research approaches common in the marketing of fast-moving consumer goods, to tourism analysis.

At the back of international moves to improve the quality of tourism statistics is an assumption that accurate data can improve the planning and marketing of tourism. Most destination agencies now gather some data, but not only does the quality of the data vary, but the uses made of it. Not all data gathered by destination agencies is analysed, summarized, circulated and acted on with anything like the systematic force one might expect. Some organizations gather but don't thoroughly analyse – research may be a political question of 'edited highlights', a publicity opportunity for the organization concerned, rather than a data set for thorough analysis and managerial direction. Some organizations may analyse, but fail to summarize. Some may summarize but fail to distribute the results. And finally, research may be summarized and distributed, but not acted upon by all those who might benefit from the results.

In practice, it is often impossible to analyse all the data collected in major studies. The UKTS, for example, which starts with a sample of 50,000, could potentially be interrogated through an infinite number of cross-tabulations and special analyses, but limitations of time and human resources means that only a number of main dimensions are commonly presented in the published report. The effective usage of research is thus as much about utility and dissemination choices as capture. This chapter is about the strategic usage of research in relation to destination-marketing issues, rather than conceptual, methodological and statistical aspects of its generation.

THE PROBLEMS OF DESTINATION MARKETING AND PROMOTION EVALUATION

The impact of marketing and promotion on destination performance is much more difficult to assess than that of most other managerial inputs. The problems lie in four areas:

- distinguishing the separate effects, on destination performance, of individual components of the marketing programme (e.g. the effect of media relations vs. advertising, or brochure distribution vs. trade exhibitions);
- separating out the impacts of uncontrollable external, environmental variables, negative (war, terrorism, health hazards etc.) or positive (a hit film featuring a destination), from impacts of NTO/ATB activity;
- separating out the effects of private sector from public sector marketing inputs: the destination agency does not control all representations of a destination; tour

operators, hotels, transport companies etc. may promote particular images of a country or region, alongside those of the NTO/ATB;

- assessing the lagged effects of promotion: promotional campaigns continue to have residual effects even after campaigns have ceased to be exposed to audiences; assessing the wear-out factor is difficult.

There are no sure ways of solving these difficulties. The start point of measuring the impact of marketing and promotion on destination success is defining objectives. Once destination objectives have been decided it becomes easier to recognize what research strategies might be necessary, who should be responsible for implementing them, how it might be done and what performance indicators might be used to evaluate achievements.

A useful demonstration of these procedures, in which research is conceived as the final, response link in a destination-marketing sequence led by a 'management by objectives' philosophy, can be illustrated from a study produced by management consultants, Touche-Ross, for the Scottish Tourist Board in 1992. The company produced a taxonomy of NTO policy that attempted to differentiate the goals, instruments, agencies and indicators relating to destination development.

The matrix demonstrates the varieties and difference of objectives that may lay behind marketing and promotion. The advantages of this kind of matrix approach to

Table 27.1 Taxonomy of NTO tourism policy

Goal	Instrument	Agency	Performance indicator
Attract more foreign visitors	International destination marketing	National Tourism Offices overseas	1. Number of foreign tourists 2. Percentage growth in visitor numbers
Generate higher expenditure per visitor	Targeted campaigns aimed at higher income groups	NTO jointly with travel trade	1. Average expenditure per tourist 2. Total foreign exchange earnings from tourism
Reduce seasonality	Out of season marketing/promotion	NTO + private sector	Annual tourist/ visitor monitors
Spread tourism geographically	Regional product development and marketing/promotion	Regional tourist agencies (ATBs/LECs)	Visitor analysis by area
Improve image of destination	Product placement in media and film	NTO or ATB	Pre-and post- awareness and attitude studies quantifying changes
Crisis management after terrorist shooting	Media visits and briefings	NTO and private sector	Recovery of visitor numbers Improved attitudes to destination

Source: Adapted and extended from Touche-Ross, 1992

destination marketing is that it locates research firmly within an overall strategic game plan so that its uses are identified, and the relevant performance indicators are specified.

PERFORMANCE INDICATORS: BEHAVIOUR AND COMMUNICATION MEASURES

There are now generally agreed to be two main approaches to performance measurements of marketing inputs, behavioural measures and communications measures. Over the last decade both approaches have been used increasingly by the more sophisticated destination planners.

Behavioural measures

Behavioural measures are those that monitor destination and destination-agency performance through tracking what people actually do. Although qualitative measures can be used, such tracking predominantly involves quantitative surveys of tourist patterns – how many went where, what their activities were, how much they spent and so on.

Visitor numbers, visitor expenditures and occupancy

Despite the problems of attributing marketing/promotional causality to visitor behaviour, visitor data remains the start point of tourism accounting and destination evaluation. Classically, there are three main kinds of data that constitute the basis of visitor profiling:

- trip or visitor numbers and profiles by type of trip, nationality, socio-economic status etc.;
- visitor revenue, calculated per head/day, and then grossed up to estimates of destination totals;
- occupancy of different accommodation types by bed and room.

The marketing uses of these three kinds of data, if kept regularly, include the identification of: economic destination trends by tourist segments and accommodation sectors; seasonality trends by tourist types and segments and accommodation types and other aspects of tourist behaviour.

A variant of the triple-destination study is the research programme of New York Convention Bureau, the destination agency for New York City, a destination of 30 million domestic visitors and 6 million international ones, making it resemble a country rather than a region (its international market is bigger than that of India and Scotland combined). NYCB's main research measures are three annual studies: a domestic study contracted to a research consultancy and implemented through a self-administered survey sent to a 46,000 national sample; an international study comprising disaggregated data on New York tourism abstracted from the national In-flight Survey of International Air Travellers; and an economic value study, Tourism's Economic Impact on New York City, that is derived from 'measures of spending, payroll and tax revenues generated by visitor spending' (New York, 1998a, 1998b, 1998c).

This triple data capture has equivalences in fmcg marketing where three kinds of data form the bedrock of monitoring: sales orders by trade intermediaries (retailers and distributors); ex-factory shipments of products; and consumer off-take (purchases actually made by consumers).

Key account monitors: critical market profiling

One of the key functions of destination research is critical market monitoring. In the marketing of fmcg, one of the on-going priorities of research is updated monitoring of key accounts. This may include analysis of a small number of big distributors who control a large proportions of total sales, or high-spend, repeat purchase consumer groups who provide significant shares of the market for a product. In the hotel market, key accounts may be corporate accounts, and in airlines groups of regular, corporate fliers.

In destination terms there are three kinds of key visitor accounts, which require regular monitoring :

1. core, repeat visitors from *specific geographic generating regions*;
2. repeat visitors from *specific types* of traveller and market segments;
3. *Emergent groups*, who may or may not be monitored in existing studies, whose potential has yet to be fully realized.

Repeat visit groups from core generating regions

One of the common features of tourism analysis is the historical dependence of most destinations upon a few markets. Tourist generation at international destinations is rather like the Eurovision Song Contest – countries that are close to each other vote for each other, and often visit each other more than more distant ones, except in certain circumstances.

There is reason to believe that this Pareto principle, whereby a few countries and regions provide the backbone of a destination's tourism, will continue in the future, and that the effects of globalization are unlikely to produce radical changes in patterns of tourist generation, however improved global communications become.

> Though world trends suggest dynamic growth in international travel few individual destinations or attractions have either a large or even spread of international visitors. The typical pattern is for both destinations and attractions, to derive their main demand from a few, often longstanding and traditional markets. This Pareto effect – the phenomenon whereby the majority of tourism generation for most countries is not equally spread across many, but concentrated among a few, nations (commonly four or less), holds good in the era of globalisation as it did in the past. This is not surprising since the main factors which commonly create tourist generation are: geographical proximity and ease of access, often with shared borders (which is why Austria attracts German tourists; Norway attracts Scandinavians; Switzerland attracts Germans; and why Finland's three main generating nations in 1998 were Sweden, Russia and Estonia); cultural homogeneity (Ireland attracts Americans; New Zealand attracts the English, the Irish and the Americans) ; and population size (which is why more Germans go to Austria than vice versa; more Americans go to

Canada and so on). For most destinations, therefore, the major generating areas tend to be the most populated countries with which they share borders and/or cultural (particularly linguistic) links.

The Pareto effect means that the past is often the most reliable indicator of the main shape of the future. For example between 1985 and 1995 main international visitors to the State of Victoria in Australia were consistently from four main country groups: New Zealand, Japan, UK/Ireland and USA/Canada (Victoria, 1996) and between 1980 and 1997 Scotland's main generating countries were England, America, Germany and France. (Seaton and Alford, 2000)

This means that the lure of new target markets offered by globalization should not be over-emphasized by destination-planners. They should be cautious in diversion of funds and effort away from old established markets because of more speculative new ones, unless there is research evidence to suggest likewise. This means that one of the major tasks of research is to monitor key markets. In the 1990s a number of NTOs rushed to divert marketing and promotional funds into special activities designed to attack new markets perceived as lucrative, particularly the Japanese, with results that rarely justified the outlay. The importance of retaining one's 'heartland' franchise is the first necessity for tourism planners. If a destination begins to lose its prime market(s) it will almost certainly be difficult to replace it with remoter, more alien ones.

There is also an additional effect: the 'squeeze on the generating regions' (Seaton, 1996b) which reflects the fact that a few countries are targeted by many. By 2010 it is predicted that over 40 per cent of all arrivals in Europe will come from five countries: France, Germany, Japan, UK and USA (WTO, 1994, p. 70). Germany is an extreme instance of a generating country that is everyone's 'key account'. In arrivals, Germany was the leading generating country in the world during the mid-1990s, only overtaken in receipts by the USA (WTO, 1995a, p. 108). Ninety per cent of German trips were taken in Europe, of which 73 per cent were in western and southern Europe in 1994. Germany has, historically, been the leading market for Austria (around 60% of arrivals between 1992 and 1994), Switzerland (around 30% in 1992–4), France (around 20% of arrivals 1992–4), Norway (around 20% of stays 1992–4) and it was third major generating country for Ireland and UK (Seaton, 1996b).

In Ireland, Bord Failte, the NTO, has produced key market studies providing in-depth profiles of main tourist 'key accounts', which are used both to improve marketing targeting and to provide data that be used longitudinally in the future for identifying trends (Bord Failte, 1995; 1996a; 1996b).

Repeat visitor types and segments

In addition to groups from prime geographic generating regions, key account analysis may also focus on specific tourist types and market segments. The types may include broad categories, such as business travellers, while the segments may include specific age groups and class groups. One category that has received attention in the UK is the Visiting Friends and Relatives category. Only a minority of international NTO provide research accounts of VFRs (Pearce, 1995), but work in the UK and in other parts of the world is reclaiming the category for serious consideration, which accounts for 20–25 per cent of travel in many places. Between 1993 and 1996, with the support of the STB and the Northern Ireland Tourist Board, special analyses of VFR tourists were made using longitudinal data derived from previous UKTS studies and Northern Ireland's International Passenger Surveys. One the special analyses (Seaton and Tagg, 1995) was able to identify major differences within the VFR category between those people visiting friends and those visiting relatives. Another (Seaton and Palmer, 1997) was able to profile the heaviest VFR travellers and specify the destinations most likely to attract them, particularly large urban conurbations. These studies also demonstrated the value of the VFR category, showing that in all categories of expenditure except accommodation and package costs, VFR travellers spent as much or more than other travellers.

Other special analyses based on retrospective, longitudinal data from the UKTS have been conducted on groupings by social class and family life-cycle status (Seaton, 1999; Smythe, 1998).

Emergent consumer groups

Key accounts are not only strong existing markets and groups. They may be those with particular growth potential, but which are currently undervalued or disregarded. These may include such groups as single travellers, women business travellers and 'grey travellers' (the important older tourist). Once they have been identified, it may be possible to profile and monitor them from special analyses, derived from existing studies, or by slightly modifying the methodology of existing studies to incorporate them. Studies such as UKTS are so data-rich that they may carry information on visitor groups that, though not examined routinely due to time and resource limitations, may be used to explore previously undervalued special market segments.

Alternatively, it may be necessary to raise special studies to track emergent groups. Internet surfers, for example, have not previously been monitored in visitor studies, but are now known to be active in scanning travel and tourism pages (Marcussen, 1999), even if their full potential has not yet been converted into bookings.

Life-style traveller segments are another kind of grouping which has, in the past, not featured prominently in destination research. These are groups of people who share similar activity patterns, attitudes and opinions that may cross the main socio-demographic dimensions commonly used in the research categories of NTOs and ATBs. Statistical techniques involving clustering and multivariate analysis may be used to mine existing data for evidence of life-style groupings, or purpose-built research schedules, like the VALs protocols used in the 1980s, may be designed for specific use as life-style research instruments. Life-style research targeting has been adopted in the Australian state of Victoria, based on tailor-made research schedules by a commercial research company, and has provided the basis for improved market targeting (Victoria State, 1996; Seaton, 1999).

In the US and Canada there has been a belated recognition of the potential of cultural travellers, as a previously unexamined emergent group, that resulted in several special studies profiling them in the 1990s (Tighe, 1991; Ontario, 1993; Travel Industry Association of America, 1997).

Benchmarking and competitive indexing

Another increasing research usage by destination agencies is benchmarking. It can be used to evaluate destination performance, as well as to provide comparative insight into destination agency performance. One such study, initiated by the Scottish Tourist Board in 1996, benchmarked Scotland's performance between 1985 and 1994, against other European destinations. A number of performance criteria were developed that

Table 27.2   Comparative dimensions of destination/destination agency benchmarking

Destination measures	Destination agency measures
Comparative visitor trends (arrivals and receipts): – versus all Europe trends (including share of European tourism) – versus selected specific countries	Visitor numbers per NTO dollar
Comparative occupancy trends	Visitor numbers per NTO promotional dollar
GDP comparisons	Visitor expenditure per NTO dollar
Balance of tourism account	Visitor expenditure per NTO promotional dollar
Balance of trade	Growth of total NTO funding 1985–94
Country 'league table' changes based on: – arrivals – receipts	Growth of NTO marketing funding 1985–94
Market dependence trends (key account analysis)	Tourist arrivals per capita of host population
Tourism employment trends	Tourist revenue per capita of host population

Source: Seaton, 1996

provided performance indicators of both the destination's progress over ten years, as well as indicators of the destination agency's effectiveness (see Table 27.2).

Benchmarking of destinations is getting easier to perform because of the mass of international tourism data gathered and disseminated by organizations like the WTC, OECD and WTO (e.g. WTO 1994, 1995a). One of the innovations to come out of the WTO five years ago was a periodic study collating data on promotional expenditure and funding of NTOs, which though imperfect and uneven in data, provides a start point for international promotional comparisons (WTO, 1995a).

Benchmarking has also been used to study specific components of destination planning. In 1997 Scottish Enterprise commissioned two studies benchmarking tourist attractions (Economic Research Associates, 1997; Scottish Enterprise, 1998). The second comprised a twelve-nation study of tourist attractions round the world, designed to gather data on best practices and innovations of relevance to Scotland. The study used twenty critical dimensions of comparison that included a number of marketing criteria, service criteria and human resource criteria. The study was the basis of a successful conference and the results were published (Scottish Enterprise, 1998). The same agency has also commissioned international benchmarking studies of activity holidays and human-resource practices.

Leverage effects

Another way of evaluating promotional efforts of destination agencies is by how much extra money the promotional budget was able to induce the private sector and other funders to invest. In destination marketing it is now generally recognized that, given the escalating price of media space and time, significant voice in the market is not likely to be achieved by NTO budgets, but through partnerships. This worked well in Ireland during the 1990s when NTO budgets, augmented by EU funds, were used in partnerships with the national carrier, Aer Lingus, to target the US markets. In the EU this partnership tendency has been encouraged by the requirement to provide match funding for destination development projects, normally 50–60 per cent, in order to qualify for grant aid.

Communication measures

None of the behavioural measures just discussed can be used to prove definitively that a destination is flourishing, or that the NTO has decisively influenced its performance, because of the difficulty of assessing the impact of other variables of influence, discussed earlier. A second approach to evaluation and research is based on communication goals. This consists in developing a model of desirable communications effects, and then measuring the achievement of each through pre- and post-measures of consumer responses. This approach was popularized among fmcg organizations in the 1960s through the publication of a book by Colley (1967), who assumed that it would always be impossible to measure marketing/promotion effects on the basis of sales because of the problem of distinguishing marketing and promotional inputs from other marketing and external variables affecting final consumer responses and decisions. What could be measured, according to Colley, and a number of others, was specified communication effects within a model of persuasion. The assumption was that product choice – purchase of car or choice of a destination – was the end of a sequential persuasion process in which the consumer went through stages of cognitive, connotative and connative knowledge that finally resulted in action. These stages were variously named by different theorists – awareness/comprehension; interest/evaluation/affective attraction; desire/purchase intention/dispositions to act; purchase, booking, action.

Pre- and post-communication measures

The prime research requirement of destination marketing evaluation through research models is the necessity of instituting pre- and post-studies that enable agencies to monitor the changes in communication effects from start to finish of a marketing or promotional programme. The organization may conduct a research survey before the marketing/promotional inputs are exposed and then repeat it at different points or, particularly, at the end of the campaign.

Qualitative techniques for destination image and branding research

In the last ten years the concept of branding has achieved wide currency as a destination concept among NTOs and ATBs in Spain and Mallorca (Kelly, 1997); Scotland, England, and London (BTA, 1997); Wales (Pritchard and Morgan, 1998; WTB, 1994); Ireland (Macrae, Parkinson and Sheerman, 1995); and the US (Nickerson and Moisey, 1999). These initiatives have been accompanied by programmes of qualitative, motivational research in order to determine the imagery, associations, beliefs and values associated with the destination, particularly those distinguishing it from those at other destinations (Dunlop, 1997; Seaton and Hay, 1998). As these destination-branding ventures multiply, it is likely that qualitative and motivational research will expand, both as a pre-communication measure, and also as a post-measure designed to provide 'image updates' over the period in which branding campaigns have been running.

Conversion studies and their problems

Conversion analysis is one of the most established methods of tourism research and, by the early 1990s, was the most widely used promotional evaluation tool (Guske and Perdue, 1992). The basic technique consists of attempting to measure trips or bookings generated through inquiries to an advertising vehicle such as print advertisement, a broadcast commercial or poster. It involves advertising with a response mechanism built in (a coded reply coupon in press adverts and a toll-free 0800 number for broadcast campaigns). Names and addresses of respondents to the advert requesting further information are recorded and samples of them re-contacted to find out whether or not they booked holidays on the strength of the information received. However, during the 1990s a number of disadvantages with the technique were raised (Burke and Gitelson 1990; Johnson and Messner, 1993). They included criticisms that the technique:

- failed to track those who did not respond to the original promotional stimulus (e.g. by coupon return/telephone inquiry), but took holidays;
- failed to identify those who had already chosen the destination, and were thus simply obtaining information to support a decision already made;
- failed to include people who might have travelled *after* the conversion study (even a year or more afterwards) had been completed (i.e. after the final questionnaires had been sent out and returned);
- failed to accommodate other variables that might induce destination choice and booking, e.g. external variables such as competitors' prices, previous destination experience, exchange rates etc; and
- held methodological flaws: Silberman and Klock (1986) enumerated several common problems with conversion studies including: improper sampling techniques; failure to correct for non-response bias (also assessed by Woodside and Ronkainen, 1984); failure to consider sampling precision; and failure to factor out those who had already decided to take a holiday in a specific destination.

A number of alternatives to conversion studies have been offered, including advertising tracking studies (Siegel and Ziff-Levine, 1990; Silberman and Klock, 1986), using panels, designed to detect movements in intentions-to-visit or similar attitudinal dimensions. Other commentators have suggested improvements in the cost effectiveness of Conversion Studies (Perdue and Merrion, 1991).

EXPERIMENTS AND TEST MARKETS

Test marketing may combine both behavioural and communication measures. The principle behind it is that a trial run of a particular combination of marketing variables – commonly a new advertising campaign or new media combination – is tried in one geographical region and expanded later if its results show improvements on results in control areas. The main research requirements are pre- and post-data for both the test area and the control one.

The test market approach was used by the Scottish Tourist Board in developing special promotional activities directed to its prime English markets in the mid-1990s. One of the features of this was its attempt to monitor responses to the new advertising through both measures of behaviour and communication effects (Seaton and Hay, 1998).

TIC/WELCOME CENTRE RESEARCH

In the 1990s, a number of studies were conducted for the first time, into the impact of tourist information centres (Welcome Centres in the US). The standard technique used was to collect names of callers, administer a short questionnaire profiling them and eliciting their reasons for stopping (commonly a comfort break!), and then recontacting them after they had returned home to find out how the stop had later influenced their trip in terms of expenditure, time spent in area, satisfaction etc. (Fesenmaier and Vogt, 1991; Lennon and Mercer, 1994; WTB, 1995). Significant progress was made in understanding the impact of TICs through these studies, particularly on the importance of maps and attractions information as vehicles for prolonging stay and expenditure in an area.

TRIANGULATION

A broad golden rule may be drawn from all the measures just examined – that given the difficulty of isolating the variables that affect destination performance, and of attributing causality to destination inputs, the best method of getting to grips with destination performance is through a combination of behavioural and communication measures – in effect, through triangulation of the research. Trips, spending and occupancy act as the basic trio of triangulated data on destination health, but they can be augmented by many of the research procedures inventoried above.

They can also be augmented by creative compilation of snapshots from specific industry sectors operating at a destination. An example of the use of multiple measures of triangulation is provided by New York Convention Bureau. NYCB augments its three main destination studies with monthly snapshots of triangulated data that comprise six performance indicators: NYC Hotel Room Nights filled; Broadway attendance; NYC airport arrivals; employment at eating/drinking establishments; attendance at selected NYC attractions; and US consumer-confidence levels. Interestingly, in December 1999 they did not all show the same general improving trends - Broadway attendances were down, against rises in all the other sectors.

THE USES OF RESEARCH – ORGANIZATIONAL OR DESTINATION PERFORMANCE MEASUREMENT?

Throughout this chapter the analysis of research practices has moved across two main functions of destination research – as destination performance measurement, and destination agency measurement. Are the two different or can the results of the former be used as indicators of the latter? In this writer's opinion they cannot because of the ultimate difficulty of relating destination visitor behaviour to NTO/ATB inputs. For example, it will always be impossible to weight the impact of *prior knowledge* and *image* of old established destinations on final tourist choices, even when the choices look like *induced* decisions, precipitated by a specific NTO/ATB campaigns. (Was it the Scottish Tourist Board's advertising that won back some of the English market in the late 1990s, or was it the residual impact of *Braveheart* and *Rob Roy*? Was it even the impact of *Braveheart* and *Rob Roy* as *discrete* visitor influences, or their effect as *reminders* that reawakened pre-existing images and attitudes to Scotland among specific visitor groups (notably, those with a historical grudge against the English!)? It will also always be difficult to weight the importance of all the external variables known to affect destinations – exchange rates, disposable income, employment security, weather etc.

Moreover, almost everywhere in the world total NGO/ATB budgets, and particularly promotional ones, will almost always be inadequate to reach even prime target market segments at a significant strike rate, let alone globally distributed subordinate ones. Compared, for instance, to the budgets, commercial time-lengths and 'opportunities to see' of promotion by car and telecommunications companies in the UK, those of destination agencies, even the more well-supported NTOs, seem trivial. This said, there are two kinds of benchmark that can be applied to destination agency monitoring: operational measures and output measures.

Operational measures

These involve monitoring the activity level of NTOs and ATBs through the quality and volume of a number of kinds of physical evidence:

1. enquiries handled per person;
2. average speed of answering visitor enquiries (by telephone, Email, letter etc.);
3. volume and 'advertising equivalent' value of press articles and other free publicity;
4. brochures distributed;
5. internet site hits recorded;
6. number and quality of media familiarization trips hosted; and
7. conference and business leads attracted or followed up.

None of these directly amounts to a visitor attracted but they indicate processual productivity on the road to achieving them.

Cost-effectiveness measures

The second kind of evidence may be assembled through cost-effectiveness measures that seek to establish quantitative relationships between tourism outputs and the inputs deemed to have produced them, such as those used in the STB benchmarking study summarized earlier (Seaton, 1996a). In fmcg marketing it is widely known that it is possible to 'buy' brand share by simply investing abnormal amounts of money in advertising promotion to produce a short-term increase in consumption, but the improvement may be not be worth the investment. There are equivalents in destination marketing. In the late 1980s and 1990s, Ireland achieved greater tourism growth than any other European country but to do so it invested more proportionally than all other countries.

The cost-effectiveness measures that can be used to monitor NTO/ATB performance include the following:

1. NTO cost-per-tourist trip (calculated by dividing the total NTO/ATB budget by the number of tourists attracted);
2. NTO cost-per-tourist £ or $ (calculated by dividing the total NTO/ATB budget by total tourist revenue produced);

3. NTO promotional cost-per-tourist trip (calculated by dividing the total NTO/ATB marketing and promotional budget by the number of tourists attracted);
4. NTO promotional cost per tourist $ spent (calculated by dividing the total NTO/ATB budget by total tourist revenue produced);
5. tourist arrivals per capita of host population (calculated by dividing the number of tourist arrivals at a destination by the total host population number);
6. tourist revenue per capita of host population (calculated by dividing total tourist revenue at a destination by the number in the host population).

(N.B. numbers 5–6 are not genuine cost-effectiveness measures but provide indications of tourism's importance at a destination that can be compared with scores at other destinations.)

How useful are these measures as destination-agency evaluation monitors? All of them, obviously, provide useful clues to the agency's approaches to destination marketing. But they will always have limitations. The operational measures are measures of *activity*, not effectiveness; all of them might be valueless if the objectives and messages of the activities are wrong or ill-judged (e.g. producing a million brochures may be futile if they are strategically ill-focused and badly presented; hosting many press familiarization trips will also be useless if they result in few stories, or ones that are hostile). Similarly, the cost-effectiveness measures are 'rough-and-ready ones', subject to the intractable issue, emphasized throughout this chapter – the assumption that tourist numbers and revenue are due to the effects of destination-agency efforts, rather than to many other variables.

In my view, though the marketing/promotional role of NTOs/ATBs will always be a major responsibility, in the future they should be equally assessed on their provision of a credible package of research initiatives that offer continuously updated situation analyses based upon research strategies and methodologies that provide a basis for multi-triangulated readings of what is going on. Such data should, of course, always include measures specifically designed to offer feedback on specific, current NGO/ATB activities, but not to be limited to that function.

THE FUTURE

What of the future? This chapter has suggested something of the range of destination-marketing evaluation modes that have emerged in the last decade, many of which represented adaptations from fmcg methodologies. These advances do not represent the end of the road in methodological innovations, or all that tourism research has to learn from fmcg techniques.

Longitudinal, destination choice models, and visitor-cycle analysis

One of the most interesting fmcg research developments, first pursued in the 1970s, was the work on brand switching by Andrew Ehrenburg at London Business School (Ehrenburg, 1959; 1968; 1969). What this sought to do was examine consumer product choices over several purchase cycles in order to identify patterns of loyalty and brand switching. The methodology comprised panels keeping weekly diaries of their purchases from which it was possible to identify purchase patterns. The results indicated that shoppers normally chose grocery goods from a 'consideration set' of only a limited number of brands, but that their actual purchase of one of them in any specific week was determined by incentives on offer for brands within the consideration set.

No comparable work has been attempted in destination marketing, although the work of Woodside, Lysonski and Sherrill (Woodside and Sherrill, 1977 and Woodside and Lysonski, 1989), has used the concepts of consideration sets. It would be useful to set up continuous panel work to track destination decisions on a long-term basis. In many destinations, Scotland being one, there is known to be a strong repeat-visitor factor, but no-one knows how frequent these repetitive trips are, how they are structured and what influences them. Research into cycles of visitation, and dimensions of repeat visitorship are long overdue. The main problem is that the panel methodologies for such work would require a long-term investment that might produce nothing of use for several years. However, a less reliable but immediate method might be retrospective report through which past visitor samples could inventory their destination choices over the last five to ten years. So potentially interesting is the issue, not just in identifying destination repeat visiting, but also changes in holiday behaviour at destinations over time, that it could be undertaken through collaborations between several destination agencies, rather than one.

Private sector organizations are already well advanced in relationship marketing programmes based on knowledge of repeat visitor purchase cycles. Cruise lines and tour operators, like Saga and Martin Randall Travel, prioritize repeat customers, not least because retaining an existing customer is cheaper than creating a new one. It is time destination agencies investigated the issues of destination-choice cycles.

Regional disaggregation analyses

Another largely unknown, but easily researched, area is the performance of areas in relation to national patterns. Large fmcg companies routinely compile regional sales data, often using TV area boundaries as sales regions, to monitor regional differences in sales performance through development-rate analyses. Such analyses depend upon indexing regional performance through a sales/population calculation against national sales/total national population averages. In destination marketing it is possible to assess the comparative total tourism strength of different regions against national patterns, and also to compare changing patterns of tourism generation within them. In the UK it would be interesting to determine to what extent Scotland or the Lake District tourism reflects total UK trends, and thus the extent to which the parameters of regional tourism may be set by trends in total arrivals in the UK.

Media impact

A growing recognition among destination agencies is the impact of media representation, particularly film, on destination choice. There is now a whole host of films that are thought to have been associated with destination visitation. The problem is that, despite some research, many of the links between film and destination influence are anecdotal and unquantified (see Appendix for some films, destinations and sources of data on them). Two steps are worthy of consideration: first, there is an urgent need for more research into the way in which film affects destination perceptions – For how long? In what ways? Among which consumer groups? If, for example, the Greek Tourist Board had some clear idea as to what impact the current production of *Captain Corelli's Mandolin* will have on Greece tourism, nationally and regionally, it might be a basis for abandoning or reducing immediate above-the-line advertising expenditures and concentrating on promotional efforts associated with the film.

The other implication is more futuristic. We are about to move into the third age of computer usage in which it is predicted that TV will be eroded by the computer as a facilitator, allowing the home-based consumer to establish direct, interactive links to activities, shopping, and films-on-demand. This could offer NTOs the possibility of important, new promotional opportunities through film. This could be achieved through the compilation of a backlist of films featuring the destination, leased from film distributors, that could be promoted on their websites, and accessed by potential tourists for viewing as part of their information search when making destination decisions. Instead of having to rely on the occasional, new, single-film releases, featuring the destination, with their limited distribution times and video shelf lives, this would enable NTOs to offer potential customers a permanent library of films featuring the destination. There is already some evidence that a single film can have significant impacts on short-term destination behaviour (Aktsoglou, 2000; Riley *et al.*, 1998; Seaton and Hay, 1998; Tooke and Baker, 1996); the strength of New York's image is very substantially related to the number of films that have featured the city. A permanent, home-accessed library of films on an NTO/ATB website could be even more powerful. Disney is already distributing free videos of its theme parks.

Researching VFR host expenditures

This chapter referred earlier to the reviving interest in VFR research, based upon the belated recognition that it may not be as insignificant in revenue terms as has sometimes been thought. This interest has been registered, not just by academics but by practitioners (Paci, Beioley; Seaton and Palmer,1997; Seaton and Tagg, 1995). One major hidden dimension of VFR remains to be investigated. In all previous accounts of the value of VFR travel the exclusive focus has been on expenditures by the visitors. There is reason to believe that this excludes an additional kind of revenue that may also have a direct benefit in regions with high proportions of VFR travel, the expenditures by hosts in entertaining their guests. These host expenditures may include the costs of hospitality at home, presents and out-of-house sight-seeing and entertainment not paid for by the traveller. At the writer's university, a programme is currently being assembled that examines this unknown dimension of VFR travel for the first time. The aim is to assemble a consortium of industy partners drawn from the hospitality industry, destination agencies and carriers with an interest in VFR (especially coach companies and budget air lines) to finance a definitive research programme that would start with qualitative explorations and finish with a nationally representative quantitative survey.

CONCLUSION

This chapter has provided an overview of some of the main issues in research addressed to the function of destination-marketing evaluation. It has shown that the last decade has seen many advances, some of them stemming from precedents from the world of fast-moving consumer-goods marketing. It has commented on the conceptual and practical distinctions between monitoring the performance of destinations and that of destination agencies. Finally, it has suggested some research agendas for the future.

REFERENCES

Aktsoglou, B. (2000) 'Paris-cinema: a passionate relationship'. *Motion*, the magazine of Olympic Airways, pp. 20–3.

Bord Failte (1995) *The Overseas Market for Seniors*. Dublin: Bord Failte.

Bord Failte (1996a) *Know your Market: United States*; *Know your Market: Great Britain*; *Know your Market: Germany*; *Know your Market: France*. Dublin: Bord Failte.

Bord Failte (1996b) *Markets 1991–1995*. Dublin: Bord Failte.

BTA (1997) *Living Britain: A Guide to Understanding the Characteristics of the Geographic Brands of Britain, London, Scotland, England and Wales*. London: British Tourist Authority.

Burke, J. and Gitelson, R. (1990) 'Conversion studies: assumptions, applications, accuracy and abuse'. *Journal of Travel Research*, **28** (3), 46–50.

Colley, R. (1967) *Defining Advertising Goals for Measured Advertising Results*. New York: Association of National Advertisers.

Dunlop, A. (1997) *Consumer Journeys*. Dublin: Bord Failte.

Economic Research Associates (1997) *Report on International Best Practice Attractions*. Glasgow: Scottish Enterprise.

Ehrenberg, A. S. C. (1959) 'The pattern of consumer purchases'. *Applied Statistics*, **8**, 26–41.

Ehrenberg, A. S. C. (1968) 'The practical meaning of the NBD/LSD theory of repeat buying'. *Applied Statistics*, **17**, 17–32.

Ehrenberg A. S. C. (1969) 'Towards an integrated theory of consumer behaviour'. *Journal of the Market Research Society*, **11**, 4.

Fesenmaier, D. R. and Vogt, C. A. (1991) 'Exploratory analysis of information use at Indiana State Welcome Centers', in *Tourism: Building Credibility for a Credible Industry*. Proceedings of 22nd Annual Conference of the Travel and Tourism Research Association, pp. 111–22, Utah: Bureau of Economic and Business Research, Graduate School of Business.

Goodall, B. (1991) 'Understanding holiday choice', in C. P. Cooper (ed.) *Progress in Tourism, Recreation and Hospitality Management*, **3**, pp. 58–77. London and New York: Belhaven Press.

Guske, L. D. and Perdue, R. R. (1992) 'The influence of multiple trips on inquiry conversion'. *Journal of Travel Research*, **30** (4), 27–30.

Johnson, R. R. and Messner D. J. (1993) 'Inquiry conversion and travel advertising effectiveness'. *Journal of Travel Research*, **31** (4), 14–21.

Kelly, T. (1997) 'You say Majorca, I say Mallorca'. *Independent on Sunday*, 3 March.

Lennon, J. J. and Mercer, A. (1994) 'Service quality in practice: customer service in Scotland's tourist information centres'. *International Journal of Hospitality Management*, **13**, (2) 231–49.

Macrae, C., Parkinson, S. and Sheerman J. (1995) 'Managing marketing's DNA: The role of branding'. *Irish Marketing Review*, **18**, 13–20.

Marcussen, Carl H. (1999) 'Internet distribution of European travel and tourism services: the market, transportation, accommodation and package tours'. Norway: Research Centre, Bornholm.

New York Convention Bureau (1998a) *'98 Domestic Travel to New York City*. New York.

New York Convention Bureau (1998b) *'98 International Travel to New York City*. New York.

New York Convention Bureau (1998c) *Tourism's Economic Impact on New York City 1998*. New York.

Nickerson, N. P. and Moisey, N. (1999) 'Branding a state from features to positioning: making it simple?'. *Journal of Vacation Marketing*, **5** (3), 217–26.

Ontario, Government of (1993) *The Cultural Tourism Handbook*. Ontario.

Pearce, P. L. (1995) (ed.) 'Special edition: the visiting friends and relatives market'. *Journal of Tourism Statistics*, **6**, 155.

Perdue, R. R. and Merrion D. (1991) 'Developing low cost, but improved conversion methodologies'. Tourism: Building Credibility for a Credible Industry, 22nd Annual Conference of the Travel and Tourism Research Association. Long Beach, California.

Pritchard, A. and Morgan N. J. (1998) 'Mood marketing: the new destination branding strategy: a case study of Wales'. *Journal of Vacation Marketing*, **4** (3), June, 215–29.

Riley, R., Baker, D. and Van Doren, C. (1998) 'Movie induced tourism'. *Annals of Tourism Research*, **25** (4), 919–35.

Scottish Enterprise (1998) 'New horizons: international benchmarking and best practice for visitor attractions'. Glasgow.

Seaton, A. V. (1996a) 'Destination marketing', in A. V. Seaton and M. M. Bennett (eds) *The Marketing of Tourism Products*. London: International Thomson Business Press, London, pp. 350–76.

Seaton, A. V. (1996b) *The Comparative Evaluation of Tourism Destination Performance: Scotland and European Tourism 1985–1994*. Edinburgh: Scottish Tourist Board.

Seaton, A. V. (1999) 'Why do people travel? Introductory perspectives on tourist behaviour', in L. Pender (ed.) *Marketing Management for Travel and Tourism*. Cheltenham: Stanley Thornes, pp. 174–214.

Seaton, A. V. and Alford, P. A. (2000) 'The promotional implications of globalisation', in C. P. Cooper and S. Wahab (eds) *Tourism in the Age of Globalisation*.

Seaton, A. V. and Hay, B. (1998) 'The marketing of Scotland as a tourist destination, 1985–1996', in R. MacLellan and R. Smith (eds) *Tourism in Scotland*. London: International Thomson Business Press, pp. 209–40.

Seaton, A. V. and Palmer, C. (1997) 'Understanding VFR tourism behaviour: the first five years of the United Kingdom tourism survey'. *Tourism Management*, **18** (6), 345–55.

Seaton, A. V. and Tagg, S. K. (1995) 'Disaggregating friends and relatives in tourism research: the Northern Ireland evidence 1990–1993', *Journal of Tourism Studies*, **6** (1), 6–18.

Siegel, W. and Ziff-Levine, W. (1990) 'Evaluating Tourism advertising campaigns: Conversion vs. advertising tracking studies'. *Journal of Travel Research*, **28** (3), 51–5.

Silberman, J. and Klock, M. (1986) 'An alternative to conversion studies for measuring the impact of travel ads'. *Journal of Travel Research*, **24** (4), 12–16.

Smythe, A. (1998) 'The impact of family life cycle status on UK travel, 1990–1996'. Unpublished dissertation, University of Strathclyde.

Tighe, A. (1991) 'Research on cultural tourism in the United States'. TTRA 22nd Annual Conference, June 9–13, California.

Tooke, N. and Baker, M. (1996) 'Seeing is believing: the effect of film on visitor numbers to screened locations'. *Tourism Management*, **17** (2), 87–94.

Touche-Ross (1992) *EC National Tourism Survey*. London.

Travel Industry Association of America (1997) 'Profile of travelers who participate in historic and cultural activities'. Travelscope Survey, Washington.

Victoria State (1996) *Tourism Victoria Research Update*. Melbourne, Australia.

Woodside, A. and Lysonski S. (1989) 'A general model of traveler destination choice'. *Journal of Travel Research*, **9** (1), 37–49.

Woodside, A. and Ronkainen I. (1984) 'How serious is non-response bias in advertising conversion research'. *Journal of Travel Research*, **22** (4), 34–7.

Woodside, A. and Sherill D. (1977) 'Traveler evoked and inept sets of vacation destinations', *Journal of Travel Research*, **16** (1), 14–18.

WTB (1994) *Tourism 2000. A strategy for Wales*. Cardiff: Wales Tourist Board.

WTB (1995) *Tourist Information Centre Users*, January. Cardiff: Wales Tourist Board.

WTO (1994) *Global Tourism Forecasts to the Year 2000*. Madrid: World Tourism Organization.

WTO (1995a) *Market trends in Europe 1994*. Madrid: World Tourism Organization.

WTO (1995b) *Budgets and Marketing Plans of National Tourism Organisations*. Madrid: World Tourism Organization.

APPENDIX: MEDIA REPRESENTATION, DESTINATION REPRESENTED AND SOURCES OF ASSERTED EFFECTS

Media representation	Destination	Source of information
Film: *Shirley Valentine*	Greek Islands	Eugenia Wickens, PhD, 1994
Film: *Cocktail*	Jamaica	Trade Press
TV soap operas and costume drama	English regional brandings in Yorkshire: Bronte Country; Emmerdale Country; Robin Hood etc.	BTA Brochures
Schindler's List/Ark (novel/film)	Auschwitz	Visitors numbers to film set
Novel/film: *Captain Corelli's Mandolin*	Greece	Corfu European Information Centre, 2000
TV soaps: *Home and Away* and *Neighbours* Film: *Crocodile Dundee*	Australia	Riley *et al.*, 1998
Many films set in Paris, e.g. *Gigi, An American in Paris*, etc.	Paris	Aktsoglou: Olympic Airways Magazine, May 2000
Films: *Braveheart, Rob Roy*	Scotland	Seaton and Hay, 1998
Film: *Close Encounters of the Third Kind*	Devils Tower National Monument, Wyoming, USA	Riley *et al.*, 1998
TV series: *Bergerac*	Jersey	Tooke and Baker, 1996
TV soap: *Dallas*	Dallas	Hearsay
The Beach, film starring di Caprio and music by All Saints	Thailand: Maya Beach, Phi Phi Island	Newspaper assertions
Film: *Thelma and Louise*	Arches National Park, Utah	Riley *et al.*, 1998

Index